DE

How Nations Serve Young Children

How Nations Serve Young Children:

Profiles of Child Care and Education in 14 Countries

Edited by
Patricia P. Olmsted
David P. Weikart
High/Scope Educational Research Foundation

With an Afterword by
Lilian G. Katz
Professor of Early Childhood Education and Director of ERIC Clearinghouse on Elementary and Early Childhood Education University of Illinois, Urbana

The High/Scope® Press
Ypsilanti, Michigan
A division of the High/Scope
Educational Research Foundation

Marge Senninger, High/Scope Press Editor

Library of Congress Cataloging-in-Publication Data

How nations serve young children / edited by Patricia P. Olmsted,
David P. Weikart : with an afterword by Lilian G. Katz.
p. cm.
Includes bibliographies.
ISBN 0-929816-07-2
1. Child care services—Cross-cultural studies. 2. Early childhood education—Cross-cultural studies. I. Olmsted, Patricia P. II. Weikart, David P.
HQ778.5.H69 1989 89-35026
362.7—dc20 CIP

International Standard Book Number: 0-929816-07-2

Printed in the United States of America

High/Scope Educational Research Foundation
600 North River Street
Ypsilanti, Michigan 48198-2898
(313)485-2000

The High/Scope Educational Research Foundation is an independent nonprofit organization formally established in 1970 by Dr. David P. Weikart. High/Scope is internationally known as a center for research, curriculum development, professional training, and public policy work. High/Scope's work centers on the learning and development of children from infancy through adolescence, with a special emphasis on the early childhood years.

A Word About IEA

"IEA" is the acronym of the International Association for the Evaluation of Educational Achievement, a nongovernmental, nonprofit organization of research institutions in 45 countries that is well known for its 25 years of comparative international surveys in science, mathematics, written composition, and other academic areas. IEA research projects have been instrumental in demonstrating the feasibility of large-scale cross-national empirical studies and advancing the methodology of comparative education.

IEA views its comparative educational surveys as a necessary first step in both national and international policy-related research. IEA findings have affected educational systems around the world, as specific educational problems have been identified and policymakers have made decisions based on these research findings.

Some of the international educational issues IEA has chosen to examine include identifying the effects of different practices in grouping or tracking students, investigating the effects of comprehensive secondary schooling, and examining the effects of specific instructional practices.

Additional information regarding IEA can be obtained from the Executive Secretary of IEA, University of Stockholm, S-10691, Stockholm, Sweden.

How Nations Serve Young Children, Patricia Olmsted and David Weikart, High/Scope Press 1989

ERRATUM in first printing:

Page 288 Table 7, delete "Children Served in" in each table heading where the words appear.

CONTENTS

TABLES *xiii*
FIGURES *xvii*
ACKNOWLEDGMENTS *xix*
PREFACE *xxi*

I. IEA PREPRIMARY PROJECT OVERVIEW AND HISTORY *3*
Worldwide Conditions Prompting the Study *3*
History of the Project *4*
Phase 1 of the Project *6*
Future Phases of the Project *10*
National Profiles as a First Step *11*
References *12*

II. EARLY CHILDHOOD CARE AND EDUCATION IN BELGIUM *13*
Introduction *13*
Day Care Options for Children Under 3 Years of Age *15*
Institutional Education for Children Aged 3 to 6 Years *24*
Two Main Concerns *31*
Endnotes *35*

III. CHILD CARE AND EARLY EDUCATION IN THE FEDERAL REPUBLIC OF GERMANY *39*
Introduction *39*
Historical and Philosophical Perspectives *40*
Demographics *51*
National Child Care Policy *59*
Options in Early Childhood Education and Care *63*
Research *76*
Child Care Issues in the Future *77*
References *81*

IV. EARLY CHILDHOOD TRAINING, CARE, AND EDUCATION IN FINLAND *87*
Introduction *87*
History *88*
Child Care Options *93*
National Child Care Policy *103*

National Child Care Issues of the Next Decade *109*
Summary and Conclusion *113*
References *115*

V. **Child Care and Early Education in Hong Kong** *119*
Introduction *119*
Historical Perspective *119*
Demographics *130*
National Child Care Policies *132*
Education and Care Arrangements *133*
Research *133*
Issues of the Next Decade *136*
Conclusions *138*
References *141*

VI. **Care and Education in Hungary for 3- to 6-Year-Olds** *143*
The Educational System *143*
Institutional Education for Children Aged 3 to 6: The Kindergarten *143*
Pedagogical and Psychological Research *148*
Endnotes *149*

VII. **Preprimary Education and Care in Italy** *151*
Introduction *151*
Preprimary Education and Care, 1831 to 1968: A Historical Overview *152*
Families, Children, and Schools Today in Italy *163*
Nursery Schools: Education and Care for Children Aged 3 to 6 *166*
An Urban Study of Children's Care and Education Services *194*
Endnotes *200*
References *202*

VIII. **Early Childhood Care and Education in Kenya** *203*
Introduction *203*
Structure of the Educational System *203*
Historical Background *205*

National Child Care Policies and Practices *207*
Demographic Information on Urban and Rural Preprimary Children *213*
Emerging Issues and Unanswered Questions *216*
Endnotes *217*

IX. EARLY CHILDHOOD CARE AND EDUCATION IN NIGERIA *219*
Introduction *219*
Background—Demographics, the Social System, and Family Policy *219*
The Child Care Picture *221*
The Preprimary Education System *224*
Summary *237*
Endnotes *239*

X. YOUNG CHILDREN'S CARE AND EDUCATION IN THE PEOPLE'S REPUBLIC OF CHINA *241*
Historical Review *241*
Brief Introduction to Early Childhood Education Since 1949 *244*
In-Progress Research Work on Early Childhood Education *253*
Current Issues *253*
Endnotes *254*

XI. PHILIPPINE CARE AND EDUCATION FOR CHILDREN AGED 3 TO 6 *255*
Historical and Philosophical Perspective *255*
Description of Child Care Options *260*
Research *264*
Child Care Issues of the Next Decade *267*
Conclusion *270*
Endnotes *271*

XII. CARE AND EDUCATION FOR CHILDREN UNDER AGE 6 IN PORTUGAL *273*
Introduction *273*
Historical and Philosophical Perspective *274*
Demographic Data *279*
National Child Care Policy *283*
Description of Child Care Options *289*

Programs and Curricula 294
Research 295
Future Needs and Issues 297
Summary 299
Endnotes 300
References 301

XIII. Child Care and Early Education in Spain 303
Introduction 303
Historical Perspective 303
Demography 311
The Care of Young Children in Spain 316
Statistics and Description of Extrafamilial Child Care Programs 318
Research 335
Future Problems 337
Conclusion 339
References 341

XIV. Child Care and Early Education in Thailand 343
Introduction 343
History of Child Care and Early Education 343
National Policy Affecting Young Children 345
Current Delivery of Preprimary Education and Care 347
Demographics 356
Problems and Issues Concerning Child Care and Early Education 359
Conclusion 361
References 362

XV. Early Childhood Care and Education in the United States 365
The Demographics Regarding Children 366
Historical Background 369
National Child Care and Education Policies 374
Early Childhood Care and Education Arrangements 377
Research on Early Childhood Care and Education 386
Issues of the Next Decade 393
Conclusion 398
References 398

Afterword:
Young Children in Cross-National Perspective by Lilian G. Katz *401*

Appendix: IEA Preprimary Project Phase 1 National Research Centers *407*

Tables

Belgium

Percentages of Populations Enrolled in Nursery School From 1960 to 1975 *27*
Auxiliary Facilities of Schools *29*
Types of Caregivers in Charge of Children in Nursery Schools During Extracurricular Hours *33*

Federal Republic of Germany

Historical Perspective of the Growth of Kindergartens *45*
Places in Krippen, Kindergartens, and Licensed Family Day Care Compared With Relevant Child-Populations in the Federal Republic of Germany, 1986 *53*
1986 Preschool Provision Rates (Krippe, Kindergarten) for Various Categories of Children Not Yet in Compulsory Schooling (Including Categories Relating to Family Type) *55*
Rate of Kindergarten Attendance for 3- to Under-6-year-olds, According to Household Income *56*
Percent of Children of Various Ages Attending Krippe/Kindergarten, According to Status of Mother *57*
Krippen and Kindergartens According to Operating Agencies *64*
Persons Employed in Kindergarten Education, According to Training *71*

Finland

Children 0–6 Years of Age in Day Care Centers, 1983 *98*
Children 0–6 Years of Age in Family Day Care, 1983 *101*

Hong Kong

Number of Kindergarten Children by Level, 1987 *131*
Distribution of Enrolled Kindergarten Children by Geographic Location, 1987 *131*
Characteristics of Kindergartens and Child Care Centers *134*

Italy

Non-State Nursery Schools, Administration and Enrollment, 1983–84 *167*
Annual Increase in State Nursery Schools, 1976–77 to 1982–1983 *181*
Trends in State Nursery School Enrollment, 1968–69 to 1983–84 *183*

Italy's Nursery School Enrollment, State and Non-State, for 3 Recent Years *185*

Kenya

Kenyan Preprimary Services, 1968 and 1986 *207*
Government and Partner Financial Contributions (in Kenyan Shillings) to Preschool Education, 1981–88 *209*
Kenya's Population for Selected Years, 1948–87 *213*
Children Aged 0–5 Years in Kenya, 1979–90 *214*
Distribution of Kenyan Population, by Specific Ages, 1979, 1984, 1989 *215*
Mortality Trends in Kenya for Selected Years, 1948–79 *215*
Demographic Factors Affecting Child Population Change in Kenya *216*

Nigeria

Available Types of Child Care *223*
Structure of Education in Nigeria *226*
Characteristics of Mothers of Children in Preprimary Institutions *229*
Number of Preprimary Institutions Compared With Number of Preprimary Schools, in Seven States *230*
Nursery School Daily Schedule *234*
Categories of Teaching Credentials in Nigeria *236*

People's Republic of China

Number of Kindergartens in China for Selected Years, 1949–85 *246*
Number of Kindergarten Staff in China for Selected Years, 1949–85 *248*
Adult-Child Ratio in Kindergartens in China, 1980–85 *249*
Educational Level of Kindergarten Administrators and Teachers, 1985 *251*
Professional Training of Kindergarten Administrators and Teachers, 1985 *251*

Philippines

Number of Philippine Children Aged 3 to 6 Years and Percent of Population They Represented, 1985 *257*

Preschool Children (Aged 3 to 6) Served by Agencies Other Than MECS-Registered Schools, 1983–84 *258*
Distribution of MECS-Registered Preschools by Region, 1983–84 *259*

Portugal

Number of Licensed Preschool Teachers Graduated From Portugal's Teacher-Training Schools per Year, 1981–86 *278*
Per-District Resident, Age 0–2, and Age 3–5 Populations, 1981 *280*
Per-District Resident Female Population (Aged 15–39) and Employed Mothers (Aged 15–39), 1981 *281*
1984 Per-District Coverage of Children Aged 0–6 by Preschool Services of the ME and the MWSS *282*
Per-District Distribution of Public and Private ME Kindergartens for Selected Years During the Last Decade *285*
Public System (ME)—Number of Operative Kindergartens and Percentage Distribution According to Enrollment, 1987–88 *287*
Institutions Under the MWSS, 1986 (1984) *288*

Spain

Reasons Mothers Give for Sending Their Children to a Preprimary Center *308*
Percentage of Women Interviewed, in Relation to Their Level of Educational Attainment, Who Place Emphasis on Academic Learning During the Preprimary Years as Preparation for the School Years *308*
Spain's Preprimary Population by Age, According to 1981 Population Census *313*
Number of Preprimary Children in Spain in 1981 and in 1986 *313*
Time Parents Play With Their Children *315*
Spain's 1970–86 Preprimary School Enrollments *320*
Distribution of Preprimary Pupils by Autonomous Community for Both State and Private Schools, 1985–86 *324*
Teacher-Pupil Ratios in State and Private Schools by Autonomous Community, 1985–86 *325*
Percentage of School Enrollment Among the Preprimary Population, 1985–86 *326*
Methods of Transporting Children to Preprimary Schools *331*
Distribution of Preprimary Schools According to Operating Hours *332*
Number of Hours Children Spend in Preprimary Schools *332*

Preprimary Education Accommodation 333
Outdoor Spaces in Preprimary Schools 333
Services Provided in Preprimary Schools 334
Percentage of Parents, According to Parent's Educational Attainment Level, Using a Preprimary School With Psychopedagogic Services 334
Percentage of Parents, According to Parent's Income Level, Using a Preprimary School With Psychopedagogic Services 335
Population Predictions for Preprimary Children in Spain 337

THAILAND

Preprimary Education and Care in Thailand, 1985 349
Numbers of Preschoolers (Aged 3 to 6) and of Preschool Institutions, 1979–87 357
Preschool Statistics, 1984–85 358

UNITED STATES

Number of 3- to 6-year-old Children and Percent of the Population They Represented, 1880–1980 366
Percent of Children (Under 18) in Poverty, by Family Structure and Race, for Selected Years 368
U.S. Early Childhood Care and Education in 1987 381

Figures

People's Republic of China

Training of Kindergarten Teachers in China *249*

Portugal

Public and Private Kindergartens of the ME From 1978 to 1986 *286*

Spain

Number of Preprimary Pupils Between 1970 and 1985 in State-Run and Private Schools *321*
Number of Classes in Preprimary Schools, Both State-Run and Private, 1985–86 *322*
State-Run and Private Sector Entities That Preprimary School Classes Are Linked With, 1985–86 *323*
Percentage of Preprimary Pupils Enrolled in Nursery Schools and Kindergartens, State-Run and Private, 1985–86 *327*
Percentage of Preprimary Teachers in State-Run and Private Schools *328*
Number of Preprimary Teachers by Degree of Specialization in Both the State-Run and Private Sectors *329*

Acknowledgments

We would like to express our gratitude to those who have assisted in making this book a reality. We acknowledge Carnegie Corporation and the Department of Health and Human Services for their support of High/Scope's Preprimary Project activities. We thank Marge Senninger for her invaluable assistance in all phases of manuscript preparation. Finally, we acknowledge the assistance of Shirley Barnes, Helena Hoas, Karen Pinner, Stephen McHugh, and Polly Neill.

PREFACE

The IEA Preprimary Project is an ongoing international study investigating the nature, quality, and effects of the experiences of children prior to formal schooling. The study includes a wide spectrum of nations that are concerned with learning more about domestic and worldwide early childhood care and education provisions and practices. At the outset of the Preprimary Project, the research team in each participating country used the most recent information available to prepare a national profile of early childhood care and education. The national profiles provide a general picture of early childhood services within the societal context of each country, the role of government in providing or supporting these services, and major historical events in the provision of these services. The profiles include descriptions of national child and family policies as well as relevant population and service data from available statistical sources; areas in which little or no data exist are also noted.

Each profile presents a statement of national policy as it affects children's early education and care. From country to country, the factors that have influenced national policy are many and complex, reflecting unique historical traditions, widely differing national attitudes, and a variety of political and economic realities. For one thing, some countries have no explicit public policy (governing young children's care and education) that applies to all families. In the United States, for example, present implicit policy reflects a historical consensus that individual families, rather than government, should be responsible for arranging for children's early experiences. In recent years, social changes have prompted the introduction of legislation to address such issues as parental leave and subsidies to families for child care. Such measures, if enacted, may eventually lead to the development of explicit early childhood care and education policies.

In contrast, the profiles of many European countries reveal extensive, explicit national early childhood care and education policies—policies that set forth specific quality standards and define optimal coverage rates. In such countries, the present emphasis is on fine-tuning existing systems and coordinating policies among governmental agencies (for example, coordinating use of part-day early education programs with employed parents' need for full-day child care). In addition, some European countries are working to increase the availability of services for specific families (those living in rural areas, those of specific racial/ethnic origin).

For developing countries, the profiles reflect yet another picture. In these countries, stated national early childhood policies are often far removed from daily reality. Although these official policies of service and support to families may be founded on a recognition of the need for such services, the policies are not implemented, owing to lack of political will and a lack of resources. High birthrates and decreasing infant mortality are increasing the number of young children in need of early childhood services. At the same time, rapid urbanization is creating a great need for many types of services, including health and sanitation as well as education and social services. These trends are placing even greater demands on already overburdened, resource-poor governments.

This book looks at how nations serve young children. It presents no solutions, and indeed, the picture it presents is only partial. The information appearing here, set in its historical context, is what nations do now—or in some instances, what nations say they do now—to serve their young children. This information sets the stage for the three interrelated phases of the Preprimary Project. Of particular interest will be a comparison of Phase 1 data with the profiles' statements of early childhood policies. (Phase 1 collects implementation data directly from families about their use of and satisfaction with early childhood care and education services). With Phase 1 information, it should be possible to assess how effectively national policies have been translated into practice.

The experiences of young children in different settings and the quality of those experiences will be explored in Phase 2. To the extent that individual national profiles have revealed explicit quality standards, comparisons can then be made between existing standards and their implementation as described by the Phase 2 data. Phase 3 data will describe later outcomes of children's early education and care experiences. This information should allow countries to examine the policies and practices described in their profiles in light of the effects on children. Thus, the overall study links policy to practice; practice, to what children experience through that practice; and what children experience, to effects in children.

In the introductory chapter, we provide an overview of the IEA Preprimary Project, present a description of the work to date, and discuss the policy implications of the first phase of the project. The national profiles written by the research teams from the project's participating countries compose the main body of the book. In the Afterword, Lilian Katz, a leading figure in early childhood education who played a major role in the planning of the Preprimary Project, integrates some of the themes found in the various national profiles and presents current international trends in early childhood care and education.

General guidelines for the national profiles were distributed to each participating country. Suggested profile topics were the following: (1) history of early childhood care and education, (2) demographics, (3) national child and family policies, (4) early childhood care and education arrangements currently in use, (5) research in early childhood care and education, and (6) issues of the next decade. Although all authors worked from the same general outline, each selected certain topics for primary consideration and covered others in a more cursory way. These decisions about emphasis sometimes reflect country-specific situations (for example, a country's historic pattern of curriculum choice); other times, emphasis is indicative of an author's areas of expertise.

The reader should interpret each profile from its national perspective: Though several authors use the same terms, the terms may have different meanings in different countries. "Kindergarten," for example, is used by several authors, but in different countries the word can refer to different types of programs serving various ages of children. We have tried to provide specific information for the reader whenever we encountered such a term in a profile. In addition, phrases such as "adequate staffing" or "well-equipped child care center" will need to be interpreted differently for countries at different stages of development or with different cultural patterns.

In any international publication, editorial decisions regarding content and style have to be made. We would like to share some of our major decisions. First, to the degree possible, we present the chapters as they were originally written or translated into English by the various project research teams. We clarified vague sections of text and reordered words within some sentences, but did not substantively revise profiles. Second, whereas the title of the work in each reference list entry is given in English, in many cases, the remainder of the entry is given only in the author's original language. In a few cases, the author has served the English-speaking reader by translating the entry in full. Also, although different formats are used across countries for endnotes, citations, and references, we have tried to standardize the information as much as possible.

It is the hope of all involved in the IEA Preprimary Project that information from the project can serve all nations, both those that are participating in the study and those that are not. With this information, policymakers in various countries can begin to think about their own policies and services for children and consider these in light of the experiences of other countries. These efforts could result in better policies and services for children and families in countries throughout the world.

Patricia P. Olmsted
David P. Weikart
May 1989

How Nations Serve Young Children

I
IEA Preprimary Project Overview and History

David P. Weikart, *President*
Patricia P. Olmsted, *Research Associate*
High/Scope Educational Research Foundation
Ypsilanti, Michigan

Now is a time when both governments and ordinary citizens in nations around the world are showing a lively interest in early childhood care and education. In country after country, the social, economic, and demographic changes occurring over the past 20 years have produced an accelerating demand for services for young children. This demand has in turn produced a need for more comprehensive information than is now available in many of these countries. Specifically, nations need the kinds of detailed information that the IEA Preprimary Project will produce—information about the varieties of care and education settings used by parents of young children, about the quality of children's experiences in those settings, and about the effects of those experiences on children's later development. Such information will help policymakers develop programs to meet the fast-growing demand for early childhood services. It will also aid government agencies in their attempts to integrate early childhood program planning with other long-term social and economic planning.

Worldwide Conditions Prompting the Study

Parents' needs for extrafamilial early childhood care and education arrangements seem to be surfacing worldwide. This expanding need for programs serving children reflects a global increase in the incidence of one-parent families and in the participation of women in the labor force (United Nations, 1965; 1966; 1974; 1976; 1982; 1986; 1988). Matters are further complicated by the increasing urbanization of developing countries and the high degree of family mobility in developed countries—two conditions that make child care by extended family members an increasingly rare option for parents. In addition, although the birthrate in most countries is leveling off or even decreasing, infant survival rates are at the same time improving. The net result in many countries is an increase in the number of young children and therefore in the need for services for these children (United Nations Children's Fund, 1987).

In the midst of all these economic, demographic, and social changes, another condition has arisen. A number of nations are at a stage of development wherein they can turn attention from children's bare survival to children's development in their early years. At the same time, a small but growing body of research is demonstrating the long-term benefits of high-quality preschool programs and thus creating widespread awareness of the importance of the early years in a child's life (see, for example, Barraio, 1988; Berrueta-Clement, Schweinhart, Barnett, Epstein, & Weikart, 1985; Weikart, in press). Both of these factors are prompting countries to plan new or expanded early childhood education programs. Thus the IEA Preprimary Project comes at a time when nations are looking for base-line information that can give them direction and when they are open to learning more about the effectiveness of preprimary services.

HISTORY OF THE PROJECT

The IEA Preprimary Project was conceived during the late 1970s by a small group of educational researchers associated with the International Association for the Evaluation of Educational Achievement (IEA) who keenly felt there was a lack of comprehensive information about the experiences of children prior to their entry into the formal educational system. Historically, IEA has focused on student performance and classroom processes in secondary schools, so it was a surprise to many professionals in the early childhood field when this research group expressed interest in sponsoring a preprimary study. One concern put forth at the time was that the national education agencies who typically have collected data for other IEA studies were not the primary groups from whom early childhood information was available within their respective countries. It was clear that those countries participating in a preprimary study would need to remain open to using procedures other than ones used in previous IEA studies. Nevertheless, by 1980 there was sufficient interest among the IEA member countries to result in the IEA General Assembly establishing a planning group to develop an international preprimary study.

The preprimary planning group met twice, once in February of 1981, in Liège, Belgium, and again in September of that year, in Nadrin, Belgium. Both planning sessions were funded by the Bernard van Leer Foundation, a Netherlands-based international nonprofit institution dedicated to aiding disadvantaged children and youth. Constituting the planning group were 14 persons representing seven countries: Marcel Crahay (Belgium); Ron Davie (Great Britain); Arlette Delhaxhe (Belgium); Gilbert De Landsheere (Belgium); Lilian Katz (United States); Suzan Montovani (Italy); Annette Marion (France); Jean-Pierre Pourtois (Belgium); Rachel Presser (Canada); Antonio Schizzerotto (Italy); Anne-Marie Thirion (Belgium); Wolfgang Tietze (Federal Republic of Germany); Bill Wall (Great Britain); and David Weikart (United States).

In 1982 the IEA General Assembly, at their annual meeting in Toronto, approved a draft proposal for the Preprimary Project. During the following year, IEA member countries received general information about the preprimary study, together with an invitation to participate. And then, at its 1983 meeting in Enschede, the Netherlands, the IEA General Assembly took two major steps towards formalizing the Preprimary Project: First, the assembly appointed a project steering committee, with Lilian Katz, of the U.S., as chair; the three other committee members appointed were Marcel Crahay (Belgium), Wolfgang Tietze (Federal Republic of Germany), and Richard Wolf (United States). Second, the assembly officially invited the High/Scope Educational Research Foundation to be the international coordinating center (ICC) for the IEA Preprimary Project. In early 1984 the final proposal for the project was completed by the project steering committee and the ICC staff (IEA Preprimary Project Steering Committee, 1984).

The first meeting of representatives from the 17 IEA member countries that had expressed interest in the Preprimary Project took place in Singapore during the 1984 IEA General Assembly meeting. The representatives discussed establishing a national research center within each country, developing instruments and procedures, and locating possible sources of funding for each country's project activities as well as for the project's international coordination activities.

During 1985 and 1986 each participating country finalized its funding arrangements, established its national research center (NRC), and identified a person to serve as its NRC director. At High/Scope, the international coordinating center, activities during this period included securing funds for the project's international activities, employing staff, and jointly developing (with NRC directors) instruments and procedures for the study. In addition, in 1986 Alan Brimer (Hong Kong) assumed the position of steering committee chair for a 1-year period.

The final operational plan for the Preprimary Project consists of three interrelated phases. Phase 1 (nearing completion at the time of this writing) employs household survey techniques to gather information from families about their use of early childhood care and education services. Phase 2 selects a sample of service settings identified in Phase 1 and uses observation and interview questionnaires to investigate the quality of life for young children in these various settings. Another part of Phase 2 consists of selecting a small number of children from each setting and assessing their development in several areas. Phase 3 is a follow-up study, at age 7, of those children assessed in Phase 2. This final phase gathers information about the children's development since their preprimary experience by using various methods, including direct assessment, examination of school records, and information from both parents and teachers.

As of mid-1989 the Phase 1 data collection has been completed, and planning for Phases 2 and 3 is under way. Fourteen countries are participating in Phase 1: Belgium (French-speaking), the Federal Republic of Germany, Finland, Hong Kong, Hungary, Italy, Kenya, Nigeria, the People's Republic of China, the Philippines, Portugal, Spain, Thailand, and the United States. (See the Appendix for a list of NRCs and directors.) As explained in the Preface, as the first major activity of Phase 1, research teams in these 14 countries prepared national profiles of early childhood care and education, and this book contains their profiles. Other countries, such as Australia and the Netherlands, have expressed general interest in the project and may conduct related studies or join Phases 2 and 3 of the Preprimary Project.

Phase 1 of the Project

So far in Phase 1, information about the use of early childhood care and education settings has been collected from nationally representative samples of families in each of the participating countries. By a joint decision of the project directors in each country, the age-range of the children to be studied by the project is 3½ to 4½ years. In most participating countries, this age-range takes in the child's last full year before entry into a formal school environment; it is also the age-range for which there is the widest variety of early childhood care and education settings.

The 14 countries participating in Phase 1 of the Preprimary Project are following a mutually agreed-upon basic international study plan that allows findings to be analyzed across nations as well as within individual countries. The cross-national analysis offers a unique opportunity to examine a wider range of variation in care and education settings than can be found within any single country. It also allows global comparisons of relationships between national policy and effects of national policies on the lives of children and families.

The Parent/Guardian Interview

Phase 1 employs a 50-minute parent/guardian interview to collect information about parents' use of early childhood care and education services. A major portion of the interview concerns the care and education arrangements parents use during a typical week. Interviewers have asked parents why they selected certain settings, what problems they encountered in any of those settings, and how satisfied they were with each setting. Information has also been collected about what parents pay for care and education arrangements, what distances children must travel, and what means of travel children use. Another part of the interview asks parents for a detailed description of a typical 24-hour day in the child's life. To obtain family background information, the interview contains questions about each child's family setting, including parental education and occupation, type of living accommodations, and family composition.

The questions just described form the core of the parent/guardian interview, which was jointly developed by the project directors from the participating countries. Questions in this core group were asked of families in all participating countries. In addition, each country has included in its interview some questions that relate to country-specific conditions and concerns. For example, because Belgium has a special interest in care and education settings used during weekends, its questionnaire requests a detailed record of caretakers and settings used for children for an entire week. As another example, in the United States, where sufficiency of services is in question, special questions provide data about (1) the availability of settings as experienced by parents seeking services and (2) parents' perceptions about the need for additional settings.

The strategy of collecting early childhood service information directly from families is unique to the preprimary study; most other studies have gone directly to care providers and teachers for such information. By interviewing families, the Preprimary Project encompasses even the most informal child care settings, those that would be missed by a study interviewing only providers and teachers. Furthermore, the family interview strategy documents parents' uses of *multiple* care and education settings, thereby giving an unprecedented total picture of care and education for each child studied. The strategy provides much-needed information about the various combinations of settings experienced by children, the proportions of their time children spend in these settings, and the time children spend traveling between settings.

SELECTION OF REPRESENTATIVE SAMPLES OF FAMILIES

In each participating country, at the outset of Phase 1, Preprimary Project staff were faced with the task of locating a representative sample of families with 3½- to 4½-year-old children. Directing this task was Preprimary Project Sampling Referee Dr. Leslie Kish from the Institute for Social Research at the University of Michigan. Dr. Kish is well known internationally in the area of survey sampling and has been a leader in the field for many years. He and ICC staff developed a sampling questionnaire to help countries design their national sampling plans.

Because of national differences in the availability of sources of information, each country's plan for locating a representative sample turned out to be unique. For example, Finland has an up-to-date computerized listing of the names, addresses, and birthdates of the entire population, which made selection of the sample of families a relatively simple task. In the People's Republic of China (PRC), lists of residents exist, but they are noncomputerized and are found in registration books kept in sub-police stations scattered throughout each province. Consequently, PRC project staff and Dr. Kish needed to devise procedures for selecting families from the listings in these registration books. PRC staff tried to locate and include all families in areas selected for the study by establishing the following guideline for their interviewers: They were to interview all families except those who could not be reached in less than 24 hours of walking. Under this guideline, only those living on the most remote farms are excluded from the PRC sample of families. For Phase 1 data collection, the number of families interviewed in the various participating countries ranged between 400 (as in Belgium and the U.S.) and 12,800 (in the PRC).

Data Analysis

The Phase 1 data analysis for each country is being conducted by the country's Preprimary Project staff. At the same time, computer tapes of the Phase 1 data will be forwarded to the ICC (High/Scope) for cross-national analysis. The first phase of the data analysis will include descriptive statistics depicting the characteristics of early child care and education settings, both formal and informal. The factors influencing family choices of arrangements, such as children's experiences, family characteristics, resources, and needs, will be explored through relational analysis. The second phase of the data analysis will attempt to build an explanatory model of early childhood care and education as it is affected by such national characteristics as family and child policies or demographics.

Public Policy Implications

Both cross-national and national findings resulting from the Preprimary Project have potential policy implications. Each participating country can view its national data within the context of the broader, international findings. For example, participants might use national data to assess how desired preschool coverage rates (the percentages of children who *should* be served) compare with actual coverage rates. They might use the international data to compare the relative effectiveness of various national systems of care and education and then use this information in planning preprimary programs for their own countries.

Portugal provides a good example of how the Preprimary Project's Phase 1 findings will be used. Today in Portugal, approximately 30 percent of preschool-aged children are being served by early childhood programs. Recently, about the time that Portugal joined the European Economic Community, the Ministry of Education issued an Educational Development Program for 1988–93. Under this program, the preschool coverage rates targeted for 1993 are 90 percent for 5-year-olds and 50 percent for 3- and 4-year-olds. To meet the 1993 objectives, Portugal will need large investments of human and other resources, as well as information to use in the planning and implementation. Gathering Phase 1 findings about Portuguese families' service needs and usage patterns is viewed as an important first step in this planning and implementation process. It is hoped that project data coming from the various regions of Portugal will clarify the regional differences that must be considered in building a new and expanded early childhood care and education system.

The People's Republic of China provides another example of the public policy uses of Phase 1 findings. Very recently, in 1987, the planning activities for PRC early childhood care and education were decentralized, with principal responsibility for these programs shifting from the State Education Commission to committees at the provincial level. Under the revised system, each province must first consider its geographic conditions (terrain, distance between towns) and the characteristics of the families living in the province and then develop the most appropriate programs. For individual provinces, this newly acquired planning function requires up-to-date information to base their preprimary plans on. The 10 provinces participating in the IEA Preprimary Project are depending on project data for this information. Guizhou Province, for example, which already has project data from a sample of 2,600 preschool children and their families, intends to use its data in developing a provincial preprimary education plan.

Future Phases of the Project

Phase 2: The Quality of Life in Settings

Phase 2 consists of collecting information about the quality of life for young children in early childhood care and education settings. A sample of the settings identified by families during Phase 1 will be selected for use in Phase 2. Employing a caregiver/teacher interview questionnaire as well as on-site observations, Preprimary Project staff will study conditions in various types of care and education settings. A core group of major types of settings (for example, in-home care by parent or guardian, group educational programs) will be studied in Phase 2 across all participating countries. Some countries will study additional types of settings, such as ones designed for specific families or children, or ones with public policy interest specific to a given country (such as Head Start in the U.S.).

The caregiver/teacher interview will focus on fixed characteristics of the setting—physical setup, management features, qualifications of staff, costs, operating schedule, child activities, ancillary services, parent participation. Observations will focus on the emotional climate, the physical surroundings, and interactions and behaviors of children and adults. Also during Phase 2, a small number of children from each type of setting will be assessed in certain areas of development. Assessment data will serve as base-line information for later assessment of the same children, in the Phase 3 follow-up study.

Phase 2 will produce detailed information about the structure and process of early childhood care and education in the participating countries. At present, structure and process data are available in only a few countries and for only some settings. Thus, even the simple descriptive statistics from Phase 2 should be of great interest to those concerned with care and education planning.

Phase 3: Assessing the Impact of Preprimary Experiences

Phase 3 of the Preprimary Project involves follow-up through age 7 of the same children evaluated in Phase 2. By this age, children from all participating countries will have completed at least 1 year of primary schooling, although the nature and substance of the primary schooling will vary widely from country to country. Thus, in order to maximize worldwide comparability, researchers may have to utilize locally appropriate means of evaluating the 7-year-olds' social competence and academic achievement. Phase 3 of the project will provide valuable information about how children's early childhood care and education experiences may influence their responses to later schooling.

National Profiles as a First Step

As noted earlier, the first step of the Preprimary Project has been the preparation of a national profile of early childhood care and education by each participating country. These profiles provide a general picture of the early childhood services available within the country, including the history and characteristics of these services, and the role of the government in supporting these services. Each country's official policies regarding the care and education of young children are also described in its profile. Following this chapter are the 14 national profiles of the participants in Phase 1 of the Preprimary Project. The wealth of information in these profiles and the diversity of the care and education systems they describe will provide the reader with a fascinating overview of how nations serve young children.

REFERENCES

Barraio, J. (1988, November). *Public policy implications from an international study of child care: Portugal.* Paper presented at the annual meeting of the National Association for the Education of Young Children, Anaheim, CA.

Berrueta-Clement, J. R., Schweinhart, L. J., Barnett, W. S., Epstein, A. S., & Weikart, D. P. (1985). *Changed lives: The effects of the Perry Preschool program on youths through age 19* (Monographs of the High/Scope Educational Research Foundation, 8). Ypsilanti, MI: High/Scope Press.

IEA Preprimary Project Steering Committee. (1984). *Preprimary Study.* (Available from High/Scope Educational Research Foundation, 600 North River Street, Ypsilanti, MI 48198.)

United Nations. (1965). *Demographic Yearbook: 1964.* New York: United Nations Department of International Economic and Social Affairs, Statistical Office.

United Nations. (1966). *Demographic Yearbook: 1965.* New York: United Nations Department of International Economic and Social Affairs, Statistical Office.

United Nations. (1974). *Demographic Yearbook: 1973.* New York: United Nations Department of International Economic and Social Affairs, Statistical Office.

United Nations. (1976). *Demographic Yearbook: 1975.* New York: United Nations Department of International Economic and Social Affairs, Statistical Office.

United Nations. (1982). *Demographic Yearbook: 1980.* New York: United Nations Department of International Economic and Social Affairs, Statistical Office.

United Nations. (1986). *Demographic Yearbook: 1984.* New York: United Nations Department of International Economic and Social Affairs, Statistical Office.

United Nations. (1988). *Demographic Yearbook: 1986.* New York: United Nations Department of International Economic and Social Affairs, Statistical Office.

United Nations Children's Fund. (1987). *The state of the world's children.* Oxford: Oxford University Press.

Weikart, D. P. (in press). Early childhood education. In T. Husen & N. Postlethwaite (Eds.), *International encyclopedia of education.* Oxford: Pergamon Press.

II

Early Childhood Care and Education in Belgium

Arlette Delhaxhe, *Researcher*
Department of Pedagogical Research
University of Liège

This case study describing the national profile of early childhood care and education in Belgium is designed to provide background information for the International Association for the Evaluation of Educational Achievement (IEA) preprimary study. It should not be considered as an exhaustive inventory of the Belgian situation. Rather, it is an attempt to integrate and report briefly the information available concerning child care conditions for Belgian preschoolers.

Our report is structured in the following way: After a brief introduction to the current socioeconomic picture and to the educational system, we give a detailed description of the present-day care options for children under 3 years of age. Then we focus on the information concerning the nursery school: history, administration, inventory, functioning, and curriculum. Finally, we discuss two main concerns regarding the existing conditions of care for 2- to 6-year-old children. This information should be relevant to defining national child care policy issues for the coming decade.[1]

Introduction

Since before the creation of the country in 1830, Belgium has had an infrastructure of care for young children—an established network of extrafamilial child care services for children under 6 years of age. Because of its charitable origins, this network was at one time primarily concerned with children's health and protection. Modern-day nursery schools (for 3- to 5-year-olds) have assumed other functions, however.

They are the places where children's socialization and personality development are nurtured. The role of the nursery school is clearly to prepare children to succeed in later schooling. Nevertheless, in the current care services for children *under* age 3, we can still feel the trace of the former aim of providing for children's health and protection.

A look at the prevailing socioeconomic situation in Belgium—in particular, at the situation of women—will perhaps provide some background for a more detailed discussion of child care.

The economic and social context of the last decade in Belgium is one of profound change. A general slowdown of the nation's economic activity has brought about a major restructuring of work organization and the employment market. Yet, despite this context of an overall economic slump, there has been an increase in the level of women's employment. (In 1982, for example, 39 percent of women over age 15 were employed, as compared with only 25 percent in 1961.[2])

This is not to say that women are proportionately represented in the country's unemployment figures. Because of women's tendency towards part-time work or short-term careers, they have been the favored targets for layoffs by employers attempting to create needed flexibility in their work force. But precisely *because* of this precarious state of work organization and employment, women are now replacing their traditionally short-term careers with continuous careers interrupted only by the birth and early upbringing of children. Today in Belgium, for 1 woman in 3, full-time rather than part-time employment is a preferred state, even for mothers of children under 3 years of age. If one considers those employed full-time, employed part-time, and actively seeking employment, 66 percent of mothers of children under age 10 are "economically active" in Belgium.[3] Thus the nation's network of extrafamilial child care is of more importance than ever.

In Belgium, employed mothers are entitled to a 3-month maternity leave (14 weeks paid). After that, the mother can obtain a 2-year child care leave without pay. When employed mothers do not choose to take this 2-year leave, from the age of 3 months their babies can be cared for outside the home in day care centers or in family day care homes. Since 1969 it has been possible for children to attend a nursery school from age 2½ to age 6. They start primary school in September of the year of their 6th birthday, and secondary school is begun normally at the age of 12. School is compulsory for children between ages 6 and 18. At present in Belgium, most 3-year-old children (95 percent) attend nursery school. As far as we know, there is no other formal system of extrafamilial day care available to them.

Day Care Options for Children Under 3 Years of Age

For children under 3 years of age who are not in parental care, there are the following official extrafamilial care options:[4]

- **Nurseries** (subsidized by government)
- **Preschool day nurseries** (subsidized and supervised by government)
- **Registered (staff) childminders** (subsidized and supervised by government)
- **Independent childminders** (not subsidized, but supervised by government)
- **Children's homes** (not subsidized, but supervised by government)

To give an idea of the extent to which these care services are utilized by parents, we can cite the following 1982 statistics[5] concerning the 361,962 children under age 3 in Belgium: The subsidized services accommodated 13.8 percent of the under-3 population; the nonsubsidized services accommodated 5 percent of the under-3 population.

Since 1969, when the age for entry into **nursery school** (*école maternelle*) was lowered to 2½, enrollment in nursery school has become another official care option for some children under age 3. In 1982, some 22,000 (about 6 percent of the under-3 population) attended nursery school. It is worth noting that among the options available to parents, only the nursery schools are free of charge (except for meals) and widely prevalent throughout the country. (Nursery schools are discussed in a later section.)

There are also "unofficial" forms of child care—the "clandestine" or "alternative" childminders, who are unsubsidized and unsupervised, and whose numbers are difficult to determine. Considering only those children in *known* extrafamilial care situations in 1982, we find that about two fifths go to a childminder (independent or registered), one third go to a nursery, and one fourth go to nursery school.

Description and Functioning of the Various Child Care Services

Nurseries

Nurseries (crèches) are institutions registered and subsidized by the Oeuvre Nationale de l'Enfance (ONE)[6] that care for children from birth up to the age of 3 years. A nursery must meet standards and regulations set by the ONE (and by the ministry of the community under whose jurisdiction it comes) concerning admission requirements, facility and site requirements, medical supervision, staff, and parental contributions.

The admission requirements are as follows: Only children "whose mothers cannot possibly provide them with the necessary care" and who are not suffering from any illness are accepted in a nursery.[7] As a result, "welfare cases" aside, most of the children in a nursery have mothers who are employed or who are students.

Most nurseries operate approximately from 7 a.m. to 6 p.m. Cared for by pediatric nurses, the nursery children are traditionally grouped into three age-ranges: youngest (under 8 months old); middle (from 8 to 18 months old); and oldest (18 to 35 months old). This grouping was linked at one time to the subsidy mode, and it determined the architecture and planning of the premises. Despite a 1981 change in the subsidy mode, this grouping system has been kept in most nurseries. It leads to an operating procedure whereby children change rooms and often pediatric nurses at least twice during their stay (at age 8–10 months and at age 18 months), and sometimes the changes are even more frequent (especially in big nurseries).

When they were initially created (in the middle of the 19th century), nurseries were charitable institutions. Their explicit role was that of "preventive hygiene"—to lower the infant mortality rate and thus keep alive the potential manual labor the country needed. The nursery was also a means for combating extreme poverty, by making it easier for mothers to hold jobs. Like similar "philanthropic" activities, nurseries were part of the movement to raise the moral standard of the working class. After the two world wars, the nurseries changed from their social safeguard role to more of a child care service role.

Beginning with the 1970s, several protest and cultural movements in favor of nurseries began to take shape: the workers' movement, the students' movement, and the women's movement. This trio of movements stirred up demands for quality and opened debate regarding provision of communal education for young children. Thus, gradually over time, nurseries have been invested with an educational role. In addition to this, the economic crisis of the last decade has endowed the nurseries once again with a social prevention function, as maltreated or at-risk children from families undergoing hardship are entrusted to nurseries by various social agencies.

The initiative to create a nursery comes from the local level. A day care center for children under 3 years of age has never been organized on the initiative of the ministry concerned (Ministry of Public Health before 1981; the executive of the French-speaking community since then). A nursery can be created by a **public authority** (state, commune,[8] province) or by a **private authority** (a social, instructional, educational, charitable, or commercial organization not under public jurisdiction). If created by a private authority, the nursery has to be set up as a nonprofit association (called an ASBL[9]). There are few nurseries (only 15) linked to companies; most nurseries are run by universities and hospitals.[10] There are no establishments run by volunteers, and only one parent-run nursery, which is a nursery established at the initiative of parents and staff in Verviers. All the nurseries, both public and private, are subject to the same standards, which are those enacted by the Ministry of Health of the French-speaking community and by the ONE.

To help combat Belgium's economic crisis, the government was forced to take restrictive measures, and among these was a 1981 measure changing the extent of adult supervision in nurseries (Royal Decree of July 15, 1981): At present, the ONE will subsidize only 1 pediatric nurse for every 7 children, whatever their age. However, this modification did not radically change the number of staff in nurseries. A staff-child ratio of 1 to 7 is inadequate if one considers the long operating hours of nurseries (staff members each work 36 to 38 hours per week, while the nursery stays open 50 to 60 hours); the need for staff time-off for leaves and illnesses; and the time staff must spend meeting with parents, supervising trainees, attending staff meetings, and undergoing various types of inservice training (on site and outside the workplace).

Parental financial contribution for a child's nursery care is required by law and is fixed every year by the Ministry of Health according to a sliding scale based on income. In 1987 the parental fee ranged from 50 to 426 Belgian francs per day. (At the time of writing, $1 U.S. fluctuates between 40 and 50 Belgian francs [BF].) The government's restrictive measures of 1980–81 have granted nurseries the option of asking parents for additional contributions (diapers, medicinal products, proper diet food, clothes) or for more money.

The 1970 ONE regulation pertaining to organizing and running nurseries (and preschool nurseries) addressed primarily hygiene, dietetics, and medical care for the children. In the 11-page regulation, only the following passages dealt with education: "Those children accepted by the nursery shall receive an education appropriate for their age which shall promote their ethical and intellectual development" (Article No.

129). "Inflicting corporal punishment on children, or modifying their diet as punishment is forbidden" (Article No. 135).[11]

The new (undated) regulation, *Minimal Normative Regulation*, shows a clear improvement. In fact, the document starts out with the principle that "in order for a child to develop harmoniously, care should be taken so that the facilities provide for the young children . . . the maximum opportunities on the physical, mental, psychological, and social levels, by making sure that hazards particular to that age are limited."

Although the standards for the supervision, architecture, and running of nurseries are uniform, diversity in ways of running nurseries has nonetheless been observed. "No single nursery is identical to another one."[12] "It is difficult to draw up very precise typology for nurseries. Each of them is a unique case, the result of an original combination of variables such as the organizing authority, size, material means, staff employed, etc."[13]

Starting with 1976, practically all the nurseries have opened their premises to parents and have adopted flexible daily schedules. But such "open" nurseries as these neither allow parents to witness their daily operations nor accommodate parents for a period of time in living quarters. Neither the staffs of the nurseries nor the parents are presently aware of how important it is to introduce a very small child gradually into a place that is strange to him or her. Rare indeed are the nurseries where parents participate in regular activities with the children.

Moreover, as a more recent survey[14] has shown, few are the nurseries that offer the parents the opportunity (in a management committee or a parents' committee) to express their opinions on how the nursery is being run, on its internal organization, on the relations with the organizing authority and with the subsidizing authority or authorities. Discussion with parents takes place mostly in conferences; parent-teacher meetings in nurseries are a recent and rather infrequent phenomenon.

The cost for nurseries is covered by three parties: the ONE (which pays staff salaries for only the quota of staff set by law), parents, and the organizing authority. The expenses for additional staff, furniture, and services (food, clothing, games) fall on the organizing authority and the parents. Funding from the National Board of Family Allowances for Salaried Workers is available in certain cases.

Preschool nurseries

Other child care institutions registered and subsidized by the ONE are the preschool nurseries, which care for children between the ages of 18 months and 3 years. At the time of their establishment, many preschool nurseries were annexed as sections of nursery schools, especially in the private educational system.[15] Thus, choosing such an annexed preschool nursery for their child may constitute for parents the first step in choosing between the private or public educational systems, which compete fiercely in Belgium. However, the preschool nursery staff is more paramedical than educational. It consists of

- A nurse (quarter-time for every 12 children) and a social worker (quarter-time for every 24 children)
- A pediatric nurse (1 for every 9 children)

In a preschool nursery, the responsibility for a group as large as, for example, 20 children may be shared either between two pediatric nurses or between a pediatric nurse and a primary school teacher. This latter solution is rarely adopted, however, because primary school teachers are not trained to care for small children, and above all because primary school teaching has certain advantages over working in a preschool nursery (for example, a primary school teacher works 27 hours per week except for school holidays; a pediatric nurse works 37 hours per week except for 3 weeks of paid holiday). Unlike nursery schools, preschool nurseries do not close during school holidays, and they provide care for children from 7:30 a.m. to 6:00 p.m.

The initiative to create and manage preschool nurseries comes in most cases from the organizing authority of a school (for example, from an ASBL or from the Municipal Authority for Public Instruction). Preschool nurseries underwent a period of expansion during the 1970s, with the result that by 1976 the day care capacity of preschool nurseries was relatively greater than that of nurseries.[16] As a day care solution, however, the preschool nursery did not appear to be meeting the needs of working parents, since it did not accommodate children under the age of 18 months. Thus, since 1980 the trend has been to transform preschool nurseries into nurseries (caring for children from birth to 3 years of age). Nevertheless, the government circular of the summer of 1986, which strictly prohibited the enrollment of any children under 2½ years old in nursery school classes, has increased parents' problems of finding day care for 2-year-olds.

Registered (staff) childminders

The private childminders who are registered and subsidized by the ONE may be attached to a nursery (Royal Decree of February 18, 1974) or to a service that is organized by a public authority, a public-service establishment, or a nonprofit association (ASBL), provided that the service employs at least 10 childminders (Royal Decree of August 18, 1975). These childminders can look after three children at most. A social worker or licensed social nurse supervises the childminders, who work in private homes. The French-speaking community pays the salary of this supervisor and remits a per-day, per-child contractual payment to the nursery or service employing the childminders. Though the contractual compensation is fixed by an executive decree, the per-child subsidy paid by the community varies to complement the amount of the parent's fee (which is determined by a sliding scale based on the parent's income). What a registered childminder earns depends on the number of children she cares for and the number of days she works per week. Her earnings are approximately 400 BF per day per child.

As to the professional recognition of registered childminders, they have a status similar to that of volunteers. Their job cannot be described as a profession; it is exempt from taxes, and it is not subject to social security charges. Thus, registered (staff) childminding services enable organizations and the communes to create child care solutions quickly and at low cost. This is evidenced by the fact that since the Royal Decree of August 18, 1975, childminding services organized by an ASBL have developed rapidly throughout the country—except in Brussels. According to ONE statistics, in 1985 there were 129 services employing 4,536 childminders, who provided care for 13,222 children.

Given the rapid growth of these services, important issues associated with childminding have to be discussed:

- **The recruitment of childminders**. Becoming affiliated with an ASBL enabled certain childminders to escape the tax authorities at the very moment when the latter were trying to uncover clandestine independent childminders, ones working "in the black market." Childminding services have probably established their own recruitment standards and criteria, but legal statutes contain no references to this subject.
- **The training of childminders**. Legal statutes are not specific at all on this subject, which leaves the question open as to training methods and course content.
- **The status of childminders**. With a volunteer status, a childminder, even a registered (staff) one, is not a full-fledged worker; because she pays no social security charges, she depends on her husband's social security (if she is married).
- **The social security exemption**. At present, a registered (staff) childminder, even though she does earn a certain income, does not pay back anything into the public treasury, because she is exempt from taxes.

■ **The childminder's image**. Whether independent or registered, with or without status, a childminder assumes—for the children of a woman who works—the traditional image of a wife at home taking care of the house and the children. This may account for the childminder's lack of recognition as a professional.

Independent childminders and children's homes

There are also childminders who, though they are accredited and supervised by the ONE, are not subsidized by it. These **independent childminders** look after children up to 7 years of age, in private homes. An independent childminder is allowed to care for no more than five children; when care of more than five children is involved, there must be multiple childminders and the setting is known as a **children's home**. Independent childminder care often takes place at the home of one of the childminders.

These independent childminders are supervised by ONE medical social workers. Medical supervision of children is compulsory and is carried out by postnatal health care services.[17] Independent childminders are paid for their services; the amount is set by the childminder. The permission of the commune is required for someone who wishes to become a childminder; granting of this permission is usually dependent on the positive recommendation of an ONE medical social worker.

Many choose the job of childminder because it enables them to stay at home and to combine family-type tasks, including bringing up one's own children, with a paid job. It means having a "job" without having to undergo job training. It also means avoiding the constraints of a salaried job: The childminder reaches an agreement with parents about the terms of her employment—about daily schedules, pay, services to be performed.

The inconveniences of independent childminding are those of freelancing (independent work) in general:

■ Paying heavy social security charges and paying tax on the cumulative income of the spouses (or working in the black market and running the risk of being fined by the tax inspection department).

■ Having working hours that equal the parents' work and commuting time and that therefore usually go beyond the 8-hour daily limit that is guaranteed for salaried workers by statutory provisions.

■ Having uncertain income with no job security. The childminder's income depends on the number of children she minds and the number of days they spend with her. When there is a break in the child's need for care, certain childminders demand a "reservation" sum from the parents—for example, during the summer holidays. But it often happens that these childminders find themselves at the mercy of parents who are late in paying the reservation sum or who contest the sum requested. Thus the child's presence is often the stake in the financial relationship between childminder and parents. Furthermore, any leave the childminder might wish to take—for illness or holiday—means not only that she cannot earn money but also that there is a deterioration of the services provided to the parents. Thus certain childminders are worried about feeling ill, and they hesitate to take holidays.

A childminder is a person whose work confines her to the house; she must combine her household chores with caring for extra children. Isolated from other women in her situation, she is alone to face the responsibilities and problems of her job. The low pay and job instability reserve the role of childminder for married women whose husbands are employed and who wish to earn some extra money while maintaining the image of "the mother at home." The price paid to a childminder for a day varies widely. It is highest in big cities (around 400 francs per day in Brussels or Liège) and can vary depending on the hours and services involved.

This type of child care is presented as being more flexible than nurseries; the childminder is supposed to be more tolerant; she spends extra time with a sick child; and so on. Some think that it is a more family-like environment and that it is easier for parents to establish a relationship with the childminder. In reality, things are quite diverse, and assessments of the situation tend to be contradictory. To date, there has been no systematic appraisal of this mode of child care. Nevertheless, it is the only child care solution for a good number of families, when there are no child care places available or when there is no other child care institution in the vicinity (as is often true in communes in the outskirts of cities, in rural communes, in villages).

Staff Training

Nurseries and preschool nurseries

The staff who care for children under 3 years of age receive their initial training in one or more of the following fields: pediatric nursing, nursing, social work, medicine, and in some rare cases, nursery school teaching.[18]

Statistics show that pediatric nurses make up the core of the people thus employed, that is, approximately 80 percent of the staff.[19] Pediatric nurse training is not university-level education; it is secondary-level education with an emphasis on health and household economics (in vocational or technical school). This initial training is quite unsatisfactory, both in terms of content and level.

A recent training-needs analysis[20] has shown how important it is for those educating very young children to develop skills like the following:

- A good command of the development processes of a young child and, in particular, of interaction processes and emotional dynamics
- An acquired sense of observation (especially regarding the behavior of adults)
- A good command of psychosocial dynamics (relations in a team and with the parents)[21]

Although there is a need for staff to have some paramedical proficiency, it becomes obvious that staff training should be directed towards promoting an educational project in every nursery.

Except for a decree adopted in June 1983 by the French-speaking community (which has not been enacted to date), there are no specific legal provisions regarding staff inservice training. However, an inventory of the resources that a continuing training program for the staff of nurseries and preschool nurseries could draw on reveals a rich array of diversified opportunities. Unfortunately, given their low income, pediatric nurses are unable to pay for this continuing training. It might be of interest here to point out that the career of a pediatric nurse working in a day care center is at a dead-end; she cannot be promoted to any higher function, status, or pay scale.

A survey[22] conducted in 49 nurseries and 35 preschool nurseries for a representative sample of all the French-speaking institutions has shown that 81 percent of the staff surveyed affirmed that they would have liked to finish their initial training. Nevertheless, the same study shows that while 80 percent of the staff questioned believed that additional training would be useful, only 12 percent reported that their studies had prepared them quite inadequately.

The earlier-mentioned decree that is awaiting enactment has prompted the ONE to investigate an altogether original inservice training program, an undertaking that covers some 60 nurseries.[23] At the beginning of 1986, the nurseries were invited to formulate an inservice training curriculum. In each nursery, the projects were conducted in coordination with the advice of a scientific (university) team and guided by psychologists. This kind of coordinated inservice training can help

- To adjust training to the real needs of each nursery
- To increase the number of psychologists and improve the coordination between them
- To regularly revise the training on the basis of a permanent evaluation

Childminders in private homes

Very few statistics are available on the initial training of childminders. The accreditation of childminders in private homes is not subject to any training criteria, either for independent childminders or for registered (staff) childminders. It goes without saying that this is a problem: Even if the experience of being a mother spares a childminder a great deal of problems in many situations, such experience is not enough to provide a young child with care and education of a professional quality, given the complexity of this task. Research is now under way concerning the staffing services and training needs for childminders.[24]

INSTITUTIONAL EDUCATION FOR CHILDREN AGED 3 TO 6 YEARS

HISTORY AND ORIGINS

Institutional day care already existed at the time of Belgium's proclamation of independence in 1830. Its aims at that time were to protect the children of the working classes from accidents and vagrancy, since the rapid industrialization and urbanization that characterized the beginning of the 19th century were shifting women from their homes to factories. Children 3 to 6 years old were cared for by the hundreds in large rooms, an arrangement called *salles d'asile* (rooms of shelter). This form of institution was organized by religious organizations or by local authorities. Benevolent women looked after the children, not only providing them safety and physical care but also attending to their moral upbringing. The aim was "to inculcate the rules of order, ethics, and religion—principles that they cannot acquire in their own families."[25]

Around 1850, Froebel's ideas about children's activities and play needs spread from Germany into Belgium, and some private kindergartens were opened. In 1880 the government published the first regulations for the institutions taking care of children aged 3 to 6 years, annexing these institutions to primary schools and calling them *écoles gardiennes*. Short-term training for teachers was organized, and educational aims were developed at the same time. The first official program was established by the Ministry of Education. It was highly inspired by Froebel's pedagogy. A passage from the first page of the regulations reads, "The nursery school (école gardienne) was meant to prepare children to succeed in primary instruction and to give them what is necessary for their physical, intellectual, and moral development."[26]

Four other institutional preschool programs have been developed during the 20th century, in 1927, 1950, 1974, and 1985. More and more, socioaffective and cognitive development of the child are the goals emphasized by the programs developed for young children. At the beginning of the 20th century, only underprivileged children attended school (8 percent of the population); nowadays, children of all social classes go to school. At the end of the 19th century, official statistics recorded 929 écoles gardiennes for the French-speaking part of Belgium; today 2,018 of these nursery schools (now called *écoles maternelles*) exist, with 7,477 classes caring for children aged 2½ to 6 years.

This significant increase in school enrollment of 3- to 6-year-old children seems to coincide with the spread of psychological knowledge to parents. It also seems to keep pace with the growth of the early childhood "market" of tapes, books, and educational aids for young children. The educational aims of preschool institutions have steadily integrated the new scientific developments in education.

It is hard to know if the transformation of the nursery school function from a caretaking one to an educational one has been brought about by increasing educational demands from privileged families that enroll their children or if the reverse is true. Families' increasing educational demands may be a *result* of the new educational opportunities afforded by preschool settings.[27]

ADMINISTRATION

The Ministry of Education is the central administrative body that is responsible for planning the programs and for regulating the establishment and functioning of schools, including the nursery schools. In Belgium, several educational networks do exist:

- A school network **organized by the state** and completely subsidized by the Ministry of Education

■ A school network funded partly by the state but **organized by local authorities** (local or provincial schools)

■ A school network funded partly by the state but **organized by private institutions** (mainly Roman Catholic schools)

Every authority (local, private, Roman Catholic) that decides to build a school has to adhere to governmental rules and norms to obtain subsidies; therefore every nursery school (école maternelle) is regulated by the same rules for the equipment norms, salaries, number of children per group, days off, and so on. Controls are centrally organized to check on the nursery schools' sanitary conditions, student-teacher ratios, and equipment norms. Supervisors, each of whom is responsible for about 250 teachers, visit nursery schools and give advice and inservice training to the teachers. Besides this inservice training, nursery school teachers must have initial postsecondary training that consists of 3 years of study in a nonuniversity vocational training school, the *école normale*. Nursery school supervisors have the same training as teachers and at least 10 years of teaching experience. They must also have passed a diploma examination.

There is no charge for a child to attend nursery school in Belgium. Private schools with a charge for admission are rare; there are perhaps, at most, only five in Belgium. Parents only pay for school lunch, when it is organized or served, and they often pay for care and supervision outside normal school hours. In the last 10 years, many centers have been created in Belgium that take care of children when schools are closed—in the morning, in the afternoon, or on school holidays during parents' working hours. These extracurricular services are called *halte garderia* (similar to babysitting), *ludothèque* (toy-lending service), sports clubs, or artistic clubs.

Inventory of Settings

Approximately 2,000 nursery schools are available for the French-speaking part of Belgium. Fifty-three percent of them depend on local authority, 37 percent are Roman Catholic schools, and only 10 percent are state schools. Children with special needs (for example, physically handicapped children, mentally retarded children) are cared for in a special institution called *école maternelle speciale*, where adapted education is provided. They benefit from special rules for equipment, norms, and ratio. In 1985 there were 651 children attending these special institutions.[28]

Actually, 98 percent of the children aged 2½ to 6 years are in nursery school (Table 1). We have no exact figures for the distribution of the remaining 2 percent: They are either at home with their families or in some other type of day care for children older than age 3; the 5-year-olds who are not in nursery school belong to the poorest part of the population.

The daily schedules are identical at nursery school and at primary school. Activities usually take place from 8:30 to 12:00 in the morning and from 1:30 to 3:30 in the afternoon for 5 days a week during the school year. (Schools are closed on Wednesday afternoons.) All 3- and 4-year-old

Table 1

Percentages of Populations Enrolled in Nursery School From 1960 to 1975

Population			Percent of Population of Each Age (in yr) Enrolled			
Birth Year	Number Born	Academic Year	Under Age 3[a]	Age 3	Age 4	Age 5
1955	148,798	—	—	—	—	—
1956	150,181	—	—	—	—	—
1957	152,388	60–61	6.8	79	90.5	92.9
1958	195,894	61–62	7.0	79.2	91.3	93.1
1959	160,662	62–63	7.7	78.6	90.8	94.4
1960	155,520	63–64	6.1	82.5	90.6	94.3
1961	158,262	64–65	6.8	84.9	94.0	94.3
1962	154,338	65–66	6.8	86.6	94.5	96.0
1963	158,196	66–67	6.8	87.5	96.2	97.6
1964	160,371	67–68	8.0	87.6	96.7	99.7
1965	154,856	68–69	7.9	80.1	96.7	99.5
1966	150,636	69–70	17.4	88.5	98.8	98.7
1967	145,899	70–71	19.3	90.3	97.0	99.2
1968	141,242	71–72	19.6	91.9	97.4	99.5
1969	140,834	72–73	20.2	93.2	98.6	99.4
1970	141,119	73–74	20.7	93.7	99.6	100.0
1971	139,104	74–75	20.8	94.2	99.7	99.9

Note. Population statistics are from the *Yearbook of Statistics of Belgium* (in French), National Institute of Statistics, Vol. 95, 1975, p. 12. Enrollment statistics are from the *Yearbook of Educational Statistics From 1960 to 1970* (in French) and *Demographic Statistics* (in French), National Institute of Statistics, No. 3, 1975.

[a]Starting with the 1969–70 school year, the age for admission to preschool dropped from 3 to 2½ years.

children are at school in the morning, and most of them attend school all day, while all 5-year-olds attend a full day of school.

In most nursery schools, children are divided into three groups composed of, respectively, those under 4, those aged 4 to 5, and those aged 5 to 6. Mixed-age groupings, however, are becoming increasingly popular. The child-adult ratio varies from setting to setting, with 15–30 children per teacher; the average, which has gradually improved over recent years, is 21 children per teacher. The rules concerning child-adult ratio allow the subdivision of a teacher's group if more than 31 children are enrolled.

Portrait of Nursery Schools

A survey being conducted in the French-speaking part of Belgium[29] on the life conditions of 4-year-old children in nursery schools gives the following picture:

The majority of schools (72 percent) are located in the center of the locality. Rural as well as urban schools are rarely (2 percent) in isolated locations. Only 20 percent of the school buildings are less than 20 years old. Building structure is generally traditional and specifically built for school use (in only 3 percent of cases are ordinary houses employed as nursery schools).

Even though all schools have playgrounds, in 10 percent of the cases the young children have to share it with the 6- to 12-year-old children. In 30 percent of the schools, there are no outdoor shelters from the rain, so children must stay in the classrooms or in another room when weather is bad. Although many schools are equipped with a gymnasium and a dining hall, other auxiliary facilities are less common. Moreover, in some cases the facilities exist, but the young children of the école maternelle do not have access to them (see Table 2). On average, the available space in the classrooms is 68 square meters, but there is considerable variability among schools.

The description of materials available in the different classrooms shows that such things as construction materials, dolls, books, table games, and painting supplies are present in a majority of cases, but more expensive materials like television sets or gardening supplies are often lacking.

More interesting are the results of the cluster analysis, which distinguishes two groups of schools according to the richness and originality of materials on hand. The "traditional" equipment (including the basic classroom items) is found in both groups. In addition to this, the first

Table 2

AUXILIARY FACILITIES OF SCHOOLS

Facility	Percent of Schools So Equipped	Percent of Schools Where Facility Is Accessible to Young Children
Gymnasium	62	49
Video room	33	26
Reading room	24	13
Projector room	20	17
Theater	12	9
Playroom	33	31
Dining hall	71	61
Workroom	9	7

Note. Data are from *Nursery School in the Plural* (in French), Research Report, by D. Lafontaine and A. Delhaxhe, University of Liège, 1987.

group is characterized by the possession of a lot of expensive and original material (miniature-shop, fancy-dress, audiovisual, gardening, cooking). So, we may distinguish "rich" schools equipped with diversified and expensive materials from "poorer" schools equipped only with the traditional materials.

The age of the building, the number and accessibility of auxiliary facilities, the richness of the materials, are all indicators that vary significantly from school to school. However, no correlation is observed between the richness of materials and the social status of the children enrolled in a setting.

The length of service of the teachers who care for 3- to 6-year-old children is important. More than a third have more than 21 years of service and thus are above 40 years old. Only 25 percent of the teachers have less than 10 years of service. This phenomenon is general in Belgian education: The average age of schoolmasters becomes older and older. In the majority of cases, one teacher is alone to care for a group of 20 children (on average) for all activities. Some schools (25 percent) benefit from the help of a nurse, especially with the youngest children.

The auxiliary personnel most often includes a cleaning woman (in 90 percent of the schools) and a supervisor for the care services during the extracurricular time (present in 50 percent of the schools). A sports teacher, for psychomotor activities, is present in only 12 percent of the schools.

If a teacher is ill, another one replaces her in a majority of cases, but the promptness of replacement varies from one setting to another. In half of the schools she is replaced immediately; in other schools it takes a week and sometimes more. The alternative solution is to parcel out the teacher's children among other teachers' classes.

Curriculum Recommendations and Practices

From the very beginning, the objective of the nursery school curriculum has been to prepare children to succeed in primary instruction. The most recent curriculum, which dates from September 1985, is the result of recommendations prepared in committee by experts, supervisors, and teachers and then approved by the ministry.

The curriculum deals with the following main fields: scientific activities (play with water, physical experiences, care of animals, exploration of the environment); language activities (stories, speeches, vocabulary); artistic activities (drawing, painting, modeling); physical education; music activities (singing, rhythm); and mathematics. The program recommends inclusion of all these fields in life activities that respect children's individuality and permit their active participation. Each age is concerned with all the different fields, but teachers have to adapt difficulty levels to the ages of the children. There is some informal evaluation at the end of the école maternelle, and some basic competencies are required of children. Tests are also given by psychologists.

A recent inquiry[30] reveals that Belgian teachers give priority to teaching children the parts of the body, distinctions between left and right, language, and logical-mathematical knowledge. Moreover, the same study also shows that the relative importance assigned to socioaffective development and to academic learning depends on the point of view of the teacher. Some teachers think that it is important to teach children discipline and academic knowledge; these teachers have a "traditional" understanding of the educational role of the école maternelle. Other, more "progressive" teachers give priority to play, social interaction, and autonomy of the children.

How Is the Program Put Into Practice?

An experimental study[31] currently being carried out to obtain a picture of the daily life experiences of 5-year-old children at school looked at 27 different classroom activities, including the following:

waiting	drama plays	manual activities
snacks	recitation	pretend play
play time	arithmetic	gardening
talks	writing	cooking
stories	painting	

The study reveals that on average, 65 percent of the school hours are devoted to educational activities; the remaining time is devoted to play, waiting, and snacks. The activities most frequently proposed to the children are painting and manual activities, preacademic learning, and talks. On the whole, the école maternelle seems more oriented to instruction than to play; the activities proposed to the children require more listening, silence, and exercise than play, sports, or relaxation. However, these percentages reflect an average calculated on the basis of overall observations and do not reveal the significant variations between schools.

A study carried out by B. Quoidbach and M. Crahay in the Liège region[32] shows how widely the duration and nature of activities offered in nursery classes differ, depending on social level of the children's families. For children of the working class, the time devoted to educational activities is reduced, and recreational activity is favored. For children from more privileged families, activities in systematic academic preparation and worksheets related to these activities are more prevalent.

At present, enrollment in école maternelle is almost universal for 3- to 6-year-old children in Belgium. But what does it really mean for a Belgian child to attend the école maternelle? The results of the surveys we have mentioned suggest that it may mean different things for different children. Indeed, in what should be similar programs, we find differences in the material characteristics (facilities, richness of material, auxiliary services, space allotments) as well as in the pedagogical aspects (educational goals and activities).

TWO MAIN CONCERNS

EXTRACURRICULAR TIME AT SCHOOL

In Belgium, if attending nursery school no longer differentiates younger children (because they all attend nursery school at least part-time), there are nevertheless important differences among children with respect to the *time* spent at school. Young children's schedules (other than their class schedules) depend on the requirements of their parents' professional lives, and in particular, on the requirements of their mothers' professional lives. In fact, a research study by V. Pieltain[33] shows that the time spent outside the home by a child correlates with the time spent outside the home by the mother. The daily schedule for the father does not influence that of the child. Thus, some children (5 percent) spend 10 hours a day in school. Others (15 percent) spend an average of 8 hours in school. Often, other childminding solutions replace the child care service at school; in these cases, grandparents principally look after children during the mothers' employment hours that are not covered by school activities.

The child care services outside of class hours (morning, noon, evening) are not the responsibility of the National Ministry of Education. These services depend exclusively on local organizing authorities. There is no regulation governing them, and the government grants only a meager subsidy (125 francs per 100 children) to the schools for the noontime care services; the organizing authorities have to contribute the rest. Critical points concerning children's extracurricular time at school include

- The large numbers of children and the noise
- The lack of possible activities for children during these periods
- Inadequate facilities
- Lack of trained staff

The previously mentioned survey being conducted in the French-speaking part of Belgium on the life conditions of 4-year-old children in preschool settings[34] has so far yielded this information:

- There is an organized child care service in 75 percent of the schools. No significant difference has been observed in this regard among the surveyed school systems.

- The presence or absence of a day care service in a school varies significantly in relation to the number of inhabitants in the area. The probability of finding a day care center in a school increases in densely populated areas.

- Facilities used for day care centers are, for the most part, school classrooms (38 percent), followed by dining halls (28 percent). Only 15 percent of nursery schools have a room specifically for child care purposes; in fact, 3.5 percent of child care centers use a corridor!

- Services can be provided in the morning (before 8:30), at noon, and in the afternoon (after 3:30). When they are organized, they last between 1/2 hour and 1 hour in the morning, for about 1 to 1½ hours at noon, and from 1½ to 2 hours in the afternoon. So, some schools open very early in the morning or close very late in the afternoon. Others are open solely during class time.

▪ When a hot meal is available at noon, parents have to pay for it in a majority of cases.

▪ The different care services offered by schools are rarely free (in only 3 percent of cases). The care service in the morning and at noon is often free; a payment is asked from parents for the care in the afternoon. The price varies from one setting to another.

No exhaustive data are available on the staffing of childminding services at school. The just-mentioned survey and the opinions of nursery school inspectors nonetheless provide us with the following information:

▪ According to the inspectors, teachers prefer not to have to perform child care tasks outside curriculum hours.

▪ These services are provided by a wide variety of individuals. Table 3 indicates the types of caregivers children are faced with during extracurricular hours. Nursery school teachers appear to be the ones least likely to provide early morning and evening day care services.

The National Ministry of Education grants a modest subsidy for supervisory duty during lunch. Since the subsidy is insufficient, the rest of the funds are provided by the organizing authority, by fundraising events in the educational community, or by direct payment on the part of the parents.

Table 3

TYPES OF CAREGIVERS IN CHARGE OF CHILDREN IN NURSERY SCHOOLS DURING EXTRACURRICULAR HOURS

	Percent of Schools With Type of Caregiver			
Time of Extracurricular Care Service	Mother	Supervisory Pediatric Nurse	Nursery School Teacher	"Rotating" Duty
Morning	26	18	11	19
Noon	29	24	14	32
Evening	27	19	7	21
Wednesday afternoon	19	17	0	4

Note. Data are from *Nursery Schools in the Plural* (in French), Research Report, by D. Lafontaine and A. Delhaxhe, University of Liège, 1987.

In conclusion, a not-yet-determined number[35] of children between ages 2½ and 6 are being cared for on the premises of nursery schools outside official curriculum hours. There is no overall care policy for these children to date (regarding caregivers, activities, child-adult ratio, quality of care, and organization of meals). The entire responsibility is left up to the local organizing authorities and may eventually be shared by parents' organizations.

Thus at the end of the 20th Century, we find in the child care services organized during the extracurricular time some characteristics reminiscent of the first preschool setting that sheltered young children in the 19th century—low wages for staff, unqualified staff, excessive noise, inadequate facilities, and grouping together of children of different ages. Moreover, since we know that the upper-class families try to choose other childminding solutions, we might question the socioeconomic level of the children who "haunt" the care services. Would we find after all these years the same social homogeneity that characterized the original preschools? It may be, however, that the critical look being given to these services and the attempts at improving them in recent years are signs that different social classes are now using the services. Whatever the case may be, the quality of life of young children has to be improved, as do the financial, social, and educational aspects of the day care services.

The Younger and Younger Enrollment in School

Today, all 5-year-old children are at school, and everybody agrees on the importance of and the necessity for 3- and 4-year-old children attending school; it is recognized as an educational and socializing environment for a young child. But there is a recent phenomenon in preschool education in Belgium: It is the school attendance by younger and younger children. Since 1970, more and more children under age 3 attend nursery school. This premature school attendance may be partly explained by the fact that parents use the nursery school as a form of free child care as opposed to using other modes of child care, such as nurseries, preschool nurseries, and family day care. Enrolling and accommodating children under 2½ years of age has been formally prohibited by a ministry circular since September 1986, but no other solutions have been proposed.

For children under 3 years of age, the emphasis is on child care (even if there is a call for an educational dimension); day care for young children remains linked to women working (even if during these last few years the "return" of children from poor families has been discerned). The fact that parents must make a financial contribution seems to indicate that women's employment is seen as a "luxury" that enables women to find fulfillment away from the household.

Can the slogan "a maximum of opportunities for a maximum of children" be retained when children 2 to 3 years of age are cared for in such widely different situations? Various kinds of social services are proliferating especially for children in the 18- to 36-month age-range. Young children are divided among different modes of child care: family care, private childminders, nurseries, preschool nurseries at school. This means child-adult ratios ranging from 1 or 2 children per adult to 25 children per adult. Inequality in degree of staffing and supervision, in funding, in facilities, and in staff training constitute the substantial differences among the various day care structures. Is this admissible when all children have equal need for high-quality day care?

ENDNOTES*

[1]Since 1980, Belgium has been divided into three communities. This subdivision is related to the linguistic regions: Flemish, Germanic, and French. Each community has its own government. At the present moment, the autonomy of each community is mostly related to cultural and social matters. In 1989, the federalization of the country is slated to increase.

Our report presents the situation of the entire country of Belgium insofar as the rules and problems are the same in all three communities. There are instances, however, when the only available statistics are from the French-speaking community, as our sources will indicate to the reader.

[2]From A. Bayar and D. Meulders, *Evolution of the Level of Women's Employment in Belgium* (in French), 2nd ed., March 15, 1985.

[3]From Bouillaguet-Bernard, Gauvin, and Provokas, *The Evolution of Work and Employment of Women in the European Economic Community*, p. 40.

[4]This part is a synthesis of a conference presented by G. Manni at the Council of Europe, Study Group on "Forms of Child Care," coordinated by Social Research Fellowships, 1986/1987 Program. It has been prepared with the collaboration of M.-L. Carels, University of Liège.

[5]Percentages are from G. Manni (1986), whose source is *ONE Statistics Yearbook, 1982* (in French).

[6]Since 1984, the ONE has been divided into two independent parts—one for the French-speaking community, the other for the Flemish-speaking community. The Flemish ONE, the Kind en Gezin (Child and Family), differs from the French ONE in that the Flemish

---

*The editors would like to express their appreciation to Arlette Delhaxhe for translating into English all reference elements in the endnotes.

allows nurseries and registered childminders to take care of children aged 3 to 6 years during extracurricular hours, days off, and holidays.

[7]From Article No. 119a and Article No. 135 of the *Rules for Nurseries and Preschool Nurseries* (in French), 1970 and 1981, which are unpublished documents available from the ONE.

[8]A commune is the lowest level of administrative area. Geographically, it gathers several villages. Each commune has a burgomaster and a council.

[9]ASBL stands for *association sans but lucratif* (association without paid purposes).

[10]The nursery of the Commission of the European Communities, which accommodates 200 children, has the status of a "children's house" and is not subsidized by the ONE.

[11]From the *Rules for Nurseries and Preschool Nurseries* (in French), 1970 and 1981.

[12]*Day Care Services* (in French), document prepared for young parents, ONE, 1985, p. 8.

[13]From B. Meunier, F. Delfosse, and R. Renard, *Infant Care Services in Brussels* (in French), Office of the Prime Minister, 1978.

[14]M. L. Carels, G. Manni , A. M. Mengels , and E. Paulet, *Nurseries, Educational Care for Children* (in French), Department of Experimental Education, University of Liège, 1985.

[15]In 1975 there were 50 preschool nurseries in Wallonia; of 41 preschool nurseries surveyed, all the private preschool nurseries (19), as opposed to only a third of the public preschool nurseries, were attached to a school. Cf. F. Delfosse under the direction of C. Presvelou, *Nurseries and Preschool Nurseries* (in French), documents of the Center for the Study of Population and the Family, Brussels, 1977.

[16]F. Delfosse under the direction of C. Presvelou, op. cit.

[17]Article No. 12, Law of September 5, 1919.

[18]This information on training has been prepared by A. Dethier, University of Liège.

[19]See C. Blondin, A. Dethier, and M. Andrien, *But What Do They Want? Training Needs* (in French), University of Liège, 1985, p. 31.

[20]For more information on this study, carried out under the direction of Professor G. DeLandsheere (Department of Experimental Education) and F. Geubelle (Clinic of Childhood Illnesses) of the University of Liège, see the following:

A. Dethier, C. Blondin, and M. Andrien, *Children and Grownups. Adults and Children in Nurseries* (in French)

C. Blondin, A. Dethier, and M. Andrien, *But What Do They Want? Training Needs* (in French)

M. Andrien, A. Dethier, and C. Blondin, *Caregiver Training. Structure and Methods* (in French)

University of Liège, Department of Experimental Education, Clinic of Childhood Illnesses, 1985.

[21]See A. Dethier, et al., op. cit.

[22]See C. Blondin, et al., op. cit.

[23]This investigation is reported by C. DeRidder and A. Dethier in *The First Steps* (in French), University of Liège, Department of Experimental Education, 1987.

[24]The study is commissioned by the ONE and is conducted by A. Dethier and C. Blondin, Univeristy of Liège, Department of Experimental Education.

[25]Translated from an extract of the *Municipal Bulletin* (in French) of Liège, Vol. 2, 1837–1839, Liège, 1840, p. 9.

[26]From Article No. 1 of the *Circular of the Minister* (in French), August 20, 1980.

[27]E. Plaisance, *The Nursery School Today* (in French), Paris, Nathan, 1977; J. C. Chamboredon, *The Job of Children, Towards a Spontaneous Education*, (in French), Research Report, Organization for Economic Cooperation and Development—Center for Educational Research and Innovation, Strasbourg, 1975.

[28]From *Stastical Documentations* (in French), 1985–86 academic year, Brussels, National Ministry of Education, 1986.

[29]D. Lafontaine and A. Delhaxhe, *Nursery School in the Plural* (in French), Research Report, University of Liège, 1987.

[30]M. Crahay and A. Delhaxhe, What Do Teachers Think About What Is Important to Do at Nursery School? (in French), Research Report, University of Liège, 1985.

[31]A. Delhaxhe, *Observing the Quality of Life of Young Children in Preschool Settings, IEA Preprimary Project Experimental Study* (in French), Paper presented at the Third Conference on Developmental Psychology, Rome, 1986.

[32]B. Quoidbach and M. Crahay, "Sociocultural Characteristics of Children and Curriculum Realized in Four Preschool Settings" (in French), *Scientia Paedagogica Experimentalis, 21*, 1, (1984): 19–49.

[33]V. Pieltain, "The Day of 4- to 6-Year-Old Children: An Inquiry in the French-Speaking Community" (in French), *Scientia Paedogogica*, in press.

[34]D. Lafontaine and A. Delhaxhe, op. cit.

[35]Ibid. The most precise information that we get are the following: 57 percent of the children stay at school at noon, 10 percent of them arrive earlier in the morning, and 9 percent are also cared for later in the afternoon.

III

Child Care and Early Education in the Federal Republic of Germany

Wolfgang Tietze, *Professor of Education*
Hans-Günther Rossbach, *Senior Researcher*
Karin Ufermann, *Research Assistant*
Department of Education
Westfälische Wilhelms-Universität Münster

Introduction

The following report offers a general profile of some aspects of the care and education of children of preschool age in the Federal Republic of Germany. The report focuses primarily on 3- to 6-year-olds. For this age group, Germany has a distinct, historical tradition of institutionalized preschool education, namely, kindergarten. Compared to other areas of care and education for young children, kindergarten is the most regulated in terms of legal provisions; it is also in the kindergarten area that the most research has been done and the most elaborate educational models have been developed. Kindergarten for 3- to 6-year-olds has been looked upon for close to 20 years as the elementary level of the general educational system, and there is a broad consensus that every child in this age group should have the opportunity to attend kindergarten (this is not the case, however, due to greatly differing regional rates of supply). Nevertheless, it is becoming clear in political and educational debates that tasks and problems currently taking shape regarding the care and education of young children can only be partly resolved within the framework of today's kindergarten.

Increasingly, questions relating to the whole age group from birth to school entry are being raised. And, in addition to the educational aspect, which dominates in the kindergarten's self-image, the child care aspect—both at kindergarten age and below—is increasingly becoming the subject of public debate. For this reason the age group of under-3-year-olds will also be considered in this report, despite the fact that the database is smaller; the literature, more limited; and the educational models, less well developed.

This profile covers historical aspects of the development of preschool care and education, documents some aspects of the present situation (as far as it is reflected in available statistics), and outlines the complete spectrum of public assistance provided for the care and education of young children in the Federal Republic of Germany. This is followed by a description of the chief child care options, in which legal, administrative, and educational angles, among others, are differentiated. In a further section, aspects and problems of the national research scene in the field of preschool education are roughly sketched. A final chapter addresses important points of departure that are emerging in today's discussions about the further development of a differentiated system of care and education for young children.

The profile does not attempt to discuss in detail the development of educational theories and concepts or of pedagogical models; it contains, in this respect, only rough sketches. Instead, a macroscopic, policy-oriented point of view is set forth, which takes into account the historical developments, the present state of affairs and its problems, and the points of departure for further development of the systems of early childhood care and education in keeping with Germany's changing social circumstances.

Historical and Philosophical Perspectives

Early childhood education and care, as a more or less clearly articulated and consciously employed educational concept, has been developing in Germany and other central European countries over the past two centuries. Its origins must be seen against the background of the formation of the bourgeois notion of the family, which came into being during the second half of the 18th century. This notion, which has generally been distinguished by an increase in warmth in the climate of family bonds, assigns a central role to the mother-child relationship (cf. Shorter, 1975). Accordingly, woman "discovers" within the family her "natural" vocation as wife and mother. Hence, the previously prevalent attitude of a certain degree of indifference towards children was replaced by one characterized by constant concern for and attention paid to children's upbringing. As a result of this cultural-historical development, childhood began to be perceived as a separate state of being (cf. Ariès, 1962), a state needing to be observed, interpreted, and subjected to deliberate molding. Educational theorists, particularly those of the circle of Philanthropism (Basedow, Wolke, Salzmann, Campe, among others), drew attention to the great importance to adulthood of the earliest phase of human life and expounded on what was pedagogically appropriate for the child (cf. Heiland, 1987).

However, members of a large number of social strata lacked the material means necessary to attain such a bourgeois family ideal. This discrepancy was further aggravated by growth of the proletarian population due to industrialization. Because of the poverty of the lower classes, all capable family members, mothers as well as older children, were obliged to work to obtain the means of subsistence. The mother's employment was ranked as more important than the care and upbringing of her small children, who represented a burden on the household and, indirectly, a further source of additional poverty. While their mothers were at work, many children, who often lacked supervision from a very early age, were left to their own resources. They were confined to their accommodations and were in some cases even given sedatives or alcohol to keep them quiet. Accidents among children were common, and a considerable number were in danger of complete dereliction (Barow-Bernstorff, Günther, Krecker, & Schuffenhauer, 1986, pp. 123 ff.; Erning, 1987a; Reyer, 1985, pp. 65 ff.). As a consequence of such a cluster of developments, various local establishments for the care and education of young children came into being. In most cases, their founding was initiated by members of the bourgeois class and the aristocracy, and the cost was borne by private societies (cf. Krecker, 1983; Reyer, 1985, pp. 133 ff.). Reyer (1987b, pp. 252 ff.) speaks of the dual motivation of publicly organized child care and education inasmuch as the objectives were to enable the mother's employment (and with this to stabilize socially and economically lower-class households) *and* to educate their small children according to bourgeois principles. In practical terms, the aims were to preclude the physical and psychological dereliction of children, to instill in them morals appropriate to the circumstances of their class, to relieve the burden on public relief funds, and to free the emerging school system from looking after young children, a task it had begun to adopt (cf. Erning, 1987a). Governmental authorities swiftly recognized the stabilizing effects such institutions had on the status quo of society and advocated their dissemination, without providing funds for their support, however.

An important role in the propagation of early childhood education was played by the writing of the Englishman Samuel Wilderspin, which was translated into German in 1826. Wilderspin propounded the importance of education for young impoverished children between the ages of 1½ and 7. About the middle of the century, parochial preschools, which had goals similar to Wilderspin's and were run according to methods described by the Protestant minister Theodor Fliedner (1800–1864), gained wide acceptance. As early as 1836, Fliedner founded in the Rhineland an establishment providing extended courses that trained women to care for and teach small children. Such trained women were then employed in the parochial preschools (cf. Erning, 1987a; Krecker, 1983). Similar efforts on the part of the established churches were made in many regions, and they formed a starting point from which, during the second half of the 19th century, the Protestant and Roman Catholic churches gained decisive influence on early childhood education and care in Germany. However, judged against the bourgeois family ideal, the institutionalized forms of early childhood care and education could offer only a poor substitute. Nevertheless, it seemed justified in a situation in which social conditions prevented the achievement of the desired quality of the mother-child relationship. The goals of such institutions were not exclusively devoted to the care and education needs of the young child outside the context of the family.

This is also true, at least partly, of the philosophy of Friedrich Froebel (1782–1852). His *Kindergarten* was not primarily intended to be a new institution. He conceived it as a pedagogical principle, with the aim of providing a new basis for the education of children *within* the family itself (cf. Heiland, 1987). Froebel's intention was to aid and instruct mothers to provide a better early education for their children by means of didactical toys and games. Froebel's conception of early childhood care and education did not intentionally relate to bourgeois children, but in fact it did so. Working-class mothers did not, for instance, have at their disposal enough leisure time to engage in the intensive preoccupation with the child that Froebel proposed.

Nevertheless, it was not the kindergarten in the form of a pedagogical model for mothers but rather the kindergarten as a pedagogical institution utilizing play and games educationally that made its reputation and created its enduring influence both in Germany and far beyond its borders. It is a mark of this influence that the term *kindergarten* as the label for preschool education has been adopted either in this form or in translated form in so many languages. Froebel's concept of the kindergarten also included intensive personnel training, the details of which he himself designed.

Froebel's conception of early childhood education and care played an important role in the aspirations and efforts to create a national plan for education during the bourgeois revolution of 1848. Together with the teachers' associations, many politically progressive individuals demanded the recognition of the kindergarten as an integral element and the very basis of a uniform national system of education. This inclusion of the kindergarten in the proposed democratic national system of education was one of the reasons for the prohibition of the kindergarten in Prussia for 10 years, from 1851 to 1861, after the failure of the bourgeois revolution (cf. Barow-Bernstorff, Günther, Krecker, & Schuffenhauer, 1986, p. 197).

A continual increase in the number of preschool institutions characterizes developments in the second half of the 19th century. Existing side by side were a number of differing types of institutions: There was the Froebel kindergarten, for instance, which emphasized educational goals. Kindergartens were generally open for only a few hours a day and attended largely by middle-class children. There were also the preschools for the poor, in which social welfare functions were emphasized. The physical environment of the preschools was not conducive to education; children often spent the whole day there. When an attempt was made to incorporate the pedagogical methods of the Froebel kindergarten into the conceptual framework of the institutions with a largely welfare character, this resulted in the establishment of the conceptual framework of the *Volkskindergarten* (people's kindergarten). Thus began a process of drawing together the various conceptions of the differing institutions.

The German Froebel Society—a union of various regional Froebel initiatives founded in 1873—and the "Pestalozzi-Froebel House," founded in 1874, played a part in the dissemination and further development of early childhood education. The Pestalozzi-Froebel House maintained a model kindergarten under the direction of Henriette Schrader-Breymann, a former pupil of Friedrich Froebel, and also trained kindergarten teachers (cf. Krecker, 1983, pp. 184 ff.). Despite the dissemination of center-based early childhood education and its gradual adoption in bourgeois strata, the idealized mother-child relationship lost, at first, little of its normative force. Women active in such institutions were guided by the spirit of motherhood, even though the children were not their own. It was because of such notions that public early childhood education developed into an exclusively female profession. Froebel himself had intended that men should also take up the profession and he had even trained some to do so (cf. von Derschau, 1985, 1987).

According to Reyer (1987c), it has been since about the turn of the last century that child-oriented motives have been advanced as a justification for center-based preschool education. At least part of the 3- to 6-year-old age group was offered a socialization that was independent of and supplementary to family upbringing. The process of becoming recognized as a system independent of specific family conditions was attended by a growing state regulation of kindergarten teacher training. In the 1908 revision of regulations governing girl's higher-school education, the Prussian board of education included kindergarten teachers' training in the curriculum of girls' schools. In 1911, standards for the examination of women completing this course were set (cf. von Derschau, 1985, 1987; Tietze, 1987). These enactments represented the beginning of an increasing commitment on the part of the state towards kindergarten education.

After the end of World War I and the transition from empire to republic, a fundamental revision of the educational system was undertaken. However, those who wished to include kindergarten in the educational system and to make it the bedplate of a uniform educational system for all children failed to achieve their objective. The regulations laid down in the 1922 Youth Welfare Act are even today still valid in principle. The law acknowledged the right of every child to an education, which the public authorities were obliged to provide indirectly or directly—if the family itself was unable to do so. The law gave priority in the founding and running of kindergartens to organizing bodies of independent social welfare organizations. This meant that kindergartens sponsored by public authorities were only established if the need for such institutions was not met by the churches or other philanthropic organizations (the principle of subsidiarity). Youth welfare offices established to operate at the level of town or county administration were to provide a public means of supplying a sufficient number of places in kindergartens, of maintaining standards of teaching and care, and of supervising all private and public institutions (cf. Reyer, 1987a). As a result of the economic crises in Germany in the 1920s and also of the growing power of politically reactionary forces, the planned system could not be fully realized. Compared with the level achieved prior to

World War I (see Table 1), there were in fact slightly fewer kindergarten places. Early childhood education was nevertheless seen from that period onwards as a peremptory public duty to be furthered and regulated by the state.

In the so-called Third Reich, kindergarten was, like all other educational institutions, placed in the service of National Socialist ideology and its desire for power (cf. Berger, 1986). The extension of National Socialist influence into the kindergarten system, which up to that time had been pluralistic in its structure, was achieved by various means. In some cases the organizing bodies were brought into line with National

Table 1

HISTORICAL PERSPECTIVE OF THE GROWTH OF KINDERGARTENS[a]

Territory	Year	Number of Institutions	Number of Children	Supply Ratio[b]
Kingdom of Prussia	ca. 1850	400	26,000	1.0%
City of Berlin	ca. 1850	33	3,800	7.5
German Empire	ca. 1910	7,300	559,000	13.0
	1930	7,300	422,000	13.0
	ca. 1940	20,000	1,123,000	31.0
Federal Republic of Germany	1950	8,600	605,000	32.3
	1960	12,300	817,000	32.8
	1965	14,100	953,000	32.7
	1970	17,500	1,161,000	38.4
	1975	23,100	1,479,000	65.5
	1980	24,000	1,394,000	78.8
	1985	24,500 [c]	1,465,000	80.0

Note. From Bundesminister für Bildung und Wissenschaft, 1987; Erning, 1987b; Reyer, 1985, 1987a; Neumann, 1987; Statistisches Bundesamt, 1988b; Statistisches Bundesamt (oral communication); partly authors' calculation.

[a]All data should be regarded as approximate. The values have been rounded off by the present authors.

[b]The supply ratio has in most cases been calculated by comparing the total number of kindergarten places with the number of all children between the ages of 3 and 6. However, because there are some kindergarten places occupied by children *under* 3 and *over* 6 years of age, the ratio should not be misinterpreted as the ratio for children *between* ages 3 and 6. For example, this tables's 1985 figure of 80 percent can be compared to a figure of only 66 percent for the age group of *exactly* 3- to 6-year-olds.

[c]Data for 1986.

Socialist ideology; in others, the church kindergartens were taken over by the National Socialist welfare organization Nationalsozialistische Volkswohlfahrt (NSV), although in many instances the NSV founded its own institutions. Kindergarten teachers' professional organizations were treated in the same manner. For instance, the Froebel association, with its long tradition, was forced to disband (cf. Reyer, 1987a). Particularly as a result of the exigencies of the war economy—women and mothers having to replace men in factory work—the number of kindergarten places was greatly increased (see Table 1).

After the end of World War II and the collapse of the structures of National Socialism, the prevailing function of the kindergarten was the one that characterized it at the time of the origin of the institution in the 19th century: Kindergartens became again institutions whose task was to save children from the threat of dereliction. The problems were, however, so great that kindergartens could only contribute partially to their resolution. A considerable number of children were orphans; many fathers had fallen at the front or were prisoners of war, so women and mothers formed the primary source of labor potential for securing their families' bare existence. The fact that many buildings—whether factories, offices, or dwellings—had been destroyed in the bombing and the fact that several million refugees and displaced persons from former German territories in the eastern part of the country had arrived in the Western Zones exacerbated the problems.

Different paths were taken in the reestablishment of the kindergarten system in East Germany (the future German Democratic Republic) and in West Germany (subsequently the Federal Republic of Germany). In East Germany the inclusion of a kindergarten level in the system of education was planned as early as 1946 and was later confirmed in law. Thus kindergarten came to be defined as an educational institution; correspondingly, it is free of charge. In contrast, the path of restoration was chosen in West Germany. As in the case of the school system, the kindergarten system turned to the example of the Weimar Republic. Kindergarten remained the administrative responsibility of the youth welfare service, and its function was limited to that of supplementing family upbringing where needed. In essence, the regulations of the 1922 act were adopted (cf. Barow-Bernstorff, Günther, Krecker, & Schuffenhauer, 1986, pp. 415 ff.; Neumann, 1987).

The state's contribution to the setting up and further development of the kindergarten system in the Federal Republic of Germany was trifling up to the second half of the 1960s. Social policy and the concomitant public debate largely reflected a return to the traditional image of the family (cf. Neumann, 1987). A widespread summary critique, although it was somewhat exaggerated, contained more than a grain of truth when it suggested that women and mothers should perceive their tasks in the triple *K* of "*Kinder*, *Küche*, *Kirche*" (children, kitchen, church). This family image implied a lack of a general need for an additional system of preschool education beyond that of the family. Such a system of care and education outside the confines of the family served its purpose only in cases in which family adversities made it unavoidable.

There was, in addition, a widespread belief that preschool education in kindergarten might even pose a threat to the family inasmuch as the institution enabled mothers to take on jobs outside the family circle. This attitude is expressed in remarks of the Minister for Social Affairs in 1957, which were made in response to the suggestion that the number of kindergartens be expanded: "We must consider very carefully to what extent the family, although protected on the outside by the creation of such social institutions, exhausts itself internally as a result" (cited in Grossmann, 1974, p. 97).

No coordinated plan existed for the extension of the kindergarten system, 80 percent of which lay in the hands of the churches. In terms of absolute numbers of institutions and of places for children within those institutions, there were increases between 1950 and 1965. However, because the birthrate rose considerably at the same time, the relative availability of places for children in kindergarten was, by the mid-1960s, the same as in 1950 (see Table 1). The program of the kindergarten at this time, corresponding with the social welfare theme that was reflected in the public attitudes towards kindergarten, was primarily concerned with the protection and custody of the child.

Embedded in conceptions of developmental psychology, according to which the child's development is effected as an internally controlled process of maturation (cf. Schmalohr, 1970), kindergarten pedagogy considered its most significant task to be providing the child with a protective environment—an environment that would secure an undisturbed development of children's talents and abilities and that would shield children both from overwhelming stimuli and from their own precocity. Regarding kindergarten, one of the most distinguished educational theorists of the period remarked: "We counteract the hothouse atmosphere of the modern world, which forces the child into a premature discrimination of its holistic response to the sensations of its environment . . . we are convinced that it is essential to offer pedagogical resistance to the precocity set in motion by our time" (Hoffmann, 1968, p. 347).

This situation changed dramatically in the mid-1960s, when a remarkable phase of expansion and reform in West Germany's education system took place. Kindergarten, although not an element in the education system, was rapidly caught up in the reform process. Indeed, early childhood education was even accorded a key role.

The immediate postwar restoration of the education system, which had been oriented towards older models, no longer seemed adequate to meet the demands of a developed industrialized nation. The conviction that the German education system was heading towards a catastrophe (cf. Picht, 1964) was widespread. As a result, the debate on education became the dominant theme in social policy during the second half of the 1960s. As an expression of a general consensus regarding the need for improving the education system, the German Council on Education, a committee consisting of scientists, members of the government, and representatives of important social groupings, was established in 1965. Its task was to make recommendations for a fundamental reform of the entire education system. Particular attention was paid to early childhood education in the hope that it would be capable of making a special contribution to the main goal of educational reform. Early childhood education would supposedly draw on the "educational reserve." It was assumed that the deficits of underprivileged children could be adjusted by compensatory early childhood education prior to school entry, thus providing equal opportunity for all children in the general school system. It was furthermore assumed that by a systematic utilization of the potential of early childhood learning, the general standard of education among all children would be raised (cf. Deutscher Bildungsrat, 1970). As a consequence, these goals caused great uncertainty in the traditional kindergarten system and led to a dramatic reorientation of its pedagogy. Kindergarten education had previously set as its task the furthering of play and games and of the child's innate developmental potential. These earlier postulates were now regarded, at least polemically, as "passive spectator" pedagogy, and the kindergartens were decried as institutions in which children were artificially kept stupid (Lückert, 1967).

Excessive enthusiasm for the imagined potentialities of early childhood education was not infrequently expressed in rather simplistic conceptions of what constitutes educational furtherance of the small child. Drill-like training of separate functions, such as cognition, language, or thinking, was introduced into kindergarten and into many families. "Games for learning" and "didactical toys" were thrown onto the market on a scale previously unknown. Irredeemable expectations were placed in particular on early literacy (cf. Schmalohr, 1973). In addition, vehement controversies about an adequate early childhood education were provoked by the concept of an antiauthoritarian education for preschool children, which arose out of the student revolt in 1968 (cf. Breiteneicher, Mauff, & Triebe, 1971; Rabe-Kleberg, 1985). Its advocates conceived antiauthoritarian education as the direct opposite of education that furthers accommodation and boosts performance in serving the interests of others. A general consensus on a suitable curriculum for kindergarten in the form of the so-called situation-oriented approach (explained in a later section) was reached only in the 1970s.

The great importance ascribed to early childhood education, regardless of the various controversies, was expressed in a new assessment of the kindergarten as an educational instrument as well as in a massive expansion of the number of kindergartens. To a much greater degree than before, kindergarten was given an educational task independent of the state of affairs in the family; it was perceived as a distinct and fundamental stage in the total system of education. The German Council on Education (Deutscher Bildungsrat, 1970) coined the term *Elementarbereich* (elementary level) for this new stage, which was to precede the primary (ages 6–9) level of education. Although kindergarten attendance would not be compulsory, it was assumed that all children would be reached by provision of an ample supply of kindergarten places that were to be filled voluntarily.

This conception of the kindergarten for 3-, 4-, and 5-year-olds as the basic stage in the total system of education necessitated a vast extension of the number of kindergarten places available at the time. The German Council on Education (Deutscher Bildungsrat, 1970) scheduled a doubling of available places by 1980. Within this period, an enormous improvement in the provision of kindergarten places was achieved in West Germany (cf. Table 1) as well as in numerous other countries (cf. Tietze & Ufermann, 1989). The strong growth in the supply ratio (percent of children served), which by 1977 had already passed the 75 percent mark, was also partly due to a substantial reduction in the birthrate during the same period.

The new conception of kindergarten as the basic level in the educational system led to the question of how best to link the two levels, the elementary stage and the primary stage. Various models for a linkage between the largely play-oriented learning in kindergarten and the school-oriented learning in primary school were developed and tested (cf. Deutscher Bildungsrat, 1975). One model provided for a 2-year school-entrance stage in primary schools (comparable to the British infants' school), into which the 5-year-olds were supposed to be admitted to be steered from play-oriented to school-oriented learning in a gradual process over the 2 years. This model involved lowering the compulsory school-entrance age from 6 years to 5 years. Another model favored a year-long preparatory class for 5-year-olds, which was latched onto the unaltered traditional first year of primary school. These preparatory classes were also located in the primary schools. The advocates of kindergarten insisted that 5-year-olds would best be served in kindergarten's mixed-age groups and that a removal of 5-year-olds from kindergarten would have a detrimental effect on the development of the 3- and 4-year-olds.

Superficially, the "contest for the 5-year-olds" was conducted with pedagogically inspired arguments, and numerous models were tested to provide an answer to the question of which institution should serve the 5-year-olds (cf. Bund-Länder-Kommission für Bildungsplanung, 1976).

Politically, however, it was a matter of whether the traditional organizing bodies, in particular the churches, should retain their influence on the education of 5-year-olds or the state should take over responsibility for the education of this age group. In the power struggle in society, the advocates of kindergarten prevailed. Compulsory school-entrance age remained fixed at 6, and in most cases, the 5-year-olds were placed in kindergarten. As a present-day remnant of the model testing, however, a small portion of the 5-year-olds take part in a preparatory phase within primary schools.

As early as the second half of the 1970s, as a result of a generalized exhaustion of educational reform efforts, kindergarten lost its position in political priorities and in public attention. Except for insignificant fluctuations, the supply ratio of kindergarten places has remained what it was in the late 1970s. Some of the reform goals put into force in the 1970s have since been revoked. For example, the goal of the annulment of kindergarten attendance fees, which was to take effect in 1982 in North Rhine-Westphalia, the largest state (*Bundesland*) in the Federal Republic of Germany, was rescinded. In other instances, there have been exceptional rulings making standards (such as the required number of teaching personnel in institutions, the required size of kindergarten groups) less binding.

Most recently, kindergarten has again been brought to public notice. Changes in the structure of the family, the increase in single-parent families, the improvement in the standard of education of young mothers and their desire for employment outside the family, as well as the remaking of woman's image that has resulted from the feminist movement, all appear to be causes for the appeal for institutions that are more capable of responding to the changing needs and lifestyles of families and children (cf. Tietze, 1987). The demands are directed at the inadequate supply of kindergarten places that, despite a relatively high average quota, exists in many residential areas. Other demands concern a greater flexibility of attendance hours—wanting them to be coordinated with family needs, for example, or wanting an increased supply of full-time kindergarten places.

One central demand relates to the improvement of care for children under age 3 years, who have not generally been counted among kindergarten clients. *Krippen*, which are institutions specializing in the care of children younger than 3 years, came into being later than the kindergartens did and have not received the same educational approval up to now (cf. Reyer, 1985). They are to be found largely in major urban centers. With some 30,000 places, they cannot serve even 2 percent of the birth-to-3 age group. In the last few years a series of mixed-age kindergartens have been established in which children from birth up to age 6 are cared for according to certain standards (cf. Siebenmorgen, 1982).

DEMOGRAPHICS

Data relating to the care and education of young children in the official statistics of the Federal Republic of Germany prove to be generally rather unsatisfactory. It is true that there are various regularly conducted statistical surveys. However, apart from the fact that in some cases the reliability regarding at least some of the survey details is doubtful, the various surveys can only be related to one another in a limited way. For example, different surveys may employ different categories and definitions; different surveys may cover different key dates within a year; and some surveys only collect data from communities larger than a given size. Many times data about characteristics that are needed to obtain a differentiated picture are not gathered. In the following, reference is chiefly made to two sets of statistics, both of which are collected by the Federal Office of Statistics. The first consists of the official statistics on youth welfare, which include records of the places available in various forms of early childhood provision. Since 1982 these statistics have only been collected once every 4 years. The second set of statistics is the annual microcensus, which is collected from a 1 percent random sample of all households. These statistics indicate the numbers of children not yet in compulsory schooling who attend an early childhood provision. The most recently available data of the two sets of statistics relate to the year 1986. The data from these statistics have been supplemented with certain selected aspects of the demographic trends in West Germany.

Table 2 compares the numbers of places in Krippen (day-care centers for children under the age of 3 years), in kindergartens (for children from age 3 to age of school entry), and in licensed family day care homes with the "under-3" and "3 to under-6" populations. The data offer a characteristic image of the Federal Republic of Germany: A relatively large supply of places in kindergarten for children from 3 years of age to school entry contrasts with a very small supply of Krippen places for children under the age of 3. Even when we consider the places in licensed family day care homes, it appears that publicly authorized places of care, center-based or not, are available for only a very small portion of the children under 3 years of age. A comparative study of the 12 member-states of the European Economic Community shows that the Federal Republic of Germany must be classed with those countries having the lowest supply of care for this age group (cf. Moss, 1988).

A breakdown by states (*Bundesländer*) of the number of Krippen places tells us little because of the small number of cases. The small number of Krippen places that exist are mostly concentrated in a few of the largest cities. Over one third of all Krippen places exist in West Berlin (with 1.86 million inhabitants), which as a result achieves a good 20 percent supply ratio for care of children under 3 years of age. If we add the other two cities with populations exceeding a million, Hamburg and Munich, the three cities are responsible for more than half of all Krippen places (cf. Vergleichende Städtestatistik, 1987).

The statistics cover only family day care homes licensed by the youth welfare offices. This number, it is safe to assume, represents a considerable underestimation of the actual proportions of day care. Estimations assume that for each licensed family day care home, there are four nonlicensed family day care homes (cf. Martin & Pettinger, 1985, p. 239).

The 1986 statistics identify 1.47 million places in kindergarten and similiar institutions. If this figure is related to the total number of all 3- to under-6-year-olds—the ratio that the Federal Republic generally uses

Table 2

PLACES IN KRIPPEN, KINDERGARTENS, AND LICENSED FAMILY DAY CARE COMPARED WITH RELEVANT CHILD-POPULATIONS IN THE FEDERAL REPUBLIC OF GERMANY, 1986

	Number of Children (thousands)		Places in Krippen		Places in Kindergartens		Places in Licensed Family Day Care Homes	
State	Aged Under 3	Aged 3 to Under-6	Total	As % of Age Group (Under-3)	Total	As % of Age Group (3 to Under-6)	Total	As % of Age Group (Under-3)
Baden-Württemberg	289	293	3,442	1.2	309,410	105.6[a]		
Bavaria	321	344	3,004	0.9	238,963	69.5		
Berlin	52	49	10,814	20.8	35,864	73.2	no data	
Bremen	22	18	142	0.6	14,542	80.8	available	
Hamburg	34	37	4,130	12.1	21,119	57.1		
Hessia	147	163	2,240	1.5	146,652	90.0		
Lower Saxony	189	200	1,841	1.0	140,448	70.2		
North Rhine-Westphalia	482	478	1,816	0.4	380,338	79.6		
Rhineland-Palatinate	108	114	408	0.4	111,007	97.4		
The Saar	32	32	115	0.4	29,261	91.4		
Schleswig-Holstein	64	66	401	0.6	45,215	68.5		
Federal Republic	1,740	1,792[b]	28,353	1.6	1,472,819	82.2	25,735[c]	0.7

Note. Data are from Statistisches Bundesamt, 1988a, 1988b.

[a]A percentage above 100 percent indicates that the number of available kindergarten places exceeds the number of children from 3 to under 6 years of age. However, kindergarten places are also occupied by children above or below the age for kindergarten.

[b]The populations for the individual states do not add up to the total of 1,792 for the Federal Republic because of the rounding used in estimating the state populations.

[c]Places for all children under 16 years of age. Experience shows that approximately half the places are claimed for children under the age of 3. The percentage value for all states is calculated in accordance with this experience.

in planning—the result is an 82.2 percent supply ratio. There are considerable differences at the state level in the supply ratios. Generally, the data reflect a historically determined north/south gradient (cf. Erning, 1987b, p. 30). In contrast to this, a comparison of supply ratios according to community size reveals less well-defined differences. Kindergarten supply in rural communities seems to be directly comparable to that in urban communities (no table).

While Krippen for children under 3 years of age are full-day institutions, this is true of only a small portion of kindergartens. Unfortunately the statistics on youth welfare do not differentiate between full-day and part-day programs. According to another set of statistics— which, however, were gathered using a similiar mode of computation—in 1985 there were, across the Federal Republic, all-day kindergarten places for 11.9 percent of the 3- to 6-year-olds ("all-day" meaning with care extending over and beyond midday; Bund-Länder-Kommission für Bildungsplanung, 1987, p. 44). According to this information, there is a high degree of full-day provision only in the cities of Berlin (98.9 percent), Hamburg (58 percent), and Bremen (about 42 percent).

The supply ratio of 82.2 percent for the 3- to under-6-year-olds (Table 2) represents a considerable overestimate of the real state of affairs (as do all ratios formed as these are). The actual supply ratio turns out to be distinctly lower for this age group, while the actual ratio for children under 3 years of age is somewhat higher than that reported in Table 2. This is because kindergarten places are occupied by a large number of 6-year-olds and by a small number of under-3-year-olds. Thus, of the 3- to under-6-year-olds, 64.9 percent attend a provision, and of the under-3-year-olds, 4.2 percent attend a provision (cf. Table 3).

The typical age of entry for kindergarten lies around the age of 4 (cf. Table 3). Of the 3-year-olds, 38.2 percent attend kindergarten; for 4-year-olds, the percentage rises to 71.4 percent. About 15 percent of all 5- and 6-year-olds not yet in compulsory schooling do not attend a kindergarten. If one assumes that they neither have already attended kindergarten nor will attend such an institution before entering school, this implies that nearly 1 out of 6 children enters school without kindergarten experience. Such an interpretation must be regarded with some caution, however, since no longitudinal data can be obtained. The trend suggested is supported by research undertaken by the present authors at the beginning of this decade. A sample survey of class teachers in 458 school-entry classes representative of North Rhine-Westphalia showed that a good 20 percent of children in the first school year had not attended kindergarten.

Table 3

1986 PRESCHOOL PROVISION RATES (KRIPPE, KINDERGARTEN) FOR VARIOUS CATEGORIES OF CHILDREN NOT YET IN COMPULSORY SCHOOLING (INCLUDING CATEGORIES RELATING TO FAMILY TYPE)

	Age Group								
Category	Under 1 yr	1 yr	2 yr	3 yr	4 yr	5 yr	6 yr and Up	Under 3 yr	3 to Under-6 yr
Total children (thousands)	591	565	576	592	594	598	460	1,732	1,784
Children in preschool provisions (thousands)	9	17	47	226	424	507	391	73	1,157
Children in preschool provisions as % of total children	1.5	3.0	8.2	38.2	71.4	84.8	85.0	4.2	64.9
German children in preschool provisions as % of all German children	—[b]	—	—	38.4	72.8	87.3	94.5	—	66.1
Foreign children in preschool provisions as % of foreign children	—	—	—	37.7	63.3	68.7	67.8	—	57.3
Children in single-parent families as % of total children	8.0	8.5	8.7	10.0	10.0	9.9	10.4	8.4	9.9
Children of employed mothers[a] as % of total children	32.0	30.6	33.7	34.8	34.7	36.6	37.0	32.2	35.1

Note. Data are from Statistisches Bundesamt, 1988a, and authors' calculations.

[a]Includes children with single employed fathers.

[b]Cannot be calculated from microcensus data.

Table 3 also demonstrates that German children attend kindergarten more frequently than their foreign contemporaries do. (According to official data [Statistisches Bundesamt, 1988a, pp. 139 ff.], foreign children make up 11.1 percent of all under-3-year-olds and 12.5 percent of all 3- to under-6-year-olds in Germany). However, kindergarten attendance proportions of the two populations have drawn closer during the last few years. While in 1978 the kindergarten attendance rate for German children was more than twice as high as that for foreign children (cf. Bund-Länder-Kommission für Bildungsplanung, 1987, pp. 34 ff.), the 1986 attendance rates of 66.1 percent for German and 57.3 percent for foreign 3- to under-6-year-olds demonstrate a clear reduction in the disparity between the two populations.

The rate of kindergarten attendance is dependent not only on the child's nationality but also on parental income, as shown in Table 4: As family income grows, the likelihood of kindergarten attendance increases. That this pattern does not hold for the two lower-income groups may be due first of all to the fact that in these income groups, the proportions of children with single mothers are significantly larger than in other income groups; because of their gainful employment, these single mothers are dependent on the child care of a kindergarten. Secondly, in the case of such low incomes, no family fees are charged, so this possible barrier to kindergarten attendance is eliminated.

The children of single-parent families and children with employed mothers belong to the group of children who are especially in need of care outside the family. According to the data of the microcensus of 1986, around 10 percent of all children under school age belong to single-parent families (cf. Table 3), which usually means families headed by single mothers. The proportion of these children has nearly doubled during the past 10 years and according to most prognoses is continuing to grow. In contrast the percentage of employed mothers with preschool children has altered only minimally during the past 10 years. For under-3-year-olds, the figure is 32.2 percent, and for preschool children aged 3 and older, it is 35.1 percent.

Table 4

Rate of Kindergarten Attendance for 3- to Under-6-year-olds, According to Household Income

	Net Monthly Household Income (DM)							
Category	Under 1000[a]	1000–1400	1400–1800	1800–2500	2500–3000	3000–5000	5000 or more	Overall
Children in kindergarten as % of all 3- to under-6-year-olds	60.7	64.9	57.9	62.5	66.7	68.8	75.0	64.9

Note. Data are from Statistisches Bundesamt, 1988a; authors' calculations.

[a]DM 2 corresponds to approximately $1 U.S. (March 1989).

Table 5

Percent of Children of Various Ages Attending Krippe/Kindergarten, According to Status of Mother

	Percent of Children by Child's Age							
Status of Mother	0 to Under 6 yr	Under 1 yr	1 yr	2 yr	3 yr	4 yr	5 yr	6 yr and More
Married	40.2	—[a]	2.7	7.4	37.1	70.8	85.2	85.2
Married and in gainful employment	45.2	—	5.2	11.0	43.8	76.1	88.4	88.2
Married but without gainful employment	37.7	—	1.6	5.9	33.9	68.2	83.4	83.6
Single	46.6	—	—	17.0	47.3	75.5	81.8	79.1
Single and in gainful employment	54.8	—	—	—	50.0	83.3	91.0	85.7
Single but without gainful employment	40.4	—	—	—	44.8	69.0	76.7	72.7

Note. Data are from Statistisches Bundesamt, 1988a; authors' calculation.

[a]Cannot be calculated from microcensus data.

Table 5 demonstrates that in all age groups, children with employed married mothers are placed in an early childhood institution more frequently than those with nonemployed married mothers are. However, the differences are essentially relevant for only the younger age groups; in the cases of 5-year-olds and older children, the differences hardly count. Similarly, the greater child care demands of families headed by mothers is reflected in the statistics; this is especially evident in the case of the employed single mother. It is striking, however, that the 5-year-olds and older children of nonemployed single mothers attend kindergarten comparatively rarely, with respective rates of 76.7 percent and 72.7 percent. These attendance rates are not very much higher than that of foreign children, and the question must be raised concerning whether these statistics reflect another marginalized group.

An increased demand for care outside the family is especially apparent in the case of the mother in full gainful employment. According to the microcensus of 1986, 37.4 percent of employed mothers with children aged 3 years to under-6 years work 40 or more hours per week. In the case of employed mothers with children under 3 years of age, the figure was 43.6 percent (no table). This is possibly explained by the fact that for economic reasons, young families in particular are frequently dependent on the full employment of the mother.

If the available all-day places are compared only with the number of children having fully employed mothers, it can be shown that all-day places are available only for every 2nd child of those aged 3 to under-6 in this group; in the case of the under-3-year-olds in this group, there are places only for every 10th child (authors' approximate calculation). Other means that may be employed to satisfy the extrafamilial care needs of these (and other children) are not indicated by these statistics. According to regionally limited investigations, the grandparents (generally the mothers' mothers) in such cases assume the care duties (cf. Martin & Pettinger, 1985, p. 239; Schindler, Born, & Schablow, 1985, p. 28; Statistisches Landesamt Baden-Württemberg, 1985, pp. 96 ff.). Grandparent care is used more frequently by mothers with lower socioeconomic status than by mothers with higher status and more prestigious professions. The capacity of grandparents to care for children appears in many cases to be limited, which necessitates adopting further arrangements for care. Thus, children in grandparent care may also be subjected to multiple care arrangements. Relatively few peer contacts for the child and a certain dissatisfaction on the part of the mother, despite low costs, appear to be common characteristics of grandparent care (cf. Schindler, Born, & Schablow, 1985).

During the past few years the debate over the kind of care and education for young children has become more pressing. In the case of children under 3 years of age, the question of a sustained increase in the number of places in public institutions has come to the fore. In the case of the older preschool children, an increase in the number of kindergarten places in the less well-provided regions of the country is a major topic of discussion. Furthermore, there is the problem of organizing the available places in such a manner that the hours of institutional operation can better correspond with the requirements and the routines of family life.

In this debate, the epochal changes in the demography and the structure of the family that have occurred in the Federal Republic of Germany are increasingly being taken into account. With the Republic's extremely low birthrate, children have almost become "scarce goods."

Since 1970 the population's proportion of children under 6 years of age has been nearly halved (cf. Statistisches Bundesamt, 1985a, p. 585). During the past two decades, the birthrate has declined from 2,600 to 1,300 children per 1,000 women in the 15–49 age group (Statistisches Bundesamt, 1985b, p. 730). A birthrate of 2,300 per 1,000 women is regarded as a prerequisite for maintaining the level of population. The patterns of living together have also changed: The proportion of households with five or more persons has been nearly halved since 1970, and the same is true of the proportion of three-generation households. The proportion of families with four or more children has also been halved since 1970, and the number of families with three children is distinctly reduced. One- and two-child families have increased in number so that they now account for respectively 51 percent and 36 percent of all families with children (cf. Statistisches Bundesamt, 1988a, pp. 186, 189, 205). The stability of the social institution "marriage" has diminished. Among marriages contracted or to be contracted since 1970, the divorce rate is or will be about twice as high as among marriages contracted during the 1950s (cf. Schwarz, 1984). We noted earlier a doubling trend since the 1970s in the number of single mothers with children under 6 years of age. However, the proportion of employed mothers with children under 6 years of age has only increased by a few percentage points, to 35.5 percent, since the beginning of the 1970s, and compared with that of other countries, it is relatively low (cf. Statistisches Bundesamt, 1988a, pp. 228, 230). Nevertheless, a fundamental change in mothers' attitudes towards gainful employment can be detected (cf. Sommerkorn, 1988), and the traditional three-phase model of gainful employment among women (employment prior to marriage, retirement at the birth of the first child, and contingent reentry into the work force at a much later age) is losing its normative effects in favor of a parallelization of employment and motherhood for women.

National Child Care Policy

A series of differing kinds of social-policy measures support and provide aid for parents and children. They relate to such differing areas as preventative medical checkups, regulations in industrial legislation, financial compensation, assistance for care and education provided by various agencies—largely the state, the social security services, and the independant welfare organizations (which receive state support). A brief synopsis of the existing provisions, particularly those for younger children or for families with children, was published by the Federal Minister for Families, Youth and Health (Bundesminister für Jugend, Familie und Gesundheit, 1980, pp. 181 ff.). We describe here only a selection of the essential measures.

With regard to the preventative medical checkups, regular checkups for pregnant women and for small children play an important role. Pregnant women are invited to attend medical checkups regularly—about every 4 weeks. Checkup results are entered into a booklet carried by the mother-to-be ("mother's passport"). From birth to 4 years of age, children can undergo eight medical checkups monitoring their health development; checkup costs are borne by the health insurance plans (legal basis: Reichsversicherungsordnung). A medical checkup in connection with school entry is obligatory (Schulpflichtgesetz). Furthermore, medical and dental serial examinations are undertaken in kindergarten and school.

A pregnant working woman can claim a 6-week paid vacation prior to giving birth. Although this is not obligatory, in most cases such claims are made. After confinement, resumption of gainful employment is forbidden for a period of 8 weeks; in the cases of premature or multiple births, this period is extended to 12 weeks. Wages and salaries are borne during this period by the employer and the health insurance. From the beginning of pregnancy to 4 months after confinement, a mother cannot be dismissed by her employer (Mutterschutzgesetz). Following the 8-week postconfinement period, the mother or the father of a child can take a 10-month parental leave, during which period the parent cannot be dismissed. The intention behind this legislation is to enable a parent to devote full time to the care of the child during its first year of life. During this parental leave, the parent concerned receives a monthly sum of DM 600 (*Erziehungsgeld*—payment for child care and education; DM 2 is equivalent to about $1 U.S. at the time of writing). Furthermore, any mother or father whether previously employed or not can obtain this child care and education payment if that parent undertakes care of the child between the 1st and the 12th months of the child's life. The child care and education benefit may also be paid to a parent who is employed less than 18 hours per week (less than half-time). During the first 6 months of the child's life, the amount of the child care and education payment is determined without regard to income; from the child's 7th month on, the benefit may be reduced on a sliding-scale basis, according to parental income (Bundeserziehungsgeldgesetz). The scale is set so that about 40 percent of parents continue to receive the full benefit beyond the 7th month, another 40 percent receive less than the DM 600, and 20 percent receive no benefit at all for child care and education.

The parental leave and the child care and education benefit represent relatively new regulations in the Federal Republic of Germany. The precursors were introduced in the 1970s but were limited to benefits for employed mothers. The present legislation was introduced in 1986, but with a limitation at the child's 10th month of life; the limit was extended to 12 months in 1988 and to 15 months in 1989; an extension to 18 months is planned for 1990. Another mode of recognition of a mother's efforts to provide for her child's education is incorporated in calculating the mother's future old-age pension. At present, she receives 1 year (per child) of credit towards old-age pension for the time she has spent away from employment, caring for the child (and thus not making the usual compulsory social security payments). Her later pension is consequently calculated as if she had been in gainful employment during this period.

In addition to other purpose-bound benefits, such as income-based payments to ensure adequate living space for the family and the children (Wohngeldgesetz), the state provides, by means of tax concessions and direct children's allowances, other benefits that are not purpose-bound. In the case of tax concessions, families with high incomes benefit more than families with low incomes do. Direct children's allowances are the same for all parents, regardless of income. Direct children's allowances are at present DM 50 for the first child, DM 100 for the second, DM 220 for the third, and DM 240 for each successive child (Bundeskindergeldgesetz). This indirect and direct support is provided at least up to each child's 16th birthday, and after that, as long as the education or vocational training of the child continues, with the maximum termination on the 27th birthday.

We have already remarked that direct public assistance in the form of Krippen for the care and education of children under 3 years of age is rare. The grounds for establishing such institutions are laid down in the youth welfare enactment and are governed by the local youth offices. Places for young children are also scarce in instances in which they are cared for in so-called mixed-aged groups (with children between 0 and 6 years of age) in kindergarten, as is the rule in the state of North Rhine-Westphalia. The placement of a child in an out-of-home provision entails a regular monetary contribution by the parents, which in cases of low parental incomes, can be assumed in part or entirely by the youth office.

Besides provisions for group care, there are also family day care homes. Attendance at these is also arranged by the youth office, and in cases of need, the costs can also be borne by the youth office. As a result of the small amount of publicly supervised care available for small children, a "grey market" of private arrangements for child care in groups and in other families has come into being. The full extent of such arrangements, many of which are strictly speaking illegal, is unknown.

In recent years there have been forms of public assistance that are intended to strengthen the educational competence of parents themselves. These include information made available to young parents in the form of periodic "letters to parents," as well as informative events and courses for parents in evening classes, in community colleges, in parent-education institutions, and in other supplementary educational institutions (cf. Ufermann, in press). In addition, there are various other informal groups for parents and small children, groups with names like "miniclub," "play-group," and "children's corner." Such groups, whose members only come together for a few hours on a week-day afternoon and whose setting is often a parental educational institution, are not so much care institutions as they are opportunities for parents to exchange information, for children and their parents to experience playing together, and for children to benefit from group interaction (cf. Tietze, in press).

For children from age 3 up to age of school entry, kindergarten is offered as a public institution. It is regarded as the first stage (the elementary level) of the general system of education, although administratively it is assigned to the youth assistance service rather than to the school system. In contrast with the free attendance in school and university, kindergarten attendance is tied to a monetary contribution on the part of the parents. Some kindergartens (for example, Waldorf and Montessori kindergartens) operate according to a particular pedagogical program. This is also true of many of the parent-initiated groups that can be placed on a legally equal footing with kindergarten (cf. Tietze, 1989). For handicapped children, special kindergartens exist—ones organized according to the type and degree of handicap—although the past few years have seen a trend to integrate handicapped children into normal institutions.

General compulsory schooling begins at age 6. For children who have reached the age of school entry but have not yet attained the requisite maturity, most states of the Federal Republic provide an opportunity to attend the *Schulkindergarten* (school kindergarten), which is a matter of retention classes that are attached to the primary school. The primary school, also designated as the primary level of the general educational system, comprises the first four grades. For a proportion of the children of primary school age, there is an additional care institution, the *Kinderhort* (day home for children; cf. Hemmer, 1985). Day home groups are usually attached to all-day kindergarten and are attended by children of working parents after school closing, into the late afternoon. With the exception of the few comprehensive schools and some model schools, there are no all-day schools. Schools in the Federal Republic usually operate from 8:00 a.m. to 1:30 p.m., 5 or 6 days per week. The number of class periods (45-minute lessons) per week varies from approximately 20 to 35, depending on the grade level. The regular schools do not provide for any school meal.

At the end of the 4th grade, parents decide, with the assistance of the school, which school their child should attend in Secondary Stage I (5th to 10th grade). The choice lies among the *Hauptschule* (a base-level secondary school that extends to the 9th or 10th grade), the *Realschule* (an intermediate-level secondary school comprising grades 5 to 10), and the *Gymnasium* (which is preparatory to university and comprises grades 5 to 10, Secondary Stage I, and grades 11 to 13, Secondary Stage II). Although secondary school education is selective, there are opportunities for students to transfer from one type of secondary school to another. There are also comprehensive schools, but these are relatively few in number. In these schools, students may choose any of three completion options. School attendance is compulsory up to age 18 in the Federal Republic of Germany. Those who receive on-the-job industrial or craft training attend concomitantly a technical school, which is conducted generally for 1 or 2 days a week.

The tertiary education beyond the compulsory schooling comprises university education and different forms of university-oriented education.

OPTIONS IN EARLY CHILDHOOD EDUCATION AND CARE

OPTIONS FOR CHILDREN UNDER 3 YEARS OF AGE

We have already noted that the opportunities for extrafamilial care of children under age 3 are few in number. All told, two types can be differentiated: care in a Krippe (day care center), which in some cases means grouping together the under-3-year-olds with older children in "mixed-age" groups, and care in a family day care home. The legal authority for both types of care is set out in the youth welfare enactment.

Care in Krippen

In the youth welfare enactment the priority of education in the family, particularly for very young children, is underscored. Public assistance is offered according to the principle of subsidiarity, that is, only if the family is unable wholly or in part to do justice to its task of care and education. Krippen are thus social service institutions providing emergency assistance. In contrast with kindergartens, they are not conceded an autonomous educational assignment.

There are neither governmental plans nor requirements regarding the rate of supply for Krippen places. Demand-supply analysis and establishment of Krippen is left to the initiative of communities and independent agencies. The church agencies, which sponsor 57.1 percent of all kindergarten institutions, remain reticent about establishing Krippen, and the reticence seems to be based on ideological grounds. Only 12.4 percent of Krippen are operated by agencies of church parishes or church welfare organizations (cf. Table 6). The demand for places greatly exceeds the present supply, and there are long waiting lists in almost all institutions. Corresponding to the philosophy of emergency assistance, social grounds are decisive for the admission of a child to the Krippe. Priority is given to children of single parents and to children from families in which both parents are employed out of economic necessity (cf. Frauenknecht, 1980, pp. 40 ff.).

Table 6

KRIPPEN AND KINDERGARTENS ACCORDING TO OPERATING AGENCIES

	Public Agencies	Nonpublic Agencies		
Institution	Communities and Higher Authorities	Churches and Church Welfare Organizations	Other Welfare Organizations	Commercial Agencies
Krippen (*N* = 1,028)	62.5%	12.4%	22.7%	2.5%
Kindergartens (*N* = 25,890)	31.2	57.1	10.8	0.9

Note. Data are from Statistisches Bundesamt, 1988b, pp. 12 ff.; authors' calculation.

The federal youth welfare enactment represents only a skeletal law; direct federal responsibility regarding Krippen is minimal. The day-to-day operation of Krippen is regulated by guiding principles laid down by the states, principles that largely contain rules about hygienic, medical, and spatial arrangements and about group-size and personnel requirements. Except in West Berlin, no standards for pedagogical planning are contained in the guiding principles.

Krippen are as a rule small institutions. Of the 1,028 Krippen existing in the Federal Republic in 1986, there were 516 with no more than 20 places each. Only 161 Krippen (15.7 percent) had at their disposal more than 40 places (cf. Statistisches Bundesamt, 1988b, p. 14). The various regulations proceed on the assumption of spatial requirements of 2.5 to 4.5 square meters (about 27 to 48 square feet) per child. In addition, there must be room for children to rest. Group size varies from 6 to 15, depending on the regulations of each state. Frequently children are grouped by age (under 1 year, 1–2 years, 2–3 years of age). The guiding principles usually schedule 2 adults for each group (cf. Bundesminister für Jugend, Familie, Frauen und Gesundheit, 1988a). Statistics indicate that in 1986, there were 4,572 full-time and 1,360 part-time personnel responsible for the care of 28,252 children in Krippen. Thus there is an average of 1 caregiver for every 5 or 6 children. Staff (about 1,000 in number), whose main duties lie in technical and economic fields or in the administration, management, and organization of the Krippen, are not taken into account in this ratio of caregivers to children (cf. Statistisches Bundesamt, 1988b, pp. 58, 61, 80, 82; authors' own calculations).

Of the Krippen personnel (about 98 percent of whom are female) directly concerned with the care of the children, 2 percent had received a college or university education, 37.2 percent were trained as *Erzieherin* (preschool teachers, who receive in fact the normal training for kindergarten teachers), 27.6 percent had been trained as *Kinderpflegerin* (care assistants, persons with shorter, less exacting, and less pedagogical training than preschool teachers), 20 percent were trained as hospital nurses or had a similiar profession in nursing care, and 10 percent had no completed training or were currently in training (cf. Statistisches Bundesamt, 1988b, pp. 68 ff.). Compared with previous years, the proportion of persons with pedagogical training has increased (cf. Frauenknecht, 1978, pp. 22 ff.). This trend corresponds with efforts to shift the focus in Krippen from a predominant concern with care towards a more educational approach. Significant impulses have come from model projects carried out initially in West Berlin and now in other large cities (cf. Beller, 1987).

Krippen are open roughly from 6 a.m. to 6 p.m. Most children in Krippen spend 9 or more hours a day there. Sample data on parent monetary contributions for the child are not available, but according to some evidence, the monthly parent contribution lies between DM 100 and DM 350 and is scaled according to parental income. In the case of low incomes, the parental contribution can be assumed by the youth office. During recent years some efforts have been made to place small children not in Krippen but in "mixed-age" kindergarten groups. Such groups contain 15 children, of whom at most 7 may be younger than 3 years of age and at most 2 or 3 may be infants.

Family day care

As in the case of care in Krippen, care in family day care homes is regulated by the youth welfare enactment. All regularly occurring kinds of care for children and youths (up to 16 years of age) outside the parental home are accordingly subject to the authority of the local youth office. Exceptions are made in the case of care by close (up to third-degree) relatives. The youth office grants permission for the child to be placed in care, is responsible for supervision, is supposed to advise and support the caregiver, and can terminate a care arrangement if it considers the child to be in danger. Supraregional standards for the actions of the youth offices do not seem to exist. The costs of family day care are borne by the parents, although in cases of need, they can be assumed by the youth office. The sum charged depends on the hours of care and the age of the child, as well as on regional fluctuation. Average rates are not available. In some family day care homes, several children are cared for. The upper limit is generally 5 children.

Compared with the institutional types of child care, family day care for under-3-year-olds is regarded as possessing various advantages: Family day care homes can be established in rural areas, in which the demand for the establishment of larger institutions is not great enough. Day care homes are usually close to the child's home, can be highly flexible, and harmonize well with the family situation. Many youth offices give preference to family day care rather than to care in Krippen. This is the result of not only ideological preference (for family-type care) but also concern with cost.

Suggestions for the pedagogical structuring of family day care are infrequent, and there is little pedagogical guidance and support on the part of youth offices. In many research reports, complaints are made about the youth offices' neglect of family day care as a field of responsibility (cf. Frauenknecht, 1980, p. 29).

In the course of the debate on the pedagogical quality of family day care for small children, a nationwide model project called "day care mothers" was carried out during the second half of the 1970s. In this model project, conditions for high-quality family day care were implemented. Among other stipulations, the number of the children cared for (including the day care mother's own children) was not allowed to exceed four children under 10 years of age. The day care mothers received preparatory practical training, and an educational advisor was at hand. Rules governing substitution as well as ones relating to a certain level of social security for the day care mothers were established, and great importance was attached to cooperation between the day care mother and the child's mother. Despite good experience with the model (cf. Martin & Pettinger, 1985), it appears to have had little impact on the general circumstances of family day care in the Federal Republic of Germany.

Illegal care arrangements and parental self-help

The limited supply of extrafamilial opportunities for very young children has led to the establishment of a "grey market" particulary for this age group. Very little is known about the extent of this market, but some estimates suggest that for every registered family day care home, there are several unregistered ones. It is probably also true that many parents and family day care mothers are not even aware of existing legal stipulations. Underground forms of group care for small children are particularly prevalent in large cities. One significant reason is that it is generally very expensive to meet the spatial and personnel standards stipulated for such groups by the youth office.

In principle, it is possible for parents to legally establish and operate parental cooperatives as children's groups. In the course of the development of the self-help movement and the concomitant reduction of cost to public authority, the establishment of such initiatives has been encouraged (cf. Bundeszentrale für gesundheitliche Aufklärung, 1983). But inasmuch as such initiatives do not succeed in obtaining public assistance, there is a danger of instability, and because of the high parental contributions, they introduce an unwelcome note of social selectivity.

OPTIONS FOR CHILDREN FROM AGE 3 TO SCHOOL ENTRY

Administrative rulings and agencies

Although **kindergarten** was able to establish itself as the elementary level of the general system of education during the 1970s, it belongs neither legally nor organizationally to the school system. It is part of the field of youth welfare and thus lies within the jurisdiction of the youth welfare enactment. The federal government possesses little jurisdiction in this field. Its task largely consists of formulating proposals and distributing information. Federal responsibilities also include developing model projects and presenting the report on youth in each legislative period. The establishment and operation of kindergarten is regulated by acts put forth at the state level, which represent the implementation of the federal youth welfare enactment. Most states have passed special kindergarten laws (cf. Herzberg & Lülf, 1985), but these deal only with the framework of finance, supply planning, equipment, parent participation, responsibilities, and so forth.

It is the duty of the local youth offices in their capacity as community authorities to encourage and promote the creation of preschool institutions according to regional needs. Following the principle of subsidiarity, precedence is accorded to the so-called independent agencies, which means primarily to parishes and church welfare organizations. Only when these agencies fail to provide the necessary institutions is the youth office (the community) obliged to act as the providing agency (public authority).

The legal precedence of the independent agencies according to the principle of subsidiarity entails most kindergartens (57.1 percent) being operated by church agencies, as can be seen in Table 6. Nevertheless the proportion of kindergartens operated by public authority has risen from 21 percent to 31 percent between 1965 and 1986. In addition to the parishes and the church and other welfare organizations, other associations serving the public interest and other legal entities can, as agencies, operate kindergartens.

The agencies act for the most part autonomously, determining their own educational philosophies and goals. Furthermore, they provide for the operation of the preschool institution, employ its personnel, supervise its running, and are responsible for pedagogical advice and inservice training of personnel.

Financing

Financing for the operation of a kindergarten comes from four sources: the respective agency, parental contributions, community subsidies, and state (Bundesland) subsidies. The proportions from these four sources vary from state to state. Parent contributions are set individually according to income and are further reduced in cases in which two or more children of the same family attend the same kindergarten. In some states, unsuccessful attempts were made at the end of the 1970s to abolish parent contributions.

As an example of the operating costs, we draw on the situation in North Rhine-Westphalia, the state with the largest population in the Federal Republic of Germany. Depending on their income, parents pay a monthly contribution of DM 35, DM 60, or DM 100. When there are two or more children of the same family, the parents' contribution is reduced by half for the second child, and there is no charge for further children. After the deduction of parent contributions, 36 percent of the remaining operating costs are carried by the agency, 32 percent by the community, and 32 percent by the state. Parent contributions generally cover between 10 percent and 15 percent of operating costs. In the case of "poor" agencies, for instance, if the parents themselves form a parent initiative to organize an agency, the share of the state can rise to 55 percent.

Size of institutions, group composition, and equipment

Kindergartens are supposed to be close to the children's homes and not too large in size. According to 1986 youth welfare statistics, 49 percent of kindergartens contained up to 50 places, 35 percent contained 51 to 80 places, and 16 percent contained more than 80 places (cf. Statistisches Bundesamt, 1988b, p. 14). The children are grouped together so that there is a maximum, depending on the state, of 20 to 30 children in a group (cf. Bundesminister für Jugend, Familie, Frauen und Gesundheit, 1988a). As a rule, no more than 25 children are included in a kindergarten group. In the case of all-day care, the group size is smaller (about 15 children). In arranging the group, care is taken to assure an age-mix, meaning children from age 3 to age of school entry are placed together in a single group. There is a principal (head) preschool teacher for each group. At best, a second person is allotted to each group. In many instances, two children's groups share the second person. According to the youth welfare statistics, the relationship in 1986 was 13 children to each fully employed preschool teacher (cf. Statistisches Bundesamt, 1988b, pp. 78 ff.).

The regulations of various states differ with regard to spatial and material provisions. Usually for each group there is a large room, which is subdivided into various functional areas. The minimal requirements in the guidelines of the states vary between 1.5 and 2.5 square meters (about 16 to 27 square feet) per child. In more fortunate instances, there is a second, smaller room that can be used to conduct special activities or to divide the group. Larger institutions also possess a gymnasium or an all-purpose room. Buildings must be equipped with sanitary arrangements suitable for children, and as a rule there is a kitchen and a separate common room for personnel. Each kindergarten should have access to an open-air play area. The guidelines for its size specify from 6 to 10 square meters (about 65 to 107 square feet) per child. All kindergartens possess a rich and multifarious supply of materials for play and games, hobby materials, various colored materials, construction games, board games, picture books, dolls and doll accessories.

Personnel

The largest portion of women employed in kindergartens (men compose only 1.8 percent of such employees) have received training as Erzieherin (preschool teachers). Training is carried out in technical colleges for social pedagogy. The entry requirement is at least a middle-range final examination (on completion of the 10th grade) and frequently a year's practical activity in social service or in social pedagogy (cf. von Derschau, 1985, p. 174). The vocational training generally lasts 3 years (in some states, 4 years) and consists of 2 years of college training and a year's practical experience with concomitant courses in college. In contrast to the university training of primary school teachers, the training of preschool teachers is nonuniversity training, and preschool teachers receive a significantly lower salary. They are usually employed as principal (head) teachers in kindergarten groups and after several years of experience can be promoted to kindergarten principal.

A smaller portion of the personnel are trained as Kinderpflegerin (care assistants). Requirement for entry to care assistant training, which lasts 1 to 2 years and usually includes practical work, is completion of Hauptschule (9th grade). Emphasis is on care and home economics. A care assistant is usually employed as the additional person caring for a group.

Only a very small portion of kindergarten personnel have been trained in pedagogy at a college or university level. Training at this level takes 4 to 5 years and includes practical work (cf. von Derschau, 1985, pp. 175 ff.). A portion of the personnel of a kindergarten have no formal training, and an almost equal portion are in training.

In addition there are a certain number of specialized kindergarten personnel, for example, special education teachers, psychologists, speech therapists, and physical therapists. These are generally present for only a few hours at a time or in the capacity of a secondary occupation.

Table 7

PERSONS EMPLOYED IN KINDERGARTEN EDUCATION, ACCORDING TO TRAINING

Level of Educator's Training	Percent of Persons at Level (N = 128,180)
Training at college/university level	1.9
Preschool teacher training	59.4
Care assistant training	16.0
In training	9.3
Without qualification	9.0
Others	4.4

Note. Data are from Statistisches Bundesamt, 1988b, pp. 68 ff.; authors' calculation.

Table 7 contains a distribution according to training of the 128,180 pedagogical employees in kindergarten in 1986. This number does not include the several thousand who are employed in technical and economic activities or those employed in administration. If the present situation with regard to personnel is compared with that of 10 or 20 years ago, one notices a strong trend toward pedagogical professionalization.

Parent participation

The regulations in all states of the Federal Republic of Germany provide for parent participation in the form of elected boards of parents. The boards advise on organizational and pedagogical questions as well as on the hiring of personnel and can represent parent interests to the kindergarten, the agency, and even the youth office. Above and beyond board participation, in many cases there is some informal participation of parents in the day-to-day running of the kindergarten, particularly in special activities. General participation of parents as volunteers is not part of the plan, however. The situation is different when a parent initiative has established a kindergarten. In such cases, the parents bear all the responsibilities of an agency. Among other things, they determine the educational philosophy and the hiring of personnel. Often they closely collaborate in the day-to-day affairs of the kindergarten (cf. Ungelenk, 1985).

Kindergarten hours

As a rule, kindergartens operate for 4 hours in the morning, generally from 8 a.m. to midday. In most provisions, activities are also offered for 2 or 3 hours in the afternoon, but not all children participate, and frequently such activities are not offered on every working day. Most kindergartens close at midday for 2 hours. The main aim of kindergarten is thus to offer half-day care. As has been noted earlier, only 12 percent of kindergarten children are cared for over and beyond midday. In most cases, such children attend specially adapted all-day provisions with, for example, smaller groups and rooms for the children to rest in. Due to pressure in recent years for greater flexibility, the number of conventional kindergartens that care for a few children over midday has also increased (cf. Tietze, 1987).

Curriculum

Since the assignment of a special educational task to kindergarten during the second half of the 1960s, a variety of didactical approaches and curricula have been developed and tested. It is possible to distinguish three main approaches: the **functionally oriented**, the **discipline-oriented**, and the **situation-oriented** (cf. Retter, 1978, pp. 138 ff.).

The **functionally oriented** approach focuses on the stimulation of children's psychological functions—such as perception, cognition, creativity, language—by the use of training programs and exercise materials. Such programs were deployed particularly at the end of the 1960s and the beginning of the 1970s and were aimed at preparing children for school entry. This approach soon came under attack for its overemphasis on cognitive abilities and its one-sided orientation towards schooling.

The **discipline-oriented** approach emphasizes orientation towards the structure of the discipline as a principle of teaching. This scientistic approach assumes that even everyday reality comes under the laws of science. Therefore, while taking the child's stage of development into account, this approach confronts the preschool child with the elementary structures and basic concepts of science. This school of thought has developed, in particular, curricula for the child's introduction to natural science and mathematics.

The early discipline-oriented and functionally oriented approaches largely designed "closed" curricula, ones that were complete systems of teaching and learning, ready-made for application by both preschool teacher and child. In reaction to such "closed" systems, demands were raised for "open" curricula, wherein the preschool teachers and the children could participate in curriculum planning, design, and execution.

The **situation-oriented** approach (cf. Zimmer, 1985) focuses on the child's life situation and its requisite social and skill competencies. In a holistically structured process of education, the children are supposed to be enabled to master the realities of their lives and to develop into autonomous individuals capable of cooperation with one another. Adults and children together inductively identify relevant life situations through exploration of the world around them. Pedagogical goals, instead of being imposed from without, are developed on the basis of common experiences with the children and in light of their (still-limited) capacities for action. The learning of elementary skills occurs not in isolation but in a social context and is subordinate to the social context. The situation-oriented approach advocates working with mixed-age groups to allow reciprocal stimulation among children; it also encourages the educational participation of parents and other adults to promote a form of learning that overlaps the generations. This entails opening the kindergarten into the community as well as redesigning the kindergarten to become a habitat for children.

Adopting the stance of the situation-oriented approach, the Deutsches Jugendinstitut (German Youth Institute; see Research section) has, together with preschool teachers and children, developed didactical materials for a spectrum of "exemplary" (typical) life situations (such as, "my family and me," "we are going to have a baby," "foreign children," "children and senior citizens," "television," "weekend," "the child in hospital"). Together with other didactical material, the situation-oriented approach was tested in a model program throughout the Federal Republic of Germany (cf. Krappmann, 1985).

In the situation-oriented approach, the kindergarten has found its own autonomous concept of education. The approach now forms a generally accepted frame of reference for kindergarten practice and for preschool teacher training. The latitude of interpretation that this approach permits evidently accounts for its wide appeal. However, sample studies on the curriculum approaches that are actually used in kindergarten have not been undertaken in the Federal Republic of Germany.

Linkages with other systems

Since the official recognition of kindergarten as the elementary level of the educational system, the question of how to link kindergarten with the subsequent primary school has arisen. As mentioned earlier, at the beginning of the 1970s, organizational models for the linkage (an entrance stage, preparatory classes) were debated and tested. Central to the discussion was the question of whether 5-year-olds should remain at the elementary level or be assigned to primary level. During the past 10 years, efforts have been made to bring kindergarten and primary school closer together didactically and methodologically and to provide a greater continuity for the children by developing forms of cooperation between the two levels. The most important outcomes of these efforts are the play-oriented learning at primary school entry; the cooperative activities, meetings, and discussions held by preschool teachers and primary school teachers; and the reciprocal visiting between the levels by both teachers and children (cf. Macholdt & Thiel, 1985).

In a number of kindergartens operated by the churches, an attempt is being made to establish a linkage to the religious life of the parish. Kindergartens are designed to be in the neighborhood of the children's dwellings. They therefore also serve as a neighborly meeting place for many parents. However, a linkage of the kindergarten to the parents' places of work is rare. It is true that there are kindergartens in companies and institutions employing large numbers of women (such as hospitals), but their number is small, and because of the high level of unemployment during recent years, there is no cause for employers to provide such an incentive to recruit mothers with small children.

There is some linkage between the kindergarten and the public medical system. Certain diseases are subject to being reported. The health authorities carry out mass medical and dental examinations, although participation is voluntary. A closer linkage to the health authorities occurs in cases involving care of handicapped children.

Special types of kindergarten

In addition to the "typical" kindergarten, there are special kindergartens that are characterized by particular educational programs. Pursuing an apparent need for a holistic life-orientation and an overarching search for meanings, a number of **Waldorf kindergartens** have been founded during the past 10 years by parent initiatives. The Waldorf kindergartens are oriented according to the anthroposophy and pedagogy of Rudolf Steiner. Their number has already reached several hundred (cf. Barz, 1984). Similarly, **kindergartens based on the Montessori model** have been established. The Montessori establishments have won a firm place, especially in the integrated education of handicapped and nonhandicapped children.

There are also **special kindergartens for children with the same or similar forms of handicap**. Groups in these institutions are generally much smaller, and the staffing includes more personnel trained in special education and various therapies. Most offer all-day care and provide transportation. Such institutions are financed in a different way than normal kindergartens are. Statistics for 1986 record 519 such institutions with approximately 21,000 places available (cf. Statistisches Bundesamt, 1988b, pp. 12, 16). This, however, includes places for older children. As a result of the efforts towards an integrated education of handicapped children in the ordinary kindergarten, the number of kindergartens for handicapped children has declined during recent years.

One aspect of the student revolt at the end of the 1960s and beginning of the 1970s was the establishment of *Kinderläden* (children stores), called so because they were frequently established in abandoned corner stores. They were founded by politically active parents who wanted their children educated in an antiauthoritarian and nonrepressive manner. The spread of this educational concept was, however, limited to a short period. Their successors, the **parent-initiative groups**, which numbered about 800 in the early 1970s and 500 ten years later (Ungelenk, 1985, pp. 22 ff.), are not committed to any particular educational concept.

Usually parent-initiative groups are organized by middle-class parents. The financial burden on parents is greater than in the case of ordinary kindergarten, since parents must assume not only their own but also the agency's portion of support. The parents, however, are free to define the educational philosophy and establish the organizational framework. They decide, for example, the hours of operation. In many cases they also work in the groups and provide such support services as cooking, cleaning, purchasing, and transportation. The focus of such parent-initiative groups has in the recent past shifted from the kindergarten level to the infant and toddler level, to serving children under 3 years of age. At this level, parental self-help is the only resource, since communities and church agencies provide few places for children under 3 years of age. Most of the parent-initiative groups for children below kindergarten level, however, receive no public assistance.

Other forms of child care

In addition to education in the family and in kindergarten, there are other forms of child care for children of kindergarten age, and these are similar to the forms of care we described earlier for younger children, namely, care within the social network of the parents (by grandparents, other relatives, friends, neighbors) or in family day care homes. Also, some might spend part of the day without supervision. Thus kindergarten-aged children, especially those of employed mothers, experience multiple care arrangements during the day. There are no national figures relating to such multiple-arrangement cases. The authors are presently conducting a sample survey of the state of care for the nation's 0- to 6-year-olds, one that investigates the many different characteristics of the individual forms of care and their concurrence in the daily routine of children.

RESEARCH

In the course of the educational reform in the mid-1960s, as the question of preschool education became highly topical, there was an inadequate research infrastructure to turn to, despite the fact that there is a noteworthy tradition in early childhood education in Germany. Actually, it was the new societal interest in the question that set in motion the establishment of the topic of early childhood as a research theme both in the universities and in certain institutes outside the universities. And frequently, there were excessive expectations regarding the feasibility of short-term, scientifically substantiated solutions.

Influenced in part by the societal pressure for action and in part by a historically and philosophically oriented educational science, there evolved an action-research approach rather than an analytically and empirically aligned approach. It was primarily a matter of developing model projects involving rather "soft" scientific supervision and evaluation. State financial assistance to research, which at the beginning of the 1970s reached substantial sums, was concentrated in such model projects. On a lesser scale, empirical research, including longitudinal studies, was carried out, but it was generally regarded as of secondary importance. Some of the topics of the research and projects were

- Early furtherance of cognitive development
- Early literacy
- Feasibility of compensatory education
- Education of 5-year-olds in kindergarten or primary school
- Preschool teachers' training and further training
- Education of foreign children
- Integration of handicapped children

Research in early childhood education is given no priority at present. State financial assistance has been drastically reduced. There is interest in early childhood education research at some universities, and in most cases, linked to such research interests are training courses for students. There are also three institutes outside the universities that have an exclusive or very strong interest in early childhood education.

These are the Deutsches Jugendinstitut (German Youth Institute) in Munich, which operates on a federal scale; the Staatsinstitut für Frühpädagogik und Familienforschung (the State Institute for Early Childhood Education and Family Research) of Bavaria, in Munich; and the Sozialpädagogische Institut für Kleinkind- und ausserschulische Erziehung (Social Pedagogical Institute for Early Childhood Education and Education Outside the School) of North Rhine-Westphalia, in Cologne. The latter two institutes, which were founded in connection with the reform of kindergarten, are state institutions and therefore operate only in their respective states, under the immediate charge of their respective state ministries.

In the future, it will be a matter of maintaining and consolidating the research infrastructure, which has already shrunk enormously during the past few years. From the viewpoint of educational science, it appears important to shift research from predominantly short-term and thematically fluctuating projects to the development of long-term research perspectives. From a policymaker's viewpoint, research questions relating to the imminent extension of early childhood care and education in its various forms and, in particular, to questions of the quality and cost of preschool education, will presumably come to the fore.

Child Care Issues in the Future

There are many indications that after the simultaneous occurrences of the late 1960s and early 1970s—the **transformation of kindergarten into part of the education system** (which has been, with regard to institutional quality, an important success) and its remarkable **quantitative expansion**—the Federal Republic of Germany is now at the beginning of a second phase of radical change in public preschool care and education. This new phase is also characterized by both qualitative and quantitative elements. Then as now, the main trends do not primarily emanate from within the care and education system; rather, they are set in motion by powerful forces from without.

Twenty years ago, the economic motive of better utilizing human capital by means of an early furtherance of the child and the constitutional motive of providing equal opportunities for children of differing social backgrounds were the fundamental driving forces. The establishment of the half-day kindergarten with the emphasis on its duties as an educational institution was, to a wide extent, an acceptable solution.

Today's emergent revisionary trends seem to draw their energy from problems confronting modern women. In contrast with the debate that led to the establishment of the half-day kindergarten as an educational institution, the present societal and political discussion points not to a single solution but to a wide spectrum of possibilities.

With the increasing participation of women (especially mothers of small children) in the work force, and the increasing participation of women in other extrafamilial activities (recreational, cultural, political), the care and education of preschool children tends to shift from being a strictly private responsibility to being a largely societal and public one. This shift to public responsibility can be perceived in the increase in external assistance offered to the family for the care and education of preschool children and in the benefits that society offers those mothers (or fathers) willing to commit their undivided attention to the care and education of their children. This constellation results in three complexes of problems, which are the object of political controversy as well as the points of crystallization for new or possible solutions regarding further development of the care and education system in its various forms. These complexes of problems are

1. **The further development of assistance in the form of extrafamilial care** by extending the supply and adapting it qualitatively to meet the needs of families and children
2. **The further development of societal benefits** as incentives for mothers (or fathers) to commit themselves for a period of time to partly or wholly abandoning gainful employment in order to care for their children
3. **The further development of regulations relating to the labor market**, allowing mothers and fathers to equate activities in the family with those in gainful employment and to make possible a smooth transition from one to the other

Further Development of the Supply and Quality of Extrafamilial Care

At present, it is possible to discern different national initiatives to expand extrafamilial care, both qualitatively and quantitatively—initiatives that will determine the course of the debates in the coming years. The federal government has submitted for public perusal a departmental draft of an amendment of the youth welfare enactment. The amendment would give every child from the age of 3 to school entry a right to a place in kindergarten. The aim of the draft is that children and families should no longer be dependent on the available supply but should have a legal right to a place. Furthermore, the draft requires local youth offices to meet the demand for all-day places for children in this age group and for places of care for children under 3 years of age (cf. Bundesminister für Jugend, Familie, Frauen und Gesundheit, 1988b).

Anticipating to some extent such goals, the umbrella organizations of all kindergarten agencies have agreed on a common basis for demand-oriented opening hours (cf. Bundesvereinigung der Kommunalen Spitzenverbände & Bundesarbeitsgemeinschaft der Freien Wohlfahrtspflege, 1987), with the intention of enlarging the supply to better reflect the differing lifestyles of families. This declaration of intent and recommendation should not be taken for actual change, however. In fact, the altercations concerning care institution expansion, which some see as undermining the family, have yet to reach their culmination.

With regard to the political discussion, allowance should be made for the fact that extending care institutions puts a financial burden on the states and the communities; thus any new approach can only succeed with their cooperation. Controversy will surely emerge over how much parents should bear of the operating costs of expanded care. It is because of such cost considerations and also because of prevailing liberal beliefs (wherein private initiatives hold high importance) that there is increasing political interest in and assistance for parent-initiative groups.

From an educational perspective, probably the most important point relates to the improvement and maintenance of institutional quality. If children will be attending institutions for the greater part of a day, a reform of the institutions' educational procedures is called for. Instead of reducing educational standards in favor of care requirements, institutions must offer children places in which their needs for protection, for a sheltered life, for social and emotional security, *and* for educational stimulation are simultaneously satisfied.

Further Development of Societal Benefits

It has been mentioned earlier that the Federal Republic of Germany—in addition to giving families tax concessions and children's allowances—has entered into a system of direct benefits for parental efforts in the education of their children, with a 1-year payment of money for the care of a child during its first year of life and the crediting of the care periods (also up to 1 year for each child) in calculating a mother's or father's future social security pension. During the coming years, it may be expected that the debate over expanding these provisions will become more intense. In some of the states, local provisions for such an expansion already exist.

Expansion on a federal level is discussed largely from two perspectives: First, with regard to extending leave beyond the period of 18 months, and second, with regard to increasing benefit payments, that is, increasing the amount of money paid for care of a child during the first year of life or increasing the credits for calculating the social security pension. The two options—extending leave or increasing benefit payments—have differing implications. Regulations relating to a leave extension combined with relatively low payments would only be attractive for mothers (not for fathers). At the same time, leave extensions could be expected to relieve the labor market (for women). Of the options being considered, only a significant increase in the size of the benefit payments could provide an effective incentive for greater participation of fathers in the education of small children.

Further Development of Labor Market Regulations

Many mothers of small children (and some fathers) desire a greater compatibility between family activities and participation in gainful employment. One way to address this need is to provide extrafamilial care opportunities in public institutions or within the social network of the family. Another would be to have a greater flexibility in the organization of employment.

As possible steps towards a family-compatible rearrangement of the work world, political demands call for an increased supply of part-time jobs together with a greater flexibility in working hours and their adaption to life rhythms. Present complaints charge that concerns about family and children are disregarded by *both* parties in collective bargaining—and this includes the unions, from whom the population expects greater concern. Due to the comparatively small degree of unionization among women, it is uncertain how much the situation will change in the foreseeable future. Under the economic system governing the Federal Republic of Germany, the state's opportunities to intervene in this regard are considered limited.

A further step towards achieving compatibility between family activities and work activities can be seen in the improved opportunities for phase-displaced combinations of both types of activity. On the basis of the enactment concerning benefits for child care during the child's first year, it has become possible for mothers or fathers to obtain leave to give this care, during which time they are protected against unlawful dismissal. It is probable that an extension of the existing regulations will be made in one way or another. Some large-scale employers have already introduced employee regulations allowing a several-year suspension of the employment contract with guaranteed opportunity to return. Regulations going even further to facilitate children's early childhood care and education—the reduction of a full-time employment contract to part-time employment or the suspension of an employment contract for several (up to 7) years while guaranteeing reemployment—are possible in public employment.

CONCLUSION

In all probability, the emerging reformation of preschool care and education in the Federal Republic of Germany will not boil down to a single solution capable of being generalized. Because of the multiplicity of lifestyles, a variety of solutions appear necessary—solutions that give young mothers and fathers choices and allow them to assume responsibility in structuring their own lives and those of their children. Accordingly, it is not merely a matter of an institutional response with regard to the preschool children's needs in care and education. In the Federal Republic of Germany, the opinion appears to be gaining ground that a sustained improvement of care and education of young children as well as the betterment of their quality of life can only be obtained through a coordinated effort involving all the differing societal subsystems.

AUTHORS' NOTE

We should like to thank Dr. Edward G. Norris for his translation of this profile.

REFERENCES

Ariès, Ph. (1962). *Centuries of childhood: A social history of family life.* New York: Knopf.

Barow-Bernstorff, E., Günther, K. -H., Krecker, M., & Schuffenhauer, H. (Eds.). (1986). *Beiträge zur Geschichte der Vorschulerziehung* [Contributions to the history of preschool education] (7th ed.). Berlin: Volk und Wissen.

Barz, H. (1984). *Der Waldorfkindergarten. Geistesgeschichtliche Ursprünge und entwicklungspsychologische Begründung seiner Praxis* [The Waldorf kindergarten. Intellectual history of its origins and its social-psychological substantiation]. Weinheim: Beltz.

Beller, E. K. (1987). Intervention in der frühen Kindheit [Intervention in early childhood]. In R. Oerter & L. Montada (Eds.), *Entwicklungspsychologie* (rev. ed.) (pp. 789–813). München/Weinheim: Psychologie Verlags Union.

Berger, M. (1986). *Vorschulerziehung im Nationalsozialismus. Recherchen zur Situation des Kindergartenwesens 1933–1945* [Preschool education under national socialism. Studies in the state of the kindergarten, 1933–1945]. Weinheim/Basel: Beltz.

Breiteneicher, H. J., Mauff, R., & Triebe, M. (1971). *Kinderläden. Revolution der Erziehung oder Erziehung zur Revolution?* [Children's stores. The revolution of education or education for revolution?]. Reinbeck: Rowohlt.

Bund-Länder-Kommission für Bildungsplanung. (1976). *Fünfjährige in Kindergärten, Vorklassen, und Eingangsstufen* [Five-year-olds in kindergarten, pre-classes and entry stages]. Stuttgart: Klett.

Bund-Länder-Kommission für Bildungsplanung. (1987). *Daten für den Elementarbereich, 1975 bis 1985* [Data for the elementary level, 1975–1985]. Bonn: Author.

Bundesminister für Bildung und Wissenschaft. (1987). *Grund- und Strukturdaten 1987/88* [Basic and structural data 1987/88]. Bad Honnef: Karl Heinrich Bock.

Bundesminister für Jugend, Familie und Gesundheit (Ed.). (1980). *Familien mit Kleinkindern* [Families with small children]. Stuttgart: Kohlhammer.

Bundesminister für Jugend, Familie, Frauen und Gesundheit. (1988a). *Zusammenstellung von landesgesetzlichen Regelungen für den Kindergarten. Stand: 1.Januar 1988* [Synopsis of state regulations for kindergarten. As of January 1, 1988]. Bonn: Author.

Bundesminister für Jugend, Familie, Frauen und Gesundheit. (1988b). *Sozialgesetzbuch (SGB)—Jugendhilfe—(Entwurf und Begründung). Stand: 5.8.1988* [Book of social service enactments—Youth welfare. As of August 5, 1988]. Bonn: Author.

Bundesvereinigung der kommunalen Spitzenverbände & Bundesarbeitsgemeinschaft der Freien Wohlfahrtspflege (Eds.). (1987). *Empfehlungen und Hinweise zur bedarfsgerechten Gestaltung von Öffnungszeiten in Kindergärten* [Recommendations and advice for need-oriented opening hours in kindergarten]. Köln/Bonn: Authors.

Bundeszentrale für gesundheitliche Aufklärung (Ed.). (1983). *Eltern helfen Eltern. Arbeitsmappe mit Informationen, Beispielen, und Tips für Selbsthilfegruppen* [Parents help parents. A desk folder with information, examples, and tips for self-help groups]. Köln: Author.

Derschau, D. von. (1985). Die Ausbildung des pädagogischen Personals [The training of educational personnel]. In J. Zimmer (Ed.), *Erziehung in früher Kindheit. Enzyklopädie Erziehungswissenschaft, Bd. 6* (pp. 169–187). Stuttgart: Klett-Cotta.

Derschau, D. von. (1987). Personal: Entwicklung der Ausbildung und der Personalstruktur im Kindergarten [Personnel: The development of training and the personnel structure of the kindergarten]. In G. Erning, K. Neumann, & J. Reyer (Eds.), *Geschichte des Kindergartens, Bd. 2* (pp. 67– 81). Freiburg: Lambertus.

Deutscher Bildungsrat. (1970). *Strukturplan für das Bildungswesen* [Structural Plan for the Educational System]. Stuttgart: Klett.

Deutscher Bildungsrat. (1975). *Bericht '75. Entwicklungen im Bildungswesen* [Report '75. Developments in the educational system]. Stuttgart: Klett.

Erning, G. (1987a). Geschichte der öffentlichen Kleinkinderziehung von den Anfängen bis zum Kaiserreich [History of public early childhood education from its beginnings to the German Reich]. In G. Erning, K. Neumann, & J. Reyer (Eds.), *Geschichte des Kindergartens, Bd. 1* (pp. 13–42). Freiburg: Lambertus.

Erning, G. (1987b). Quantitative Entwicklung der Angebote öffentlicher Kleinkindererziehung [Quantitative development of the supply of public early childhood education]. In G. Erning, K. Neumann, & J. Reyer (Eds.), *Geschichte des Kindergartens, Bd. 2* (pp. 29–39). Freiburg: Lambertus.

Frauenknecht, B. (1978). *Institutionelle Kleinkindbetreuung in der BRD* [Early childhood care in provisions in the FRG]. München: Deutsches Jugendinstitut.

Frauenknecht, B. (1980). *Die Situation in der Tagespflege insbesondere für Kinder bis zu 3 Jahren von erwerbstätigen Müttern* [The situation in early childhood day care, especially for children from 3 years of age of working mothers]. München: Deutsches Jugendinstitut.

Grossmann, W. (1974). *Vorschulerziehung. Historische Entwicklungen und alternative Modelle* [Preschool education. Historical developments and alternative models]. Köln: Kiepenheuer & Witsch.

Heiland, H. (1987). Erziehungskonzepte der Klassiker der Frühpädagogik [Educational conceptions in the classics of early childhood education]. In G. Erning, K. Neumann, & J. Reyer (Eds.), *Geschichte des Kindergartens, Bd. 2* (pp. 148–184). Freiburg: Lambertus.

Hemmer, K. P. (1985). Der Kinderhort [Day care home for school children]. In K. P. Hemmer & H. Wudtke (Eds.), *Erziehung im Primarschulalter. Enzyklopädie Erziehungswissenschaft, Bd. 7* (pp. 289–300). Stuttgart: Klett-Cotta.

Herzberg, I., & Lülf, U. (1985). Administrative Rahmenbedingungen und quantitative Entwicklungen im Elementarbereich [Administrative frameworks and quantitative developments at the elementary level]. In J. Zimmer (Ed.), *Erziehung in früher Kindheit. Enzyklopädie Erziehungswissenschaft, Bd. 6* (pp. 99–113). Stuttgart: Klett-Cotta.

Hoffmann, E. (1968). Frühkindliche Bildung und Schulanfang [Early Childhood Education and School Entry]. In G. Bittner & E. Schmid-Cords (Eds.), *Erziehung in früher Kindheit* (pp. 17–34). München: Piper.

Krappmann, L. (1985). Das Erprobungsprogramm und seine Folgen [Model Programs and their effects]. In J. Zimmer (Ed.), *Erziehung in früher Kindheit. Enzyklopädie Erziehungswissenschaft, Bd. 6* (pp. 39–54). Stuttgart: Klett-Cotta.

Krecker, M. (Ed.) (1983). *Quellen zur Geschichte der Vorschulerziehung* [Sources for a history of early childhood education] (4th ed.). Berlin: Volk und Wissen.

Lückert, H. -R. (1967). Begabungsforschung und basale Bildungsförderung [Research on cognitive development and cognitive stimulation]. *Schule und Psychologie, 14*(1), 9–22.

Machholdt, T., & Thiel, T. (1985). Der Übergang vom Elementar- zum Primarbereich [The transition from the elementary to the primary level]. In J. Zimmer (Ed.), *Erziehung in früher Kindheit. Enzyklopädie Erziehungswissenschaft, Bd. 6* (pp. 138–152). Stuttgart: Klett-Cotta.

Martin, B., & Pettinger, R. (1985). Frühkindliche institutionalisierte Sozialisation [Socialization in early childhood provisions]. In J. Zimmer (Ed.), *Erziehung in früher Kindheit. Enzyklopädie Erziehungswissenschaft, Bd. 6* (pp. 235–252). Stuttgart: Klett-Cotta.

Moss, P. (1988). *Child care and equality of opportunity. Consolidated report to the European Commission.* Brussels: Commission of the European Communities.

Neumann, K. (1987). Geschichte der öffentlichen Kleinkindererziehung von 1945 bis in die

Gegenwart [History of public early childhood education from 1945 to the present]. In J. Erning, K. Neumann, & J. Reyer (Eds.), *Geschichte des Kindergartens, Bd. 1* (pp. 83–116). Freiburg: Lambertus.

Picht, G. (1964). *Die deutsche Bildungskatastrophe. Analyse und Dokumentation* [The German education catastrophe. Analysis and documentation]. Olten/Freiburg: Walter.

Rabe-Kleberg, U. (1985). Erziehung, antiautoritäre [Education, antiauthoritarian]. In J. Zimmer (Ed.), *Erziehung in früher Kindheit. Enzyklopädie Erziehungswissenschaft, Bd. 6* (pp. 290–292). Stuttgart: Klett-Cotta.

Retter, H. (1978). Typen pädagogischer und didaktischer Ansätze im Elementarbereich [Types of pedagogical and didactical approaches at the elementary level]. In R. Dollase (Ed.), *Handbuch der Früh- und Vorschulpädagogik, Bd. 2* (pp. 135–150). Düsseldorf: Schwann.

Reyer, J. (1985). *Wenn die Mütter arbeiten gingen—Eine sozialhistorische Studie zur Entstehung der öffentlichen Kleinkinderziehung im 19. Jahrhundert in Deutschland* [When mothers go to work—A social and historical study of the origins of public early childhood education in Germany in the 19th century] (2nd ed.). Köln: Pahl-Rugenstein.

Reyer, J. (1987a). Geschichte der öffentlichen Kleinkindererziehung im deutschen Kaiserreich, in der Weimarer Republik und in der Zeit des Nationalsozialismus [History of public early childhood education in the German Reich, in the Weimar Republic, and in the period of National Socialism]. In G. Erning, K. Neumann, & J. Reyer (Eds.), *Geschichte des Kindergartens, Bd. 1* (pp.43–82). Freiburg: Lambertus.

Reyer, J. (1987b). Entwicklung der Trägerstruktur in der öffentlichen Kleinkindererziehung [The development of the structure of the agencies in public early childhood education]. In J. Erning, K. Neumann, & J. Reyer (Eds.), *Geschichte des Kindergartens, Bd. 2* (pp. 40–66). Freiburg: Lambertus.

Reyer, J. (1987c). Kindheit zwischen privat-familialer Lebenswelt und öffentlicher veranstalteter Kleinkindererziehung [Childhood between the world of the family and publically organized early childhood education]. In J. Erning, K. Neumann, & J. Reyer (Eds.), *Geschichte des Kindergartens, Bd. 2* (pp. 232–310). Freiburg: Lambertus.

Schindler, H., Born, C., & Schablow, M. (1985). *Die Lebenssituation von Kindern unter 3 Jahren und ihren Eltern in Bremen: Ergebnisse einer Befragung von mehr als 2000 Familien* [The condition of under 3-year-old children's lives and that of their parents in Bremen. The results of an inquiry into more than 2,000 families]. Bremen: Universität Bremen.

Schmalohr, E. (1970). Möglichkeiten und Grenzen einer kognitiven Frühförderung [The possibilities and limits of the early encouragement of cognitive development]. *Zeitschrift für Pädagogik, 16*(1), 1–26.

Schmalohr, E. (1973). *Frühes Lesenlernen* [Early literacy]. Heidelberg: Quelle & Meyer.

Schwarz, K. (1984). Eltern und Kinder unvollständiger Familien [Parents and children in incomplete families]. *Zeitschrift für Bevölkerungswissenschaft, 10*(1), 3–36.

Shorter, E. (1975). *The making of the modern family.* New York: Basic Books.

Siebenmorgen, E. (1982). 0- bis 6-jährige Kinder in einer Gruppe? [0- to 6- year-olds in one group?]. In H. Merker & J. Schulte (Eds.), *Tageseinrichtungen für Kinder—Beiträge aus der Praxis* (pp. 17–25). Köln: Deutscher Gemeindeverlag und Kohlhammer.

Sommerkorn, I. (1988). Die erwerbstätige Mutter in der Bundesrepublik: Einstellungs- und Problemveränderungen [The gainfully employed mother in the FRG: Changes in attitudes and problems]. In R. Nave-Herz (Ed.), *Wandel und Kontinuität in der Bundesrepublik Deutschland* (pp. 115–144). Stuttgart: Enke.

Statistisches Bundesamt (Ed.). (1985a). Jugendhilfe 1983 [Youth Welfare 1983]. *Wirtschaft und Statistik, 1985* (7), 585–591.

Statistisches Bundesamt (Ed.). (1985b). Bevölkerungsentwicklung 1984 [Demographic developments 1984]. *Wirtschaft und Statistik, 1985* (9), 729–733.

Statistisches Bundesamt (Ed.). (1988a). *Bevölkerung und Erwerbstätigkeit. Fachserie 1, Reihe 3: Haushalte und Familien. Ergebnisse des Mikrozensus 1986* [Population and employment. Technical series 1, series 3, households and families. Results of the microcensus 1986]. Stuttgart/Mainz: W. Kohlhammer.

Statistisches Bundesamt (Ed.). (1988b). *Statistik der Jugendhilfe. Teil III Einrichtungen und tätige Personen in der Jugendhilfe am 31.12.1986* (Arbeitsunterlage) [Statistics of youth welfare. Part III. Institutions and persons active in youth welfare on the 31st of December, 1986 (Working material)]. Wiesbaden: Author.

Statistisches Landesamt Baden-Württemberg (Ed.). (1985). *Die Erwerbstätigkeit von Müttern und die Betreuung ihrer Kinder in Baden-Württemberg* [The gainful employment of mothers and the provision of their children in Baden-Württemberg]. Stuttgart: Author.

Tietze, W. (1987). Flexibility in preschool education: Current issues in West Germany's kindergartens. In M. M. Clark (Ed.), *Roles, responsibilities, and relationships in the education of the young child* (pp. 40–48). Birmingham: University of Birmingham.

Tietze, W. (1989). Vorschulerziehung [Preschool education]. In D. Lenzen (Ed.), *Pädagogischer Grundbegriffe, Bd. 2* (pp. 1590–1604). Reinbeck: Rowohlt.

Tietze, W. (in press). Familienerziehung und Kleinkindpädagogik [Early education in families and in provisions]. In L. Roth (Ed.), *Pädagogik. Handbuch für Studium und Praxis.* München: Ehrenwirth.

Tietze, W., & Ufermann, K. (1989). An international perspective on schooling for fours. *Theory into practice*, 28(1), 63–77.

Ufermann, K. (in press). Elternbildung und Elternarbeit im Rahmen der Vorschulerziehung [Parent education and working with parents in preschool education]. In J. Hohmeier & H. Mair (Eds.), *Familien- und Angehörigenarbeit.* Freiburg: Lambertus.

Ungelenk, B. (1985). Die gegenwärtige Situation der Eltern-Initiativ-Gruppen [The present situation of parent initiative groups]. In H. Nickel (Ed.), *Sozialisation im Vorschulalter* (pp. 18–25). Weinheim/Deerfield Beach, FL: Edition Psychologie, VCH.

Vergleichende Städtestatistik. (1987). Kindergärten, Kinderhorte, Krippen/Krabbelstuben sowie Sonderkindergärten am 1.1.1986 in den Gemeinden mit 20.000 und mehr Einwohner [Kindergarten, day care home for school children, Krippen, crawl parlors, as well as special kindergartens on the 1st of January, 1986, in communities of 20,000 and more inhabitants]. *Der Städtetag (8)*, 491–500.

Zimmer, J. (1985). Der Situationsansatz als Bezugsrahmen der Kindergartenreform [The situational approach as a framework for kindergarten reform]. In J. Zimmer (Ed.), *Erziehung in früher Kindheit. Enzyklopädie Erziehungswissenschaft, Bd. 6* (pp. 21–38). Stuttgart: Klett-Cotta.

IV

Early Childhood Training, Care, and Education in Finland

Mikko Ojala, *Professor of Early Childhood Education*
Department of Education
University of Joensuu

Introduction

The Finnish educational and training system is composed of four consecutive stages, namely, the preschool (ages 0–7), basic (ages 7–16), middle (generally ages 16–19), and higher (generally ages 19–23). During the past two decades, this Finnish system has undergone massive development and reform at all levels (Nurmi, 1981).

The **preschool stage** is composed of home care, day care, and a voluntary preschool for 6-year-olds. In the year they reach the age of 7, children shift to the **basic stage**, the publicly sponsored 9-year mandatory comprehensive school that is further broken up into a 6-year lower stage and a 3-year upper stage. The **middle stage** of the educational system is composed of vocational schools and institutes and a 3-year gymnasium. The length of vocational training varies from 2 to 5 years. An aim of educational policy has been to direct about half of each age cohort towards high school and the other half towards vocational training. The **higher stage** is formed by the colleges and universities. About 20 percent of the age cohort are placed in higher education.

This profile's goal is to depict and analyze on the national level the basic ideals of the training, care, and education for preschool-aged children in Finland. First, I will consider the history of early childhood education in Finland from the early 19th century up through the 1970s. Next, I will explore the training, care, and educational conditions and framework in the 1980s. The final section of this study will analyze and describe Finland's family policy goals and the measures that Finland employs to support families with children. Before drawing conclusions, I intend to investigate the future prospects of early childhood education.

History

The Froebelian kindergarten ideals that arose in Germany in the early 19th century (cf. Ojala, 1984b) were a significant historical factor affecting the training, care, and education of preschool-aged children in Finland. Froebel's ideas spread very quickly from Germany to Finland. The founder of the Finnish public education system, Uno Cygnaeus, was personally acquainted with the operations of kindergartens and teacher training in Germany in the mid-19th century. Cygnaeus, who was delighted by the kindergarten ideal and assured of the need for kindergarten, once said, "Every humanitarian came to hope that this blessing would produce an institution that would become common in our country" (Salo, 1939). When the first teacher-training college was established in Finland in 1863, an elementary school, kindergarten, and nursery school were founded in conjunction with it, in accord with Cygnaeus's proposal. The nursery school was designed for children under 4 years of age, and the kindergarten, for children 4 to 10 years of age.

Comparing Germany and Finland, one finds great similarities in the early stages of the development of the kindergarten ideal (Ojala, 1984b). Both Froebel and Cygnaeus viewed the kindergarten primarily as a center of enlightenment. Both saw the pedagogical insufficiency of the institutions that were functioning on the bases of social services (for example, *salles d'asiles* in France, *Warteschule* and *Kinder-Bewahranstalt* in Germany) and believed in working towards an intellectual and practical reform of education, one that would begin prior to school-age. They felt that only in this way could the national level of education be raised. They stressed that mothers and child nurses be trained in educational tasks and that new methods of activity and equipment that were pedagogically appropriate to the education of small children be developed and introduced.

Following the deaths of Froebel (in 1852) and Cygnaeus (in 1888), however, the development of the kindergarten ideal changed in both Finland and Germany (cf. Ojala, 1984b, 1985b). Hanna Rothman, who was Finland's successor to Cygnaeus, began to develop kindergartens according to the German model that was based primarily on social services. The example was taken from the already existing social welfare institutions and workshops. The Finnish kindergartens became popular kindergartens, which since 1888 had been established primarily "for children of poor families who were left to walk the streets uncared for" (Committee Report, 1974:15). Ironically enough, with the changeover of kindergartens to "popular" kindergartens, the notion of the kindergartens being instrumental in improving the national level of education became somewhat secondary.

The kindergartens were at first (in 1897) placed under the administration of the school authorities (Nurmi, 1981). Since 1924, however, the kindergartens have been governed by the social welfare authorities. Evidently, a main reason for this administrative change was the Civil War in 1918, which strengthened the social service tasks of the kindergartens.

The number of kindergartens in Finland increased relatively slowly until the late 1940s. By the turn of the century some 10 kindergartens had been established in Finland (Social Service Journal, 1970, June). By the late 1920s the number had risen to approximately 80 (Hänninen & Valli, 1986). A decade later there were nearly 100 kindergartens, but growth stopped during World War II in Finland. The interruption caused by the war was, however, rapidly remedied by the late 1940s. Statistics show that by the end of that decade, there were almost 150 kindergartens, and by the end of the following decade, the number had reached almost 230. Prior to the enactment of the 1973 Day Care Law (when kindergartens became "day care centers"), the number of kindergartens had peaked at over 350 in the late 1960s (Social Service Journal, 1970, June).

Until the enactment of the 1973 Day Care Law, **kindergartens** enrolled 3- to 7-year-olds. (The nature of enrollment after the enactment is discussed in a later section.) With certain exceptions, kindergarten group size was set at 25 children per teacher (Law 296/1927, Statute 80/1936). Generally, each kindergarten had separate sections for full-day and half-day (4-hour) operations. A kindergarten could, however, function solely on a full-day or half-day basis (Social Service Journal, 1970, June). In cities and residential areas the minimum enrollment of a kindergarten was set at 50 children; in the countryside and sparsely populated areas the minimum enrollment had to be 15 children (Statute 297/1927). In cities and residential areas it was usual for a kindergarten to care for 75–150 children. Institutions caring for more than 100 children were built chiefly in the postwar years of the 1940s and 1950s (Hänninen & Valli, 1986).

Kindergartens could be either public or private. From their inception in Finland, most kindergartens have been public. For instance, by the late 1960s about two thirds of the kindergartens were public and one third were private (Social Service Journal, 1970, June). Since 1913, both public and private kindergartens that fulfill certain conditions of operation have been eligible for state subsidies (Hänninen & Valli, 1986; Statute 297/1927; Statute 80/1936).

In addition to kindergartens, in the late 19th century **nursery schools** were established in Finland. Their growth followed the same pattern as kindergarten growth. Like the kindergartens, nursery schools could be either public or private. There were eventually two types (Hänninen & Valli, 1986): (1) Some were designed solely for infants and toddlers up to 3 years old, with the average number of children enrolled being slightly under 30 (Social Service Journal, 1970, June). (2) In the early 20th century, "expanded nurseries" were also established. These were meant for children from birth to age 7 (Hänninen & Valli, 1986), and the average number of children enrolled was slightly above 30 (Social Service Journal, 1970, June). By the late 1960s nurseries and expanded nurseries numbered over 300. Unlike kindergartens, prior to the enactment of the 1973 Day Care Law, the nursery schools were not eligible for state aid.

Finland's third main form of institutionalized care for preschool-aged children has been the **dayclub**. Churches have generally been responsible for this form of care. The earliest forerunner of the dayclub was probably the 18th century playschool in Holland, which later spread to Germany and Scandinavia. Dayclub operation in Finland began in the late 1940s and gradually spread to different parts of the country (Hänninen & Valli, 1986). By the late 1960s there were about 200 dayclubs in Finland (Social Service Journal, 1970, June). With few exceptions, dayclubs have not been public. Neither have they been eligible for state aid. A general directive for dayclub operations, issued in 1970, stipulates that the dayclub is to serve 4- to 7-year-olds and sets the maximum group size at 20 children. Activities are organized so that the same group of children meets three to five times per week, for a maximum of 3 hours per meeting (Hänninen & Valli, 1986).

Two less-formal types of publicly sponsored care outside the home for preschool-aged children have been the **playground programs** and the **park aunts** (Hänninen & Valli, 1986). Playground operations began in the 1910s, providing services to 4- to 10-year-olds for 2 to 8 hours daily. There were slightly over 300 playgrounds by the late 1960s. Park aunts, caregivers meant chiefly for children under age 4, were employed at slightly over 200 locations in the late 1960s.

Care and training for preschool-aged children with special needs has long existed in Finland (Hänninen & Valli, 1986). As early as the beginning of the 20th century, the forms of operations of the kindergartens were adapted to children who were forced to spend long periods of time in hospitals (for example, children with rheumatism or tuberculosis). A kindergarten was established in the 1920s for the mentally retarded. More special kindergartens and special groups at normal kindergartens were instituted in the 1950s. The number of special care centers was not, however, large. By the late 1960s these special facilities numbered only six, two public and four private (Social Service Journal, 1970, June).

Firing Up the Day Care and Preschool Training Discussion

In the late 1960s the public began to pay serious attention to the need for day care (Ojala, 1986b). Commissions and committees meeting between 1966 and 1972 formulated a "sharply increasing reorganization of day care" (Committee Report, 1967:B46, 1969:B104, 1971:A20, 1972:B44). The reorganization efforts were prompted by abrupt changes in the nation's social and occupational structure (Ojala, 1985b). The shift from an agrarian society to one built-up and town-centered occurred in Finland later and more rapidly than in many other European countries. Finland saw its greatest change in the 1950s and 1960s. The speed of urbanization and industrialization is well described by this comparison: The change that occurred in Finland over a 25-year period required a period three times as long in the other Nordic countries (Committee Report, 1980:31).

As a result of the changes in the social and occupational structures, industrialization increased rapidly and created new jobs, chiefly in towns in southern Finland and in the capital city region. Also as a result of structural changes, a significant number of women entered the work force. Throughout World War II the proportion of women employed outside the home had been about 10 percent (Jallinoja, 1976). After the war, the situation changed quickly. In 1950, 34 percent of women were gainfully employed outside the home. The corresponding figure for 1960 was 48 percent, and for 1970, 58 percent.

Since the retail shops and businesses employing much of the new work force wanted full-time employees, demand for full-day child care, in particular, began to grow in the early 1970s. In addition, the need for day care services for children under age 3 increased (Ojala, 1985b). The general public, however, did not support a substantive increase in the number of nursery schools (Committee Report, 1967:B46). Family day care became the object of discussion and interest and was seen to have potential for functioning as a better form of child care, to complement institutionalized day care, especially for children under age 3.

In the ensuing discussion, "home care" and "day care" were occasionally set up as opposites. The most critical of parliamentary speeches considered the proposed day care reform to be too institutionally centered. A part of the then-sitting Parliament even proposed that the Day Care Bill contain a clause providing for home care support payments, which could be in the form of a care benefit, child allowance, or mother's salary (Parliament Proceedings, 1972).

Paralleling the late-1960s day care discussion in Finland was discussion of the issue of preschool training. This issue was not completely new. As early as the turn of the century, kindergartens in Finland had been operating according to the Froebelian model, with intermediary classes (preschool classes) for 5½- to 6-year-olds. These classes aimed at developing school readiness (Ojala, 1986b). The prevailing conditions changed significantly, however, when the school system became interested in the preschool training issue. A concrete indication of the awakening of activity was the inauguration of the preschool trial programs, first in the schools and later in conjunction with the day care centers (National Board of Education, 1982).

The effects of Finland's preschool training discussion were not purely domestic. In the summer of 1969 the International Federation of Teachers' Associations met in Helsinki, and out of this meeting grew an extensive declaration concerning preschool training. Influence from the enrichment programs of the 1960s in the United States also played a part in the formulation of the declaration (Committee Report, 1972:A13).

A Finnish national plan for the resolution of the preschool training issue first emerged in 1970. In 1972 the Preschool Committee that was established to resolve the issue published its proposal for the goals, curriculum, and organization of preschool training (Committee Report, 1972:A13). Though in the late 1970s yet a second committee made an attempt at instituting national preschool training (Committee Report, 1978:5), this final goal has not been accomplished. Nevertheless, at present, Finnish 6- year-olds can voluntarily participate in preschool training either at school or at a day care center.

THE CHILDREN'S DAY CARE LAW

The work begun in 1966 concerning the reorganization of day care culminated, after several stages, in the enactment of the 1973 Children's Day Care Law. This law requires each municipality to provide publicly organized or supervised day care to such an extent and in such forms as the need demands (Law 36/1973). It requires municipalities to insure that day care be provided in the child's mother tongue, be it Finnish, Swedish, or Lapp.

According to a statute associated with the Day Care Law, prime consideration must be given to enrollment of children requiring day care on the basis of social or educational grounds (Statute 239/1973). Children admitted on social grounds are those whose parents are gainfully employed outside the home, are students, or are ill or otherwise unable to care for their children. Children admitted on educational grounds are those requiring special education services. Also, children of Finland's returning emigrants, children in minority groups, and those in children's homes are given special consideration regarding day care services (Circular A3/1984/pe).

Day care in Finland is chiefly a full- or part-time public operation. A private individual or corporation may also provide day care services. The Day Care Law demands, however, that any individual or corporation charging for day care services make a formal announcement of operations to the social welfare board of the municipality at least 2 weeks prior to commencing operations. In addition, the law requires municipal social welfare boards to supervise the operations of private day care suppliers.

CHILD CARE OPTIONS

Only after the enactment of the Day Care Law did a more extensive discussion of the goals and curriculum of day care develop. A significant report on the educational goals of day care was released in 1980 (Committee Report, 1980:31). Its proposals led to the inclusion of a separate goals paragraph in the 1973 Day Care Law. This paragraph defines the national educational goals for day care as follows:

■ The goal of day care is to support the educational function of the home and to work with the home in furthering the balanced development of the child's personality.

■ Day care should offer the child continuing, safe, and warm human relations, provide activities supporting the child's all-around development, and create a favorable growth environment for the child.

■ Day care should, according to the needs of the child and in keeping with the general cultural tradition, further the child's physical, social, and emotional development and support the child's aesthetic, intellectual, ethical, and religious growth. Supporting religious growth should include respecting the convictions of the child's parents or guardians.

■ In fostering the child's development, day care should support the child's growth towards being responsible, peace-loving, and caring of the environment.

Besides being influenced by the educational goals established by the law, educational activity is also guided by goals set by subareas, which are based on the report of the Committee on Educational Goals (Committee Report, 1980:31). Subarea goals include separate content goals for physical, social, emotional, intellectual, aesthetic, ethical, and religious growth.

The educational activities of day care in Finland are not strictly based on any single theory of developmental psychology (Ojala, 1985b). Instead, special consideration is given to cultural and social conditions of development. In conjunction with this, the quality of the care environment is considered to be central to the realization of the day care training goals. The following qualitative demands are made on the young child's care and educational environment:

■ The child's care and educational environment must be safe, healthy, homelike, and conducive to a close contact with nature.

■ The child must have a permanent day care locale that together with the home forms an organized and logical growth environment, where the care provided is suitable to the child's normal daily activities.

■ In care and education, the child must be shown morally valuable models and be protected from mental and physical violence and other unsuitable influences.

■ The child must have permanent carepersons who provide love, acceptance of children's individuality, and understanding of children's developmental stages and needs.

■ Education must offer the child multifaceted perceptions, activity totalities, our cultural traditions, and favorable opportunities to experience the year's changing seasons, both commonplace and festive events, both restful and active endeavors.

■ The child must have suitable facilities and equipment for physical exercise and games, and experiences that enrich development, in the form of activity periods and small tasks.

The realization of the educational goals of day care also influences educational methods. In realizing these goals, basic care situations, games, small tasks, arts and crafts, teaching and activity periods, contact with the environment, celebrations, and excursions are employed. The celebrations and excursions serve to create the emotional highlights of day care (Committee Report, 1980:31).

Since the early 1980s the responsibility in Finland for the publicly organized care, training, and education of preschool-aged children has chiefly resided in the day care system. According to the Day Care Law, day care is implemented in three operational modes, which are described in the three sections that follow (Law 36/1973). Besides these three modes of day care, there is also preschool training for 6-year-olds, which is provided by the school system (*Government Decision*, 1985, March 14).

Day Care Centers

Following the enactment of the Day Care Law, kindergartens in Finland began to be referred to as day care centers, meaning physical and operational entities that are established for child care purposes (Circular A3/1984/pe). Most of the day care centers in Finland are public, but it is also possible to establish private day care centers, which, like the public ones, can receive state aid.

As conditions for receiving state aid, there are guidelines and norms to be met concerning the physical layout of Finnish day care centers (Circular A6/1980/pe). A day care facility must set aside an area of 50–70 square meters for each day care place (slot). This figure includes the surface area of the building, the outdoor playground, open areas and driveways, and parking space. The facility's equipped outdoor playground must allow 10–20 square meters per day care place. Separate outdoor areas must be designed for children under age 3 and children over age 3, and this design must take into consideration activities involving both construction and movement. For full-time day care, interior space must be at least 6 square meters per child over age 3, at least 8.5 square meters per child aged 1 through 2, and at least 10 square meters per child under age 1. Interior space per child over age 3 in part-time day care must be at least 4 square meters. The minimal requirement for generally used space, such as a gymnasium or auditorium, is 36 square meters of free space. This space can be designed to be combined with other space (as multipurpose space). Multipurpose space should allow

1 square meter per child. There are norms and guidelines concerning other day care center areas (staff social facilities, dining rooms, first aid rooms).

A day care center can have places for 5–100 children. In certain exceptional situations, the number of places can slightly exceed 100. Children come to the day care center 4 to 10 hours a day. Part-time care lasts 4 to 5 hours, and full-time, generally 8 to 10 hours. A center can function, if necessary, to provide evening and night care to children of shift-workers. Part-time care can also be organized in sparsely populated areas a few days a week (Circular A3/1984/pe).

For their daily activities, children are divided into groups that are formed on the basis of age and of care and educational factors. Generally the maximum allowed is twenty 3-year-olds per group. If, however, the 3- year-olds are in day care for only 4 hours a day, the group may include 25. A maximum of 12 per group is set for 1- to 2-year-olds. For groups of children under 1 year of age, the maximum is 6. In the 1980s it has been desirable to compose groups so that they insure the most favorable care and educational conditions, facilitate operations, and in part increase the child's feelings of security. This means that the same group might contain both full- and part-time children, 1- to 6-year-olds (sibling groups), some children requiring special care and training, or chiefly 6-year-olds.

Children in full-time day care arrive at the facility between 6:30 and 8:30 a.m. First they have breakfast, after which they all participate in guided activities or a teaching period (either together or in small groups). The guided activities last from a few minutes to an hour, depending on the age level. After these activities the children play, draw, do arts and crafts, on their own. Afterwards they go outside until about 11:00 a.m., which is lunch time. Following this lunch is a rest period lasting about 2 hours. This is followed by an afternoon snack and either a short guided period or free play. At the end of the day the children go outside again to play and await their parents.

Children requiring special care and training are usually cared for in the same groups as other children are. This integration affects the size of the groups in such a way as to reduce the group size by two for each child requiring special care and training. Occasionally an entire day care center or part of one is used solely for children requiring special care and training, in which case the day care group is half the normal size (Law 36/1973).

Special arrangements are also employed in organizing day care in sparsely populated areas (Ojala, 1983, September). If the available space does not conform to the general norms, the group size can be reduced. Activities can be organized for a reduced portion of the year (at least 76 days) or week (2–3 days). This partial-year or partial-week arrangement often means that the same teacher handles the activities of several day care centers (mobile day care activity).

The Day Care Law requires a sufficient number of qualified staff (Law 36/1973). The requirements regarding number and training of staff are dependent on the composition of the group. Since 1981, staff requirements have been the following:

- For full-time groups of 1- to 2-year-olds—one preschool teacher/social pedagog and two child nurses
- For full-time groups of children over age 3—two preschool teachers/social pedagogs and one child nurse
- For part-time groups of children over age 3—one preschool teacher/social pedagog and one child nurse (Circular A3/1984/pe)

Though the preschool teacher, social pedagog, and child nurse are jointly responsible for the child's care and education, the training they receive differs in nature and length. Since 1983 **preschool teachers** have received 3 years of training at either a teacher-training college or a preschool teacher institute, both of which require a high school diploma for admission. **Social pedagog** training consists of 4 years of vocational training. **Child nurses** receive child nurse training or other comparable training approved by the Ministry of Social Affairs and Health. This training lasts 1 year for high school graduates and 2½ years for those who have only completed comprehensive school.

The responsibilities and duties of the staff groups are based on training (Circular A3/1984/pe). The preschool teachers/social pedagogs are wholly responsible for the planning, implementation, and evaluation of day care educational activity. Their training qualifies them to function as group leaders. The task of the child nurse is to participate in planning, implementation, and evaluating day care activity and to function as a back- up in care and education. Each day care center has a director, who can be either a preschool teacher or a social pedagog.

Day care centers require other staff for kitchen duty, cleaning, clothing-care, and other organizational tasks. The number of staff is dependent on such factors as the size of the facility, the time of operation, and the special structure of the groups.

In 1983 about 20 percent of 4-year-olds were in day care centers (Table 1). Table 1 shows that day care participation increases with age. For example, in 1983 slightly less than 9 percent of 1-year-olds were in day care, but nearly 49 percent of 6-year-olds were in day care. Of the children in Finnish day care centers in 1983, almost 70 percent were in full-time care.

Evaluations of the training, care, and education provided by day care vary (Boström & Sundquist, 1976; Kamppinen, 1979; Kiviluoto & Parkkinen, 1976; Munter, 1984; National Board of Social Welfare, National Board of Health, & University of Helsinki Child Psychiatry Clinic, 1981, 1982, 1984; Ruoppila & Korkiakangas, 1975). Generally speaking, the readiness and development of children in day care compares with that of children in home care (Ojala, 1985a). Day care neither hinders nor substantially furthers the child's development. Some studies indicate that day care has, for example, furthered the child's creativity (Heikkilä, 1973; Ruoppila & Korkiakangas, 1975) or intellectual and motor development (Kyöstiö, Luukkonen, & Koskenrauta, 1975). In contrast, it has been noted that children under 3 years old, in particular, have in some cases had difficulties in adapting to day care (Lahikainen & Sundquist, 1979) and that children from day care centers have had shorter attention spans or been more disruptive when entering school (Kamppinen, 1979).

In recent years particular attention has been given to the care of children under 3 years old in day care centers, because it has been observed that the length of the care day, together with unstable living conditions of the family, can cause the child to undergo psychophysical stress (Munter, 1984). Of children in full-time day care, about half are there 9 hours, and a quarter are there as long as 11 hours. Long day care hours may disturb the child's normal bedtime, which may rob the child of needed sleep. Also, the child's psychophysical stress increases with a

Table 1

Children 0–6 Years of Age in Day Care Centers, 1983

Age (in yr)	Number	Percent of Total Age Group
0	359	0.5
1	5,708	8.6
2	7,245	11.4
3	9,667	15.3
4	12,406	19.5
5	15,985	25.0
6	31,646	48.4

Note. The figures, based on the situation existing on December 31, 1983, are from the National Board of Social Welfare, 1985, July.

large turnover among the children in the day care group. Only about 4 percent of the groups reported no turnover during the entire year.

Finnish parents trust in the day care system, despite its shortcomings: About 43 percent are satisfied, while about 45 percent are very satisfied (Munter, 1984). When questioned, parents cite the positive aspects more often than the negative ones. In particular, parents emphasize the opportunity day care centers provide for the expansion of the child's social contacts, the growing importance of the day care center, and the competence of the staff. Negative aspects cited include particularly the children's susceptibility to illness and the large group size.

FAMILY DAY CARE

Family day care is also subject to the provisions of the Day Care Law. **"Family day care"** is defined by the law as child care in private homes or in other familylike settings (Law, 36/1973). A locale in which family day care is provided is referred to as a family day care center. Family day care can be performed at the day care provider's home or at the child's home. In a situation referred to as **three-family care** (Circular A3/1984/pe), two to four homes (the children's) compose the rotating care locale for a maximum of four preschool-aged children.

Family day care in Finland can be either public or private. Public family day care is guided by a municipal family day care supervisor. In public family day care, the caregiver is a municipal employee. Private family day care is based on an agreement between the caregiver and the child's guardians. The duty of the municipalities is also to supervise and guide private family day care. Unlike public family day care, private family day care is not eligible for state aid (Circular A3/1984/pe).

The law demands that the family day care center be suitable to the child's care and education. Therefore, prior to being approved for public use, the center is inspected regarding heating, ventilation, lighting, availability of pure drinking water, and level of sanitary facilities. Special attention is paid to whether the locale is suitable for the child's favorable development and free of anything threatening to the child's security (Law 36/1973). To insure the child's basic care, the center must have areas appropriate for hygienic care, eating, and undisturbed rest. Play areas in the family day care center must be at least 7 square meters per child. Outdoor areas are also inspected to insure that they meet the guidelines set for family day care.

No more than four children (including the caregiver's own children under age 7) can be cared for at one time (Law 36/1973). Before the children are brought to the family day care center, an agreement is drawn up by the child's parents, the family day care supervisor, and the caregiver. This agreement sets out the details of the child's daily care and training (Circular A3/1984/pe).

Family day care is recommended in particular for children below 1 year of age (Circular A3/1984/pe). In principle, however, this mode of day care is meant for all ages and all types of children, either on a part- or full- time basis. In practice it is used primarily for care and education of children below 3 years of age.

In forming family day care groups, consideration is given both to the caregiver and to the child (Circular A3/1984/pe). Group composition depends on the resources afforded by the family day care center, the caregiver's own family situation, and the ages of her children. It is important for all children in the group to have the opportunity for age-appropriate activity. Children requiring special care and training can also be placed in family day care, and when they are, special consideration is given to the composition of the group.

The Day Care Law requires the caregiver to be capable of looking after children (Law 36/1973). To guarantee this, each family caregiver is trained specifically for the job at a course approved by the National Board of Vocational Education. Since 1985 this course has been 250 hours in length. Caregivers must also take a 16-hour first aid course. Besides training, it is also important for caregivers to have personal suitability and experience. Selection is made on the basis of application, visits to the home, and an interview that is carried out by two persons, usually the family day care supervisor and a psychologist, nurse, or social welfare officer (Circular A3/1984/pe).

In 1983 about 16 percent of Finnish 4-year-olds were in family day care (Table 2). In contrast to the situation in day care centers, children aged 1 to 3 years form the majority in family day care, which in most cases is a full-time form of care. Statistics for 1983 indicate that slightly over 90 percent of family day care children were cared for on a full-time basis.

Positive aspects of family day care are the small group size, homelike care environment, and operational flexibility (National Board of Social Welfare et al., 1984; Ojala, Lius, & Pänttönen, 1981). Consequently the training methods of family day care resemble home methods more than day care center methods do (Huttunen, 1984). Experience has shown that family day care is an especially suitable mode of care for children

Table 2

CHILDREN 0–6 YEARS OF AGE IN FAMILY DAY CARE, 1983

Age (in yr)	Number	Percent of Total Age Group
0	1,267	1.9
1	11,213	17.0
2	11,496	18.0
3	10,854	17.1
4	9,990	15.7
5	8,929	14.0
6	6,758	10.3

Note. The figures, based on the situation existing on December 31, 1983, are from the National Board of Social Welfare, 1985, July.

under age 3, for those susceptible to infection, for those with parents working irregular hours, and for those who have tired of large groups in day care centers (National Board of Social Welfare, 1980; Ståhlberg, 1980). Negative aspects of family day care are the low education level of caregivers, the short duration of the caregiver's vocational training, the length of the caregiver's workday (averaging about 10 hours), and the frequent caregiver turnover (Aho & Kuokkanen, 1980). Though family day care providers receive course-structured vocational training, most work in this job only temporarily or only until their own children reach school age.

PLAY ACTIVITY

The Day Care Law defines "play activity" in Finland as indoor or outdoor children's games or activities guided and supervised in a place or area designed for this purpose (Law 36/1973). The purpose of play activity is primarily to complement other modes of day care (Circular A3/1984/pe). It is recommended for children in home care or family day care and in day care for special groups, and it can be either public or private. Play activity is concerned with four modes of operation (Circular A3/1984/pe): playclubs, playgrounds, equipment-lending facilities, and the Open Day Care Center operations. These four modes of operation can exist separately or in combination.

Private play activity is centered to a large degree in **playclub** operations. Playclubs are a regular play and hobby activity designed for children over 3 years of age (Circular A3/1984/pe). Meeting once or twice a week, the clubs generally function less than 4 hours a day. The number of children may not exceed 15. Private playclubs clearly outnumber public ones (National Board of Social Welfare, 1985, July). According to 1983 figures, 6,500 private playclubs served slightly more than 95,000 children, about 21 percent of Finland's preschool population. In contrast, in 1983 almost 900 publicly sponsored playclubs served about 15,000 participants, or merely 3 percent of the preschool population.

Playground operations are a regular form of play and hobby activity for children of different ages (Circular A3/1984/pe). Playground operations can begin when there are at least 5 to 10 participating children in the neighborhood. Parents and other children from the area can also occasionally join in playground operations. Operations include regularly scheduled activity periods. Public playgrounds functioning in 1983 numbered just under 2,000, serving about 30,000 children (National Board of Social Welfare, 1985, July). This figure represents about 6.5 percent of the preschool population.

Equipment-lending facilities are designed to serve children of different ages and adults who direct children in regularly scheduled play (Circular A3/1984/pe). Lending facilities can be established when 20 to 30 children requiring this service are found in a neighborhood.

Open Day Care Center operations are meant to simultaneously serve children of different ages, as a training and guidance activity, and adults, as a means through which social contacts between families can be increased (Circular A3/1984/pe). The operations attempt to facilitate the training task of parents and family day care providers. Generally, Open Day Care Center operations provide for a maximum of 15 children and 15 adults at one time. Participating children must always be accompanied by an adult. Open Day Care Centers are still new in Finland and operate partially on a trial basis. Thirteen of them existed in 1983 and served over 4,000 children (National Board of Social Welfare, 1985, July). This figure represents about 1 percent of the preschool population. Parent evaluations of the Open Day Care Center have been positive (Huttunen, 1983, 1984). More so than with either family day care or center day care, parents report positive changes in their children's behavior, for example.

Preschool

Since not all Finnish 6-year-olds are in day care, the school system also engages in preschool training for 6-year-olds. In accord with the school law and by consent of the Ministry of Education, Finnish comprehensive schools can organize a maximum of 1 year of training for 6-year-olds who are not yet required to attend school (Law 476/1983).

Children's participation in preschool training is voluntary. The goal of preschool training, according to the goals set for educational and training activities of the comprehensive school, is to further the child's balanced development and to increase learning opportunities. The curriculum, which does not include any division into subject areas, employs the principle of integrated learning, as is the case with the children's training at day care centers (*Government Decision*, 1985, March 14). According to the evaluations of trial preschool programs since 1971, preschool training has furthered the child's development in all areas, but most clearly in the area of socioemotional development (National Board of Education, 1982).

Preschool can function either in conjunction with the lowest grade of the lower stage of comprehensive school or as a separate preschool class. This separate class can be established if there are at least 7 children to participate in preschool training in the district of the lower-stage school. Such a class may have no more than 25 children, however (*Government Decision*, 1985, March 14). In 1985 the number of 6-year-olds in classes that combined preschool with first grade was from 1 to 7 per class. In all, 950 pupils participated in preschool training in conjunction with the schools in the academic year 1985–86 (National Board of Education, 1986).

NATIONAL CHILD CARE POLICY

In the *Government Family Policy Report* released on March 25, 1980, the basic guidelines for Finnish family policy were outlined. This report considered the position of the family in society in light of the latest available information. A slowdown in population growth and the prospect of eventual population decline have prompted a strengthening of family policy in Finland. Achieving a steady birthrate and a balanced age-structure is now viewed as important to many areas of social activity. Family policy measures are increasingly seen as methods for achieving social justice and equality.

SUPPORT MEASURES CONNECTED WITH CHILDBIRTH

In Finland, the family-support measure of longest standing has been one connected with childbirth. Since 1937, expectant mothers have recieved a **maternity benefit**, obtainable either as money or as a package containing clothing and supplies for newborns. The monetary value of the benefit is not great—in 1986, 540 Finnish marks (FIM). (4 FIM is equivalent to $1 U.S. at the time of writing.) The public health aspect of the benefit has been substantial, since the benefit's prerequisite of a prenatal medical exam has directed expectant mothers to maternity clinics (Lindgren, 1983).

In addition to this longstanding benefit, Finland has recently developed other forms of assistance centering on childbirth. An expectant mother can now receive a **maternity allowance** in addition to the maternity benefit, to compensate for her loss of salary due to pregnancy and childbirth and to improve her own and her child's health care. This maternity allowance is paid for 25 days prior to the counted date of birth and for 233 days after birth. This allowance can instead be paid to the father if the mother consents and if the father remains home from work to care for the child. The father can take leave and receive allowance immediately after the child is born, for a period of 6 to 12 workdays and, beginning about 3 months after the birth, for a period of 158 days (Lindgren, 1983). The maternity allowance amounts to 70 to 80 percent of the mother's or father's daily salary. In 1986 the minimum maternity allowance was 40 FIM per day.

The first 100 workdays of the maternity allowance period compose the **maternity leave**. During this period, the allowance is paid only to the mother, unless the father, with the mother's consent, takes a 6- to 12-workday **paternity leave** after the birth of the child. This so-called extended paternity leave reduces the total length of the parent's leave. In the early 1980s about 17 percent of Finnish fathers used the paternity leave (Lindgren, 1983). Following the first 100 workdays of the maternity allowance period, the remaining days can be used towards either parent's leave. This 158-day **parent's leave** can, with the mother's consent, be used in its entirety or in part by the father. The father and mother cannot, however, take parent's leave at the same time. Each taking leave separately, they can divide the leave period into two parts; the minimum length of either's part must be 12 days (Siltanen, 1985).

Maternity and child health care is provided by the municipal health center in conjunction with the maternity and children's clinics. Expectant mothers come to the maternity clinic by their fourth month of pregnancy. The newborn comes under the auspices of the maternity clinic for 2 weeks. During the prenatal and postnatal periods, the maternity clinic provides the mother with guidance concerning her health and prepares both parents for the birth. From the age of 2 weeks up to the age of school entry, the child is covered by the services of the children's clinic. The children's clinic advises the parents in child care, regularly checks the child's health, offers help when the child is ill, and provides vaccinations. Both maternity and children's clinics presently also attempt to provide counseling services (Lindgren, 1983).

Both the maternity and children's clinics offer free services to their users. Obviously these services have been successful, since Finland's infant mortality rate (now 6.5 per thousand) and maternal mortality rate are both among the lowest in the world (Lindgren, 1983).

MEASURES FOR IMPROVING THE CONDITIONS OF FAMILIES WITH CHILDREN

A comparison of the income levels of families with and without children under school age has shown that each additional child weakens the family's economic position. In order that families with children might also achieve a moderate economic standard, Finland employs special measures for the improvement of the conditions of these families.

In addition to the maternity allowance, there is a **child benefit system** to compensate for the long-term costs incurred with the birth of a child (*Government Family Policy Report*, 1980, March 25). Child benefits are paid to families with any children under age 17. In 1986 these payments were as follows: 2,088 FIM per year for the first child, 2,420 FIM per year for the second, 2,928 FIM per year for the third, 3,808 FIM per year for the fourth, and 4,592 FIM per year for the fifth and succeeding children.

Families can under certain circumstances receive a **housing subsidy** (Siltanen, 1985). The average size of this subsidy was about 300 FIM per month in the early 1980s. Young parents with children, in particular, can receive a **low-interest** and **long-term mortgage** for buying their own home. Finland also grants **child support payments** to insure children's maintenance in the case of a parent's inability to meet family responsibility. In the early 1980s this payment was about 200 FIM per month. Families with children can also deduct a specified annual sum as a **child deduction** in their taxes for each child under age 18 maintained during the tax year.

ALTERNATIVE CHILD CARE ARRANGEMENTS

The 1980s witnessed a brisk discussion in Finland concerning child care arrangements. The discussion has shown that no general solution to the problems of child care exists. The government maintains that alternative child care systems should be available for families, so that each child's and family's particular circumstances might be accommodated. For the care of infants, family policy allowing parents to care for the child at home seems to be a solution. In the case of toddlers, the idea that the parents should be able to choose home care as an alternative to center or family day care has been stressed (*Government Family Policy Report*, 1980, March 25).

The possibility of caring for children under age 3 primarily at home has improved greatly in Finland in the 1980s. A law concerning the **support of home care** was enacted in 1984. For parents of children under age 3 the law provides economic support that can include a basic payment, a sibling payment, and a supplementary payment. These three payments, which were in 1986 respectively about 1,000 FIM, 200 FIM, and 800 FIM per month, are available to families with three preschool-aged children. Families with two preschool-aged children, if one is under 3 years old, are also eligible for home care payments, as are families with one child under 15 months old. The goal is that by the end of the decade, home care payments should be available to all families that are providing care for their child or children under 3 years old at home.

Since 1985, fathers and mothers have also had the opportunity to take a leave, after the so-called parent's leave, to care for children under age 3 at home. This later leave can be taken by either the father or the mother in a maximum of four periods, with the minimum length of each period being 2 months. Both parents cannot be on leave at the same time. During this leave, the parent's job is unaffected. Currently the length of the leave is determined by the number and ages of the children in the family. The goal is that by the end of the decade all parents of children under 3 years old should have the right to this leave (Siltanen, 1985).

The costs of center day care are paid by the national government, the municipalities, and the users. In 1983 the national government's share of the costs was 43 percent; the municipalities', 39 percent; and the users', 14 percent. Corresponding figures for family day care were 37 percent, 43 percent, and 18 percent (National Board of Social Welfare, 1985, July). Day care services for low-income families are free; others pay a fee dependent on the family income. The 1986 fees are as follows: full-time day care for 6-year-olds—100 to 700 FIM per month; for 3- to 5-year-olds—125 to 875 FIM per month; and for children under 3 years—0 to 625 FIM per month. Part-time day care costs 30 to 120 FIM per month for 6-year-olds, 65 to 445 FIM per month for 3- to 5-year-olds, and 0 to 325 FIM per month for children under 3 years old.

Day care is directed from the national, provincial, and local levels. Overall power lies with the national government, which approves the proposal of the Ministry of Social Affairs and Health concerning the national plan devised by the National Board of Social Welfare for social welfare and health care. The plan contains the provisions for children's day care and covers a period of 5 years.

General control, direction, and supervision of day care lies with the National Board of Social Welfare. It is responsible for the preparation of the national plan; the directives concerning day care staff, facilities, and operational equipment; and the development of the day care curriculum. On the provincial level (in the 12 provinces), day care is directed and supervised by the provincial governments and subject to the approval of the National Board of Social Welfare. The duties of the provincial governments are to approve municipal day care plans, inspect day care facilities, and approve in certain cases the maximum size of day care groups. Local decision making about day care organization is left to Finland's 464 municipalities. Municipalities must insure that the supply of day care meets the local demand. Municipal responsibility is given to social welfare boards, and in some large cities, to the day care department.

The operational responsibility for the direction, education, and teaching in each day care center lies with the center's director. Family day care supervisors are in charge of family day care operations. In some municipalities there are also educational activity directors, who direct all modes of day care activities in the municipality.

Regardless of the fact that the Day Care Law has been in effect since 1973, the children's day care system demands continuing development. In the early 1980s about 60 percent of the nation's preschool-aged children were in the care of their father, mother, or other family members (Official Statistics of Finland XXI B:22). During this period, about 80 percent of mothers were working outside the home. The pressure just for quantitative development of day care has been so great that day care services are currently insufficient. Statistics indicate that in 1983, Finland could provide for 60 percent of its day care needs. Regional differences, however, are great. There are many municipalities in which the number of day care places is almost sufficient. In the capital city region and in large towns, the need for places is still enormous.

Development of day care operations centers on full-time day care places (*Government Family Policy Report*, 1980, March 25). Full-time places made up almost 80 percent of the total number of places in 1983. Family day care is the most common mode of service in the rural areas and for children under age 3, whereas day care centers serve primarily towns and large residential centers in the training, care, and education of 3- to 6-year-olds. Statistics indicate that in 1983, almost 60 percent of family day care places were outside the cities, and just over 70 percent of the nation's day care centers were located in the cities (National Board of Social Welfare, 1985, July).

The development of day care services is also affected by their relative costs. According to estimates made at the beginning of the decade, the average cost for establishing each day care place was about 30,000 FIM, and per-child operational costs were about 1,300 FIM per month (*Government Family Policy Report*, 1980, March 25). During the same period, the cost to society for home care support came to 700 FIM per month per child.

There were about 175,000 day care places in Finland in 1985. The goals set for 1986–90 envision an annual increase of 7,000 places (Ministry of Social Affairs and Health, 1985).

Special Support and Services Needed by Families With Children

In addition to the general forms of support available to families with children, there are also special support services available for the individual needs of children and families with children.

One special service available to families is **municipal household assistance**. The most common reasons for needing this household assistance are the birth of a child or illness of the person taking care of the household. It is also needed when a child in public day care is ill. Household assistance is provided by a housekeeper, whose services at home can be requested. A separate assistance system has been developed for farm families and is called **substitute aid** (*Government Family Policy Report*, 1980, March 25). Household assistance is not completely free. The fee charged is dependent on the family's wealth.

Under certain conditions, the wife and children of an individual completing his compulsory military service can receive **soldier's benefits**. This assistance is provided if it can be demonstrated that the military service will substantially weaken the family's financial position (Siltanen, 1985).

Care for handicapped and chronically ill children under 16 years of age is supported through a **special care subsidy**. This subsidy is not dependent on the parents' wealth or income (Siltanen, 1985). A special subsidy is paid to extremely handicapped children. In 1986 this special subsidy amounted to about 900 FIM per month. Care subsidies for chronically ill children were about 600 FIM per month for the same year.

In crisis situations, the family and child can be aided through **child welfare measures** and the **child guidance clinics**. Child welfare aid entails the family and child being assisted by the personal support of a social worker, by the use of a support person, or by arrangement of summer or other recreational activities. Child guidance clinics provide family and educational counseling. A recent development, however, has been the attempt to concentrate educational counseling for preschool-aged children in the maternity and children's clinics (*Government Family Policy Report*, 1980, March 25).

NATIONAL CHILD CARE ISSUES OF THE NEXT DECADE

Finland, unlike the other Nordic countries, has not experienced a stagnation in economic growth. This has laid a good foundation for the continued increase in day care places. If the goal of 7,000 new places per year is met, the need and demand for day care places will be in balance by the mid-1990s at the latest.

In the future, the need for places will still be greatest in the capital city region and in other large towns. Experience gained in the capital city region indicates, however, that concentrating solely on a quantitative increase in the number of places will not entirely solve the region's day care problems, which have proved to be complicated—a constant lack of qualified personnel, rapid staff turnover, and oversized groups of children.

The shortage of staff can be partly reduced by increasing the number of trainees. This increase should be chiefly in preschool teachers and child nurses, with about 700 trainees annually in each. In the capital city region there are other reasons for increasing the number of trainees, besides the shortage of personnel. Because day care personnel are mainly female and young, there should be an additional reserve of trained personnel to fill vacancies left by maternity leaves. Also, if day care personnel participate in graduate and continuing education—another increasing need—this will require an expanded personnel reserve.

In addition to increasing trainee numbers, increased consideration should be given to the internal and external working conditions of day care personnel. For example, the continuing personnel shortage in the capital city region is caused in part by such factors as the expensive housing and the high cost of living, the long distances that must be traveled to work, and the mental stress of the work. It is also more common in this region to resort to enlarging the maximum size of groups at day care centers because of both the personnel shortage and children's frequent absences. In doing so, however, little serious attention is paid to the numerous disadvantages that large groups cause for both staff and children (Belsky, Steinberg, & Walker, 1982; Ojala 1985a). The conclusion, based on research results, that 15 to 18 is the optimal group size for 3-year-olds in day care should be duly considered in Finland, as well as in other countries, as a basis for decision making.

Since the early 1980s the period of training for all day care personnel groups has been extended. Therefore, it is not particularly necessary to do this in the near future. However, special attention should be given to the coordination of personnel training and to the provision of graduate and continuing education.

The training for preschool teachers in particular should be standardized. Preschool teachers are now trained in several ways: in social service institutes (social pedagog training), in preschool teacher colleges, and at universities. Since special demands for several different training systems no longer exist, future training for preschool teachers should be more systematic. In the early 1970s a proposal was made that preschool teacher training be shifted wholly to universities. This solution would not only standardize training, it would also lay the foundation for a close relationship between early childhood education and the schools. This in itself is significant, because the separation in Finland between schools and day care centers has traditionally been quite distinct.

Providing continuing education for day care personnel is also an important future task in Finland. The new social welfare laws enacted in 1984 require municipalities to arrange continuing education for day care personnel at least every 5 years. This should promote the development of the curriculum of day care, which until now has been of secondary importance. The laws state that the purpose of day care is to support the home in its training tasks and to further, in conjunction with the home, the balanced development of the child's personality. The scope of this task and, more important, its analysis are also significant topics for continuing education. There is reason to believe that in the near future, day care personnel will need to show an increased willingness towards cooperation not only with parents but also with co-workers and various community agencies (Taipale, 1985). Continuing education should support personnel in taking on new tasks, since reforms often are accompanied by feelings of insecurity on the part of staff.

The continued development of day care also requires additional research and experimental activity. Research in early childhood education is conducted by universities (cf. Ojala, 1984a), by the National Board of Social Welfare, and by the municipalities.

The research activities of **universities** have chiefly been in applied early childhood education research; the education, developmental psychology, and special education areas, in particular, have formed the scientific basis. In the near future, Finland will also need basic research and early childhood education research institutes (Ojala, 1986b). This will lay the groundwork for early childhood education reform that is based on scientific rather than pragmatic ideas.

Financing by the **National Board of Social Welfare** has made it possible to carry out university-affiliated research and experimentation concerning day care. Research topics have been, for instance, sibling groups in day care centers, three-family day care, development of day care in sparsely populated areas, and Open Day Care Center operations. Research and experimentation have been hindered, however, by the short duration of the experiments, and the results achieved have been generally rather superficial. Future research should concentrate on longer-term, more thorough research projects, and experimental activity should be increasingly directed towards the educational issues of day care. Longer-term and more thorough research is also needed in the areas of basic and continued training of day care personnel.

Small-scale experiments, arising mainly out of local interest, are also carried on by the **municipalities**, often in cooperation with the local university. Since the municipalities are ultimately responsible for running day care, they should in the near future consider establishing day care commissions composed of experts, administrators, and day care personnel. In this way, the municipalities could take a more active role in developing day care.

Responsibility for direction and administration of day care in Finland lies with the Ministry of Social Affairs and Health and with the National Board of Social Welfare. The clear direction of day care has resulted primarily from having national laws and guidelines. The new social welfare law enacted in 1984, however, is a departure from this situation in that it reduces central government control. A goal in the near future is for the municipalities to take an even greater responsibility, not only in controlling the economic aspects and maintenance of day care, but also in determining the form and content of day care operations. As previously noted, the municipalities will become responsible for the continuing education of day care personnel and for research and experimentation.

This reduction in central government control is an attempt to bring day care services closer to their users and to benefit from local expertise and new ideas (Taipale, 1985). The success of the change will probably mean increased activity in the development of day care. It can also mean increased motivation on the part of administrators and day care personnel. However, an obstacle could arise if a quite different view of day care development is taken by the municipalities. Numerous examples of this have already been noted. Central administration should closely monitor these municipalities, providing follow-up, advice, and guidance wherever possible. One possible strategy might be the use of different forms of development seminars, which could be organized in the municipalities or participated in by the municipalities.

Day care development is not influenced only by quantitative and qualitative considerations. Since Finnish day care is primarily publicly organized, it is strongly connected to the nation's prevailing labor, family, and educational policies (Ojala, 1985b). For instance, it appears that the view arising at the beginning of the 1980s favoring development of at-home, parental child care will receive further support in the near future (Jallinoja, 1985). Already the extended maternity leave, the home care benefits, and the mother's assured right to return to work after caring for her child have had a positive effect on such development.

Measures concerning the arrangement of work hours for parents also seem to have gained support, especially in regard to making home care possible. A work group established by the Ministry of Social Affairs and Health has recently proposed that parents of children under age 5 and in the first grade at school should be able to reduce their regular workday to 6 hours. In addition, it has proposed that workers be granted flexible work hours and a statutory 3-day leave for the care of sick children.

As parents begin to take on even greater responsibility, especially in the care of children under 3 years of age, there will be many interesting consequences. If development continues in this parent-care direction, the pressure to increase the number of day care places will be less than anticipated; there might also be a marked reduction in family day care, possibly a complete abandonment of this form of child care (Jallinoja, 1985). Also, if preschool training for 6-year-olds is strengthened and leads in the near future to the lowering of the school age to 6 years, day care will then be centered chiefly on the task of caring for and educating 3- to 5-year-olds. This would resemble the situation day care centers (kindergartens) were in prior to the enactment of the Day Care Law.

The view of development I have just described represents new challenges for day care centers. In the future, parents will seek more flexible care arrangements; maintaining the present full- and part-time hours will no longer work. Families will also need increased support, counseling, and guidance in educational matters, and pressures and expectations for the provision of this educational guidance will probably be placed on the day care centers. Day care centers will also be expected to become more involved with experimentation and research in early childhood education. Perhaps care centers in the future will be better able to answer the new challenges if a reduced demand for day care places substantially reduces the size of both the centers and the groups of children served. Then the day care centers will function well and perhaps provide real opportunities in support of the child's and family's total growth according to their individual needs.

SUMMARY AND CONCLUSION

The Finnish society's system of early childhood education has a history of development of more than 100 years. Froebel's ideas were quite rapidly brought to Finland, and Cygnaeus started to develop the kindergarten ideal along the lines of Froebel. The goals were reform of the intellectual and practical training given prior to going to school, raising the national level of education, training mothers and nurses, and developing new, pedagogically appropriate equipment and modes of operation. This development only partially succeeded. After the death of Cygnaeus the kindergarten ideal began to develop chiefly on social welfare bases. The original desire to increase the national level of education on an intellectual basis was abandoned. Instead of emphasizing intellectual development, early childhood education placed its greatest attention on practical matters. Practical educational activity was designed for the most part according to the operational modes and equipment developed by Froebel. Finnish preschool programs have to the present day developed mainly along Froebelian lines. (This is not the case in the other Nordic countries.)

Early childhood education in Finland has for almost 100 years developed under national control. For this reason the number of private kindergartens and day care programs has not been great. It is also significant that the national government supervises the private day care operations, although responsibility for their direction has not proved to be clearly defined. For example, prior to 1924, kindergartens in Finland were under the control of the school authorities, and thereafter they transferred to control of the social welfare authorities. Though the national responsibility for the development and control of day care today still rests with the social welfare authorities, the school authorities also participate in the arrangement of day care and early childhood education by organizing preschool training for 6-year-olds and by training preschool teachers.

Though the participation of two different agencies in directing early childhood education may make its attempts to develop more difficult, it could also be beneficial. The social welfare authorities concentrate on the sufficiency and appropriateness of children's care arrangements. The school authorities, for their part, are more interested in what kind of education and training preschool-aged children get. It could be that the differing perspectives of the two agencies are needed to create the most favorable conditions for children.

The government's determination to involve itself in the development of day care and the enactment of the Day Care Law in the early 1970s were essential for the creation of new day care places. The importance of the law is evident from the fact that after its enactment, the number of places nearly tripled in the period from 1973 to 1983. At first, however, the law did not contain norms for the development of the content of day care operations. Later, the law was amended to include a special clause specifying the national educational goals of day care. The educational goals contained in the law and the goals included in the report by the National Committee on Day Care Educational Goals together have laid the foundation for development of the curriculum of day care in the near future. It is significant that only through these two documents does Finland for the first time have the real possibility of carrying out a complete national evaluation of day care.

The defined educational goals of day care are also important from a historical perspective. The goals contain the same basic ideas found in the far-reaching ideals of early childhood education set forth by Froebel and Cygnaeus. These basic ideas concern not only the education of the child but also that of the whole family. In emphasizing the educational tasks of the kindergarten, Cygnaeus was convinced that his ideas would remain alive. With the 1984 inclusion in the Day Care Law of a set of educational goals, we may have reason to believe that Cygnaeus's prediction has come true, at least in part, after almost a hundred years of waiting.

There is reason to believe that in the near future, additional attention will be paid to the development of the curriculum of day care. It will still, however, be necessary to create more day care places. Current trends indicate that additional day care places will be necessary through the early 1990s. Moreover, there may be more effective family policy measures to improve the home care possibilities for children. The government will attempt to create still better conditions for the care of children under 3 years of age primarily at home and for the care of 3- to 6-year-olds in day care centers. Although family day care will still be needed temporarily, especially for children under age 3, it will in the short-run be reduced and eventually even disappear. Then preschool-aged children will be cared for mainly at home and in day care centers.

In any case, new family policy measures, the likely increase in preschool training organized by schools, and the likely peaking of demand for day care places (perhaps even a reduction in demand) could soon bring about marked changes in the Finnish day care system.

REFERENCES*

Aho, H., & Kuokkanen, J. (1980). *Municipal family day care as seen by family day care persons* (in Finnish). Unpublished master's thesis, University of Joensuu, Finland.

Belsky, J., Steinberg, L., & Walker, A. (1982). The ecology of day care. In M. Lamb (Ed.), *Nontraditional families: Parenting and child development* (pp. 71–116). Hillsdale, NJ: Lawrence Erlbaum Associates.

Boström, C., & Sundquist, K. (1976). *The influence of day care on children's intellectual development* (Psykologiska Rapporter No. 8) (in Swedish). Turku, Finland: University of Turku.

Circular A6/1980/pe. *Plan for day care facilities* (in Finnish). Helsinki: National Board of Social Welfare.

Circular A3/1984/pe. *Children's day care* (in Finnish). Helsinki: National Board of Social Welfare.

---

*The editors would like to express their appreciation to Mikko Ojala for translating into English all reference elements that originally were in Finnish.

Committee Report 1967:B46. *Report of the Commission of Children's Day Care* (in Finnish). Helsinki: National Publication Center.

Committee Report 1969:B104. *Report of the Regulations Committee of the Commission on Children's Day Care* (in Finnish). Helsinki: National Publication Center.

Committee Report 1971:A20. *Report of the Committee on Children's Day Care* (in Finnish). Helsinki: National Publication Center.

Committee Report 1972:A13. *Report of the Preschool Committee* (in Finnish). Helsinki: National Publication Center.

Committee Report 1972:B44. *Report of the Regulations Committee on Children's Day Care* (in Finnish). Helsinki: National Publication Center.

Committee Report 1974:15. *Report of the Committee on Training Early Childhood Education Personnel* (in Finnish). Helsinki: National Publication Center.

Committee Report 1978:5. *Report of the Commission on Growth and Education of Six-year-olds* (in Finnish). Helsinki: National Publication Center.

Committee Report 1980:31. *Report of the Commission on the Educational Goals of Day Care* (in Finnish). Helsinki: National Publication Center.

Government Decision Concerning the Bases for Organizing Preschool Training in the Comprehensive Schools (in Finnish). (1985, March 14). Helsinki: National Publication Center.

Government family policy report (in Finnish). (1980, March 25). Helsinki: National Publication Center.

Heikkilä, J. (1973). *Differences in creative thinking in first- and second-graders who have or have not attended kindergartens* (Research Reports in Education, No. A:22) (in Finnish). Turku, Finland: University of Turku.

Huttunen, E. (1983). *Fruitfulness of open day care trial operations in Nurmes* (in Finnish). Nurmes: Office of Social Welfare.

Huttunen, E. (1984). *Family and day care cooperation as a supporting factor of education and the child's development* (Research Reports in Education, No. 2) (in Finnish). Joensuu, Finland: University of Joensuu.

Hänninen, S. -L., & Valli, S. (1986). *The history of Finnish kindergarten work and early childhood education* (in Finnish). Helsinki: Otava.

Jallinoja, R. (1976). *Study on the development characteristics of day care in Finland* (Working Papers, No. 1) (in Finnish). Helsinki: University of Helsinki, Department of Sociology.

Jallinoja, R. (1985). *Introduction to family sociology* (in Finnish). Porvoo, Finland: Werner Söderström.

Kamppinen, V. (1979). *On the connections between development environments and the child's behavior at school* (in Finnish). Unpublished master's thesis, University of Helsinki.

Kiviluoto, H., & Parkkinen, T. (1976). *The effects of different early childhood care environments on the child's development* (Reports From the Department of Psychology, No. 21) (in Finnish). Turku, Finland: University of Turku.

Kyöstiö, O. K., Luukkonen, J., & Koskenrauta, P. (1975). *Preschool training without a school. Report on trial programs on integrating teaching in preschool training* (Research From Department of the Behavioral Sciences, No. 25) (in Finnish). Oulu, Finland: University of Oulu.

Lahikainen, A. -R., & Sundquist, S. (1979). *Reactions of children three years old and younger to day care* (Research Reports From the Department of Social Psychology, No. 1) (in Finnish). Helsinki: University of Helsinki.

Law 296/1927. *State Aid to Kindergartens Law* (in Finnish).

Law 36/1973. *Children's Day Care Law* (in Finnish).

Law 476/1983. *Comprehensive School Law* (in Finnish).

Lindgren, J. (1983). *Fundamentals of social security* (in Finnish). Porvoo, Finland: Werner Söderström.

Ministry of Social Affairs and Health. (1985). *National plan for the organization of social welfare and health 1986–90* (in Finnish). Helsinki: Author.

Munter, H. (1984). Psychophysical strain on small children (in Finnish). *Sosiaaliviesti, 3,* 43–48.

National Board of Education. (1982). *Ten years of preschool activity* (in Finnish). (Bulletins on School Trial Programs and Research, No. 2). Helsinki: Author.

National Board of Education. (1986). *Report on preschool teaching in comprehensive schools in the academic year 1985–86* (in Finnish). Helsinki: Author.

National Board of Social Welfare. (1980). *Report of the Work Group to Examine and Develop Family Day Care: The development of family day care* (Publications of the National Board of Social Welfare, No. 6) (in Finnish). Helsinki: Author.

National Board of Social Welfare. (1985, July). 0- to 6-year-old children in day care, December 31, 1983 (in Finnish). *Statistical Bulletin of the National Board of Social Welfare.*

National Board of Social Welfare, National Board of Health, & University of Helsinki Child Psychiatry Clinic. (1981). *Children's Development Study, Part 1: The first year of age* (Official Statistics of Finland, Social Special Research 32:72) (in Finnish). Helsinki: National Publication Center.

National Board of Social Welfare, National Board of Health, & University of Helsinki Child Psychiatry Clinic. (1982). *Children's Development Study, Part 2: The second year of age* (Official Statistics of Finland, Social Special Research 32:83) (in Finnish). Helsinki: National Publication Center.

National Board of Social Welfare, National Board of Health, & University of Helsinki Child Psychiatry Clinic. (1984). *Children's Development Study, Part 3: The third year of age* (Official Statistics of Finland, Social Special Research 32:102) (in Finnish). Helsinki: National Publication Center.

Nurmi, V. (1981). *The Finnish school system* (in Finnish). Helsinki: Werner Söderström.

Official Statistics of Finland XXI B:22. *Social welfare 1980* (Social Welfare Annual) (in Finnish). Helsinki: National Board of Social Welfare, Planning and Statistical Office.

Ojala, M. (1983, September). Education for children living in sparsely populated areas in Finland. *Seminar papers presented at the International Standing Conference for History of Education. Seminar group 6: Science, technology, and society since 1954* (pp. 79–82). Westminster College, Oxford, England, September 5–8, 1983.

Ojala, M. (Ed.). (1984a). *Early childhood education research in Finland* (in Finnish). Helsinki: Lastensuojelun keskusliitto.

Ojala, M. (1984b). Friedrich Froebel and the Kindergarten movement in Finland. *Informationen für Erziehungs- und Bildungshistorischen Forshung* (Heft 25, pp. 202–212). Universität Hannover.

Ojala, M. (1985a). *Fundamentals of early childhood education* (in Finnish). Helsinki: Kirjayhtymä.

Ojala, M. (1985b). A portrait of Finnish day care: Before and after 1973. In E. Catarsi (Ed.), *Twentieth century preschool education: Times, ideas, and portraits* (pp. 179–191). Milan, Italy: Franco Angeli Libri.

Ojala, M. (1986a). Day care research, trial program, and development operations as a part of early childhood education research (in Finnish). In H. Salminen (Ed.), *Scenarios of day care* (pp. 137–140). Helsinki: National Publication Center.

Ojala, M. (1986b). A major educational controversy in Finland: Are 6-year- olds ready for school? In G. Giovanni (Ed.), *Conference for the History of Education. Vol. 2. Compulsory education: Schools, pupils, teachers, programs, and methods* (pp.33–42). Universitá di Parma—"Bollettino" C.I.R.S.E.

Ojala, M., Lius, E., & Pänttönen, P. (1981). *Family day care as a part of day care and early childhood education. Research project report* (Publications of the National Board of Social Welfare, No. 4) (in Finnish). Helsinki: National Publication Center.

Parliament Proceedings 1972. *Documents, appendices, and minutes* (in Finnish). Helsinki: Library of Parliament.

Ruoppila, I., & Korkiakangas, M. (1975). *Effects of preschool, kindergarten, and the home on children's development 2. Results concerning the effects* (Publications of the Department of Psychology, No. 17) (in Finnish). Jyväskylä, Finland: University of Jyväskylä.

Salo, A. (1939). *The education of small children in the educational system of Uno Cygnaeus* (in Finnish). Hämeenlinna, Finland: Karisto.

Siltanen, A. R. (1985). *Carousel of life and the Finnish family* (in Finnish). Helsinki: Yhteistyö.

Social Service Journal. (1970, June). *Municipal and private nursery schools, expanded nursery schools, and kindergartens and their placement by type of municipality in 1969* (in Finnish).

Statute 297/1927. *Statute on Kindergartens Receiving State Aid.*

Statute 80/1936. *Statute on Kindergartens Receiving State Aid.*

Statute 239/1973. *Children's Day Care Statute.*

Ståhlberg, M. -R. (1980). *The influence of form of day care on occurrence of acute respiratory tract infections among young children* (in Finnish). Turku, Finland: University of Turku, Department of Pediatrics.

Taipale, V. (1985). *Annual Meeting for Cooperation in Child Care* (in Swedish). Helsinki: Socialstyrelsen.

V

Child Care and Early Education in Hong Kong

Sylvia Opper, *Lecturer*
Department of Education
University of Hong Kong

Introduction

This profile describes the present situation in Hong Kong regarding early education and care for children from 3 to 6 years of age. Aimed at policymakers, researchers, and practitioners, it sets out a perspective for future decisions regarding training, standards, curriculum development, and research. By providing some background information and an overview of existing strengths and weaknesses as well as of accomplishments and achievements of the early childhood system, the profile might suggest future directions for action aimed at improving the quality of life of young children.

The profile surveys the history of the systematic provision of early education and care in Hong Kong from the immediate postwar origins until the present day. It considers the various sectors of kindergarten education, child care, and early childhood special education and refers to major features of government policy and involvement in preprimary services. It also looks at research in the field and raises some important issues that will need to be addressed within the next decade.

Historical Perspective

In Hong Kong approximately 250,000 children between ages 3 and 6 attend preprimary institutions (HK Govt., Education Department, Statistics Section, 1988; HK Govt., 1986–87b). In 1986, kindergarten enrollment represented 89 percent of the relevant population (Education

Commission, 1986). This high proportion reflects the value that the Chinese traditionally attach to education, but it also reflects the economic and educational situation. Although a university degree has distinct economic advantages in Hong Kong, university places are only available for 2 percent of the population. Consequently university entrance competition is very keen, and success in previous schooling becomes a crucial factor. Formal schooling is an important avenue to social and economic mobility, and preschool is perceived as the first step along this avenue.

Two executive government branches are responsible for preprimary education and care in Hong Kong. The first is the Education and Manpower branch administered by the Education Department. The second is the Health and Welfare branch administered by the Social Welfare Department. **Kindergartens** are regulated by the Education Department and provide a 2- to 3-year course of education suitable for children between the age of 3 years and the age of entry to primary school (approximately age 6). They usually offer daily 3-hour programs in either morning or afternoon sessions. **Child care centers** are regulated by the Social Welfare Department and consist of establishments "at which more than five children who are under the age of 6 years are habitually received for the purposes of care and supervision" (HK Govt., 1982a). Types of child care centers include whole-day centers, residential centers, half-day nurseries, and playgroups.

The two types of preschool—kindergartens and child care centers—have similarities as well as major differences. They both provide services for a common pool of children aged 3 to 6 years. Moreover, with the exception of one demonstration nursery run by the Social Welfare Department Training Section, they are all in the hands of private organizations. In the kindergarten sector a number of these organizations are profit-making, whereas in the child care sector the majority of them are charitable (these are called voluntary agencies).

Differences exist, however, between kindergarten and child care center philosophies, job titles, standards, and staff training. In kindergartens the emphasis is on education, and kindergarten educators, like their counterparts in Hong Kong primary and secondary schools, are called teachers. In child care centers the emphasis is on care and supervision, and educators are referred to as child care workers. Regulations for the two types of preschool (regarding space, adult-child ratio, curriculum methods, and materials) are somewhat different and are discussed later in this profile. Staff training also differs between the two sectors, so that qualifications accepted in one sector are not recognized in the other; a trained child care worker wanting to move to a kindergarten would have to undergo the kindergarten teacher training, and vice versa.

The historical development of early education and care in Hong Kong helps to explain some of the reasons for the distinctions between the two sectors.

ORIGINS AND EARLY DEVELOPMENT (IMMEDIATE POST–WORLD WAR II YEARS)

Although an experimental Montessori infant class in a primary school was recorded as early as 1913 (HK Govt., 1913), and institutions for abandoned children were set up by charitable organizations during the early part of this century, it was not until the immediate post–World War II period that the number of preschools expanded considerably. Their development is closely related to the recent history of the territory and in particular to the rapid increase in Hong Kong's population over the years. The 1945 Hong Kong Government *Annual Report* estimated the population to be approximately 600,000. The 1957 *Annual Report* estimate was 2,670,000. By 1987 the *Annual Report* puts the figure at 5,588,000.

The rapid increase in population between 1945 and 1957, due partly to a high birthrate and to the return of residents to their homes after the Japanese occupation but mostly to the influx of refugees from the civil war and turmoil of mainland China, caused significant economic and social problems. The newly arrived parents were anxious to get their children into schools, but financial resources and land for building these schools were scarce. In addition, there were few facilities to care for children who had been separated from their parents or abandoned. The overall postwar situation placed enormous strains on a precarious economy already struggling to recover from the devastation of the Japanese occupation, and this naturally had repercussions in the kindergarten and child care sectors.

Development of kindergartens

During the immediate postwar years, the new immigrants needed work, and in many families both parents were employed. This created a "noticeable local demand for kindergartens" (HK Govt., 1955) that the existing few kindergartens (attached to primary schools) were unable to meet. Consequently, private kindergartens operated by untrained persons in their own homes were set up for small groups of children. Since no registration or official inspection was required for these establishments, it is difficult to estimate the number of children involved in such arrangements.

During the period 1950–70, kindergarten enrollment increased dramatically. In 1957 only 19,000 children attended kindergarten (HK Govt., 1957–58). By 1961 this figure had risen to 29,529 (HK Govt., 1961–62), and by 1971 it was 140,960 (HK Govt., 1971–72). The population explosion, a growing awareness of the benefits of early education for young children, and an increase in family income that allowed parents to send their children to kindergarten all contributed to this growth. Another major cause was the increasingly stiff competition to get children into prestigious or elite primary schools, which often selected their incoming primary-one pupils by means of entrance examinations. Parents responded to this practice by enrolling their children in kindergartens, in the belief that preschool education would help their children pass these exams. According to the Hong Kong government *Education Report* for 1967–68, approximately 50 percent of the children entering the first year of primary school had received some preprimary preparation.

More and more private kindergartens were set up to meet the demand for preschool education. These were usually located in residential flats whose rooms were converted into classrooms. The high demand for kindergarten places, coupled with the shortage of space, resulted in serious overcrowding. Moreover, as more and more children enrolled in these kindergartens, unqualified young women were taken on as teachers. However, the number of teachers did not increase in proportion to the growing number of children, so kindergarten operators increased class size, causing the teacher-child ratio to deteriorate; this ratio, which had been 1 to 25 in 1958 (HK Govt., 1958–59a), by 1971 was 1 to 35 (HK Govt., 1971–72).

As class size grew, the proportion of kindergarten teachers who were trained declined from 35 percent in 1958 to 20 percent in 1971. There were many reasons for this. First, the existing teacher-training system was unable to train sufficient numbers of teachers to meet the rapid increase in kindergarten enrollment. Second, a number of kindergarten operators and administrators did not believe that training was necessary for teachers of young children. Furthermore, untrained teachers could be paid lower salaries, thus reducing the operating costs of a kindergarten, and this was an important consideration in a profit-making enterprise.

As long as kindergarten operators and parents seemed willing to accept this situation of overcrowding and untrained staff, the government, which had other, more pressing priorities in primary and secondary schooling, was only minimally involved at the kindergarten level. However, in 1953 a Kindergarten Section was set up within the Education Department to help kindergarten teachers in program planning and implementation (HK Govt., 1953–54). This section continued to provide professional advice throughout the period.

Development of child care centers

During the early postwar years, the child care sector was also facing tremendous problems, although their concerns, which centered on the provision of child care for needy working mothers and on the protection of children, were of a slightly different nature.

In 1948 a Social Welfare Office was set up within the Secretariat for Chinese Affairs to protect women and children (HK Govt., 1948). It was staffed by five female social workers, who had the necessary powers of inspection and prosecution to enable them to keep an official eye on families where children might be in danger of sale or ill-treatment. The main duties of these children's officers, as they came to be called in 1950, were related to child welfare (HK Govt., 1948–54).

The increase in the number of employed mothers from needy families during the immediate postwar years sparked a growing demand for child care. Voluntary agencies set up crèches and nurseries to help these families. In 1958 seven nurseries and crèches, with a total enrollment of 345 children, were registered with the newly established Child Welfare Section of the Social Welfare Department and visited regularly by the children's officers (HK Govt., 1958–59b). By 1960 there were 13 registered nurseries and play centers, with an enrollment of 1,532 children (HK Govt., 1960–61). By 1962 this had risen to 20 crèches and nurseries and 5 play centers, which provided places for 3,900 children (HK Govt., 1962–63).

The government provided grants of land or premises to organizations deemed capable of running efficient nurseries, gave financial subsidies to centers needing assistance, and organized ad hoc courses for child care staff.

In brief, during the early postwar years, both the kindergarten and child care sectors went through a rapid period of expansion, with a sharp increase in demand for places, particularly in kindergartens. This placed considerable pressure on the system in terms of space, class size, adult-child ratios, and teacher training, and the quality of programs inevitably suffered. Since there was little control of program quality, it is difficult to know precisely what effects this situation had on the children. Profit-making organizations to a large extent met the demand for kindergarten places, and voluntary agencies provided child care.

RECENT DEVELOPMENTS (1975 TO PRESENT)

The same trends and problems that were noted during the early stages have persisted during recent years, although measures to solve the problems have differed between the two sectors.

Kindergartens

The major recent milestones affecting policy in kindergarten education were the publication of the government *White Paper on Primary Education and Preprimary Services* in 1981, the Lewellyn Report in 1982, and the Education Commission's *Report No. 2* in 1986.

▪ ***White Paper on Primary Education and Preprimary Services*, 1981:** In 1980, with 85 percent of the kindergarten teaching staff untrained (Hong Kong Council of Early Childhood Education and Services, 1986), professional bodies and the public in general were becoming more vocal in expressing their unease and dissatisfaction at this state of affairs. They argued that government needed to become more involved in the preprimary sector. Consequently, in 1980 the government published a green paper, and in 1981 it adopted a *White Paper on Primary Education and Preprimary Services*. This document was the first to publicly set out government policy on early education and care.

In an attempt to rationalize the existing system of early education and care in which both kindergartens and child care centers accepted children of the same age group, the white paper proposed that child care centers should serve the 2- to 3-year-olds and kindergartens should accept 4- to 6-year-olds. Because of pressure in particular from kindergarten operators, the age of enrollment in kindergartens was subsequently lowered from age 4 to age 3.

The white paper highlighted the need to improve kindergarten teacher training and to increase the proportion of trained teachers in the kindergartens. In addition, it stated a government intention to set up a Joint Training Institute to coordinate training courses for both child care and kindergarten staff. Other proposals included the introduction of a fee-assistance scheme for low-income families; recommendations on minimum space, materials, and equipment for kindergartens; and suggestions for improving curriculum methods.

The proposed fee-assistance scheme, which was to be administered by the Social Welfare Department, was introduced in 1982 to help low-income families meet the fees for both kindergartens and day nurseries. In the academic year 1982–83, the average number of children enrolled in nonprofit day nurseries was 12,085. Of these children, 76 percent were receiving some financial assistance under this scheme (HK Govt., 1982–83).

To help nonprofit kindergartens, the white paper also proposed such measures as government reimbursement of rents and property taxes and a 5 percent subsidy on their approved fees. Government did not, however, envisage helping with staffing costs of preschools, with the exception of special child care centers serving disabled children.

Despite all the measures it proposed, the 1981 white paper made clear that government involvement in kindergartens would continue at a low level.

▪ **The Lewellyn Report, 1982:** In 1982 a panel of internationally recognized educators was invited to Hong Kong to evaluate the entire education system. This resulted in the publication of what has become known as the "Lewellyn Report," formally entitled *A Perspective on Education in Hong Kong* (Visiting Panel, 1982). In the report the panel argued that very high priority should be given to the training of early childhood professional and ancillary staff. The panel also proposed that in the long run, kindergartens should become part of the aided sector, which would essentially mean government subsidization of kindergarten education.

A serious economic recession during the early 1980s resulted in the postponement of many of the measures suggested in the 1981 white paper and in the Lewellyn Report. There were also problems incurred in trying to implement some of their recommendations. Kindergarten operators were often reluctant to release their staff for training, partly because of the costs involved in recruiting substitute teachers and partly because of the anticipated need to increase salaries once the teachers had been trained. Although the white paper proposed a target of having 45 percent of kindergarten teachers trained by 1986, in reality, only 28 percent were trained by then (HK Govt., 1986–87a), which was an increase of 13 percentage points from 1980 (HK Govt., 1980–81).

▪ **Education Commission *Report No. 2*, 1986:** In 1986 the Education Commission, a body comprising eminent local business persons and educators, published *Report No. 2*, which includes a chapter dealing with preprimary education. This report presented a wide range of recommendations affecting kindergartens, including a restructured fee-assistance scheme, a set of salary scales for kindergarten staff, a proposal for the expansion of kindergarten training efforts, and suggestions for research into the effects of preschools in Hong Kong. In addition the commission proposed a teacher-child ratio of 1 to 15, the unification of standards for the two preprimary sectors, and the setting up of a joint committee to implement this unification. Some 18 months have passed since the publication of this report, and the chapter on preprimary services still remains to be discussed by the legislature.

Child care centers

A recent major milestone in the development of child care was the government's adoption in 1975–76 of ordinances and regulations for child care centers (HK Govt., 1982a, 1982b). This legislation—the *Child Care Centers Ordinance* and *Child Care Centers Regulations*—governs the operation of child care centers; staff training; qualifications; the staff-child ratio; and minimum space, safety, and health standards.

At the same time, a Child Care Centers Advisory Inspectorate was set up within the Social Welfare Department (HK Govt., 1976–77). This section was responsible for the registration, inspection, and control of child care centers.

The *Child Care Centers Ordinance* stipulated that child care workers must successfully complete a recognized course of training within a year of entering service. This created an urgent need to provide suitable training. The intense training efforts carried out during the years immediately following the adoption of the ordinance resulted in the majority of child care workers being trained by 1983 (HK Govt., 1983–84). Particulars of this training are given later in this section.

At present some 225,108 children in Hong Kong attend 829 kindergartens (HK Govt., Education Department, Statistics Section, 1988) and about 26,819 children attend some 230 child care centers (HK Govt., Social Welfare Department, personal communication, 1988). The greater popularity of kindergartens is due to differences in the public perception of the roles and functions of the two types of preschool. Parents generally believe that kindergartens, with their more formal approach, provide "education," while child care centers, with their learning-through-play approach, provide only "care." Kindergartens therefore are perceived as a better preparation for primary school.

Because of the tendency for parents to withdraw their children from whole-day child care centers at age 5 (or even, increasingly, at age 4), so they can send them to a kindergarten, the whole-day centers are becoming establishments serving predominantly the youngest preschool children. Child care center operators are deeply concerned about this and are trying to change public attitudes. For instance, a joint committee consisting of members from the Social Welfare Department and from government-subsidized child care centers has been set up to develop activity guidelines for nurseries. These are intended to help the workers meet the developmental needs of the young children in their care and to persuade parents that child care centers are also able to prepare children adequately for primary school.

Other preschool institutions

In addition to the regular kindergartens and child care centers, a certain number of other institutions serve preschool children with special needs. Under the Education Department, there are kindergarten classes of special schools, such as schools for the blind, deaf, or otherwise handicapped, that provide services for handicapped preschool children who are age 4 and older. Under the Social Welfare Department there are special child care centers that provide services for handicapped children from birth to age 6. Mainstreaming (integration) of mildly handicapped preschool children is found quite extensively in the child care sector but only on a very small scale in private kindergartens.

Preschool Staff Training (History and Current Status)

There is a considerable difference between the two sectors of early education and care in Hong Kong with regard to the history and philosophy of staff training, even though all recognized teacher training for both sectors is either conducted or sponsored by government.

Training for kindergarten staff

Although a small number of infant and kindergarten classes existed within primary schools as early as 1913, no systematic provision for kindergarten teacher training existed until 1950. Kindergarten staff for these early classes were trained in Taiwan, Macau, mainland China, or the United Kingdom.

In 1950–52 the first official 2-year part-time training course for teachers was introduced at the Northcote Teacher Training College, a training institute for primary teachers. This course, which was run by a

Froebel-trained kindergarten teacher, accepted 20 students and was discontinued some 2 years later. In 1953 the teacher of the course was appointed Education Officer within the newly set-up Kindergarten Section of the Education Department. In 1956 this Kindergarten Section started running 2-year part-time training courses with an intake of approximately 50 students every 2 years. The intake was not, however, sufficient to meet the ever-increasing demand for kindergarten teachers caused by the proliferation of kindergartens during the 1960s and 1970s. As a result the proportion of trained kindergarten teachers grew steadily worse during this period. By 1981 only 15 percent of the 5,316 kindergarten teachers were trained (HK Govt., 1980–81).

The 1981 *White Paper on Primary Education and Preprimary Services* proposed measures to improve the situation. It set target dates by which a certain proportion of kindergarten staff were expected to be trained: By 1986, 45 percent were to have undergone training, and by 1988, the proportion of trained staff was expected to reach 60 percent. The *White Paper* also stated the intention to provide preservice initial training for kindergarten teachers similar to that already provided for primary school teachers.

To achieve these goals, an overall inservice training program was implemented. This consisted of a short, 12-week part-time course offered by the Kindergarten Advisory Inspectorate to teachers with lower educational qualifications, and a 2-year part-time course run by a unit of a regular training institute for primary teachers, the Grantham College of Education. This latter course was intended for persons with more advanced educational qualifications. A person completing the short course is designated as a "Qualified Assistant Kindergarten Teacher," a qualification that is not recognized by the Hong Kong government's *Education Regulations* (1980) or *Education Ordinance* (1985), whereas the longer course leads to the title of "Qualified Kindergarten Teacher" and entitles the person to become a registered kindergarten teacher.

The new training program did not seem to have the expected impact on staff training. By 1986 only 28 percent of teachers, rather than the projected 45 percent, had been trained, and therefore in this same year the Education Commission proposed an increase in intake by both types of courses. Thus, by 1994 an estimated 84 percent of kindergarten staff would be trained, for the most part by the short course. Two 1981 white paper recommendations to improve kindergarten teacher training, namely, the introduction of preservice kindergarten training similar to that for primary school teachers and the establishment of a Joint Training Institute for the two sectors of early education and care, were deferred.

Training for child care center staff

The first recorded training for nursery teachers was a course run by the Young Women's Christian Association (YWCA) in 1949 to train 20 nursery supervisors and teachers (*South China Morning Post*, 1950). In 1958 the government, in partnership with the YWCA, introduced a 5-week part-time course for the training of 20 nursery staff (HK Govt., 1958–59b). This was taken over by the Training Section of the Social Welfare Department in 1962 (HK Govt., 1962–63), and the enrollment increased to 50 nursery workers each year.

After the introduction in 1976 of compulsory training for child care workers within a year of their employment, training efforts were increased. A series of 4-month part-time courses and a 1-year full-time course were offered by the Social Welfare Department. The latter was contracted out to the Hong Kong Polytechnic in 1977, and in 1979 an additional 2-year part-time Certificate in Child Care course was introduced for workers who were unable to follow full-time studies. In 1980 a 2-year full-time course for child care workers with lower educational qualifications was introduced in the Lee Wai Lee Technical Institute.

By 1983 the majority of child care workers had been trained by one of these courses, and the short courses were also contracted out to the Polytechnic. In 1985 the Lee Wai Lee Technical Institute took over the certificate course from the Polytechnic, and in 1986 the Polytechnic introduced a 2-year part-time course leading to a Higher Certificate in Child Care for experienced child care workers having already obtained the basic Certificate in Child Care (HK Govt., 1986–87b).

Training for staff of other preschool institutions

Training for teachers of preschool children with special needs is also contracted out to the Polytechnic, which has offered a 6-month course since 1985 for workers in special child care centers. In 1987 this was expanded to a 1-year course.

In conclusion, recognized training for kindergarten staff is the monopoly of the Education Department, whereas that for child care workers is carried out either by the Vocational Training Council (Technical Institute) or by joint effort of the Social Welfare Department and the Polytechnic. Qualifications gained in the kindergarten sector are not recognized by the child care sector, and vice versa. Until now, the emphasis has been on providing initial training for untrained teachers/

workers, or short ad hoc staff development courses. The field is, however, gradually moving towards providing more extensive training for other types of early education and care staff, such as supervisors and experienced teachers/child care workers. The University of Hong Kong offers a 2-year part-time masters degree in education program for teacher-trainers, inspectors, and other persons in leadership positions in the field when and if there is sufficient demand. One program was offered in 1982–84, and a second program will be conducted in 1988–90.

Current Status of Early Childhood Education and Care

To summarize, attendance in preschools is very high in Hong Kong, with almost every child between 3 and 6 years of age attending some kind of preschool institution. Early childhood education and care in the territory is divided into two categories, kindergartens and child care centers, under the respective control of the Education Department and Social Welfare Department. All preschools, with one exception, are run by private organizations, and in the case of kindergartens, a number of the sponsoring organizations are profit-making. Most preschool children with special needs go to special schools or child care centers or to program units that practice mainstreaming in day nurseries and kindergartens.

The distinction between kindergartens and child care centers results in anomalies and discrepancies in the delivery of services to young children. Despite the fact that the stricter legislation governing child care centers generally results in conditions that are more suitable for early education and care, many parents prefer to send their children to kindergartens, which they perceive as providing a better preparation for primary school.

Government involvement in preschools, particularly in the kindergarten sector, is limited to minimal fee-assistance, provision of subsidized premises for nonprofit preschools, inspection and control of preschool premises, curriculum leadership, and staff training.

Demographics

In 1987 there were 225,108 children enrolled in 829 kindergartens, and 26,819 children enrolled in 230 child care centers or nurseries. In other words, 90 percent of the children enrolled in some kind of preschool are in kindergartens, whereas 10 percent are in child care centers. The breakdown of enrolled kindergarten children by level in 1987 is given in Table 1.

The distribution of the kindergartens among the three geographical areas of Hong Kong Island, Kowloon, and the New Territories in 1987 is given in Table 2. From this it can be seen that overall there is 1 kindergarten in Hong Kong for every 272 children. In Hong Kong Island the ratio is 1 for every 230 children; in Kowloon it is 1 for every 301 children; and in the New Territories it is 1 for every 271 children.

Table 1

NUMBER OF KINDERGARTEN CHILDREN BY LEVEL, 1987

Class (Age in yr)	Number of Children	Percent
Nursery (3–4)	66,524	29
Lower K (4–5)	78,034	35
Upper K (5–6)	80,550	36
Total	225,108	100

Note. From *Enrollment Summary September 1987*, by Hong Kong Government, Education Department, Statistics Section, 1988, Hong Kong, Government Printer.

Table 2

DISTRIBUTION OF ENROLLED KINDERGARTEN CHILDREN BY GEOGRAPHIC LOCATION, 1987

Location	No. of Children (%)	No. of Kindergartens (%)	Percent of Hong Kong Population Residing in Location
Hong Kong Island	43,394 (19)	189 (23)	22
Kowloon	84,807 (38)	282 (34)	43
New Territories	96,907 (43)	358 (43)	35
Total	225,108 (100)	829 (100)	100

Note. From *Enrollment Summary September 1987*, by Hong Kong Government, Education Department, Statistics Section, 1988, Hong Kong, Government Printer.

In Hong Kong Island the percentage of kindergartens closely corresponds to the percentage of Hong Kong's overall population distribution (23 percent versus 22 percent), whereas in Kowloon the percentage of kindergartens is lower than the population distribution percentage (34 percent versus 43 percent), and in the New Territories it is higher (43 percent versus 35 percent) (HK Govt., Census and Statistics Department, 1987). In other words, the figures suggest that the New Territories have a higher relative proportion of Hong Kong's young children compared with their percentage of the overall population. This finding is consistent with the fact that many of the new towns and large residential estates, which consist to a large extent of young families, are found in the New Territories.

National Child Care Policies

In Hong Kong there is no single overall policy governing child care and education, although certain legislative measures have been adopted that relate directly or indirectly to the protection, rights, and obligations of children throughout the period from before birth until the end of schooling.

The care and welfare of pregnant women is an individual and personal matter. Most mothers ensure prenatal care privately or by some form of subsidized service provided by their employer. Free medical services including maternity care are provided in government hospitals for needy persons. All pregnant women are entitled to maternity leave of 10 weeks—4 before and 6 after the birth of the child—during which employers must continue payment of wages. Female workers may not be dismissed on maternity grounds.

At the end of the period of maternity leave, employed mothers use a variety of child care arrangements. A few day or residential crèches are available, but most babies of employed mothers are either cared for by household maids (many of whom come from the Philippines—an estimated 34,000 Filipino maids worked in Hong Kong in 1987), relatives, friends, or neighbors. Some paid home child care is also available. Since only programs serving more than five children under the age of 6 years need to be registered with the Social Welfare Department, statistics on these different care arrangements are not available. However, the sizable drop in the percentage of employed women during the child-raising years (from 79 percent of the group 20–29 years of age to 56 percent of the group 30–39 years of age) would suggest that many mothers stay at home to take care of their children.

At age 2, children are eligible for entry into a nursery, and at age 3, they can start kindergarten. For the half day when they are not in the preschool, children who attend half-day kindergarten sessions presumably have the types of informal care arrangements already mentioned.

At approximately age 6, all children start compulsory primary schooling. All primary schools are fully subsidized by the government, although the majority are operated by private organizations. Only 8 percent of the primary schools are government-run (HK Govt., Education Department, Statistics Section, 1988). After 6 years of primary schooling, children move on to 3 years of compulsory secondary schooling. The majority of the secondary schools are also privately run but government-subsidized, and only a few of them are government-operated.

Although schooling is not compulsory beyond secondary form-3 level, the majority of children continue until secondary form 5, when they take the Hong Kong Certificate of Education examination. Results of this examination determine whether the person will leave school to continue a vocational or technical education or to join the work force, or will continue on to the two matriculation classes of secondary forms 6 and 7, the respective prerequisites for entry to the Chinese University of Hong Kong and the University of Hong Kong.

Education and Care Arrangements

The characteristics of kindergartens and child care centers are shown in Table 3 on pages 134 and 135.

Research

Past research into early childhood has consisted of relatively small-scale surveys conducted either by the Social Welfare Department or by voluntary agencies with a view to assessing the effectiveness of existing programs or to providing some basis for setting up new child care arrangements. The topics covered practical questions, such as the conditions of child care centers, parental satisfaction with various caretaking

Table 3

CHARACTERISTICS OF KINDERGARTENS AND CHILD CARE CENTERS

Characteristic	Kindergarten	Child Care Center
Relevant legislation	*Education Ordinance* (rev. 1985), *Education Regulations* (rev. 1980)	*Child Care Centers Ordinance* (rev. 1982), *Regulations* (rev. 1982)
Practice guide	*Manual of Kindergarten Practice* (1984)	*Code of Practice* (1976, rev. 1982)
Government department	Education	Social Welfare
Purpose	Education	Care and supervision, education
Sponsorship	Private organizations	Private organizations, government-aided organizations
Income	Monthly fees approved by Education Dept.	Monthly fees approved by Social Welfare Dept.
Government support	Rent/rates refund for non-profit-making; fee assistance for needy parents	Rent refund and 5% subsidy for non-profit-making; fee assistance for needy parents
Registering body	Registration Section for Director of Education	Child Care Centers Advisory Inspectorate for Director of Social Welfare
Inspection responsibility	Education Inspectorate	Child Care Centers Advisory Inspectorate
Staffing	Supervisor to keep accounts Registered teacher Permitted teacher	Registered supervisor to ■ Manage center ■ Maintain records ■ Plan, organize, and implement programs ■ Plan menus ■ Deal with all staff matters Registered child care workers to ■ Be responsible for well-being and safety of children under care ■ Carry out program of activities ■ Prepare and arrange educational materials ■ Keep room clean and tidy and maintain equipment Trainee worker
Staff qualifications	Registered teacher: ■ Certificate of Education	Supervisor: ■ School Certificate with 2

Table 3—Cont.

CHARACTERISTICS OF KINDERGARTENS AND CHILD CARE CENTERS

Characteristic	Kindergarten	Child Care Center
	■ 10 years of experience ■ Degree and Teacher Certificate ■ Degree and 3 years of teaching experience ■ Certificate of Education or equivalent and 10 years of teaching experience Permitted teacher: ■ Certificate of Education or equivalent ■ Same qualifications as above but without 10 years of teaching experience	passes or equivalent ■ Successful completion of approved training ■ 3 years of experience ■ At least 25 years old Child care worker: ■ Completion of form 3 ■ Completion of approved training Trainee worker: ■ Completion of Form 3 ■ 18 years old ■ Intention to complete training
Approved staff training	12-week inservice course at Advisory Inspectorate, Education Dept., or college of education leading to Qualified Assistant Kindergarten Teacher (QKT) 2 years of inservice at college of education leading to Qualified Kindergarten Teacher (QKT)	8-week inservice course at Polytechnic Certificate in Child Care course: ■ 2-year full-time for form-3 graduates ■ 1-year full-time for form-5 graduates ■ 2-year part-time for form-5 graduates
Staff-child ratio	1 to 45	1 to 14
Salaries	No salary scale, but range from HK$2000 to HK$5000 monthly[a]	Government pay scale ranging from HK$2835 to HK$5855 monthly
Operating hours	3–3.5-hour sessions either in a.m. or p.m.	Whole day: 8 a.m.–6 p.m. Half day: 9 a.m.–12 noon 1–5 p.m.
Space (minimum)	1.2 m² per child 2.4 m² per teacher	1.8 m² per child
Curriculum	Thematic approach, Activity approach, Traditional approach	Learning through play
Age	3–5 years inclusive	2–6 years
Parent involvement	Parent-Teacher Assn.	Parent-Teacher Assn.
Links with other systems	No formal links	No formal links

[a]$1 U.S. = $7.8 HK (approximately) at time of writing.

arrangements, needs of employed mothers or of various groups of children.

A number of surveys under the sponsorship of Hong Kong's two universities, the University of Hong Kong and the Chinese University of Hong Kong, are in progress at present to examine the following topics:

- Burn injuries of young children less than 12 years old (Chinese University of Hong Kong)
- Behavioral problems of preschool children (University of Hong Kong)
- Music facilities in kindergartens (University of Hong Kong)
- Effects of caretaking forms and styles on child development (Chinese University of Hong Kong)
- Preprimary provisions and development of preschool children (IEA study sponsored by University of Hong Kong)

Given the paucity of studies in all areas of early childhood, a great deal of research still needs to be done, particularly in such areas as curriculum, program development and evaluation, training impact, and child development.

Issues of the Next Decade

The situation of early education and care in Hong Kong gives rise to a great deal of professional concern. On the one hand, the almost universal preschool attendance of young children between ages 3 and 6 is a clear indication that parents believe some form of early education is important for their child. On the other hand, the existence of 1 kindergarten for every 272 children would suggest that many kindergartens are fairly large in size. This average, combined with the fact that many kindergartens are located in converted residential flats, is not a promising indicator of high-quality programs. One of the major issues needing to be addressed, therefore, is **program quality**, which includes a number of other related issues.

One of these issues is **training**. A teacher's qualifications, knowledge, expertise, and training contribute significantly to the quality of a program. Not only has a large proportion of kindergarten staff received no training, but even staff who have had some recognized training (in either the child care or kindergarten sectors) have only received the equivalent of a 12-week part-time or (for a small minority) of a 1-year full-time course. This is insufficient to provide the teacher with the specialized knowledge and expertise required for teaching young children. Moreover, the duration of these courses compares unfavorably with that of the 3-year full-time course offered to primary school teachers.

The current rate of kindergarten teacher training is also inadequate. If continued it will result in barely 50 percent of kindergarten teachers being trained by the end of the next 10 years. Training, therefore, is an urgent issue that calls for adopting large-scale corrective measures.

Programs of high quality also require adequate **space**, suitable **adult-child ratios**, and developmentally appropriate **teaching methods**. At present the per-child space requirement for child care centers is 1.8 square meters, and for kindergartens it is 1.2 square meters. The adult-child ratio is 1 to 14 in child care centers and 1 to 45 in kindergartens, a discrepancy that has caused much concern. Although the Education Commission in their 1986 *Report No. 2* recommended the adoption of a 1 to 15 adult-child ratio for kindergartens "over time," they gave no target date for this ratio to come into effect. Lack of space and inappropriate teacher-child ratios in kindergartens contribute towards overcrowding and preclude the types of activities and experiences that promote learning in young children.

Moreover, the use of learning tasks that often consist of the rote memorization of concepts more suitable to the older, primary child is widespread. They derive from the preschool teacher's lack of training and from inappropriate pressure from parents. There is a serious need for parent education about children's learning and about developmentally appropriate educational practices. The notion and dimensions of high-quality early education and care programs within the Hong Kong context need to be specified, and appropriate measures should be taken to ensure that such programs are achieved in all preschools.

All these issues of program quality are in turn related to **government involvement** in early education and care. High-quality programs involve added costs. Not only is adequate staff training required, but also, once staff is trained, appropriate financial incentives are required to encourage them to remain in the field. Since the kindergarten sector is to a large extent controlled by commercial interests, official measures are needed to require training and to provide the incentives for it, possibly in the form of subsidized salaries for trained kindergarten teachers.

Another issue of serious concern is the **unification of standards and of delivery** of early educational services. The existing discrepancies between the two sectors result in inequality of educational provision and discrimination against the children in lower-quality programs. Both child care centers and kindergartens need to be seen as offering the same type of services, since they are serving a common pool of young children. Here again, as with the issue of program quality, common standards need to be specified and measures then need to be taken to ensure that they are universally applied.

Curriculum development is another issue that needs to be addressed. At present the child care centers have no recommended curriculum, although one is being prepared. The Hong Kong Government's Kindergarten Inspectorate, however, published a *Guide to the Kindergarten Curriculum* (1984) using a thematic or unit approach that most kindergartens feel obliged to follow. Rather than being made to adopt a single type of curriculum, preschool staff should be helped to engage in curriculum development themselves. In this way they would be able to produce curriculum materials appropriate to the needs and interests of the children and to the goals and objectives of their particular preschool.

The mainstreaming (integration) of handicapped children into regular preschools has yet to be seriously addressed. So far, mainstreaming is only practiced in a very limited way, in some child care centers, for the mildly handicapped children. Much more will need to be done in the future.

In brief, there are a number of crucial issues facing the field of early education and care in Hong Kong. Several of these—such as staff training, curriculum, low status, and inadequate financing—are common to many other countries. One problem unique to Hong Kong, however, is the uncertainty about early childhood education in the light of the future reversion of Hong Kong to China in 1997. What, for example, should be the language of instruction? At present the language used in preschools is the Cantonese dialect. In a few years, preschool children will undoubtedly need to study standard Chinese (*putonghua*) more intensively. The question has not been seriously considered yet, but it will require a solution in the next few years.

Conclusions

To conclude this profile, it might be appropriate to highlight some of the strengths of the system of early education and care in Hong Kong, to indicate some areas in need of improvement, and to suggest some ways in which government and the private sector might upgrade the quality of services provided to young children.

On the positive side, Hong Kong is fortunate in having universal preschool education and care for all children between ages 3 and 6. Some 260,000 children of this age group attend over 1,000 preprimary institutions. This high enrollment rate reflects both parents' recognition of the benefits of preschool and the positive response of private enterprise to their demand for preschools. As a result, no child is denied a place in preschool.

Government and professional bodies are increasingly aware of the requirements for high-quality early educational programs—comprehensive staff training, favorable adult-child ratios, adequate space, and appropriate teaching methods and curriculum materials. There has been a gradual attempt to improve on some of these. For instance, there is a projected increase in the training rate of kindergarten teachers. Curriculum development is being conducted by the two government sectors and by private preschool organizations. The Education Commission's 1986 *Report No. 2* cites the need to improve teacher-child ratios and increase space in kindergartens. All these are promising signs of progress.

The other side of the coin, however, is that the system is being "stretched" to serve the large number of children that use it. In many cases, quantity is emphasized at the expense of quality. The lack of adequate measures for quality control results in educational practices that are not conducive to the mental and physical well-being of young children.

Early education and care in Hong Kong is almost exclusively in the hands of private organizations, and while some of these offer outstanding programs, too many seem to place profit above any genuine concern about children. Government, by adopting a laissez-faire approach to kindergartens, has not adequately protected the welfare of young children. For example, standards for kindergarten practices are few, and those that exist are not strictly enforced. A more stringent control of the quality of educational programs is urgently required.

Another weakness is the fragmentation of the control and implementation of early education between different government departments and even between different sections within these departments. Some deal with registration and inspection of premises, while others deal with program inspection, training, and curriculum development. Some training is carried out in institutes of higher education; other training is carried out within government departments. This diversification makes it difficult to achieve cohesive policy and to unify standards. Although recommendations for unification have been made, these need to be implemented as soon as possible. One way to achieve unification would be to set up a single body to deal with the whole field of early childhood education.

Kindergarten teacher training is perhaps the single greatest area of need. The present training system is inadequate, both in quantity and quality. It is limited in scope and does not provide an overall structure to serve early childhood professionals at all levels. The existing system provides only initial training, but as the teacher proceeds along her career, gains more expertise and experience, and goes beyond this initial "survival" stage, she is faced with a lack of opportunities to meet her changing professional needs. Furthermore, there is little incentive for a kindergarten teacher to undergo training, since not only is there no requirement, but there seems to be no guarantee of any financial reward for training. Without the opportunity for acquiring additional qualifications or training, besides accumulating years of experience, there is little a teacher can do to improve her status. Insufficient training leads to low salaries, low status, and low morale—the major causes of the burnout and the high rate of attrition among kindergarten teachers.

Morever, there is little coordination between the training for kindergarten teachers and the training for child care workers. The split system of training needs to be looked at as a whole, both with an eye to unification across the two sectors and with an eye to the need for continuing professional growth among early childhood educators.

In sum, the crucial underlying weakness seems to be a lack of steadfast commitment by government to an overall policy for the field of early education and care. Government involvement tends to be piecemeal, ad hoc, and crisis-oriented. If parents or professionals complain too loudly, something is done; if no pressure is exerted, government adopts a policy of seeming indifference. In the final analysis it is the well-being of young children that suffers from this neglect and lack of concern.

Author's Note

I wish to express my appreciation to Mrs. Miranda Tse and Mrs. Amy Lee, Department of Education, University of Hong Kong, for their contributions to this chapter.

REFERENCES

Education Commission. (1986). *Report No. 2.* Hong Kong: Government Printer.

Hong Kong Council of Early Childhood Education and Services (CECES). (1986). *Report on Training in Early Childhood Education in Hong Kong.*

Hong Kong Government. (1913). *Education Report.* Hong Kong: Government Printer.

Hong Kong Government. (1945). *Annual Report.* Hong Kong: Government Printer.

Hong Kong Government. (1948). *Annual Report.* Hong Kong: Government Printer.

Hong Kong Government. (1948–54). *Social Welfare Department Report.* Hong Kong: Government Printer.

Hong Kong Government. (1953–54). *Education Report.* Hong Kong: Government Printer.

Hong Kong Government. (1955). *Education Summary.* Hong Kong: Government Printer.

Hong Kong Government. (1957). *Annual Report.* Hong Kong: Government Printer.

Hong Kong Government. (1957–58). *Education Report.* Hong Kong: Government Printer.

Hong Kong Government. (1958–59a). *Education Report.* Hong Kong: Government Printer.

Hong Kong Government. (1958–59b). *Social Welfare Department Report.* Hong Kong: Government Printer.

Hong Kong Government. (1960–61). *Social Welfare Department Report.* Hong Kong: Government Printer.

Hong Kong Government. (1961–62). *Education Report.* Hong Kong: Government Printer.

Hong Kong Government. (1962–63). *Social Welfare Department Report.* Hong Kong: Government Printer.

Hong Kong Government. (1967–68). *Education Report.* Hong Kong: Government Printer.

Hong Kong Government. (1971–72). *Education Report.* Hong Kong: Government Printer.

Hong Kong Government. (1976–77). *Social Welfare Department Report.* Hong Kong: Government Printer.

Hong Kong Government. (1980). *Education Regulations* (rev. ed.). Hong Kong: Government Printer.

Hong Kong Government. (1980–81). *Education Report.* Hong Kong: Government Printer.

Hong Kong Government. (1981). *White Paper on Primary Education and Preprimary Services.* Hong Kong: Government Printer.

Hong Kong Government. (1982a). *Child Care Centers Ordinance* (rev. ed.). Hong Kong: Government Printer.

Hong Kong Government. (1982b). *Child Care Centers Regulations* (rev. ed.). Hong Kong: Government Printer.

Hong Kong Government. (1982–83). *Social Welfare Department Report.* Hong Kong: Government Printer.

Hong Kong Government. (1983–84). *Social Welfare Department Report.* Hong Kong: Government Printer.

Hong Kong Government. (1985). *Education Ordinance* (rev. ed.). Hong Kong: Government Printer.

Hong Kong Government. (1986–87a). *Education Report.* Hong Kong: Government Printer.

Hong Kong Government. (1986–87b). *Social Welfare Department Report.* Hong Kong: Government Printer.

Hong Kong Government. (1987). *Annual Report*. Hong Kong: Government Printer.

Hong Kong Government, Census and Statistics Department. (1987). *Annual Digest of Statistics*. Hong Kong: Government Printer.

Hong Kong Government, Education Department, Statistics Section. (1988). *Enrollment Summary September 1987*. Hong Kong: Government Printer.

Hong Kong Government, Kindergarten Inspectorate. (1984). *Guide to the Kindergarten Curriculum*. Hong Kong: Government Printer.

South China Morning Post, July 19, 1950, p. 3.

Visiting Panel. (1982). *A Perspective on Education in Hong Kong*. Hong Kong: Government Printer.

VI

Care and Education in Hungary for 3- to 6-Year-Olds

Péter Vári
Center for Evaluation
National Institute of Education
Budapest

The Educational System

In Hungary, although employed mothers can take a 3-year child care leave to care for their infants and toddlers, there is also institutional care—the crèche—available for children aged 6 months to 3 years.[1] (About 10 percent of children under 3 years old are in crèche care.) From age 3 to age 6, nearly all children (about 90 percent) attend kindergarten.[2] In the September after their 6th birthday, they start the eight-grade general school, where in each of the first four grades, they have one teacher for all subjects; in each of the upper four grades, they have a specialized teacher for each subject. Education is compulsory from age 6 to age 16. Following successful completion of general school, students can attend secondary academic, vocational, or trade school. Only the academic and vocational secondary schools prepare students for tertiary (college or university) education.

Institutional Education for Children Aged 3 to 6: The Kindergarten

Kindergarten Origins and Aims

The first kindergarten in Hungary (which was among the first in Europe) was founded in 1828 and followed the example of Samuel Wilderspin's kindergarten in England.[3] The first training school for kindergarten teachers opened shortly thereafter, in 1837. By the end of the 19th century, when Hungary had a total population of 15 million, there were already 700 kindergartens. Today (in 1985), with a national population of 10.6 million, Hungary has over 4,800 kindergartens serving about 424,000 children aged 3 to 6 years. The aim of today's kindergarten is both social and pedagogical: It is a help for the employed mother, and care and education for the child.

Administration of Kindergartens

The national Ministry of Cultural Affairs is the central administrative body responsible for planning the kindergarten program. The establishment of new kindergartens depends, however, on the decision of local (town or community) authorities called councils. Also, some factories and firms establish their own kindergartens.

There are certain government regulations for the establishment of new kindergartens (both government- and factory/firm-sponsored). For example, the classroom must allow at least 2 square meters per child, and each classroom must contain the equipment prescribed in the so-called equipment norm. All costs (including construction, equipment, and salaries) are covered by the authority establishing the new kindergarten. Parents pay only a meal fee, which is based on their income and number of children. The government's per pupil expenditure for kindergarten in 1983 was 12,000 forints (which was roughly equivalent to $280 U.S.).[4]

Kindergartens are administered by the educational departments of the local councils and by the staffs of the kindergartens. Supervision is organized centrally, with the supervisor being a trained kindergarten teacher (who teaches no class of her own). Kindergartens established by factories and firms are supervised either by local council supervisors or by their own supervisors.

A kindergarten may be made up of several groups of children. A group consists of about 26 children with two teachers, each of whom takes a 6½-hour shift with the children (with both teachers on duty at midday). The same teachers remain with a class throughout the entire 3-year program, and most children attend kindergarten for 3 years. Teachers use a curriculum that is prepared by the National Institute for Education with the collaboration of many experts and kindergarten teachers and under the supervision of the Ministry of Cultural Affairs.

INVENTORY OF KINDERGARTEN SETTINGS

In 1985, 91.3 percent of Hungary's 3- to 6-year-old population attended kindergarten. (The attendance rate was even higher among 5- to 6-year-olds, 96 percent.) Of all children in kindergarten in 1985, 91.8 percent attended council kindergartens, and 8.2 percent attended others. Of the 8.7 percent of the 3- to 6-year-old population not participating in institutional kindergarten education, about one third were living in very disadvantaged sociocultural circumstances (mainly in Gypsy families) and two thirds were at home with their mothers (on child care leave), with grandparents, with a paid nanny, or attending a private kindergarten. We have no exact figures concerning the distribution of this latter group (the two thirds). Those children not attending any kindergarten take part in a 192-hour course between age 5 and age 6 to prepare them for first grade of the general school. The percentage of children needing this school-preparation course has decreased significantly over the years—from 54 percent in 1965, to 29 percent in 1975, to less than 10 percent in 1985.[5]

Because of a shortage of kindergarten places, in 1985 there were 1,960 children (with employed mothers) who were not allowed entry into kindergarten.[6] In the event of an overcrowded kindergarten, a committee consisting of a senior teacher, the teachers, members of the parents' panel, and the representative of the establishing authority must decide who shall be turned down for admission. Enrollment priority is given to children living with single parents (with broken families, with fathers doing military service, and so on) and to children living in disadvantaged families. Usually only kindergartens in large towns find it necessary to refuse children. Another kindergarten enrollment problem involves families living in very disadvantaged circumstances who sometimes fail to apply for kindergarten admission for their children. For example, only 32.4 percent of 3- to 6-year-old Gypsy children attended kindergartens in 1985.[7]

In 1983 there were kindergartens in each town and in 78 percent of Hungary's communities; out of 3,003 existing communities, there were 976 with no kindergarten, and of these communities, 732 had fewer than 500 inhabitants (no source provided).

Slightly disabled children are educated together with healthy children, while children with severe mental and physical handicaps are taught in special institutions. Altogether, in 1986 there were 175 special institutions of this type serving 28,579 children, of whom 630 were kindergartners.

Kindergarten teachers have secondary or tertiary degrees. In 1985 there were 68 percent with tertiary-degree teacher training, 20 percent with secondary-degree teacher training, and 12 percent with no teaching qualifications (no source provided). A teacher with a **secondary degree** has finished the eight-grade general school and then graduated from a secondary vocational school that trains kindergarten teachers. A teacher with a **tertiary degree** has attended a kindergarten teacher-training college (for 2 years) after finishing the general school and a four-grade secondary school (either academic or vocational). The training for kindergarten teaching includes courses in the following: history of education; theory of education; didactics; general, developmental, and educational psychology; pedagogy of play; language; literature; physical education; mathematics; music; methodology; and kindergarten practice. This training consists of both theoretical courses (90 percent) and practical courses (10 percent). A teacher having **no teaching qualifications** has graduated from an academic secondary school (offering general, college-preparatory education) but has not attended any specialized kindergarten teacher-training institution (either secondary or tertiary).

A 1983 figure for the number of teachers in Hungary's kindergartens is 28,820.[8] In the approximately 4,800 kindergartens existing in 1985, besides the teachers, there were more than 12,000 adult staff members—nannies, kitchen workers, food managers, caretakers, cleaners, and secretaries.[9]

In most kindergartens (81.6 percent of them) children are divided into three groups (classes), according to age: 3- to 4-year-olds, 4- to 5-year-olds, and 5- to 6-year-olds. Statistics from 1985 indicate that in 14.2 percent of the kindergartens, there were only two age-groups (3- to 4½-year-olds and 4½- to 6-year-olds); 4.2 percent of kindergartens had only one age-group (3- to 6-year-olds). On the average, there were 25.9 children in a group.

The kindergartens are open for at most 12 hours a day (from 6 a.m. to 6 p.m.), to coincide with the working hours of parents. A few children spend only half of the day in kindergarten, but most of them are there all day. Thus 99.5 percent of the kindergartens provide children with three meals a day (the rest provide no meals). Except for a 1-month holiday in summer, kindergarten operation is year-round.

In 1985, 78 percent of the kindergarten facilities were independent, 18 percent were attached to general schools, and 4 percent were part of educational centers (an institution consisting of a crèche, a kindergarten, a general school, a community center for different cultural activities, and a public library).

Each group of children has its own classroom, and there is a bathroom for every two classrooms. New kindergartens include a gymnasium, as well. The classrooms are used for play, meals, and obligatory activities (ones in which all children must participate). Most of them are supplied with facilities and equipment for drama, role play, and construction activities. The 1985 statistics reveal that 4.1 percent of kindergarten classes are held in facilities not built to be used as classrooms.

PROGRAM CONTENT

The routine of the youngest children (aged 3 to 4) is rather different from that of the older ones. The children arrive between 6:00 and 8:30 a.m. (depending on the parents' work schedules). Their day is spent in play with breaks for meals and naps. Though, in principle, children's initiative is allowed to develop without interference, the teacher sometimes joins their play, perhaps to bring the play to a higher level, to make suggestions for new activities, or to resolve conflicts.

At a suitable moment, the teacher may initiate some activity according to a fixed plan. For example, using puppets, she may demonstrate family life or she may name the parts of the body; she may model something in clay, sing a song, or tell a story. The children who are interested join her; those who are not may continue playing. There is only one activity in which all children have to participate—gymnastics—which lasts for 10 to 15 minutes and occurs only once a week.

The daily schedule of the two older groups (aged 4 to 5 and aged 5 to 6) is somewhat different. Their day—before breakfast time—also begins with play. At breakfast and other meals, there is a system of "on-duty" service whereby children take daily turns setting and clearing the tables and serving one another. Their breakfast is followed by obligatory activities that last about 25 minutes for the 4-year-olds and 50 minutes (split into two sessions) for the 5-year-olds. These activities deal with such subjects as art, gymnastics, music, mathematics, and knowledge of surroundings. There are also activities in literature—stories, poems, films, and puppet shows—but these are not obligatory (children participate only if they want to).

Each government and factory/firm kindergarten operates according to the standard curriculum prepared by the National Institute for Education and approved by the Ministry of Cultural Affairs. The curriculum lists the following main areas of study: health habits, civics, play, work, mother tongue, physical education, knowledge of surroundings, mathematics, literature, art, and music. It outlines the educational tasks of each area, describes the general level of development a 4- to 6-year-old child can achieve in each area, and suggests appropriate teaching methods and activities.

Learning in the kindergarten differs from that in general school in three main ways: In kindergarten, children acquire knowledge not intentionally but incidentally; they learn mostly through their own activity; and the educational philosophy and principles of social learning determine the teaching approach even more than they do in later schooling.

PEDAGOGICAL AND PSYCHOLOGICAL RESEARCH

Research relating to the child from infancy to age 6 is carried out by several organizations, including coordinating offices of various ministries, universities, teacher-training colleges, the National Institute of Education, the Hungarian Pedagogic Society, and the Hungarian Psychological Society. Neither the coordination nor the financial support of research is satisfactory.

We consider three research projects as most important: (1) a study of the social penetrance (socialization) of 3- to 6-year-olds (Ferenc Merei, 1970); (2) a study of the effects of kindergarten curriculum (Agnes Bakonyi-Vincze, Ilona Szabode, 1983); and (3) the ongoing kindergarten-school experiments conducted by Otto Mihaly, National Institute of Education. The main point of Mihaly's study is this: Researchers, assuming that children between ages 3 and 6 learn primarily through personal contacts, have organized classes where children can stay together from age 3 until age 10. They hope this will facilitate the children's transition to general school. One teacher works with the class for 5 years, while the children are between ages 3 and 7 (in kindergarten and the first 2 years of general school); a second teacher begins working with the same class when the children are age 5. She also stays with the class for 5 years, until the end of the fourth grade of the general school. An analysis of the findings of this project is under way.

ENDNOTES

[1]According to United Nations Department of International Economic and Social Affairs, Statistical Office, *Demographic Yearbook, 1984* (New York: United Nations, 1986), Hungary's rate of female labor force participation (women 25 to 54 years of age) is 76.99 percent.

[2]Unless another source is mentioned, statistics in this profile are from the Hungarian Central Statistical Office, *Statistical Yearbook, 1985* and *Statistical Yearbook, 1986* (Budapest: Author).

[3]Wilderspin's kindergarten provided education for children 1½ to 7 years old who were living in poverty.

[4]Statistic is from Z. Báthory, "Hungary," in *The Encyclopedia of Comparative Education and National Systems of Education*, ed. T. Neville Postlethwaite (Oxford: Pergamon Press, 1988), p. 343.

[5]Z. Báthory, op. cit., p. 340.

[6]The Central Statistical Office *Statistical Yearbook, 1985* reports only 413,803 kindergarten places but 424,678 kindergarten pupils.

[7]The Gypsies in Hungary are estimated to be well under 5 percent of the population (personal communication from Dr. Leslie Kish, University of Michigan).

[8]Z. Báthory, op. cit., p. 343.

[9]For this and the remainder of the statistics in Inventory of Kindergarten Settings, no source was provided by the author. (Editors' note.)

VII

Preprimary Education and Care in Italy

Filomena Pistillo
European Center for Education
Ministry of Public Instruction
Frascati

Introduction

The history of preschool provisions in Italy is intimately tied to the country's overall development and to the political, social, economic, and structural changes that have taken place.

From the early 1800s to the eventful 1960s, two factors have constantly weighed against the development of a proper preschool educational system in Italy, negatively influencing its extension, organization, and quality of service. On the one hand, government has pursued a policy of calculated unconcern; on the other, the Roman Catholic church[1] has made an ever more open and insistent bid to take over. The care and education of young children, often considered a terrain on which to defend rival interests, has thus ended up as a political battleground.

A knowledge of the background to public (and, in particular, governmental) involvement in preschool provision is necessary to fully comprehend the status quo and to foresee likely trends. Thus a major part of this report describes the history of child care institutions in relation to the major political and social changes occurring in Italy from 1831 to the end of the 1960s.

Our historical résumé emphasizes those problems still besetting scholars and educational authorities today, for certain choices made in the period preceding national unification have conditioned preschooling to this day. Teacher training, for example, has consistently been handled in the most superficial and impractical manner possible. This apparent paradox cannot be understood until the various interests and the typically opportunistic, adult-centered conception of child care institutions have been fully elucidated.

It should be added, to be fair, that a better idea of children's well-being and a greater interest in early childhood have emerged with time. But legislative changes have been slow in coming. This fact alone shows how much resistance has had to be overcome to attract attention to the quality of life offered young children by their educational setting, by their relationships with the adults caring for them, and by the relationship of their school to home and neighborhood.

A second major part of this report deals with the range of preschool provisions available in Italy today. After discussing the Italian family and the Italian education system as these relate to preschool provisions, we give a rather detailed description of the nursery schools for 3- to 6-year-olds. This is followed by a section devoted to the main issues of debate and research concerning preschool in Italy. A concluding section discusses the more interesting aspects of a recent national study on the use of preschool provisions by Italian families.

Preprimary Education and Care, 1831 to 1968: A Historical Overview

The years 1831 and 1968 are indeed historic: During the former, Italy's first preschool for poor children was opened, while the latter marks the institution of a system of public nursery schools. The two years frame the period that this historical overview will cover.[2]

It should be remembered while reading it that during the period 1831 through 1968, Italy's political and economic organization was completely revolutionized by the following events: the Risorgimento (nationalistic) movement led by the liberal bourgeoisie; national unification in 1860; the Fascist dictatorship and the Liberation (1922–45); the proclamation of the Italian republic and the approval of the Constitution in the years 1946 and 1947.

The 19th Century—From Charitable Shelters to Kindergartens

Abbot Ferrante Aporti introduced the first modern Italian preschools when he opened his first *asilo di carità* (charitable shelter) for young children in the economically backward and chiefly agrarian Italy of 1831. The liberals became immediately interested in the methodology of Aporti's preschools and favored their spread. But after 1848, when the liberal enthusiasm for educating the populace began to wane, support fell off (not only for the preschools but for all forms of public education as well), and no new Aporti preschools were opened.

The unification of Italy in 1860 gave fresh impetus to public education projects, although they were by no means among the priorities in liberal political platforms. The superficial attitude towards education in general can be seen from the policies designed to eliminate illiteracy and guarantee elementary education for the whole population. The cornerstone of these policies, the so-called **Casati law** (legge Casati), immediately revealed its inadequacy and actually contributed to defeating the fight against illiteracy (it must, of course, be recognized that social and economic backwardness made the task overwhelmingly difficult). Not only was the Casati law inefficient in facing up to the task of public instruction, it did not even attempt to further what little had been done up to then in the field of preschool education. It considered that a citizen's formal education was to begin with the first year of elementary school and thus established that obligatory schooling was to start at 6 years of age.

A simplistic view of early childhood, high child-mortality during the first 5 years of life, and a relatively small national budget for education all helped to favor the choice of age 6 as the bottom threshold for obligatory schooling; there was a consequent lack of interest in preschools. But these were only the contingent causes. Deeper sociopolitical reasons were also at work. Entrusting young children's care and education to private (and in particular church-run) concerns fit in with the prevalent philosophy of limiting government involvement and favoring private enterprise. It also repaid the Roman Catholic church somewhat for the economic losses it had suffered during the process of national unification. Finally, it saved the government from involving itself in a deficit-prone, educationally "useless," and politically dangerous public service, while safeguarding the principle of freedom of private interests to establish educational institutions. Meanwhile, the church began emphasizing the charitable aspect of its preschools; the state (national government) followed suit, turning those it had opened in the past over to the Ministry of the Interior, which ran all public assistance programs. Leaving future development of preschool education to private enterprise provoked, of course, an unequal and unplanned distribution of new institutions throughout the country. Northern and central Italy, whose poverty and illiteracy levels were less disastrous than elsewhere, naturally received the lion's share.

The number of preschools created and their staffing were, in any case, inferior to real needs in terms of enrollment. In the school year 1862–63 there were 1,806 preschools with a total of 2,568 teachers and assistants; by the school year 1899–1900 these figures had risen to only 3,280 preschools and 7,725 teachers and assistants (who had 355,703 children placed under their care).

The quality of the service offered in the preschools of the late 19th century was, by our standards, distressing: The rooms were numerically and logistically insufficient; there was a scarcity of educational materials and equipment; methodology was totally unplanned guesswork. Many preschools were simply parking lots where, because of the lack of space and pedagogical training, the children were kept quiet and immobile all day. In others, the staff went to the opposite extreme: Children were taught reading, writing, arithmetic, science, as though they were already in elementary school. At the bottom of such disparity and methodological confusion lay the untouched problem of how to choose and train preschool staff.

The assignment of preschool provision to the Ministry of the Interior impeded improvements. While the Ministry of Education had the authority to decide pedagogical questions, it could exert only minimal influence through its inspectors and could do nothing to combat the serious structural and organizational shortcomings. It took the popularity of the Froebel method and the *giardini d'infanzia* (kindergartens) to raise consciousness over the quality of preschools, and it was to be on this terrain that the Agazzi sisters' method and the Montessori method were to take root in Italy.

The first kindergarten was founded in Venice in 1869, although Froebel's method had been partially applied in a few preschools in the North as early as 1867. While several educators declared their admiration for the method and openly espoused it, there was also a fair degree of opposition and even hostility, especially in Roman Catholic circles. It was considered too "geometric" and play-centered; it supposedly restricted the child's liberty and fantasy; it did not include religious education; last but not least, it was a foreign and Protestant invention. Catholic hostility was to be expected, given the kind of people who were promoting Froebel's method in Italy: Among them were Protestants and Jews, lay activists in favor of the separation of church and state, Masons, and the Ministry of Education, which at that time was dominated by anticlerical and Masonic appointees.

The debate between supporters and opposers of Froebel's method led to a compromise solution. A "mixed method" was devised by combining what was generally recognized as valid in Aporti's method with the best in Froebel's method. Although the amalgamation was artificial and theoretically questionable, the mixed method was a great practical success, mostly because of the lack of pedagogical and cultural awareness on the part of preschool staff and also because of the ambiguous approval of educational theorists.

Thus the spread of Freobel's method and kindergartens did not actually mean that teaching was improving noticeably in most Italian preschools. Still, changes were afoot, and Aporti's methodology started to be gradually abandoned. By 1889, 10 percent of preschools in Italy declared that they followed Froebel's method, 74 percent (1,562) said they used the mixed method, and the remaining 16 percent claimed they were implementing some kind of undefined "Italian experimental method" (that is, their own method).

The beginnings of change were more noticeable in officialdom, where Froebel's method (with extensive retouching) had continued to gain ground among educational experts and school authorities. A decree in 1880 provided that students of teachers' colleges (*scuole normali*) had to undergo training in kindergartens using Froebel's method and that preschool teachers had to have 3 years of practice in a kindergarten. A law in 1889 actually annexed the Froebel kindergartens to the teachers' colleges, thus facilitating the training program.

The Early 20th Century—Major Progress in Theory and Practice

The early 20th century brought the beginnings of economic transformation to Italy, as industrialization finally began to get off the ground. Giovanni Giolitti[3] headed the government. Industry began recruiting women in sizable numbers, and this made it urgent to solve social questions that had been idly debated for years, namely, questions about welfare and working conditions for women and children. Spurred on by the Socialists, the government approved a law in 1902 that set the minimum working age at 12 years and permitted women to suspend work during pregnancy (although without pay or benefits or any form of aid). With Filippo Turati at its head, the Socialist party became more and more interested in educational questions, in the defense of young children's rights, and in the spread of preschools throughout the country. Educators also began to show increased interest in early childhood and preprimary education. Their 1898 congress called for more state intervention and the assignment of nursery schools to the Ministry of Education, so the ministry could define the status and provide for the recruitment of preschool staff and also define the educational and pedagogical objectives the schools should attain. The National Union of Educators for Infancy, through its review *The Voice of Preschool Teachers*, begun in 1904, called for the same kind of measures. Finally, the Ministry of Education itself conducted a survey in 1910 that denounced the pitiful state of preschools and of staff qualifications and called for the same remedies.

As a consequence of the survey, a committee of experts was formed to draw up a plan for reorganizing preschool provisions. The efforts of this committee led to the approval of the **New Programs** in 1914. In the meantime, another law approved in 1911 transferred control over elementary schooling from communal to national government; the law also created a network of **School Assistance Centers**, which were primarily charged with making sure that underprivileged children could attend elementary school but which were also to be responsible for encouraging the creation of other kinds of educational institutions, including preschools. While educators were discussing just how to prepare preprimary teachers, a law passed in 1913 instituted 2-year technical secondary schools for the practical preparation of preschool staff, the so-called ***scuole pratiche magistrali***.

In this very same period, Rosa Agazzi and her sister Carolina were developing their own educational method while Maria Montessori was setting up the first of her "Children's Homes" (Casa dei Bambini) in Rome. These two educational innovations attracted immediate attention and provoked hot debate in educational circles between Agazzi and Montessori partisans. The Italian Union for Public Education held a convention in 1911 to submit the various positions to reasoned, scientifically founded analysis. This is the first instance of serious methodological inquiry and confrontation in the field of preprimary education in Italy. Unfortunately, the convention concluded without the participants having taken a clear-cut stand on any of the issues.

This was, as can be seen, a particularly fertile moment in Italy for child education in general and nursery schooling in particular; major progress was being made in both theory and practice. Still, government was singularly absent from the scene; the progress made in extending and upgrading preschool provisions was by no means due to any organic policy promoted by the Ministry of Education. In fact, the admirable efforts of private individuals during the early 1900s were matched by zero-growth in public preschools, when responsibility was in the hands of communal government, and near zero-growth after the law was passed obliging the communes to institute School Assistance Centers. Existing preschools were verging on economic collapse. Whatever progress was made in strengthening and extending the preprimary system may be attributed exclusively to the Roman Catholic church. In fact, making a bid for control over the entire field of preprimary educaton, the church started founding new preschools and assigning its religious orders to run the ones already in operation.

Statistical data on preschools during the first two decades of this century reveal two peaks in the overall growth rate: 1911–12 and 1920–21, each with an average annual increase of about 109 facilities. It is difficult, however, to say how many of these institutions endorsed a given view of preschool education, whether it be Aporti's, Froebel's, the Agazzis', Montessori's, an eclectic one, or the one that simply considered children as baggage to be held in deposit. In 1900 there were 320,000 young children enrolled in 3,280 institutions run by 6,815 teachers and assistants. In 1920 enrollment rose to 501,000 and the number of schools, to 5,455, but the sharpest rise was in staff, which grew to 12,320. It is calculated that the ratio of enrollment to demand improved just as positively: from 4.4 percent in 1861 to 14.3 percent in 1900 and to 25 percent in 1920.

These favorable statistics for 1920 should not lead us to forget, however, that 75 percent of children between 3 and 5 years of age received no preprimary care or education. The 25 percent that did receive preschool services, most of whom were to receive no other form of schooling afterwards, were packed into overcrowded rooms with teacher-pupil ratios of 1 to 45. Furthermore, official data reveals that whatever preschool education existed was confined to the better-off parts of the country. The figures for schools, teachers, and enrollment show that northern Italy was one-and-a-half times better-off than central Italy, two-and-a-half times better-off than Sicily or Sardinia, and three times better-off than the rest of the South in preprimary facilities.

FASCIST REFORM—"SHELTERS" BECOME "NURSERY SCHOOLS"

As fascism reared its head over the country, the situation of preprimary education in Italy was far from rosy, either quantitatively or qualitatively.

In October 1922 the Fascist party, with power now in its hands, felt it necessary to revamp educational policy with an eye both to inculcating its principles in the populace and to creating intermediary party leadership (which was sorely lacking). The Fascist party, having no clear ideas on pedagogy or education and no ready-made program of its own, took over remnants of preceding policies and sewed them together with the ideology of the neoidealist philosopher Giovanni Gentile. It then proceeded to reform the school system accordingly.

In 1923 the **Gentile Reform Law** was passed. As was the case before, the law left preprimary education to one side, solving none of its problems and, if anything, accentuating the negative effects of the preceding system. The name for preschools was changed from *asili* (shelters) to *scuole materne* (nursery schools); these nursery schools were supposed to be the first stage (lasting 3 years) of elementary education. Attendance was not, however, made obligatory; the public institutions were still (confusingly) run both by the Ministry of the Interior and the Ministry of Education; preprimary schooling was still conceived of in terms of custody and recreation instead of education; even more leeway was given to private (and especially church) initiative in creating new facilities. In 1933 over 60 percent of preschools were run by religious orders, and nuns constituted over two thirds of the staff.

The Gentile Reform Law brought only a few additions and clarifications to the program outlined in 1914. The numerical increase in preschools was quite modest during this period—3.6 percent as compared with the 3.3 percent increase of the preceding two decades. The increase in enrollment was likewise a modest 1 percent. The numbers of teachers rose by 0.5 percent, and the teacher-pupil ratio was 1 to 44. The reform also provided for "schools of methodology" for preprimary education, but only on paper. Creating and running them was left to private (mostly church) initiative. The Fascist government never exercised effective control over the preprimary sector, which remained a virtual church monopoly.

During their first years in power, the Fascists promoted the Montessori method, but after having flirted with the Montessori methodology for only a few years, the Fascist regime switched over to the method of the Agazzi sisters. Since the latter method was already firmly established in Roman Catholic nursery schools, the regime thus avoided contrasts with the church. Fascist Education Minister Giovanni Bottai went so far as to proclaim the Agazzis' method as "the method of the Italian preschool system."

Minister Bottai proclaimed a **School Charter** in 1939. Because of the war, the only practical implementation was to circulate among the schools a 1940 ministry letter suggesting experimental preschool programs. On February 9, 1945, the government newly decreed **Programs and Instructional Models to Be Implemented in Elementary and Preprimary Schools**. But the programs did not find favor among the teachers.

After Fascism—More Ardent Ideological Battles

After the Liberation, the new government continued to pursue a policy of indifference combined with encouragement of church initiative in the preprimary sector, which was the policy that it had inherited from its predecessors and which continued to pay politically. While various national leaders (especially the elected representatives of the Left) began to take interest in early childhood, their interest was confined to resolving the primary needs of young children. Lay Roman Catholics began to become more and more interested in the question of preschool education, and it is not hard to see why. The Christian Democrats won majority control over Parliament in the 1948 elections, with no small help from the church; it became clear that a preferential relationship between Christian Democrat politicians and the ecclesiastical hierarchy would be of mutual benefit, and this union characterized Italy all through the 1950s. Since private schools and, in particular, preschools were the fief of the church, it does not come as a surprise to see government finally paying attention to the educational needs of young children.

In 1947 Minister of Public Instruction Guido Gonella promoted a **National Committee for School Reform** whose job was to determine the needs of the schools and make proposals for improvement. The study inevitably showed that preschools were not promoting children's education; they were too often considered child-custody centers; there was a shortage of suitable rooms, furniture, educational materials; teachers had often been recruited without qualifications and given no contract; their pay was inadequate for the functions they had been assigned. There was a unanimous request to replace the teacher-training secondary schools (scuole magistrali) with a new, more highly qualified training system. The geographical disparity in the distribution of preschools became clear from the study, as did the dismal relationship between number of schools and potential demand.

Church leaders, not wanting to lose their monopoly over preprimary education, spoke out against any direct government intervention in this sector. They were promptly reassured by the minister of public instruction (Gonella). Speaking at the inauguration of the National Center for Preschool Education at Brescia in 1950, he reaffirmed that the government was ready to help private initiative in expanding the preschool system; it would be, he claimed, impossible for the state to intervene directly or to try to support the entire system. The principle of government subsidization of private concerns opening new preschools, he concluded, would in any case eliminate the need for direct state intervention for many years to come. It was on this same occasion that Gonella reaffirmed that the Agazzi method was and should remain *the* method practiced in Italian preschools.

Towards the mid-1950s lay political parties began to awaken to the educational needs of early childhood: They denounced the excessive religious control over preschools, the lack of involvement by public institutions, the absolute dearth of facilities in the South. The writings of educators such as Lamberto Borghi and Francesco de Bartolomeis were particularly significant.

The boom years from 1951 to 1961, the "Italian miracle," brought exceptional industrial development and with it profound changes in social values and lifestyles. Family patterns changed, as did the conception of early childhood. Italy became a consumer society, although public service infrastructure was still sorely lacking. People migrated from the countryside to the cities, especially southerners to the North in search of jobs; male labor became prevalently industrial instead of agricultural; and female labor increased sharply, especially in the period 1958–63.

The Italian family started to become nuclear. Children had fewer possibilities for acquiring social roles and education from within a densely populated and stratified home. The number of children per family began to decline visibly, especially in the North.

Against this economic and sociological backdrop, Roman Catholic and lay political forces waged ever more ardent ideological battles over the solution to the new social problems that had arisen. The prime minister, beaten in Parliament, declared a political crisis in 1958 and called for general elections. Again, the church did not hesitate to make its weight felt during the election campaign. The Christian Democrat party ended up the winner, increasing the number of its seats in Parliament. But the Socialist party picked up votes too, and although the Communist party and the Social Democrats did not rise above their 1953 figures, the political scene was modified.

The government won approval for its newly published ***Guidelines for Educational Activities in Preschools*** and then, in the person of Amintore Fanfani, attempted to push through Parliament a **Ten-Year School Plan** that contained two articles specifically regarding preprimary education. But the question of preprimary teacher training was still dividing educators, and the government measures, which to all effects permitted public financing of private schools, ignited once again the long-standing feud over the respective roles of public and private involvement in education.

THE 1960s—ESTABLISHMENT OF A PUBLIC SYSTEM

In 1960 the Communist party presented a legislative proposal for direct state involvement in preprimary education. A center-left government, formed in 1962 with Fanfani at its head, had to abandon the 1958 Ten-Year Plan in favor of a **Three-Year Plan**, easier to implement. This plan included an allocation of 700 million lire (1.1 million dollars U.S.) to build a few state-run preschools, over and above the 2 billion lire (3.2 million dollars U.S.) in grants to local bodies (provinces, communes, nonprofit welfare agencies, charitable organizations, or other institutions) for the building of preprimary facilities. This compromise measure between Christian Democrats and Socialists paved the way for a network of semipublic preschools (although its actual implementaion took a number of years and more political battles).

The 1963 **Agreement on a Common Political Program for the Formation of a Center-Left Government** included a provision whereby the government would sponsor a law to regulate preschools nationwide.

The mid-1960s witnessed a rebirth of interest in preprimary education on a local level in various cities. The most interesting examples are found in the Emilia region. In 1962 the local government voted to construct the first four of a series of preschools throughout the region, while from 1960 to 1969 Bologna, the main city in the area, doubled the number of preschools it ran and the total enrollment of young children under its care. In the last 5 years of the period, the quality of Bologna's preschools improved noticeably as well, thanks to the dedication of Bruno Ciari. Ciari felt that preprimary education was a privileged means of giving every child, of whatever social background, a common cultural foundation upon which to grow as a person and as a citizen. He also believed that educational theories should grow out of daily contact with the job of educating; his **New Model for Educational Practice** is the fruit of this endeavor. Far from breaking ties with the past, the New Model was one with roots in the tradition leading from Aporti to Froebel to the Agazzis and Montessori.

In the 1964 *Report on the State of Public Instruction*, Minister Gui revealed the ever more disastrous state of the preprimary teacher-training secondary schools (scuole magistrali). In the same year, he presented a law for the **Institution of State Nursery Schools** that diverged radically both from the Communists' proposal and from the Socialists' proposal. The main point of contention was over the future teacher-training-school system, and even the fact that Minister Gui's proposal excluded males from the teacher-training schools was a source of bitter controversy.

The battle over the law was a battle of endurance. Its final rejection caused the second Moro government to resign. In 1966 under the third Moro government, Minister Gui presented a new proposal for the **Regulation of State Nursery Schools**; it again provided for all-female staff and subordinated nursery education to family care. This time, after a stiff battle (again over the question of the teacher-training secondary schools), the law was passed and took effect on March 18, 1968 (see the section entitled Legislation: Law No. 444 (1968) and addenda). This **Law No. 444**, which was called "the 444" in Parliament, finally officially recognized the government's right to be directly involved in preprimary education. Other than that, however, the law was hardly satisfactory, since it was the result of too many compromises. In 1969 the newly issued ***Guidelines for Educational Activities in State Nursery Schools*** (explained in a later section) was approved.

Since the foundation of an official state preprimary educational system, attempts to improve that system either quantitatively or qualitatively have met with various obstacles. There has been only a modest increase in new facilities, due to insufficient funding that does not take into consideraion inflation. At any rate, most of the funding goes simply to pay staff and current expenses. Special fundings are obtained only when the government is put into a corner. Those parts of "the 444" that at the time were considered innovative are now far behind what many local administrations have been doing in their communal nursery schools since the end of the 1960s. In particular, communal nursery schools in north-central Italy have come up with the newest and most exciting proposals for the education and care of young children, proposals that are progressive not only in an educational sense but also in a social sense. Again, the Emilia region has distinguished itself in this field.

The positive example of these locally run schools has in turn caused people to begin thinking of nursery schools as semiautonomous institutions whose educational policies are a social product and not simply a reflection of the whims of individual families or of the decrees promulgated by state bureaucracies.

FAMILIES, CHILDREN, AND SCHOOLS TODAY IN ITALY

The preschool provisions available to Italian families today are **day nurseries**, for children aged 0 to 3 years, and **nursery schools**, for children from age 3 to age 6. The historical development of each service has been different. Different, too, are their respective supply-demand ratios. Nevertheless, for some years now, both have had to meet family demands for new and more complex services. To do so adequately, they have had to reorganize and diversify. The profound changes in user profile in the last decade have been particularly marked with respect to day nurseries.

The role of nurseries and nursery schools has changed, basically because families and society as a whole have changed. This is particularly true of day nurseries. The amount of sociopedagogical value that these are accorded has recently increased enormously, in light of the reservations and prejudices that marked their beginnings.[4] In addition, the social and educational value of nursery schools has become widely established and socially accepted. (There is an increasing tendency to talk about "nursery education," a term that incorporates both day nurseries and nursery schools, as run by local authorities in northern and central Italy. Educators are happy to adopt this term, since it is a felicitous interpretation of what nursery schools currently provide.) Whereas Italy's most recent organizational changes affecting work, the family, and society have redefined and clarified the need for and usefulness of these services, they have also emphasized the need for the services to adapt to the wider social context.

CHANGES IN FAMILIES' NEEDS, ATTITUDES

Among the recent changes having the strongest impact on families and children (and hence on the preschool institutions under study), are (1) the family's greater social isolation; (2) the lack of peer relationships available to children outside of preschool institutions; (3) the spread of parents' work activity and changes in their working hours, especially in industry; (4) a greater parental desire to fully experience parenthood and not entrust children too much to educational or supervisory institutions; (5) increased family concern about choosing an educational institution that meets their specific requirements; and (6) nursery attendance by children from all social classes.

The attitude of young Italian families towards nursery education remains very ambivalent. Making use of extrafamilial services is often seen as a last resort, especially for the care of children under age 3. Yet families are increasingly feeling the need to entrust their young children to specialist services for long periods of the day. At the same time, families are becoming more demanding than in the past, wanting better services and tighter guarantees. Moreover, they also seek to maximize compatibility between the needs of each family member and what the institutions and society in general can offer. However, this need of the families for checks and guarantees regarding services does not generally lead parents to involvement with the institution, in the sense of participation in management or monitoring bodies, nor does it lead parents to make any direct contribution towards improving the services. All in all, one can say that although entrusting children to the institution is done more responsibly than in the past, it is still seen as an unavoidable necessity; too often it becomes more like "abandoning" than "responsibly entrusting."

The continual increase in both the quantity and quality of families' demands is a fact, yet families have difficulty expressing their quality requirements clearly. There exists a tension between a service that tends to fall into line with both the explicit and the implicit demands of those who use it (at the same time partly modifying family behavior) and families for whom entrusting their children to educational institutions is increasingly problematic and contradictory. Italy's young families have a growing investment (not just a material one) in their children and want to ensure them every opportunity for growth and well-being; at the same time, they feel the real fragility of the nuclear family and the eroding of traditional family roles. Because families are gradually convincing themselves that preprimary institutions have a significant impact on their children's overall development, their choice for preschool care and education comes to hold great importance for their children.

THE EDUCATIONAL SYSTEM

In Italy, children have 8 years of compulsory schooling, from age 6 to age 14. But nursery school enrollment of children aged 3 to 6 is becoming increasingly common, so schooling in fact starts before the legally established age. Although the falling birthrate has caused a continuing drop in the number of nursery school pupils and in the number of nursery schools (there were 30,027 schools in 1981–82 and only 28,613 in 1985–86), the percentage of the catchment age group enrolled has continued to rise and by 1986 was only about 13 percent away from 100 percent enrollment of Italy's 2,529,092 preschool-aged children.[5]

Compulsory schooling is divided into two cycles; 5 years of elementary school (*scuola elementare*), followed by 3 years of middle school (*scuola media*) or first-level secondary school.

Primary school enrollment has stood at 100 percent for several years now. The falling birthrate, however, has brought down absolute numbers. Middle school provides the student with a general education. It also has 100 percent enrollment, but this was first attained later than that for elementary school; however, in some regions, middle school has a limited dropout phenomenon. Until the last few years, enrollment numbers were constantly on the increase, but here too, the falling birthrate is beginning to have an effect.

If they have a diploma, students can leave school at age 14 to take up a job or an apprenticeship. Most, however, continue their studies. Those who do not succeed in gaining the middle school diploma (*licenza media*) are required to stay on until they are 15. Those pupils who for some reason have not gained the middle school diploma, such as those who have started work with only an elementary school diploma, can attend one of the "150 hours" courses designed to help them obtain the diploma.

Once compulsory schooling has ended, programs are no longer uniform. Upper secondary schools (*scuole secondarie superiori*), are remarkable for their great diversity. Classical and science-oriented high schools follow an established program that prepares students for university studies, while technical and professional institutes offer a wide choice of subjects that may be combined in various ways.

Among those institutes offering vocational training is the earlier-mentioned scuola magistrale, which trains nursery school teachers but does not lead to a matriculation-type exam or qualify one for university entrance. In contrast, after 4 years at the *istituto magistrale* and successful completion of a final exam, students are qualified to teach in both nursery and elementary school. They may directly enter a university education department (*facoltà di magistero*) for a degree in pedagogy, languages, or literature, but to enter any other university department, they must first take a year's supplementary studies.

Nursery Schools: Education and Care for Children Aged 3 to 6

Serving the educational needs of 3- to 6-year-olds, nursery schools in Italy are divided into **state** institutions (run directly by a ministry or agency of the national government) and **non-state** institutions (run by other kinds of government bodies or by private organizations). Corresponding to these differently sponsored institutions are different kinds of enabling legislation and different principles of management. In the final analysis, this means differences in service quality and in the degree to which services meet people's needs.

The ties between state and non-state nursery schools are of a very complex nature. This is true administratively (one has only to think of current relations between national and local governments!) as well as politically. The political complexity derives from the necessity of using public funds to maintain non-state nursery schools in spite of the economic losses they habitually incur. But the national government is loath to take them over directly, partly because of the sheer magnitude of both the undertaking and its required financing, but mostly because of the principle (guaranteed by the Constitution) that calls for maintaining economic pluralism and freedom of choice. This does not mean that better-defined relations between the private and public sectors could not be attained; recent proposals for an **integrated national system** (which we discuss further on) in fact offer an alternative model of relations between state/non-state agencies and national/local governments.

At any rate, both state and non-state nursery schools are placed under the authority of the Ministry of Education—the former, directly; the latter, indirectly through local school board officials.

Non-State Nursery Schools

Non-state nursery schools include those run by private organizations (religious bodies, private lay organizations, or single individuals) as well as those run by local (communal, provincial, regional)[6] government, public corporations, or the like. Table 1 summarizes the non-state nursery school enrollment for 1983–84.

Nursery schools in the autonomous provinces and regions

Of Italy's 20 regions and the 95 provinces making up those regions, the 2 provinces of Trento and Bolzano/Bozen and the 4 autonomous regions—

Table 1

Non-State Nursery Schools, Administration and Enrollment, 1983–84

	Local Government		Other Public Organizations		Religious Institutions		Private (Lay) Organizations		Total	
Geographical Location	Schools	Pupils	Schools	Pupils	Schools	Pupils	Schools	Pupils	Schools	Pupils
Northern Italy	2,014	132,730	685	45,151	2,755	165,680	1,824	103,755	7,278	447,316
Central Italy	749	62,188	71	3,826	1,377	78,018	275	9,984	2,472	154,016
Southern Italy	678	42,777	178	10,329	1,687	102,286	1,685	65,503	4,228	220,895
Islands of Sardinia & Sicily	668	29,486	180	9,275	810	38,915	635	21,330	2,293	99,006
Italy	4,109	267,181	1,114	68,581	6,629	384,899	4,419	200,572	16,271	921,233

Note. From the *Central Statistics Institute Bulletin* (*ISTAT Notizàrio*), Rome, 1986, 2.

Friuli-Venezia Giulia, Valle d'Aosta, Sardinia, and Sicily—enjoy the greatest latitude in the field of school legislation, especially with regard to preschool education. The provinces of Bolzano/Bozen and Trento, for example, have completely taken over the functions of national government in this domain. The province of Trento has even approved its own constitutive law that not only brings together the various pieces of national legislation but goes beyond them. In fact, it innovates in a number of fields, since it takes into consideration the development of educational theory since the 1970s.

The regions of Valle d'Aosta and Friuli-Venezia Giulia have more limited powers with regard to education; indeed, they can only decide the regulations that implement national laws. Thus the nursery school system in these two regions is that created by Law No. 444 and addenda, in other words, the laws regulating state nursery schools in Italy. In Sicily, the regional government enjoys greater freedom; it can "complete" national school programs with innovations of its own. Nonetheless, up to now, the Sicilian nursery school system has been a faithful reproduction of the national model. The regional government in Sardinia has likewise not yet intervened substantially in the state legislation that governs nursery schooling.

Nursery schools run by local government, public corporations, and private organizations

These schools are still run under the provisions of the **Omnibus Elementary School Law** of February 5, 1928, and by the ordinances implementing it, which were issued the same year. Since the Italian Constitution provides for pluralism in education, Law No. 444 (passed in 1968 to regulate state nursery schools) does not apply to non-state nursery schools. But non-state nursery schools can, if they so desire, follow the state norms.

The legislation that currently applies to non-state nursery school is three-tiered, and each one of the tiers offers a differing degree of elasticity: (1) There are thc obligatory dispositions of the 1928 Omnibus Law. (2) There are the dispositions contained in the civil code that regulate the relations between school management and personnel. (3) There are the dispositions of Law No. 444, to which non-state nursery schools may freely subscribe, with respect to the overall educational goals and the general administrative setup. The total effect of this accumulation of laws is that the authorities find it difficult to know just what to enforce. A unified piece of legislation is obviously called for, as experts have long said.

Operations

All non-state nursery schools are placed under the supervision of the Ministry of Education. The ministry's powers include authorizing the institution to open or revoking authorization and closing the school. The head of the local elementary school performs these tasks for the area under his supervision. For authorization to open a school, the proprietor must send a written request before the beginning of the school year to the local elementary school, with documents certifying Italian citizenship, the qualifications and good moral standing of the proprietor and of the teachers, and the fitness of the building to be used (this means submitting a floor plan and proof of health and safety inspections). Authorization to open is granted for 1 year and is renewed tacitly from year to year if the original conditions at the time of the first issuance do not change.

Non-state nursery schools may opt to follow the dispositions enacted for state schools with respect to operations and furnishings; in particular, they may opt to follow the 1969 ***Guidelines for Educational Activities in State Nursery Schools*** instead of the guidelines written specifically for non-state schools in 1958. As to the maximum number of children per class, the limit for non-state schools may only be surmised from an old 1928 regulation that established that no more than 60 children could be assigned to a single teacher.

Financing

Article 31 of Law No. 1073 (enacted in 1972) provides for partial financing of locally run nursery schools by the national government, on a yearly basis, if the institutions so request. The funds are meant to cover part of the normal running expenses and cannot by any means cover the entire cost of operations, much less such expenses as building repair and upkeep or transportation. To be eligible for state funds, schools must offer free tuition and/or refectory rights to all or part of their students. The request for funds is presented to the local school board by the proprietor or organization running the nursery school. The school board supervisor, who must inspect the school and personally ascertain the school's real financial needs, determines in effect whether state funds will be granted and how much. Before being forwarded to the ministry for official approval, the request must however be approved by various provincial bodies.

Personnel

The credentials required for teaching in non-state nursery schools is a diploma from a secondary school that trains preschool teachers (scuola magistrale), as per the 1928 law already described; elementary school teachers may also teach in nursery schools if they pass a specific test, as described in Law No. 444 (1968). The maximum and minimum age-limits for personnel are established by the party running a nursery school, according to specific internal regulations; otherwise, common-law norms hold. The work contract between proprietor and staff member is considered private. The local state supervisor, who is responsible for seeing that all regulations are observed, can ask to check up on the physical and pedagogical fitness of non-state nursery school staff.

STATE NURSERY SCHOOLS

As the first part of this profile shows, the state's interest in preprimary education has changed over time, progressing from blind trust in private initiative to the regulation of private nursery schools to the creation of a network of public schools (Law No. 444, March 18, 1968).[7]

To be fair, it should be added that the state did intervene directly in preprimary education before 1968, although its impact was insignificant. The nursery schools annexed to secondary teacher-training schools and to teachers' colleges were run directly by the Ministry of Education. Moreover, the national government created two agencies dealing with the preprimary sector: the National Agency for Child Care in the border areas and the Agency for Nursery Schools in Sardinia. The first agency was eliminated in 1975, but the second is still active in Sardinia. However, the first *massive* intervention was Law No. 444, which was the result of extenuating political haggling and, above all, grassroots pressure placed on the government during the eventful 1960s. The interest in nursery schools in that highly politicized period is not hard to understand: The preprimary age is the ideal moment to remove the social disadvantages that a child may have acquired in coming from a less-privileged home or neighborhood. But psychology and pedagogy also lent their findings to promoting improved nursery schooling: The early years in a child's life were seen as a vital, never-to-be-had-again moment in which basic mental processes evolved; society therefore realized that it had a responsibility towards the child in those areas in which families do not generally have the means of assuring proper growth.

Legislation: Law No. 444 (1968) and addenda

The fundamental characteristics of the state nursery school system were given by Law No. 444 (1968); but since then, there have been other legislative acts, such as the **Decreti Delegati**,[8] that have sought to adapt the original model to the changing times.

Law No. 444 got off to a difficult start. The economic slump, which began just when the law was to be put into effect, caused a slowdown in allocations; this meant that the coordination between the overall planning of the nursery school network and the building construction program was thrown off. Many nursery schools were simply not built or "temporarily" housed in whatever accommodations local government bodies could come up with (in accordance with the "transition process" measure contained in Law No. 444, Article 29). The application of the law was also hindered by the fact that planning was not tied to a norm regulating how the law was to be put into effect (a so-called *regolamento di esecuzione della legge*); more precisely, the law called on the Ministry of Education to produce such a norm, but the ministry never did.

However, the operation of the nursery school system has been ensured through ordinances and ministry recommendations. It was only when the Decreti Delegati appeared that certain activities, such as the hiring of teachers, were adequately provided for; at the same time, other activities, such as recruiting the heads of the local elementary schools in charge of nursery schools, to this very day go on without any specific norm governing them.

Without a doubt, Law No. 444 was extremely important. It is not, however, universally acclaimed. Article 3 of the law, for example, is still criticized as keeping the state system subordinate to the private system. The criticisms, it should be added, do not all come from those who favor a generalized state educational system; even those who believe in the legitimacy of private initiative in education feel that the relationship between state and non-state schools should be better balanced. A solution to this controversy is hard to see. The very principle of a "plurality of regimes" within a society leads to inevitable deadlocks.

Criticism has also been leveled at the educational goals that the law proposes. In particular, there is dissent over the concept of "preparing the child for elementary school." This could jeopardize the autonomous role of nursery schools in deciding just how to help a child develop his faculties; it could also introduce dangerous forms of premature education. Law No. 444 authorizes state intervention in preprimary education, but its purpose is to permit the state to provide for *supplementary services in geographical areas where the demand has not been satisfied.* It therefore does not make the state a true competitor of private institutions. State nursery schools, as preprimary schools, accept children from 3 to 6 years of age; their purpose is to educate them, help them develop their personalities, prepare them for elementary school, and thus complete the training received in the family. Attendance is not obligatory and is free of charge. Children may, if so desired, attend only the morning or afternoon session.

Number and size of classes

Schools are normally composed of three classes corresponding to the ages of the children (3, 4, and 5 years). The maximum number of classes allowed is nine. Mixed classes (ones with children of various ages) are permitted. In small towns, a single-class school is permitted. Classes may be composed of not more than 30 and not less than 15 children.

Timetable and school year

At present, timetables vary from a minimum of 5 to a maximum of 10 hours. The school year may not be shorter than 10 months. Law No. 444 states that the daily timetable cannot be shorter than 7 hours, except for certain local requirements, amply documented. In 1978, **Law No. 463** raised the daily timetable to 8 hours (with a 10-hour maximum), divided into two sessions (morning/afternoon). Given that a previous decree (No. 417, 1974) had reduced the daily teaching load for state schoolteachers, it became necessary to nominate two teachers for each class. Thus it became possible for nursery schools to remain open for more than 7 hours a day and more than 10 months a year, through rotation of personnel.

Enrollment

State nursery schools open on September 1 and close on June 30. Parents generally enroll their children in May for the following school year. Enrollment for a given school year is open to children who by December 31 are at least 3 and no more than 6 years of age. If places are available, a child turning 3 in January may be enrolled, but only after the 3rd birthday.

The admission of handicapped children over 6 years of age constitutes a very delicate problem; the problem lies in determining a child's mental age, which must be in the 3–6 bracket in order for admission to be legal. The Teachers' Council makes the decision, case by case, after hearing the opinion of medical, social, psychological, and educational experts.

Creation of new schools or new classes

Article 3 of Law No. 444 states that schools will be created "taking into consideration those places where the greatest need is found, in particular the economically depressed areas and the areas of rapid urban growth."

Each year, a disposition of the Ministry of Education establishes what criteria and what procedures will be followed; it is a complex process indeed, involving the communes, the local elementary school head, the local School Council, the local Ministry of Education representatives, the provincial school board, and the regional government. At the completion of the process, the Ministry of Education, after obtaining the necessary approval from the Ministry of the Treasury for funding, issues the decree instituting the nursery school. When the decree becomes effective (the regularity of all acts has to be certified by a special body), the local ministry representative issues an order formally establishing the nursery school.

Personnel

Staff was meant to be, according to Law No. 444, exclusively female. The positions it provided for were teacher, co-teacher, assistant, and on an executive level, headmaster and national inspectors. Maintenance staff, on the other hand, was meant to be provided by communes wishing to have a nursery school in their area. The positions of co-teacher and assistant were abolished in 1978 by Law No. 463, which also specified that new nursery school teachers have to go through a selection process and do a year of practice teaching.

Unfortunately, a regulation for putting Law No. 444 into practice was never issued; thus it was legally impossible to recruit head teachers or nursery school inspectors. The law did provide for a transitory measure to fill vacancies: These executive positions were turned over to elementary school heads and elementary school inspectors. Moreover, before the appearance of the Decreti Delegati in 1974, it was not possible to hire teachers for the new nursery schools. The recruiting of teachers has now become possible, but the executive positions are still in the hands of elementary school officials, who were to occupy them "temporarily" 18 years ago. Not only is it impossible to recruit specifically trained executive personnel, but it is impossible to put into practice certain functions attributed to nursery school Teachers' Councils (by Decree No. 416, 1974) in the absence of regularly nominated school heads.

Law No. 463 (1978) not only abolished co-teachers and assistants but also, as mentioned earlier, raised the daily timetable to 8 hours (with a maximum of 10), divided into two sessions (morning and afternoon). Each session has two teachers who work 30 hours a week with the children and who put in up to 20 hours a month on top of that for the other activities connected with running a school. Thus, in a school that is open 8 or 9 hours a day, there are necessarily 1 or 2 hours of double-staffing within the same class. But this is not the only interesting side effect to the disposition regarding timetables. The need to recruit extra teachers resulted in opening up nursery school positions to those elementary school teachers who were waiting to be nominated to an elementary school; this has meant that for the first time, male teachers have made their appearance within the hallowed walls of a nursery school.

These modifications have changed the face of the nursery school provided for by Law No. 444. They have also raised some new questions—what to do with the extended schedule and the time of double-staffing and how to get the jobs done that the former assistant used to do, given the lack of qualified maintenance staff. A few sporadic ordinances will certainly not be enough to smooth over these rough edges as well as those caused by the lack of coordination between national and local government (the latter being responsible for important services in the proper functioning of a nursery school).

Teacher training

Present regulations provide for the training of future nursery school teachers either in 3-year scuole magistrali or in 4-year istituti magistrali. (These are both secondary schools that accept middle school graduates, who are approximately 14 years of age.) The magistrale diploma is not considered by itself, however, proof of teaching ability. The would-be teacher must therefore pass a competency test as part of admission to state employment in the preschool system within a particular province. The test is, of course, purely verbal (a written exam followed by an interview). Furthermore, the first year of actual teaching is considered a practice period during which the candidate "learns the trade." A school head must have higher qualifications: a special diploma in school administration, a university degree in education, and a record of regular employment teaching in the state system for at least 3 years. To become a local inspector, a candidate must have a university degree in education and 4 years experience as head of a school. The position of national inspector carries some additional requirements, which are the same as those for the analogous job in the elementary school system.

Teacher training and the general question of teaching standards has been a crucial question in political and educational debates concerning preprimary education over the past several years. The question is complex, and there are no clear-cut solutions. Or rather, no attempt has been made to face the question squarely and *make* clear-cut decisions. Thus, more than half a century after the creation of secondary schools to train teachers (the scuole pratiche magistrali instituted in 1913) things have not changed appreciably. Indeed, qualifications expected of nursery school teachers may be considered to have worsened in comparison with the present-day higher cultural levels and expectations of the overall population, and thus the more sophisticated professional profile Italian preschool teachers ought to have. Neither the training provided by the istituti magistrali (too old-fashioned) or that provided by the scuole magistrali (too short and skimpy) can meet today's demands. Both teachers and educational theorists increasingly call for an improved system of basic teacher training. In response to these demands, in 1974 Parliament passed Decree No. 417 that would make a university degree obligatory for all teaching jobs, including nursery school. The law cannot, however, be adequately applied until the secondary school system is reformed—a controversial topic that has been tossed about for years and to which no solution seems anywhere in sight. Thus, the legal qualifications of preschool teachers have not in effect changed. A partial attempt at reforming teacher training may however be found in a proposed law that would alter the requirements for secondary school diplomas. The proposal would temporarily maintain the existence of both istituti and scuole magistrali but would make them both 5-year institutions until the overall secondary school reform law abolishes them.

Thus, the major characteristics of future nursery school teacher training are already visible in present attempts at legislation. First of all, training in special secondary schools will last 5 years (and content will obviously increase proportionately). Secondly, university instruction, as required by Decree No. 417, will be provided along the following lines (what follows is a synthesis of recent proposals):

■ **A 2- or 3-year university program:** Various proposals of this kind provide for (1) a standard short program open to any future nursery school or elementary school teacher; (2) a 2-year specialized program for future nursery school teachers, plus a 3-year specialized program for future elementary school teachers; or (3) a special short course open only to potential nursery school teachers.

■ **A 4-year university-degree course:** This proposal for training nursery school and elementary school teachers includes two possible alternatives, namely, (1) two distinct programs leading to two distinct degrees and (2) a common program for prospective nursery school and prospective elementary school teachers for the first 2 years of university instruction, followed by 2 years of specialization for each in their chosen fields.

■ **A 4-year university-degree course:** This proposed course would qualify the student to teach in secondary schools and be followed by specialized training for those graduates intending to teach in nursery schools or elementary schools.

Frabboni (1984) gives us an idea of what a future nursery school teacher ought to have in the way of university instruction. He clearly opts for the longer kind of program. First of all, however, he recalls the need for a *new* kind of university-degree course in educational sciences, one that would ensure specific professional ability to solve pedagogical and didactic problems: "The new degree course, although it would still have to satisfy traditional requirements not yet abolished, would provide for (a) a functional program of studies . . . (functional with respect to the capacities to be acquired) . . . , (b) three levels of professional competence . . . (theoretical, practical, and interactional, or in other terms, knowledge, know-how, and relational skill)." As far as inservice training is concerned, he proposes "diversified programs providing for both individual and group retraining, either in the teacher's own community or elsewhere" (p. 98).

Frabboni's proposals are obviously a far cry from the situation in present-day Italy, where inservice training depends on spontaneous, personal initiatives undertaken by individual teachers. Courses are inevitably outside their home communities, thus requiring them to face the expenses of room and board. The courses themselves are spontaneously organized by "experts," self-styled or otherwise, who often lack firsthand knowledge of the teachers' real needs; teachers generally find these courses too abstract and of little use. Frabboni's idea of inservice training involves organizing the teachers *within* a given community into a permanent retraining program that would be based on whatever experimental work any of them might be involved in.

Local government participation and financing

Current law attributes preprimary education both to national and local government, the latter including communal and regional administrations. This many-sided approach is most felt in the areas of "scholastic assistance,"[9] logistics, and current operations. Scholastic assistance has been the responsibility of regional administrations since 1977; the administrative functions are handled by communal officials according to guidelines established by the regional administrations. The old School Assistance Centers (created in 1911) have been eliminated, and their services and facilities have been transferred to the communes. Thus, the economics of preprimary education involves communal, regional, and national government.

Specifically, the **communes** are responsible for medical and psychological services for students; assistance for handicapped students; the furnishing of suitable buildings and their upkeep, heating, and lighting; the installation of a telephone and the payment of all charges; cleaning and surveillance personnel; school bus service; furnishing and running a school cafeteria or meal service. (Bus and meal services were subsequently attributed to local agencies by Presidential Decrees No. 3/1972 and No. 616/1977.) The **regional administrations** are responsible for building new schools (Decree No. 616/1977 transferred the responsibility of school construction from national government, as had been specified under Law No. 444, to the regional administrations). Finally, **national government** has the exclusive responsibility of taking care of nursery school staff payrolls, nursery school furnishings, teaching materials, and all other equipment used in the care and education of the children. Once installed, the furniture and supplies become the property of the communes, with the proviso that the material be used permanently in the nursery schools.

It is worth dwelling for a moment on two important communal responsiblities that influence and interact with the nursery schools' educational program: the meal and school bus services. These services have caused a flurry of discussions among the teachers and also among communal and national authorities. Since the law does not state clearly who is responsible for what, the elimination of assistants in the nursery schools has meant that teachers themselves have been called upon to accompany the children when they are riding the bus to and from school and when they are eating lunch. Certain technical problems arise: The law obliges the teachers to be present in the school at the same time it would have them out in a school bus; it is apparently the teachers who are to watch over the children during lunch, yet the law specifically forbids meal services for the teachers themselves. Are they to skip lunch to watch over the children eating?

Bus and meal services are being increasingly requested by families. Between the 1970–71 and 1984–85 school years, the number of children served by busses went from 15,208 to 117,212; the number using meal services went from 103,595 to 643,359. The 1984–85 figures represent, out of the total student population, a 27 percent participation in the bus service and an 82 percent participation in the meal service.

The national government budget for nursery schools has increased continually to keep up with the demand. The overall allocation has grown from 24,995,000,000 lires in 1970 to 547,806,156,000 lires in 1980. (At the time, this was equivalent to growing from about 40 million to 365 million dollars U.S.) The payroll absorbs an increasingly larger share of available funds; in 1980 it took up 85 percent of the budget (*La scuola materna in Italia*, 1982).

The 1969 *Guidelines for Educational Activities*

The Ministry of Education *Guidelines for Educational Activities in State Nursery Schools* was issued in 1969 to satisfy the requirements of Article 2 of Law No. 444 passed the previous year. In the first part of the publication, the ministry states general goals. The headings of the various sections, as listed below, give an idea of the contents:

- Aims of nursery school care and what education should strive for
- The teacher's freedom and responsibilities in the classroom
- Nursery schools and the family
- The need for nursery schools in present-day society
- The child's personality
- Children in a changing world
- The personalities of teachers and assistants
- The educational aspects of child care
- Specific forms of educational activities

In the second part of the publication, the ministry deals specifically with educational questions. Again, the headings will give an idea of the contents:

- Religious education
- Sentimental, emotional, moral, and social education
- Play and constructive activities; everyday activities
- Educating the mind

- Linguistic skills
- Free expression in drawing, painting, or modeling
- Musical education
- Physical education
- Individual and group activities

The *Guidelines* takes into consideration the most advanced psycho-pedagogical research available at the time. The child is to be rooted in the historical reality in which he lives. His childhood needs are to be respected, in particular his need to move, to explore, to assert himself, to make believe, to communicate, and to socialize. The didactic observations and suggestions offered in the *Guidelines* appear quite acceptable. This makes the parts dedicated to religious considerations seem even more contradictory. But even that part of the publication represents a definite step forward with respect to the 1958 *Guidelines* published for non-state nursery schools, so much so that getting the 1969 edition to press took a strenuous tug-of-war with Vatican authorities (who went so far as to remind the ministry, while the *Guidelines* was being written, of the commitments contained in the concordat signed by Mussolini—an intrusion contrasting with the church's public declarations in favor of freedom of religious beliefs and with the liberal attitudes that had been emphasized during Vatican Council II). Although the 1969 *Guidelines* bears the traces of traditional Roman Catholic influence, it does remind teachers that all children are to be considered equal insofar as religious beliefs are concerned. Also, although the *Guidelines* continues to pay homage to such outworn stereotypes as the teacher "mother-figure" and the teacher "missionary," it does mention the need for specific professional skills. The teacher must "have sound training in the basics, which means a high level of overall instruction and knowledge of the specific fields of pedagogy, psychology, and sociology. She must have personality traits that permit her to establish a well-balanced emotional relationship with the children. Her inner emotional equilibrium should be enriched with optimism, a sense of humor, lightheartedness; by no means should she be given to anxiety, overexcitability, bad temper, intolerance, distrust. She should have a diagnostic ability in order to bring to the attention of the medical authorities any illness, physical disturbances, or irregular development a child may have; she should likewise be able to diagnose problems involving the child's character and mental development. She should be able to lend a hand in whatever treatment is called for" (paragraph 5). This then, is the portrait of what a teacher should be like according to the *Guidelines*. One can only marvel at the scant preparation that the self-same ministry continued to provide for teachers in the years that followed.

There are, of course, unclear and ambiguous affirmations in the *Guidelines*. But as a rule, it certainly does give us a glimpse of a new kind of educator in the nursery school classroom, from both cultural and pedagogical standpoints. Furthermore, it tends to confer a specific autonomy to nursery school education, as distinct from elementary schooling. Thus, the *Guidelines* represents a positive chapter in the history of child care in Italy, notwithstanding that it is now outdated and that the principles it espoused were actually put into practice in very few places.

The future of the *Guidelines*

Many factors, some extrinsic and some intrinsic to the *Guidelines*, have led educators to request a new edition or its complete replacement. Since it appeared, there have been many developments both in educational policy and in social, psychological, and educational research; social and economic conditions in Italy have changed greatly as well.

The 1984 inspectors' reports (Serena, 1986) show that there is a widespread request among teachers for a revised edition of the *Guidelines*. They want a revision that takes into consideration the concept of educational programming and gives specific educational goals to reach instead of general talk about mental processes, one that takes into consideration the "points of contact with the elementary school" (these points involve didactics, curriculum, and schoolroom procedures).

Frabboni (1985) claims that the weak points in the *Guidelines* are (1) its incertitude as to contents and methods in teaching and (2) its vagueness as to intermediate and final educational goals. The didactic value of the *Guidelines* is beginning to wear thin; the theoretical foundations invoked are not organic; the cognitive aspects of education are superficially treated and divided into eight "pre-subjects" (taken lock, stock, and barrel from elementary school curriculum). There is no idea as to how to formulate a coherent curriculum. The real solution, Frabboni concludes, would be the approval of a detailed program for nursery schools that would connect them with and give them a status similar to that of elementary and middle schools. Nursery school would then be a genuine first step. Frabboni's suggestion is a program based on Bruno Ciari's New Model for Educational Practice.

Extension and distribution of the state nursery school system

The geographical distribution of the new nursery schools and classes has strictly followed the dispositions contained in Law No. 444. This means that the ministry has given priority to those areas where preprimary schooling was totally absent, to the economically depressed areas, and to the areas with accelerated urban growth (through immigration or a natural increase in population).

Up to the school year 1977–78 the number of schools increased steadily each year (except for 1969–70, in which no new schools were instituted because funds were not allocated). From 1978 on, however, the annual increase began to slow down. This was mainly due to the rising financial demands placed on the state nursery school budget by the schools already built (and specifically by the operating costs, which skyrocketed when two teachers were assigned to every class, as provided by Law No. 463 in 1978). The slowdown in school construction was also due to the general policy of cuts in public spending that had come into effect. A slight drop in the total demand for nursery school services was only a marginal cause (see Table 2).

The geographical increase in nursery schools was strongest in the South and on the Islands (principally Sicily and Sardinia). Given the initial disadvantage of these areas with respect to northern and central Italy, one might surmise that all inequality has been definitively wiped out. In reality, one has only to examine the general socioeconomic conditions in the South to realize that it would not be wise to sit back satisfied;

Table 2

ANNUAL INCREASE IN STATE NURSERY SCHOOLS, 1976–77 TO 1982–83

School Year	School Units	Annual Increase
1976–77	10,434	
1977–78	11,430	+996
1978–79	11,890	+460
1979–80	12,334	+444
1980–81	12,633	+299
1981–82	12,861	+228
1982–83	13,202	+341

Note. Reelaboration of data from the Central Statistics Institute (ISTAT), *Annuario Statistico dell'Istruzione* [Annual Abstract of Educational Statistics], and the Ministry of Education, *La Scuola Materna in Italia* [Nursery Schools in Italy] (1982).

if anything, more and more timely school construction is needed, despite the favorable comparisons with growth in other areas.

The gap between the North and South still remains and is not simply a question of number. In fact, the gap is qualitative and involves the kind of service offered. What happens is that requests for new nursery schools are generously met by the national government, but local administrations are not able to assure the financing necessary to cover the operational costs of the new institutions. This general lack of funds for important social services characterizes southern administrations and has dire effects on schools, both from the standpoint of daily operations and from the standpoint of educational goals achieved.

Trends in state nursery school enrollment

Enrollment in the state nursery school system rose from 68,462 in the first year of its existence (of which 31,465 was enrollment in southern Italy) to 787,913 in the school year 1985–86. In spite of a fall in birthrate during recent years, statistics show an overall steady increase in nursery school enrollment (Table 3).

After the state system's first year, up through 1975–76, the annual percent of increase was greater in the Center and North than in the South. (For example, the increase for 1972–73 was 61 percent in the North, 50 percent in the Center, and only 36 percent in the South.) The more rapid increase in the North may be explained in two ways: (1) The North had to make up for an initial disadvantage in state services available (due to a certain resistance to the state system, the North did not take full advantage of the law immediately after its passage). (2) Previous to the law, the North had already been obliged to institute a locally administered nursery school system to handle the large increase in childhood population (in Lombardy and Piedmont), which was due to immigration of workers from the South; this situation had already favored massive state grants in the years 1970–75, aimed at helping these economically disadvantaged areas to face the problems caused by such factors as urban concentration, a largely employed female population, and the coexistence of different cultures and extractions.

This being said, and in spite of the percentage increases in enrollment in the various geographical areas, statistics still show a clear advantage of the Center and South over the North with respect to the availability of state nursery school services. Even if one compares potential demand and services offered, the South comes out more favorably.

Table 3

TRENDS IN STATE NURSERY SCHOOL ENROLLMENT, 1968–69 TO 1983–84

School Year	Northern Italy	Central Italy	Southern Italy	Islands	Total
1968–69	13,171	9,183	31,465	14,643	68,462
1969–70	16,266	12,263	37,522	18,735	84,786
1970–71	30,079	22,559	56,866	24,292	133,796
1971–72	48,327	39,121	86,860	32,509	206,817
1972–73	77,635	58,799	117,868	40,875	295,177
1973–74	102,228	76,751	144,723	47,524	371,226
1974–75	127,619	92,957	168,828	56,340	445,744
1975–76	151,717	106,930	192,578	67,019	518,244
1976–77	172,535	123,724	218,362	75,998	590,619
1977–78	189,958	132,153	242,022	84,969	649,102
1978–79	200,402	138,240	261,542	94,259	694,443
1979–80	204,749	144,173	283,872	98,953	731,747
1980–81	209,837	148,107	295,897	104,881	758,722
1981–82	204,463	148,623	300,884	108,731	762,701
1982–83	202,524	148,927	309,454	111,165	772,070
1983–84	198,588	146,004	313,597	114,489	774,678

Note. Data are from the Central Statistics Institute (ISTAT), *Annuario Statistico dell'Istruzione* [Annual Abstract of Educational Statistics], and the Ministry of Education, *La Scuola Materna in Italia* [Nursery Schools in Italy] (1982).

Data regarding staff: The student-teacher ratio

The increase in enrollment has generated a similar increase in staff. In the 1983–84 school year, the Italian state employed 61,120 nursery school teachers; that figure rose to 64,773 the following year. A comparison between increases in enrollment and increases in staff shows a greater proportional increase in the *latter*; thus the student-teacher ratio has gradually improved, going from 24 to 1 in the 1968–69 school year to 12 to 1 in 1980–81. The much-improved student-teacher ratio is due not to a decrease in student population but rather to the widepread implementation, beginning in 1979, of the extended child care schedules; when most state nursery schools began to remain open 8, 9, or 10 hours a day, it became necessary to have 2 teachers per class. Thus, although the 1984–85 student-teacher ratio was only 12.1 to 1, there were nevertheless 24.6 children per class. Male staff members have slowly begun to appear in nursery schools, but there were only 135 male teachers employed in

1985–86 (in 1980–81, male staff members in *any* capacity constituted only 0.21 percent of total personnel).

Utilization of different timetables

In the 1984–85 school year 20,098 (out of 31,811) schools followed a daily timetable of 8, 9, or 10 hours. These figures reflect a general tendency towards full-day provision. Schools that have a 5-hour timetable are for the most part located in the South and have not been provided with either a meal service or supporting staff by their local authority. For the longer timetable, the norm is 8 hours, while a 9th hour may be used for travel. A 10th hour is only provided in a very few cases, usually in areas of heavy industry. There is also an increasing provision of a "short week" timetable, which consists of 6 hours a day for 5 days a week. This model allows staff to have Saturdays off and, where a full-day program is in operation, increases double-staffing.

STATE NURSERY SCHOOLS COMPARED WITH OTHERS

In this section we summarize the main points that emerge from the inspectors' reports of 1984–85 (Serena, 1986; Lucchini, 1986) and from the latest available data. We then take a closer look at issues affecting both state and non-state institutions.

Nursery school enrollments—including state and non-state schools—in 1983–84 numbered 1,695,911 and covered 84.9 percent of 3- to 5-year-olds; in 1984–85 they stood at 1,639,000, covering 86.2 percent of 3- to 5-year-olds; in 1985–86 the figure was 1,633,000, covering 87.8 percent of the relevant population. During these 3 school years, as Table 4 indicates, there was some growth in state nursery schools (ISTAT data for the last 3 years show this growth to be mainly in the South and the Islands). State schools represent almost half of the total national figure for each of the years shown in the table. Population decline, however, has slowed state enrollment increases.

Non-state nursery schools, in contrast, have experienced a steady drop-off, according to Table 4. The reasons for this decline are many and complex. The main ones can be identified as (1) population decline; (2) local authorities' economic difficulties; and (3) increased running costs coupled, in the case of those run by religious bodies, with staffing problems due to the crisis affecting religious vocations. As a result, the last few years have seen several non-state schools close, to be replaced by state nursery schools. This tendency holds not only for nursery schools

Table 4

ITALY'S NURSERY SCHOOL ENROLLMENT, STATE AND NON-STATE, FOR 3 RECENT YEARS

School Year	Non-State	State	Total	% Coverage of 3–5's
83–84	921,233	774,678	1,695,911	84.9
84–85	853,699	795,708	1,639,000	86.2
85–86	835,149	787,913	1,633,000	87.8

Note. Statistics are from the Central Statistics Institute (ISTAT).

run by private individuals and by religious or lay bodies, but also for communal nursery schools, due to cuts in funding. This phenomenon has so far affected only certain communes, but it has brought out a need for institutional changes, for an overall strategy of halting this gradual passive handing-over of communal schools to the state, for a strategy that would instead bring the two kinds of public nursery schools together. However, we must point out that increased enrollments in state nursery schools are due not only to takeovers of non-state institutions but also to the setting up, over the last few years, of state nursery schools in areas that previously had none at all. Apart from having falling enrollments, however, non-state nursery schools, especially those that are privately run, are presently the better-organized ones in the large and medium-sized population centers, where they most frequently compete with state schools. They are known to have greater flexibility (regarding such things as hours of operation, enrollment deadlines, and adaptation to foreign languages). They also provide educational services that some families demand, such as so-called *primine* (explained in a later section). Since non-state nursery schools concentrate primarily on urban areas, outer suburbs and rural areas are being progressively abandoned, at least until the state decides to take action. Agricultural and needy areas may have one or two state nursery schools, at times with only one or two classes; they will have no others.

As things stand, an estimated 350,000 preschool-aged children remain outside the nursery school system. "The main reasons why children remain outside the school system are a lack of school buildings (especially in the South and Islands); female unemployment due to the crisis in production; the survival of a type of family structure, in certain areas, that makes nursery schools redundant; and the veto on setting up a state nursery school for fewer than 13 children, or for fewer than 10 if this includes a handicapped child. Those most likely to suffer exclusion are children living in such out-of-the-way places as mountain areas and small islands. For them, the only educational opportunities come from the family or the small local community, but they come in a non-systematic, informal form; the only alternative source is the mass media, which may at times produce a rather negative conditioning" (Serena, 1986, p. 200).

Educational Innovation and Experimentation

Experimentation—or more generally speaking, innovation—in state-run nursery schools dates back to the 1960s. It has been concentrated in certain parts of northern and central Italy. There are also at present many examples of "experimentation" in non-state nursery schools. Indeed, one can state that the liveliest innovative tradition belongs to certain private- or local-authority schools. Unfortunately, it is impossible to draw a precise map of the phenomenon. There are few published records, and the evidence they provide is often incomplete. Moreover, since non-state schools are not obliged to have their experimentation officially sanctioned, even schools that experiment all the time and in very advanced ways may well not be registered as experimental schools. However, the practice of circulating information via professional magazines and through conferences at both the regional and the national level is becoming increasingly established.

The most striking examples of innovation are to be found among particularly active and inventive schools run by local authorities in various parts of northern, central and, more recently, even southern Italy. Perspicacious administrators have organized refresher courses for staff, forms of collaboration with universities, and teams to monitor the schools. They have also offered financial help with the implementation of specific innovative proposals. Current innovation in these schools nearly always follows the line developed in the Emilia region (more specifically, in Bologna) in the 1960s, namely, Bruno Ciari's New Model for Educational Practice.

Experimentation, understood as an expression of teachers' didactic autonomy, was introduced into state schools of every type and every level by Decree No. 419[10] in 1974, although it did not become a reality until 1977. The decree categorized experimentation as (1) research and innovation regarding teaching methods and (2) research and innovation regarding regulations and structures. The experimentation must take the form of research and study and must be concrete.

Category-1 experimentation, concerned primarily with how to teach, can be proposed by teachers and approved by the Teachers' Council, with no need for any authorization by the ministry (Article 2). Category-2 experimentation, which is institutional, must be authorized by the Ministry of Education. A proposal must be forwarded to the Ministry of Education by the school, together with the opinion of the regional research institutes (IRRSAE). The proposal sets out the question to be studied, the working hypotheses, the organization and means, the costs, the methodological procedures, and the assessment procedures. The ministry authorizes such experiments annually, at the same time that it decides on subjects and timetables and deals with the make-up of pedagogic committees (Article 3). The final administrative stage comes with the transmission of the results, and their assessment, to the school's bureaucratic and elected bodies, to the regional research institutes, and to the minister, who passes them on to the National Council.

Compared with other types of school research, the research in state nursery schools is a relatively recent phenomenon. "There are still only a few state schools that have completed experimental projects and can be considered innovative. Their [the projects'] distribution has hardly been rational, either. Nevertheless, they have multiplied over the last few years, partly as a result of fashion and partly due to a greater awareness of the issues on the part of teachers and administrators. Often, however, associated problems involving logistics or availability of material militate against any innovation, or even against the continuation of any activity after 1 p.m." (Kanizza, 1986).

Institutional experiments (as per Decree 419/1974, Article 3) generally concern curricular and organizational continuity between nursery school and elementary school; earlier schooling; early bilingualism; integrating handicapped children into the schools; nonadaptation to school; organization of educational spaces, timetables, and activities; psychomotor education; and teaching models for nursery schools and the first cycle of primary school. Some projects involve more than one type of school; others are specific to the 3–6 age group. Some are spread over several years; others are completed within a single school year.

These are the common features of experiments governed by Article 3 of Decree 419/1974: The experimenting teachers wish to ensure continuity with elementary school, so that they can measure the long-term effects of what they are doing; refresher courses and inservice training precede and accompany the experiment; the study and use of means of assessment is widespread. Experimenters, without exception, want their own experiments to be taken note of and discussed.

Experiments took place in 1977–78 in 22 schools in 6 provinces; in 1978–79, in 43 schools in 10 provinces; in 1979–80, in 10 provinces; in 1980–81, in 64 schools in 16 provinces; in 1981–82, in 44 schools in 13 provinces. In 1985–86 around 30 institutions were experimenting. The number of schools involved, however, was higher than 30, since several experiments involved more than a single school. The experiments were concentrated in the North and Center of Italy; except for one experiment in Sicily, the South and the Islands remained uninvolved. Although there are more state nursery schools in the South, experiments have been concentrated in the North and Center, areas in which the cultural influence of nursery schools run by local authorities is more strongly felt.

The precise number of these institutional experiments is known, and documentation regarding them is complete. But there have also been numerous other innovative measures (in line with Article 2 of Decree 419/1974) as well as attempts at cultural and professional renewal by teachers. Regarding these measures and attempts, it is hard to assess their worth, get access to documentation, or glean full information. "It is usually a case of experiments carried out without full scientific rigor. They nevertheless bear witness to the demand for research into innovative procedures. They are also a valid cultural stimulus for many teachers and lead to practical improvements in educational performance" (Serena, 1986, p. 200).

Silvia Kanizza (1986, pp. 286–304) has correctly pointed out the salient features of experimentation and of the literature on the subject, as regards both state and non-state nursery schools, and highlights from her analysis are given here. The literature includes expertly drawn-up proposals that are well developed and based on sound pedagogical and psychological criteria, as well as accounts of experiments that are rich in photographs but poor in detailed comment. The few well-thought-out analyses tend to be signed by the "experts" who assisted the teacher, while the more fragmentary descriptions come from groups of teachers or collectives. Kanizza writes, "Experimental projects and experiments that are correct from every point of view (that is, complete with hypotheses, method, evaluation, and control groups) are in fact almost nonexistent in infant [early childhood] schools. . . . In the majority of cases, even in those in which the term *experiment* is used, many features that are essential for the project as a whole are missing. For example, the hypotheses are taken for granted, and evaluation is not carried out at all but simply indicated generically as being possible, or else taken as redundant, in view of the manifest 'happiness' of the children. [Furthermore] . . . the term *experimental* is used inaccurately. Almost any kind of alteration in habitual procedure, however sketchily designed, gets labeled 'experimental.' In this way, the distinction between experiment and innovation, that is, between a scientifically based procedure and potential attempts at improving teaching practice, cannot hold for everyday practice, in which the two terms are used and abused to describe practices that have very little that is experimental or innovative about them."

Kanizza's analysis continues, "What even the best attempts completely lack is any comparison with different models and different educational situations; these could serve as a control. . . . In general the only accepted assessment criterion is whether the children or their parents were pleased, that is, 'social validation' as opposed to validation based on an analysis of changes that took place or of differences between divergent systems. . . . Innovations are accepted on the basis of political or ideological convictions, at most for timeliness, but never for subsequent testing. This is apparent, too, from the highly didactic tone given to the proposals. The very idea of experimentation, or even semiexperimentation, has gone missing in recent years. . . . The idea that nursery schools are simply parking areas, with no significant educational implications, may have had an influence on the lack of any experimental planning that took into account points of departure and subsequent learning. So far, then, we have gone no further than a first level, that of changing structures, either wholly or in part. Some experiments have taken a further step, that of a reasoned approach, but we are still far from genuine experimentation. We may indeed feel that these are the first steps, considering also the general level of preparation of the staff, who—and this is important—seem unable to implement changes by themselves. . . . Things only work when there are experts on hand to help and supervise."

The Politico-Pedagogical Debate: Issues and Perspectives

The principal current issues in the politico-pedagogical debate on nursery education are as follows:

a. Staff training, a long-standing but still heated issue, which we dealt with in an earlier section.

b. Reform of the *Guidelines*; the issues involved were discussed in an earlier section.

c. Organization of both state and non-state nursery schools into a single national system.

d. Establishment of continuity between day nurseries and nursery schools, and between the latter and compulsory schooling.

e. Establishment of independent headships and elected governing bodies for nursery schools.

f. Lowering the starting age for compulsory education.

g. Improvement of nursery schools in the South of Italy, including the Islands.

Experts in the field have been concerned with these issues for several years now, and lately families have become interested as well. Recent episodes have added to this list two further issues, which we will discuss first:

h. Teaching of the Roman Catholic religion, and Education Minister Falcucci's program for doing it.

i. Adjustment of the nursery school calendar.

In the wake of the new 1984 Concordat between the Holy See and the Italian government and the subsequent 1985 Accord between the minister of education, Falcucci, and the chairman of the Italian Episcopal Commission, ministerial circulars have been issued regarding the application of the Accord as it affects religious teaching in state schools. The ministerial measures have aroused discontent and opposition among all types of people who work in schools, at every level. In particular the "new" religious programs for nursery schools (which are also the first), have aroused a great deal of puzzlement and opposition.

Lamberto Borghi, Egle Becchi, and Loris Malaguzzi have helped to clarify the basic issues with interesting articles from which we have taken the following remarks:

"State schools cannot set themselves up as propagators of specific religious faiths without abdicating their essential function, that of guaranteeing equal freedom of education to all pupils" (Borghi, 1986, pp. 6–7).

"There is a real risk that introducing religious instruction in nursery schools would impose upon them a rigid organization that negates the atmosphere of play and free discovery that ought to be theirs. Moreover, pedagogical and psychological principles warn against inculcating the idea of God too early" (Becchi, 1986, pp. 8–9).

"Teaching the Catholic religion—as stipulated in the Accord—would leave the pedagogical and cultural raison d'être of nursery schools deformed. It would mean inflicting absolutely unacceptable violence on children, families, and teachers" (Malaguzzi, 1986, pp. 3–5).

With regard to adjustment of the nursery school calendar, there is a demand for it to be brought into line with that for other types of school. A significant consensus in favor of this change has even emerged within the National Educational Council, though only as regards sharply cutting the number of days of attendance.

Now let us take a closer look at the other issues we have not yet discussed, points c, d, e, f, and g.

A single national system

A Christian Democrat proposal (No. 1839, June 26, 1984) regarding non-state education looked to an "integrated system" for nursery schools, in which state, communal, and "autonomous" schools (the last-named being those run by private individuals or by religious or lay organizations) would be placed on the same footing, with autonomous schools becoming almost totally state-financed. This has sparked off a lively debate, from which new proposals are emerging. Everyone accepts the idea of a national system capable of overseeing relations between the various managements and of unifying nursery education, but diversity and the principle of institutional pluralism must be respected, as provided by the Constitution. The distinction between schools for everyone (meaning those under state and local authority—clearly public) and those with ideological connotations must also be respected. There is agreement that the latter should not be ignored, but neither should they be placed on the same level as the others. An alternative proposal to the Christian Democrat one could be summed up in the following terms: a national public system (state plus local-authority nursery schools), backed up by a set of national-level guidelines (a national Convention) that would regulate state, regional, and local authority measures to support autonomous schools and that would set certain conditions for the autonomous schools. This would supersede the existing intricate network of conventions.

Continuity between school levels

The issue of continuity between nursery school and elementary school has been given new impetus following publication of the **New Elementary School Programs** (the Falcucci Programs, Decree No. 104, February 12, 1985, in effect from 1987). These recognize the need to build links with nursery education at the pedagogical, curricular, and organizational levels. The proposal to recognize nursery schools as the first rung of basic education (nursery, elementary, middle) falls within this framework, as does that of bringing the compulsory school-starting age forward to cover the final year of nursery school. The demand for a genuine curriculum to be provided for nursery schools can be seen in the same light. Well-conducted studies (under the guidance of university experts) have continuously enriched the debate on continuity between nursery schools and both day nurseries and primary schools.

Headships and governing bodies

Falcucci's contested proposal to legally bring nursery and elementary schools together under joint administration also follows the path of continuity, at least as regards organization. Since 1968, the administration of nursery schools has been "provisionally" entrusted to the head of the local primary school. The idea that nursery schools should be completely autonomous, even in this respect, has had majority support ever since. Insistent demands for autonomy within the ministry, through the setting up of a specific General Directorate, are being added to those for institutional autonomy at lower levels.

The precarious, marginalized position in which nursery schools often have to operate, because the problem of how to manage them has been left unresolved, also affects the working of their elected governing bodies. According to Decree No. 416/1974, state nursery schools are not administratively autonomous, but dependent on the elementary school to which they are linked. Only two teachers from each nursery school can become elected participants on the district School Council of their associated elementary school. Nursery school parents, moreover, cannot elect even a single representative to these management bodies. In contrast to this, in many local-authority nursery schools, there are rather progressive regulations regarding management and parent participation. As for autonomous nursery schools, various models are followed—conservative in some cases, progressive in others. Overall then, just as autonomous administration is being sought, so too are autonomous, participatory nursery-school management bodies. A legislative project for a "national public nursery school system" must deal adequately with this issue, too.

School-starting age

The debate on the school-starting age began several years ago. People are sharply divided in favor of either age 5 or age 6. At present, the age is 6. Those who favor 5, however, are further divided between those who hold that 5-year-olds should begin with an extra year of elementary school and those who hold that 5-year-olds should attend a final year of nursery school—reformed nursery school, of course. A further alternative has also been put forward: that there should be a specially designed 2-year bridging period between nursery school and primary school, jointly supervised by both schools, to serve both 5- and 6-year-olds. Some of these arguments were settled, and new ones started, by Falcucci's draft bill of 1985, which made it possible to enroll children aged 5½ in elementary school. Having children accepted into primary school earlier meets some of the demands and requests put forward by families. It also puts an end to the lucrative (especially for nursery schools under Roman Catholic control) phenomenon of so-called *primine*, whereby the child covers the first year of elementary school privately, after which he or she sits for admission to the second year of elementary school and thus gets a year ahead of peers. Falcucci's draft bill measure may also, at least in part, bring the debate on lowering the school-starting age, and the effects of this on both nursery schools and elementary schools, to a premature conclusion.

School improvement in the South and Islands

One must also denounce the grave disparity still existing between preschool services in the North and those in the South, in spite of the development of nursery education over the last few years. As well as needing more of them, the South suffers severe problems regarding the conditions of its nursery school buildings. Sixty percent of southern nursery schools are housed on temporary sites: in flats within apartment blocks, in shops, in historical buildings, in basements, or else within primary schools. Many schools in the South cannot provide canteen services; only 52 percent of them provide a hot meal, as against 98 percent in the North. Because they lack canteen or meal service, the schools can only operate for 5 hours a day. Social and health support facilities are often lacking as well. Transport services are equally inadequate, and in some inland areas, almost nonexistent.

One of the most conspicuous causes of the North-South divide, in both quantitative and qualitative terms, is southern local authorities' lack of involvement in preschool provision. Although it is they who are entrusted with opening state nursery schools, these local authorities are often not in a position to perform the tasks attributed to them by law, or else they simply do not try. In the view of experts on services for very young children in the South and on the Islands, the current refusal of many southern local authorities to encourage nursery schools (and day nurseries) and provide them with adequate support is due not so much to their objective economic difficulties as to their lack of an ethos oriented towards organizing, programming, and managing services. These administrators therefore need to be involved more directly in the problems and management of such services and not relegated to a merely bureaucratic or welfare role. To improve the nursery school service in the South, the state must provide a more realistic, better-programmed southern policy (in line with the current policy of giving the South priority when it comes to implementing new measures).

In planning new measures, which are wanted, the state must not only concern itself with providing services where none exist and with strengthening those that do exist; it must also concern itself with the quality of its measures. This it can do by means of (1) programmed development of nursery school buildings (including improvement of school building regulations, so as to avoid the usual nonspending of regional funds); (2) widening canteen services to include all nursery schools; (3) improving teaching quality, by encouraging research and innovation and by implementing a wide-ranging program of inservice refresher courses for existing staff.

AN URBAN STUDY OF CHILDREN'S CARE AND EDUCATION SERVICES

This section summarizes the situation regarding services for very young children in towns and cities, outlining service characteristics on the basis of a survey carried out in 1982–83 in eight urban areas. The survey was an inquiry into the quality of services and levels of parental satisfaction with them. Subjects were 2,000 urban Italian families with children in the 0–5 age-bracket. The choice of Milan, Treviso, Bologna, Ascoli Piceno, Napoli, Matera, Trapani, and Sassari was made because each has geographic and economic features that make it particularly interesting and significant. The survey was carried out by the Centro Studi Investimenti Sociali (CENSIS) on behalf of the Direzione Generale dei Servizi Civili of the Ministero dell'Interno.

Two items from the CENSIS survey seem of particular significance for the aims of this report: (1) the choice and utilization of services and (2) family organization and the role of relatives in the care and education of children 0 to 5 years of age. It also seems worthwhile to take a very brief glance at health and welfare services designed for very young children.

"The available services for very young children . . . are still, overall, quantitatively insufficient. They are especially insufficient

- For the under-3's (compared to the 3- to 6-year-olds)
- With regard to prevention and integration (compared to treatment and welfare)
- In new working-class urban areas (compared to inner-city and residential areas)
- Regarding social welfare (compared to health care)
- In terms of recreation, green spaces, play equipment, and play leadership" (CENSIS, 1984, p. 22)

The number and range of services available, the supply of equipment, and the presence of qualified staff is markedly less in central and southern Italy, where private enterprise takes on a more active role to fill gaps left by the state.

The welfare situtation differs among the eight cities, yet the quality and variety of services has scarcely evolved in any of them. Most measures taken are of a traditional, economic nature. There is a lack of any service such as home help. Although the number of needy and abandoned children taken into institutional care remains high, it is in decline almost everywhere. Still, neither the number of institutions nor the number of bed places has fallen. In Milan, such institutions are run in conjunction with the commune, which oversees them, whereas the other communes in the sample often delegated this service to private institutions and failed to supervise the welfare services provided.

Almost all the communes in the sample have sought to limit institutionalization and to replace it with care within the family. Only in Bologna, however, has the latter overtaken the former. "The most innovative alternative to institutionalization is to be found in Bologna, which has the lowest percentage of children taken into institutional care. There an Infant Welfare Protection body has been set up. Organized on an apartment-group basis, it tries to resolve the 'toughest' cases by taking charge of the children until the best family solution can be found, whether this involves the original family nucleus or an adopted one. . . . 'Families at risk' are given priority almost everywhere, using the existing facilities for minors and reducing or waiving charges (for example, for day nurseries). Only in Naples is a partly boarding approach applied to minors from 3 to 18 years old: The Province of Naples has 80 purpose-built units which in 1981 functioned as full-time schools for around 7,000 children and adolescents" (CENSIS, 1984, pp. 21–22).

On the health front, the main deficiencies concern school medical services (except in Milan and Bologna) and early preventive measures (except in Milan). There are not enough public pediatric services anywhere, so parents have to turn to private practioners, even regarding disturbances of a rather serious nature. Second-level pediatric services, however, are vastly more organized and numerous in terms of both location and utilization. This demonstrates how priority is given to treatment rather than to monitoring the child's development. The health services have played a fundamental role in cutting the rate of infant mortality, especially in the last 10 years. Nevertheless, the national rate for Italy is still higher than the average for the more-advanced European countries.

Education and the child

Regarding nursery schools, supply almost meets demand in all of the sample cities (95 percent of children obtain nursery school places), but what nursery schools offer children varies according to the local authority. Offerings can also vary from one school to another within the same commune's jurisdiction. Further variation stems from competition among the various types of management: state, local-authority, or private (35 percent of day nurseries and nursery schools are private). The differences primarily have to do with service infrastructures (meals and transportation), the condition of the buildings, landscaping, staff numbers and qualifications, and medical help. Northern commune facilities are the ones that work best. Placement and care of handicapped children is best in public schools. Private establishments serve primarily children who come from the upper and middle classes, whereas public services have a more socially heterogeneous clientele, especially in the big cities. Working-class children and children from broken homes are granted a reduction in the monthly fees to encourage attendance, at both day nurseries and nursery schools. Parent participation in the running of either kind of institution is uniformly minimal.

What can be said about the quality of the services is less satisfactory than what has been said about their quantity. Overall, the provision and maturity of services is greater in the large cities of northern Italy— cities with a well-developed advanced-service sector, where one finds more employed women, where very small families are more isolated and more fragile, and where the people give more voice to their needs. In the towns and cities of central and southern Italy (but also in smaller towns in the North), "the supply side goes its own way, often without involving the population or knowing its needs, with no real planning, without efficiency and with dubious efficacy" (CENSIS, 1984, p. 36).

Families' behavior with regard to the relationship between supply and demand is often contradictory—using yet distrusting (or remaining indifferent to) the services offered; asking for free public services, yet paying for private ones—a mixture of criticism and passive exploitation at the same time. In general, families "cobble together" solutions by taking advantage of some public services, backing these up with domestic help, and spending something on private services, too.

Public versus private services

Private services do not always aim to fill gaps left by public services. There is no coordination between the two. The resulting duplication, waste of resources, and competition reduce the efficacy of the whole operation. It is commonly felt that private setups go further towards meeting consumer demand. Private services aim to compete with public ones in (curative) health treatment and in education—areas in which people are more disposed to choose private services so they can avoid the real or supposed malfunctioning of the public services.

The role of family

Family organization in Italy is based on the mother's presence and commitment. She remains the central figure, with an over-heavy load regarding the care and upbringing of children. Her main source of support is usually a network of her relatives. The survey found that what the relatives do—the functions of grandparents, uncles, and aunts—varies according to the type of family profile.

Grandparents mainly help families when there is just a single child in the 0–5 age bracket (daily, in 30.7 percent of cases) or else when both parents work (27 percent). Uncles and aunts do an enormous amount for larger families (and do it daily for 88 percent of them) and for those with low overall socioeconomic status. They have a replacement function or play a welfare and subsidizing role mainly in the case of problem families,[11] whereas grandparents perform more limited functions and perform them for a different type of family.

North and South do not noticeably differ as regards the roles of relatives. Grandparents' foremost role seems to be giving their grandchildren frequent presents (46.2 percent). Next in importance is the advice they offer parents on nutrition, hygiene, and upbringing practices. Their third most frequently performed function is direct education of their grandchildren, since the children are often put in their charge (in 30 percent of cases). The grandparents perform entertainment, play, and socialization functions. These advising and upbringing functions are performed far less often by uncles and aunts, who are less frequently around or available.

Relatives play a greater upbringing role in families in which the parents have a lower level of education or in which both parents are absent for long periods of the day. In addition, new families often start up relationships with couples with small children (38.5 percent) and with other families. These are usually neighbors (51 percent), friends (44 percent), or work colleagues and parents of children attending the same day nursery or nursery school as their own. If the bond with the family circle is fairly tight, the relationships that the new family embarks on with friends and neighbors are no less significant, especially when these too are going through the experience of looking after children and bringing them up.

Fathers rarely involve themselves in looking after their children, especially as regards instrumental, service functions, which they usually leave to the mother. When they concern themselves with their children, it is usually to give them presents, play with them, take them for walks, or watch television together. Whereas the mother "immediately takes upon herself or is allotted the heaviest child care duties, the father, being less harassed, can devote himself to more distinctly 'qualitative' interactions with the child. Both father and mother take on only to a minimal extent the task of teaching reading and writing. This function is delegated to outside educational agents almost everywhere" (CENSIS, 1984, p. 64).

For 32.5 percent of the 2,577 children in the survey, the family experience is the central one during the morning; for 59.5 percent, during the afternoon; and for 95.2 percent, in the evening. In the morning, it is almost always the mother who is the principal caretaker (57.2 percent); the father is on hand in only 8.7 percent of cases. In the evening, 83.9 percent of fathers and 94.3 percent of mothers spend time with their children. Children who spend the most time with their parents or relatives in all three periods of the day typically belong to large families with low socioeconomic status. The extent to which a child is handed over to outsiders or to grandparents, baby sitters, neighbors, and friends correlates strongly with the father's occupational status and degree of education.

Educational services: Choice, use, and satisfaction

The survey found that 54.8 percent of the children spend their mornings mainly in socializing institutions. Only 26.5 percent do so in the afternoon, when the family environment becomes the dominant one. Use of services for infants differs significantly from use of services for young children. It is estimated that only 8 or 9 percent of those entitled to do so actually attend day nurseries, whereas a good 95 percent attend nursery school. Families in the eight areas surveyed tend not to send their children to nurseries before they are 1 year old, and then only if they cannot be looked after within the family. Once the children reach age 3, or even a few months beforehand, parents feel the time is ripe to enroll them in a nursery school.

Prime users of educational facilities for very young children tend to be upper- or middle-class families in which the mother goes out to work and in which there are two children 0 to 5 years of age. They are also primarily families living in the North of Italy, where afternoon attendance of nurseries and nursery schools is also higher. The smaller the number of children in the family, the more likely they are to be entrusted to relatives or baby sitters. Relatives are more often employed by lower- and lower-middle-class families; baby sitters, by upper- and upper-middle-class families. The mother stays at home to look after small children more frequently in working-class and southern families.

Choosing between public and private services

The main reason families give for choosing private structures is "proximity to home," followed by "good training," "hygiene," and "qualified staff." In the South, private schools are chosen primarily on grounds of hygiene and long opening hours; in the North and Center, primarily because of proximity to home. Working-class and other families of low socioeconomic status look particularly for long opening hours (in the private sector) and for absence of fees (in the public sector). Those most satisfied about having enrolled their children in public schools are members of the middle and upper classes and people living in northern urban areas, whereas those most satisfied with private sector services tend to come from the working classes. In fact, it is the public services that prove more attractive overall. Given a free choice, 57 parents out of 100 would entrust their children to them.

The main demands parents make of socioeducational services for very young children have to do with assurances about hygiene, nutrition, and facilities. Secondary considerations have to do with the staff (that they should be qualified, sensitive to childrens' needs, and cooperative towards their families). After these comes interest in the quality of institutional socialization, in the training, and in the education given the children.

In conclusion, parental satisfaction with educational structures correlates with the extent to which these guarantee both the physical well-being of their children and a good staff-child relationship. Educational content and atmosphere are held as secondary or seen as factors that are difficult or troublesome to control.

AUTHOR'S NOTE

Thanks to Enzo Catarsi and Giovanni Genovesi for allowing me free use of their publication *L'infanzia a scuola*; to Patrizia Ghedini for information on communal day nurseries; to the staff of the demography and education sections of the Central Statistics Institute; to the staff of Servizio di Medicina Sociale of the Ministry of Health; to my colleagues in the Department "Programmazione e Costi dei Sistemi Formativi" at Centro Europeo dell'Educazione; and to Philip Swann for a revision of the translation.

ENDNOTES

[1]The Roman Catholic church has always been the almost official religion in Italy. Approximately 98 percent of the Italian population is "officially" Roman Catholic. A large number of schools—nurseries through primary schools, high schools, and universities—are run by religious groups. During the school year 1983–84, 6,629 preprimary schools run by religious groups served a population of 384,899 children. Unless specified otherwise, we will use "the church" to mean the Roman Catholic church throughout the report.

[2]The principal source of information for this overview is *Infanzia a scuola* [Infancy at School] by E. Catarsi and G. Genovesi, published by Juvenilia, Bergamo, 1985.

[3]Giolitti was a Piedmontese politician who headed a series of dynamic and enlightened governments for the first 15 years of the 20th century.

[4]The concept of "protecting motherhood," according to the rhetoric of the Fascist regime, followed by the company logic of providing a minimum of assistance to the working mother, gave way to the idea of socioeducational services for very young children in the 1970s. It was not until 1971 that Law No. 1044 declared that around 3,800 day nurseries should be set up throughout the country.

[5]Statistics are from the *Central Statistics Institute Bulletin* (*ISTAT Notiziàrio*), Rome, 1986, 2. The Central Statistics Institute (ISTAT) produces twice-yearly reports on the main aspects of education in Italy, as they stand in October and in December, in conjunction with the local education offices and the universities, on behalf of the Ministry of Education. The first furnishes some provisional basic data, issued immediately in the form of a short bulletin and as a supplement to the monthly statistical digest. The second provides definitive data, with an in-depth treatment of various aspects of the educational system. These are published in the *Annual Abstract of Educational Statistics* 3 to 4 years later. The figures vary by about 1 percent between the two reports, although the discrepancy is about 3 percent in relation to nursery schools, because of enrollments after October 1.

[6]The Republic of Italy is divided into 20 regions. These are divided into provinces (95 in all), and each province consists of a number of communes. The regions are autonomous bodies with powers and attributes assigned by the Constitution. The regions of Sicily, Sardinia, Trentino-Alto Adige, Friuli- Venezia Giulia, and Valle d'Aosta have special statutes and enjoy particular autonomy.

Communal nursery schools are considered private institutions by law. This is because schooling is not a communal responsibility, and thus any initiative in that domain is considered entrepreneurship by present-day legislation. In other words, communal administrations running nursery schools have the same legal status as the head of a private school.

[7]The *Constitution of the Republic of Italy* already conferred on the state the right to intervene where necessary: Article 3, in fact, states that "all citizens have equal social dignity and are equal before the law, without distinction as to sex, race, language, religion, political opinion, or personal or social condition. It is the duty of the republic to remove those obstacles of an economic or social nature that, by limiting in practice the liberty and equality of all citizens, impede the full development of their human personality." Article 37 declares: "Women workers have the same rights. . . . Their working conditions must permit them to fulfill their essential functions in the home and assure mothers and children a special and adequate protection." (Law No. 1204, December 30, 1971, deals with "the protection of working mothers.") Article 33 affirms that the state is to institute schools at all levels.

[8]The **Decreti Delegati** (which were "decrees delegating" power) appeared in 1974. **Decree No. 416**: "Institution and reorganization of the decisional bodies in nursery, elementary, secondary, and art schools." **Decree No. 417**: "Norms regarding the legal attributes of teachers, administrators, and inspectors of the state nursery, elementary, secondary, and art school system." **Decree No. 418**: "Payment of salary increases to cover extra workloads for administrators and inspectors." **Decree No. 419**: "Educational experimentation and research; cultural and professional inservice training; institution of appropriate bodies." **Decree No. 420**: "Norms on legal attributes of nonteaching personnel." This is not the place to discuss the high points and shortcomings of the decrees; it suffices to say that they represent the most important step towards facing the problems of the school system that the public authorities have taken in many years.

[9]"Scholastic assistance" covers all those activities that try to compensate for the disadvantages caused by the sociocultural background of a child. Law No. 444 (1968) and the 1969 *Guidelines* strongly expressed the desire to make children's second infancy a moment of social and cultural advancement for the underprivileged. This was to be achieved by educational means but also by "aid and assistance" aimed at removing the social handicaps most directly influencing the child's development.

[10]Decree No. 419/1974: "Educational experimentation and research; cultural and professional inservice training; institution of appropriate bodies" (Articles 2 and 3).

[11]Such families totalled 168, out of the 2,000 surveyed. They were characterized by low income, one parent, handicapped children, unemployed family head (or even two unemployed parents), and four or more children. They differed from the rest of the families in the sample by having at least two of the aforementioned features.

REFERENCES

Becchi, E. (1986). Il Dio dei bambini [Children's God]. *Bambini, 3,* 8–9.

Borghi, L. (1986). L'insegnamento della religione nel "Nuovo Concordato" [Religious education according to the "New Concordat"]. *Bambini, 3,* 6–7.

CENSIS. (1984). *La condizione dell'infanzia tra famiglia e istituzioni* [Children and their families and institutions]. Roma: Ministero dell'Interno. Direzione Generale dei servizi civili.

Frabboni, F. (1984). *La programmazione nella scuola materna* [Curriculum planning in nursery schools]. Firenze: La Nuova Italia.

Frabboni, F. (1985). Una scuola che si dà il voto: "insufficiente" in politica, "buono" in pedagogia [Schools grade themselves an "F" in politics, a "B" in didactics]. *Infanzia,* 2, 5–13.

Kanizza, S. (1986). Scuola dell'infanzia e sperimentazione di base [Infant school and basic experimentation]. In E. Becchi & B. Vertecchi (Eds.), *Manuale critico della sperimentazione e della ricerca educativa* (pp. 286–304). Milano: Franco Angeli.

Lucchini, E. (1986). Dove va la scuola materna? [Where is nursery school going?]. *Infanzia, 6,* 5–12.

Malaguzzi, L. (1986). I bambini del "si" e quelli del "no" ["Yes" children and "no" children]. *Rivista dell'Istruzione, 3,* 3–5.

Serena, O. (1986). In margine alla relazione ispettiva sulla scuola materna [Notes on an inspection of nursery schools]. *Rivista dell'Istruzione* (Monografico: La Materna nel 1984), 2, 195–202.

VIII
EARLY CHILDHOOD CARE AND EDUCATION IN KENYA

Pauline Riak, *Senior Researcher*
Ruth Rono, *Researcher*
Florence Kiragu, *Researcher*
M. Nyukuri, *Researcher*
Bureau of Educational Research
Kenyatta University
Nairobi

INTRODUCTION

This profile is designed to give background information for the IEA preprimary study. It is not an exhaustive report but an attempt to document available information about the nature of education and care for young children in Kenya. The profile includes the following:

- A brief overview of the structure of formal schooling
- Historical information on the development of "out-of-home" care for children under age 6
- A description of national policies regarding families and children, which includes information on the current status of early childhood education and care
- Demographic information on rural and urban preprimary children
- Future directions in preprimary education, care, and research

STRUCTURE OF THE EDUCATIONAL SYSTEM

Although there is no document in Kenya that stipulates mandatory formal schooling, school enrollment has risen sharply since Kenya became an independent republic in 1963. While the proliferating primary schools are mostly government owned, private primary schools run by individuals or church organizations are also on the increase. More and more Kenyans have come to recognize the need for schooling, which at the moment seems to be the only pathway to a good job. The age of entry for Kenyans into a formal primary school is 6 years. In 1979 the proportion of Kenyan 6-year-olds entering formal schooling was 64.1 percent.[1]

For children under age 6, there are various forms of care and education. Child care for those aged 0 to 2 years is usually provided in homes by mothers or other female relatives, by older siblings, or—in the case of employed mothers—by paid *ayahs* (childminders), who oftentimes are dropouts of the formal school system. These childminders tend to be young, untrained, and often poorly paid and poorly treated by their employers.

For those children who enroll in a preprimary institution, the normal age of entry is 3 years. For the first 2 years, they attend what is known as nursery school or kindergarten, where the main activities are playing and learning the alphabet and numbers. To serve children approaching age 6, however, there are preprimary classes aimed strictly at preparation for entry into standard 1 in the primary school. In such classes, children learn how to read, write their names, and perform basic arithmetic operations. Some of these "preparatory" preprimary classes are housed in the formal primary schools, while some are housed in the kindergartens or nursery schools.

Prior to 1984 the progression up the education ladder for those who attended formal schools was 7 years of primary school, 4 years of secondary school, 2 years of higher secondary school, and 3 years of university. In 1985 the government introduced the 8:4:4 system of education, in which the progression up the education ladder is as follows: 8 years of primary, 4 years of secondary, and 4 years of university. This new system is in the process of implementation, and so far three cohorts have passed through the primary cycle; the first batch of secondary pupils will complete the secondary cycle in 1989.

After secondary schooling, some students go into formal training in postsecondary institutions, while others go into self-employment or private/public-sector employment. It is intended that at the end of the primary and secondary cycles, students will have acquired skills enabling them to become self-reliant.

Historical Background

Early childhood education and care have been a part of every society throughout history. In the past in Kenya, children's development occurred naturally, within a framework of caring in a traditional community of predominantly rural families. Though this system presented limits to children's development and mobility within the group, it provided children with the security of acceptance because of the clearly defined roles and relationships.

Kenyan childrearing traditionally has been characterized by great care and concern, with the mother playing a very important role in establishing a warm relationship between herself and the child. This close relationship with the child often extends to other members of the family as well, mainly to adult females and siblings. Children have been viewed mainly as a resource to the family and community, as someone to help on the farms or with the livestock, and later, to provide security for parents and younger siblings. Boys would carry on the family names, and girls would bring wealth to the family when they marry.

Recent decades, however, have seen major changes in social structures and a great widening of perspectives, with greater demands being made on each new generation. The slackening of ties of the extended family has occurred simultaneously with technological changes and a sustained movement towards urban centers. Even the more recent phenomenon of the nuclear family is no longer the norm in Kenya. Now, thousands of single parents must bring up their children by themselves. The early childhood education and care that once occurred naturally and without much conscious planning, in small communities of extended families, is now fractured and ill defined in many parts of urban and rural Kenya.

Kenya's young parents today, especially the rural mothers and single parents, are carrying a heavy burden, since they must combine childrearing with economic activities—without the traditional support system. The overall result is that parents who cannot afford to pay childminders and whose children cannot accompany them to the workplace often leave their children in the care of other children who should themselves be in school, or they leave their children to fend for themselves. These are the children—urban and rural—who may be malnourished; may become victims of fire, abuse, and other environmental hazards; and later in life, may become adult social misfits through no initial fault of their own.

Kenya's contemporary concepts and values of childrearing are a result of the nation's rapid socioeconomic changes. These changes, which have developed within a context of diverse cultural and linguistic traditions and of uneven resource allocations, have affected not only the basic perceptions about childrearing practices but also the material base of socialization and care.

The growth of "away-from-home" institutions for young children in Kenya is a relatively new phenomenon. During the 1940s a few institutions were established by the wives of Europeans for their own children and for Asians. The first of these institutions that served African children were started in African locations in urban areas and on tea and sugar plantations, where all able-bodied females were expected to work away from their homes. Later, during the Mau Mau wars of the 1950s, similar centers were established in the emergency villages. These were never intended to be centers of learning. They were essentially a bureaucratic control-mechanism for children left behind by freedom fighters and for other victims of the war. In these early institutions, custodial care and security of the young children were the main concern. The educational components were least pronounced.

Today, the establishment of "away-from-home" educational and care centers for young children in Kenya is often a community affair. Usually, individuals (mainly mothers) get together and decide to establish a learning center for their children who are not yet in formal schools. They identify the land on which it is to be built and start gathering building materials. With the support of others in the community, they complete the construction of the center and then appoint one of their members (who has been at least to primary school) to be the teacher. They also decide on a salary for the teacher and on how monies for the salary should be collected. In urban areas, individual entrepreneurs often establish the preprimary institutions.

Various factors have contributed to the rapid and continuous growth of education and care institutions in Kenya for children under age 6. The effects of World War II, the introduction of a cash crop economy, the drive for national sovereignty, the increased access to formal schooling, the postindependence mobilization of the society, and the rural-urban migration have all resulted in changes in settlement patterns that have worked together to quicken the disintegration of the extended family

Table 1

KENYAN PREPRIMARY SERVICES, 1968 AND 1986

Year	No. of Institutions	No. of 3- to Under-6- year-olds Served	No. of Teachers	
			Trained	Untrained
1968	4,300	177,036	—	5,184
1986	12,058	650,700	5,012	11,441

Note. Data are from the Ministry of Education, Science, and Technology, *Evaluation of NACECE/DICECE Programme* (Nairobi: Kenya Institute of Education, 1987 August), p. 2.

unit in a large number of Kenyan families and have necessitated "out-of-home" assistance in childrearing.

No information on the number of preindependence (pre-1963) institutions for early childhood education and care is available. However, since 1963 there has been rapid establishment of these institutions, as shown by the figures for two representative years in Table 1.

NATIONAL CHILD CARE POLICIES AND PRACTICES

MATERNAL AND INFANT CARE

At the time of this writing, June 1988, it was difficult to find a document stipulating the government policy on care for children from the prenatal stage through age 2. However, throughout the Republic of Kenya there are local government health centers known as maternal and child care centers, where mothers receive both prenatal and postnatal care as well as advice on how to feed their babies and how to keep them healthy and free from diseases. There are also maternity hospitals, where women obtain the necessary care and where children receive all necessary immunizations.

Mothers employed in the government sector are granted a 2-month maternity leave with pay but with forfeiture of their 30-day vacation for that year.[2] This, however, affects only a small proportion of the women of child-bearing age in Kenya, since most Kenyan women in the 15 to 45 age group are not in formal employment. According to a 1977/78 labor force survey, 87 percent of the adult female population were employed, but mostly in agriculture-related occupations.[3]

PREPRIMARY CARE

Since gaining independence, the government has shown some concern with the problems facing preprimary education and care, though to date, financial constraints have not allowed full involvement. Preprimary education prior to 1980 was under the Ministry of Culture and Social Services, with over 80 percent of preprimary institutions being run and financed by private groups and individuals. In 1980, however, through the *Presidential Circular No. 1*, preprimary institutions were placed under the Ministry of Education, Science, and Technology. The National Center for Early Childhood Education (NACECE), based at the Curriculum Development Center, Kenya Institute of Education, was established as the professional body to implement government policy on early childhood education. The center is developing a network of subcenters, District Centers for Early Childhood Education (DICECEs), whose officers serve as facilitators and trainers for early childhood programs. The first 9 DICECEs were established in January 1985. A year later 6 more were added, and by January 1987 there were 18 DICECEs in Kenya. It is anticipated that their number will continue to grow.[4]

NACECE has a close working relationship with the DICECEs and with partners that have agreed to collaborate with the government to set up DICECEs across the country. (The Bernard van Leer Foundation, UNICEF, and the Aga Kahn Foundation are such partners.) Together the NACECE and DICECEs conduct programs for parents and other community members to promote awareness of the role of preprimary education. The preprimary programs are supervised at the district level by qualified and experienced teams composed of officers from the DICECEs, district inspectors of schools, and preprimary supervisors from county and municipal councils.

There also is a national implementation committee that is appointed by the director of education. Chaired by the chief inspector of schools, this group is consultative in nature and has the mandate to advise the director of education on matters related to early childhood education and to implement the national and district programs for early childhood education.

Finance and other resources

Many government ministries and agencies are now involved in supervision, guidance, and personnel training for preprimary programs. However, there is still gross underprovision of the finances necessary for

Table 2

GOVERNMENT AND PARTNER FINANCIAL CONTRIBUTIONS (IN KENYAN SHILLINGS[a]) TO PRESCHOOL EDUCATION, 1981–88

Year	Kenyan Government	UNICEF	Aga Khan Foundation	Bernard van Leer Foundation
1981	1,568,000	—	—	384,900
1982	1,809,200	1,326,360	—	—
1983	2,133,520	3,129,300	—	—
1984	2,901,800	3,603,000	—	—
1985	4,005,060	1,626,000	—	2,000,000
1986	4,050,300	3,102,000	2,075,000	3,101,500
1987	5,977,660	2,640,000	2,084,000	3,038,800
1988	7,806,480	2,640,000	2,104,000	—
Total	16,467,880	18,066,660	6,263,000	8,140,300

Note. Data are from Ministry of Education, Science, and Technology, *Evaluation of NACECE/DICECE Programme* (Nairobi: Kenya Institute of Education, 1987 August), p. 45.

[a]At the time of writing, 19 Kenyan shillings is approximately equivalent to $1 U.S.

effective and efficient implementation of preprimary programs; existing programs (nursery schools and preprimary preparatory classes) are able to serve only about 25 percent of the total 3- to under-6-year-old population (which meant serving 25 percent of almost 2½ million children in 1987).[5]

The role of local government through the local authorities has been mainly confined to professional advice through inspection and supervision, curriculum development, and the training and employment of teachers. However, alongside the increased national government spending for preschool education, there has been a greater level of funding by parents, local committees, churches, voluntary organizations, and individual investors. Table 2 illustrates the extent of contributions by the main funding partners. It is somewhat more difficult to quantify the contributions made by the thousands of parents, communities, organizations, and groups throughout the republic, who since independence have given time and resources (financial and material) to the development of preprimary institutions. Their contributions have been substantial and are growing. In addition, parents must pay fees ranging from 25 to 850 Kenyan shillings per month. (At the time of writing, 19 Kenyan shillings is approximately equivalent to $1 U.S.)

Research and evaluation

An integral and ongoing part of the NACECE/DICECE programs is curriculum research. In addition to their well-established curriculum development projects in 13 different local languages, curriculum research is currently being initiatied in 6 other linguistic areas. In these research projects, project leaders train trainers and teachers, develop the curriculum and the syllabus for teachers' courses, and establish guidelines for schools, bearing in mind community participation at all levels of program development. For these various projects, the NACECE has established a national dissemination network.

General objectives

The preprimary programs are intended to provide an informal education geared towards developing the child's mental capabilities and his physical growth. Their stated goals are to do the following:

- Enable the child to enjoy living and learning through play
- Enable the child to build good habits for effective living as an individual and member of a group
- Enable the child to appreciate his/her cultural background and customs
- Foster spiritual and moral growth of the child
- Develop the child's imagination, self-reliance, and thinking skills
- Enrich the child's experience in a way that enables him/her to cope better with primary school life[6]

The programs are further aimed at raising parents' and community members' awareness of early childhood services in their districts. Parents are given advice on child care, nutrition, and health during prenatal stages, as well as on immunization and other services available for children. They are also advised on general care of toddlers before preprimary and after preprimary age.

Preprimary programs address the following recognized needs for 3- to under-6-year-olds:

Physical development—

- There should be activities to increase coordination of hand, leg, and eye muscles. Most of the children can, for example, feed themselves, throw objects, kick balls, climb, and jump low heights. While 3-year-olds cannot do such things as catch balls or keep rhythm during dancing, 5- and 6-year-olds can do this well.
- In the small-motor area, the 3-year-olds have less control of their muscles and would therefore not color within defined areas, but older

children can do this properly. For example, the youngest children will not be able to write and draw proper figures, but most of the older children can do this. The 3-year-olds will also not be able to repeat designs, but most older children can do so. The 3-year-olds do not draw or model things that resemble the real objects, animals, or people they want to draw or model. Older children can do this quite well.

■ To stimulate children to develop properly, the parents and teachers should provide adequate materials to play with. Safety must be ensured, especially where it involves climbing or throwing things that can be dangerous. The parents and teacher should avoid pushing the younger children to do things that they may not be able to do, as this may destroy their confidence and self-image.

■ Most children are very choosy about food at this age, but they should be given a balanced diet to ensure proper growth. Teachers should monitor children's growth and also advise parents on a balanced diet for their children.

Socioemotional development—

■ Play is still a very important means of learning and socialization for children. For 3-year-olds, parallel play and fantasy play are still very common, but at this age, children do not like to share materials and facilities. With the older children, role play becomes increasingly important. They start playing in groups and are more prepared to share materials and facilities. During their play, the older children start to form simple rules that all those playing must obey. This becomes a very important foundation for the development of the concepts of rules, regulations, and discipline.

■ Social needs should be satisfied and developed. These needs include self-image, independence, confidence, concern for others, responsibility, love, and security. Teachers can help to develop children's self-image by encouraging, praising, and rewarding them, and also by providing activities within their capabilities. Independence can be developed by encouraging children to feed themselves, dress themselves, and perform other small tasks for themselves both at home and school.

■ Regarding discipline, the teacher should help the children to control their emotions and behavior. The adult should, however, be consistent and firm, so that children feel secure and know what is expected of them. There must also be consistency in discipline between home and school. The parents and teachers must therefore work closely together to ensure that this consistency in discipline exists.

■ Teachers must be made aware of some problems that children at this age might have, such as aggression, taking things they like from school and from others' homes, bullying, fighting, shyness, unnecessary fears, thumb-sucking, temper tantrums. When the teacher notices any behavior problems in any child, she should try to find the underlying cause of the problem, and in so doing, she will be able to assist the child. The teacher should also contact the child's parents, so that both can work together to solve the problem.

Mental development—

■ Children at this age learn best through use of concrete materials that they can manipulate; concept development continues. At this age, children can only handle one attribute of an object at any given time. In sorting tasks, for example, children can sort by one attribute only, such as by color or by shape. Between ages 3 and 4, children are not able to distinguish colors and shapes, but older children can.

■ Children's vocabulary increases rapidly between ages 3 and 6. Language assists them to understand some abstract concepts, for example, color, shape, feelings. They use language to describe past events, to describe things that are absent, and to some extent, to describe future events.

■ Children imitate language and actions, and these help to clarify their concepts and ideas. It is important therefore that parents and teachers provide models, so that children develop proper conduct and concepts.

■ Children at this age are still very curious and have endless questions. Those living with the children should answer their questions as meaningfully as possible. Parents and teachers should also provide materials and opportunities that enable children to explore the environment around them and to satisfy their curiosity.

Special needs—

■ Teachers should be able to identify children with special needs, and they should give these children the care and assistance required. They should also be aware of the services available for these children. Teachers should be able to pass all the information to the parents and the other family members. Children with special needs include the highly gifted children, physically and mentally handicapped children, and emotionally disturbed children.[7]

DEMOGRAPHIC INFORMATION ON URBAN AND RURAL PREPRIMARY CHILDREN

Kenya's population growth has accelerated tremendously since the first national census in 1948, as reflected in Table 3. The most recent Kenyan population census, in 1979, reported a population of 15,327,061. This figure made Kenya the 6th most populous country in sub-Saharan Africa; the 10th in the African continent; and the 47th in the world. The high population growth rate that was used to predict the 1987 population—4.1 percent per year—is based on a combination of changes that have occurred in Kenya: a lowering of mortality rates and an increase in birthrates.

Tables 4 and 5 emphasize the need for massive planning if Kenya is to serve effectively the growing numbers of children at the preprimary and primary levels. Table 4 gives the number of children from 0 to 5 years of age from 1979 through 1990. Table 5 shows that according to estimates, by 1989, 56 percent of the total population of Kenya will be 16 years of age or under, and 24.8 percent of the population will be aged 5 and under. From both of these tables, there is clear and consistent evidence that Kenya is experiencing a sharp decline in infant and child mortality rates. This decline is due to rising family incomes, remarkable advances in public health care, and the increasing provision of other social services.

Table 3

KENYA'S POPULATION FOR SELECTED YEARS, 1948–87

Year	Population	
1948	5,405,966	
1962	8,636,263	
1969	10,942,705	
1979	15,327,061	
1980	16,667,015	a
1987	approximately 22,000,000	b

Note. Data are from Central Bureau of Statistics, *Kenya Population Census, 1948, 1962, 1969, 1979*, Vol. 1 of each; Republic of Kenya, *Population Projections for Kenya 1980–2000* (Nairobi: Central Bureau of Statistics, 1983 March), pp. 3, 23.

[a]The 1980 figure is a corrected figure for underenumeration in the 1979 census; it has been updated by a 3.3 percent pro rata increase.

[b]Estimate based on a 4.1 percent annual growth rate since 1980.

Table 4

CHILDREN AGED 0–5 YEARS IN KENYA, 1979–90

Year	No. of Children Aged 0–2 yr	No. of Children Aged 3–5 yr
1979[a]	1,705,000	1,677,000
1980[b]	2,220,000	1,920,000
1981[c]	2,295,000	2,002,000
1982	2,371,000	2,081,000
1983	2,452,000	2,162,000
1984	2,545,000	2,236,000
1985	2,686,000	2,319,000
1986	2,801,000	2,405,000
1987	2,933,000	2,489,000
1988	3,065,000	2,584,000
1989	3,206,000	2,733,000
1990	3,333,000	2,827,000

Note. Data are from Central Bureau of Statistics, *Kenya Population Census, 1979*, Vol. 1, p. 180; UNESCO, *Statistical Analysis of Demographic and Educational Data in Kenya*, SEM/KENYA—Pans April 1984, Serial No. ST- 24/WS/10, pp. 90–93; Republic of Kenya, *Population Projections for Kenya 1980–2000* (Nairobi: Central Bureau of Statistics, 1983 March), p. 23.

[a]Figures for 1979 are actual from population census.

[b]Figures for 1980 are corrected figures for underenumeration in 1979; they have been updated by a 3.3 percent pro rata increase.

[c]Figures for 1981–90 are projections assuming constant levels of mortality and fertility.

Table 6 summarizes Kenya's mortality trends since the first census in 1948. The crude death rate, which was 25 per 1,000 in 1948, fell by 1969 to 17 per 1,000 and further fell by 1979 to 14 per 1,000. The child mortality rate, which in 1948 was 184 per 1,000, fell to 138 per 1,000 by 1979 (no table). Infant mortality (deaths per 1,000 live births) also declined from 160 per year in the 1948–57 decade to about 110 per year in the 1958–67 decade, and then to 94 per year in the 1968–76 period. By 1979 an estimate of 87 infant deaths per 1,000 live births was recorded. As also shown in Table 6, the life expectancy at birth, which in 1948 was only 35 years, increased to 44 years by 1962, then to 49 years by 1969, and finally to 54 years by 1979.

Among other factors, education has played a substantial role in the decline of infant and child mortality. In fact, mortality studies in Kenya suggest that a significant factor in the reduction of infant and child mortality is increased female education. It is therefore likely that with the recent implementation of universal primary education in Kenya,

Table 5

DISTRIBUTION OF KENYAN POPULATION, BY SPECIFIC AGES, 1979, 1984, 1989

Age (yr)	1979 (Actual)	1984 (Projected)	1989 (Projected)
0	3.7%	4.5%	4.8%
0–2	11.2	13.0	13.4
0–4	18.6	20.9	21.1
3–5	10.9	11.5	11.4
6–12	21.3	21.7	21.3
13–16	9.7	9.7	9.9
17–18	4.6	4.2	4.3
15–49	42.6	41.2	41.6
15–59	46.8	45.2	45.5
60+	4.6	3.5	3.3

Note. Data are from Central Bureau of Statistics, *Kenya Population Census, 1979*, Vol. 1; Republic of Kenya, *Population Projections for Kenya 1980–2000* (Nairobi: Central Bureau of Statistics, 1983 March), p. 23.

Table 6

MORTALITY TRENDS IN KENYA FOR SELECTED YEARS, 1948–79

Year	Infant Mortality Estimates (per 1,000 Live Births)	Life Expectancy at Birth (yr)	Crude Death Rate (per 1,000 Population)
1948	160	35	25
1962	110	44	20
1969	94	49	17
1979	87	54	14

Note. Data are from Central Bureau of Statistics, *Kenya Population Census, 1948, 1962, 1969, 1979*, Vol. 2 of each, *Analytic Report*.

further declines in infant and child mortality will be experienced owing to the rising educational level of the population. Moreover, the implementation of preprimary education since 1981 and the subsequent initiation of maternal and child care programs in Kenya should aid substantially in reducing the nation's infant and child mortality rates.

At this time, the overall difference between infant mortality rates in urban and rural areas is small. As a result of the rapid decline in infant mortality for rural women, the difference is now only half as great as in

Table 7

DEMOGRAPHIC FACTORS AFFECTING CHILD POPULATION CHANGE IN KENYA

	Infant Mortality		Neo-natal Deaths	Nutrition Status & Selected Indicators of Welfare					
Province	Pre-1967	1967–76	as Percent of Infant Deaths	Total Mortality	Children Sick	Mothers With No Education	No Piped Water	No Sewage Facilities	No Milk Feeding
Nyanza	162	128	30	220	59%	52%	98%	38%	39%
Western	118	109	49	187	57	46	95	19	47
Rift Valley	103	64	47	132	39	55	89	50	13
Central	88	56	51	85	37	30	77	2	8
Nairobi	100	75	40	93	—	—	—	—	—
Eastern	100	77	52	128	43	46	88	38	23
Coast	156	129	59	206	54	77	79	62	65

Note. Adapted from Republic of Kenya, Central Bureau of Statistics, *Nutrition Survey III*, 1982; Central Bureau of Statistics, *Population Census, 1979*, Vol. 2, *Analytic Report*.

the period before the 1970s. However, beyond infancy, rural-urban differentials widen considerably. Childhood mortality rates indicate that the young child faces much higher risks in rural than in urban areas. Furthermore, the rates suggest that these risks have not declined over time.

It is also evident from mortality studies in Kenya that the most dramatic differentials in infant and child mortality are regional in character. According to these studies, the general geographical pattern in Kenya is that infant and child mortality tend to be lower towards the central part of the country and higher in the coastal and western parts. Besides geographical location, there are many other differences—ecological, social, and cultural—among Kenya's provinces, as shown in Table 7, and these may account for their mortality differentials. Researchers have also found that malaria endemicity has a significant correlation with the mortality levels.

EMERGING ISSUES AND UNANSWERED QUESTIONS

Much research is needed to clarify the many issues related to the care and education of the young child in a changing Kenyan society. This research would give guidance to policymakers for future directions for both mothers and their children. Some questions needing answers are these:

- Do preprimary institutions really make a difference, and if so, in what way?
- What are the shared characteristics of those young children (0 to under-6 years of age) who do not have access to preprimary institutions or whose parents do not allow them to attend formal institutions?
- What are the working relationships at the community level between various ministries that are responsible for services for the 0 to under-6 age group?
- If employed mothers get only 2 months of maternity leave, should organizations, both public and private, be encouraged to have nursery schools at the workplace to meet the needs of these mothers returning to work?
- What are the needs for training childminders and for regulating terms and conditions of service?

The trends of increasing population and overall improvements in health and education suggest that large numbers of young children will need protection by the government if they are not to become victims of poverty and related diseases. The NACECE must be given a wider mandate and greater resources, so that it can effectively coordinate and implement sustainable programs to improve child care and early childhood socialization. Besides addressing child care and education needs, preprimary institutions are poised to accommodate a multifaceted approach to the problems of rural development. Since they are district focused, community based, and community owned, they could be used as adult training and recreation centers for passing on development ideas that could be initiated and sustained by the community.

ENDNOTES

[1]This statistic is based on data from the Republic of Kenya, *Ministry of Education Annual Report, 1979* (Nairobi: Government Printer), p. 32 and Central Bureau of Statistics, *Kenya Population Census, 1979*, Vol. 2, *Analytic Report*, p. 21.

[2]Waruhiu Commission, *Report of the Civil Service Review Committee 1979–80* (Nairobi: Government Printer, 1980), p. 177.

[3]From Republic of Kenya and United Nations Children's Fund (UNICEF), *Situation Analysis of Women and Children in Kenya, 1988* (in press).

[4]Statistics are from Ministry of Education, Science, and Technology, *Evaluation of NACECE/DICECE Programme* (Nairobi: Kenya Institute of Education, 1987 August). As

described earlier, many Kenyan preschools are established by local communites; this is the case for about 79 percent of preschools. Another 11 percent are founded by church organizations. In those districts where NACECE is involved, it has encouraged communities to build more schools, select teachers, make arrangements to pay the teachers, and through the DICECE, to make arrangements for teacher training. (See J. Kagia, *Integration of Education, Health, and Care for the Total Development of the Child*, paper presented at Seminar on Early Childhood Education in Kenya: Implications on Policy and Practice in Mombasa, August 31–September 4, 1987.)

[5]Statistic is from the Ministry of Education, Science, and Technology, *Evaluation of NACECE/DICECE Programme* (Nairobi: Kenya Institute of Education, 1987 August).

[6]From Ministry of Education, Science, and Technology, *Guidelines for Preschool Education in Kenya* (Nairobi: Jomo Kenyatta Foundation, 1984).

[7]From Republic of Kenya, *Republic of Kenya: Early Childhood Education Programme. The DICECE Component (1985–1989)* (Nairobi: Ministry of Education, Science, and Technology, 1984).

IX

Early Childhood Care and Education in Nigeria

Olayemi M. Onibokun, *Senior Research Fellow*
Institute of Education
University of Ibadan

Introduction

This profile provides base-line data for the IEA preprimary study by describing and documenting the full range of care and education services available for Nigerian children between 3 and 6 years of age. In it, we take a fresh look at the past and current practices in child care and education, focusing on care arrangements, patronage, curriculum, teacher education, and research efforts. We also analyze the administrative, political, and economic factors influencing the child. Because of the scanty information available from some states, our report may not be exhaustive of the Nigerian situation. This notwithstanding, we envisage that the profile will be of use to planners, policymakers, teachers, and researchers in effecting appropriate care and education for young children.

Background—Demographics, the Social System, and Family Policy

Demographics

Nigeria, which derives its name from the river that constitutes the most remarkable geographic feature of the country, became a fully independent and sovereign nation in 1960 and a republic in 1963. With an area of 923,768 square kilometers and an estimated population of 100.8 million in 1985 (50.9 million males, 49.9 million females), it is divided into 22 regions (including 21 states and the federal capital territory, Abuja).[1] Lagos, the commercial capital, constitutes Africa's third-largest urban area, following Cairo and Johannesburg.

Nigeria has a relatively youthful population, with children below the age of 10 years making up almost 32 percent of the population in 1985.[2] Moreover, National Population Bureau Statistics show a rapid increase in the young population in the last decade. One of the reasons for this is the decline in infant mortality: In the 1950s at least 250 children per 1,000 died before the age of 5 years. This had decreased to about 150 per 1,000 by the early 1970s,[3] and the 1985 Nigeria fertility study report shows that presently the infant mortality rate (deaths per 1,000 live births) is about 90 per 1,000, with the corresponding figure for childhood mortality (between ages 1 and 5 years) about 75 per 1,000.[4] These latter two statistics indicate that over 10 percent of Nigerian children die before the age of 5 years. Not surprisingly, child mortality is higher in the rural areas than in the urban areas, where children have the advantage of exposure to such modern facilities and amenities as electricity, plumbing, hospitals, and preprimary care services.

THE SOCIAL SYSTEM

The family unit in Nigerian society is traditionally very close. The concept of mother and father in the Western sense applies only among the highly educated. Generally, in the extended family (which is still prevalent in the traditional sections of urban areas and in rural areas), every adult male is regarded as "father" and every adult female as "mother." A relationship such as cousin is too distant and therefore unrecognized; to a young child, every older child is either "brother" or "sister." Under such a system, it is not surprising that some of the costs of childrearing are borne by members of the extended family. Relatives or older siblings might care for the child while the parents go to work, or they might directly bear financial responsibility for the education of the child.

Since a social security system in the form of health, welfare, and pension programs is minimal or nonexistent in Nigeria, children act as the main source of old-age security for their parents. Furthermore, parents seem to derive psychological satisfaction from their children. By Western standards, Nigerians would appear to have many children—according to the National Population Bureau, 6.34 children per family. Faced with the rapidly growing population, however, the federal government is currently advocating reducing this birthrate. Fathers are granted tax-relief for up to 4 children only.

FAMILY POLICY

Government policy promoting infant and child welfare is almost nonexistent. There are laws against child abuse and child labor, for example, but they are not enforced. There are no facilities for educating couples for parenting. Prenatal care is not free, although such drugs as folic acid and vitamin tablets are given to pregnant women free of charge. A pregnant woman, if she is employed, is entitled to a 3-month maternity leave—6 weeks before and 6 weeks after delivery. (Paternity leave is unheard of.) Delivery is done in private hospitals, government institutions, herbalist homes, churches, and private homes with the help of neighboring women. Free medical consultation and immunization are available for children, but parents have to bear the cost of drugs and hospitalization.

THE CHILD CARE PICTURE

CHILD CARE NEEDS

The vast majority (95 percent) of Nigerian women, whether in urban or in rural areas, whether educated or illiterate, are economically active to insure their immediate families against financial inadequacy.[5] The age pattern of women's labor force participation suggests that motherhood and work are frequently combined. Mothers working in the informal sector of the economy (on the farms, in the markets) often work and care for their children at the same time. However, those urban mothers employed in the formal sector of the economy must work outside the home for a fixed period each day, and these women require some kind of substitute care for their infants, toddlers, and preschool-aged children. (The Federal Ministry of Labor has no statistic regarding the percentage of Nigerian women employed in the formal sector.)

In the past, employed urban mothers could recruit house-help among the young school-leavers and dropouts migrating into the cities, or they could seek the help of unemployed relatives. Nowadays the availability of better-paying jobs in service industries has reduced the number of such helpers, making the existence of other forms of child care a critical issue.

The loss of traditional child care resources has spurred a rapid growth in urban day care centers set up to meet the needs of employed mothers. More than 90 percent of children of employed mothers in urban centers are placed in such institutions (editors' note: no source provided), with some children being enrolled as early as 4 to 6 weeks after birth. There is no law governing the earliest age at which children may be in institutional care. Only a small percentage of mothers hire in-home nannies (charging 80 to 140 naira per month) or take their children to be cared for at the homes of childminders.[6] A 1981 study by Bamisaiye and Oyediran found a positive relationship between income and type of care mothers patronized.[7] Mothers at the lowest (salary) grade levels (01–06) patronize babyminders, while those at the higher grade levels (07–17) use day care centers. Babyminders and nannies are neither accredited nor registered, and therefore data on their number are not available in any state. Ad hoc child care arrangements abound. For instance, babies may be taken to homes of relatives when the house-help suddenly resigns, or in desperate cases, babies have been kept by their mothers in their offices.

Day Care Centers

Day care centers have not received the same level of attention in Nigeria as preprimary institutions have. Care services for children under age 3 in Nigeria seem to be uncoordinated and unregulated. Day care centers are registered and controlled by the Ministry of Health in each state. This means that permission to set up a center should be obtained from the area medical officer and that area health supervisors should supervise the centers. However, owing to inadequate staffing and poor record keeping in many state ministries, the exact number of existing day care centers is not on record. While the medical officer in a town in Oyo State had records of only 1 such center, this author was able to locate 17 others. Also, although all day care centers and other institutions serving children below 3 years of age are supposed to be under the supervision of the Ministry of Health, because some centers may include children of nursery age and kindergarten age, they are supervised instead by the Ministry of Education or the Ministry of Social Welfare.

Services

Day care centers, which often operate between 7 a.m. and 6 p.m., provide custodial care only. The centers are usually equipped with some toys and play equipment, but mothers are expected to bring such supplies as food and diapers for their children each day. There are no dental services, and many centers do not have medical supervision. Facilities to promote the child's physical, intellectual, emotional, and social development are lacking in many centers. However, any attempt to distinguish "day care" from "play group" from "nursery" in the Nigerian context is rather complex. It is common to see one center providing custodial care to babies, social and physical training to 3- and 4-year-olds, and educational services to 4- and 5-year-olds. Table 1 provides a summary of the types of care available to children aged 0 to 6 years.

Center staffing and size

Day care centers are set up by nurses, teachers, secretaries, or any interested persons. It is felt that any mother is qualified to set up care services for children; there is a preponderance of women in the day care field. Since there is no regulation of child-adult ratios, some centers are adequately staffed, while others have too few staff. In the Nigerian context, 1 staff person for 35 children is considered adequate.

Some centers are small and manageable, while others are quite large. In this author's 1988 survey of day care in Oyo State,[8] the number of children per center ranged from 25 to 141. A total of 604 children were registered in the eight centers visited.

Fees

Fees charged depend on the quality of services provided. It also appears as though the more commercialized the location, the higher the charges for child care. For example, in Lagos and Port Harcourt, which are state

Table 1

AVAILABLE TYPES OF CHILD CARE

Age-Range (yr)	Facility	Function	Setting[a]
0–2+	Nanny, babyminder, day care center	Custodial (Type A)	Home/extra-familial/institution
2–4	Nursery school	Custodial (Type A)/ preparatory (Type B)	Institution
3–5	Kindergarten	Preparatory (Type C)	Institution
5 or 6	Primary-one class	Formal education (Type D)	Institution

[a]Proprietors of any type of setting are allowed to perform any of the four types of functions. Some homes provide only type-A service, and some homes are involved in type-B care only. Most institutions provide care of types B, C, and D.

governmental and commercial centers, the day care fees range between 100 and 150 naira per month; in Oyo State, which is less prosperous, the range is 50 to 80 naira per month.

The Preprimary Education System

Origins

The first school in Nigeria was established by missionaries in Badagry in the 1840s and called the Nursery of the Infant Church. Contrary to what the name implies, it was not a nursery but a primary school. Thus, education was introduced by the missionaries and propagated for their converts. The colonial authorities paid no attention to preprimary education, or if they did, they left no documentary evidence. Birth registration was not common then, so no strict or specific age was defined for school enrollment. Maturity for schooling was evident when a child could use his or her hand to touch the ear opposite that hand, a physical feat that can usually be performed when the child is about 7 to 8 years old. That being the school-readiness criterion, there was no need to even consider school entry for 3- to 6-year-olds.

By the 1950s, Nigerians had become more politically active. This period consequently witnessed bold innovative educational efforts, such as the highly successful Universal Free Education by the Western State government (1955) and the ill-fated Universal Primary Education Scheme of the Eastern Region government (1957–58).[9] Another innovation during this period was the establishment of child care institutions—preschools—to meet the needs of educated women who brought their children home after completing studies abroad. Most of the early preschool proprietors and their clients had lived in Great Britain and were familiar with that country's out-of-home care for children of working parents; the preschools they established were elitist, serving children of educated parents in the major urban centers. An expatriate education officer in eastern Nigeria is quoted as saying that "there is no obligation at present [for the government] to provide education for children before they enter primary school."[10]

This noninterference of the government in preprimary education continued until the 1969 National Curriculum Conference, when the first official statement on the age of admission to the primary school was made and when, for the first time, official mention was made of "younger children between 3 and 5 years old who may be enrolled in nursery and kindergarten classes to prepare them for lower primary classes."[11] Since this declaration, successive government policies have emphasized the *preparatory* role of preschool institutions, a fact that may explain the rigorous academic content of Nigerian preschool programs (to be discussed more fully in another section). During Nigeria's oil-boom era of the 1970s, the business of setting up preschools also boomed. Many of the state governments belatedly recognized the existence of these institutions, and a preprimary section was set up in the Ministry of Education to draw guidelines for establishment and supervision of the schools.

FEDERAL GOVERNMENT POLICY

Currently the federal government of Nigeria makes policy statements but, perhaps because of its huge financial outlay for primary, secondary, and tertiary education, does not participate directly in early childhood education; the control, supervision, and administration of preprimary programs is delegated to the states. The states, in turn, which also finance education at the primary, secondary, and tertiary level, leave responsibility for *provision* of preprimary education in private/corporate hands: Religious groups, philanthropic organizations, private owners, secular universities or colleges, and labor organizations are the preschool providers. Table 2 outlines the present-day structure of education in Nigeria. The only free education is primary school, which is provided by the state governments and subsidized by the federal government for children aged 6 to 12.

The first preschool policy of the federal government was outlined as follows in the *New National Policy on Education* (1981):

> Preprimary education as referred to in this document is the education given in an educational institution to children aged 3 to 5+, prior to their entering the primary school. The purposes of preprimary education should be
>
> - Effecting a smooth transition from the home to the school
> - Preparing the child for the primary level of education
> - Providing adequate care and supervision for children while their parents are at work (on the farms, in the markets, in offices, and so on)
> - Inculcating social norms
> - Inculcating in the child the spirit of inquiry and creativity through the exploration of nature and the local environment,

Table 2

STRUCTURE OF EDUCATION IN NIGERIA[a]

Duration (yr)	Type	Statutory System	Type of Control	Content
0–3	Custodial care	Home nannies/day care	State	Physical and emotional care
3–6	Preacademic	Preprimary schools	State	Preacademic
6	Basic	Primary schools	State	General
3	Basic	Junior secondary	Federal/state	General
3	Quasi-professional	Senior secondary	Federal/state	Academic/pre-vocational
4	Professional	University/technical colleges	Federal/state	Vocational

[a]This 6-3-3-4 structure of education (primary through tertiary level) was launched in 1977 and took effect in September 1982.

through playing with toys, through artistic and musical activities, and so on

- Teaching cooperation and team spirit
- Teaching the rudiments of numbers, letters, colors, shapes, forms, and so on, through play
- Teaching good habits, especially good health habits

To achieve the above objectives, government will

1. Encourage private efforts in the provision of preprimary education.

2. Make provision in teacher-training institutions for student teachers who want to specialize in preprimary education.

3. Ensure that the medium of instruction will be principally the mother tongue or the language of the immediate community; and to this end will

a. Develop the study of spelling for many more Nigerian languages.

b. Produce textbooks in Nigerian languages. Some of these developments are already being pursued in the linguistics departments of universities and under the auspices of some State Ministries of Education. The federal government has also set up a language center as part of the educational services complex under the Federal Ministry of Education. This language center will be expanded so as to have a wider scope.

4. Ensure that the main method of teaching in the preprimary institution will be through play and that the curriculum of teacher-training colleges is appropriately oriented to achieve this.

5. Regulate and control the operation of preprimary education as well as ensure that the staff of preprimary institutions are adequately trained and that essential equipment is provided.

To achieve these aims, the appropriate level of government will review and enforce the educational laws that relate to the establishment of nursery schools, to make sure that schools that are opened are well run and that preprimary teachers are qualified and that other academic infrastructure is provided. Ministries of Education will make regular inspections to ensure maintenance of high standards.[12]

Many states have worked out their own guidelines for operating preprimary programs. For example, Anambra State prepared as far back as 1977 a detailed application form for permission to establish a nursery school. The form seeks information on the prospective proprietor and spells out policy on organization, staffing, curriculum, buildings, equipment, and school closings. A zonal inspector of education must give approval of the application. The Anambra State government was the first to prepare a document titled *Nursery School Regulations*.[13]

To insure uniformity of practice and maintain standards in the states, the Federal Ministry of Education has prepared *Guidelines on Preprimary Education* (1987)[14]—a yardstick for inspecting officers to use in assessing the standard of work in preprimary schools. The *Guidelines* covers the following topics:

- Objectives of preprimary education (as stated in the *National Policy on Education*)
- Government attitude towards preprimary education (advocating participation by the private sector)
- Requirements regarding type of establishment, siting, facilities, equipment, space (for instance, prohibition of residential nursery schools except for those serving the handicapped)
- Specifications on playgrounds, furniture, fees, teacher and aide qualifications
- Teacher-pupil ratio (recommending 1:25)
- Language of instruction (mother tongue/market language)

- Books (recommending ones with local background)
- Record keeping (administrative and academic)
- Inspections (by officers of the State Ministry of Education)
- Conformance to federal education law
- Provision for handicapped
- Criteria for school closure (noncompliance, inadequate facilities, unqualified staff)
- Institutions of higher learning providing training in preprimary education (eight, including University of Ibadan)
- Religion (conformance with religion of parents)
- Health (including hygiene and sanitation)

This document can be regarded as the first working document on preprimary education in Nigeria.

CURRENT STATUS OF PREPRIMARY EDUCATION

Proprietorships

Although all state governments are actively interested in care and education for their children, response to this author's 1987–88 survey of preprimary institutions in seven states reveals that 85 percent are privately run by individuals and religious bodies; 5 percent are run by voluntary organizations, such as the National Council of Women's Societies; and only about 10 percent are government sponsored—either set up as model schools or attached to government institutions of higher education (all universities, teacher-training colleges, and polytechnics have preprimary schools, for example).[15] Exceptions to this categorization are a UNICEF-sponsored center set up in Benin, Bendel State, in 1972 and a Danish-government-sponsored nursery set up in Ebute-Ero, Lagos, in 1966.

Patronage

A 1977 Nigerian Institute of Social and Economic Research (NISER) survey in metropolitan areas in seven states indicated that about 60 percent of preschool-aged children of working mothers in urban centers were receiving extrafamilial care (this included those in institutions and those cared for at home by paid helpers.)[16] The remaining 40 percent were either cared for by relatives or by mothers who combined this responsibility with gainful employment. In urban areas, economic and social changes since 1977 have pushed up considerably the percentage of 0- to 6-year-old children cared for in institutions. With the availability of relatively "cheap" day care (some centers serving low-income families charge as little as 20 naira per month per child), all children in urban areas can be said to have the opportunity to *attend some place* while their mothers are at work.

The 1977 NISER survey also describes the characteristics of mothers patronizing the available institutions, as shown in Table 3. From the table, one gets the impression that most of the mothers of children in preschool institutions were married, had at least a primary-school education (6 years or more of schooling), and were either self-employed or employed as civil servants.

Availability of preprimary programs

It is difficult to know at present the total number of preschool institutions—nurseries and kindergartens—in Nigeria, because each state keeps its own records. Moreover, since most of the preschool institutions are privately owned, information about the per-center populations,

Table 3

CHARACTERISTICS OF MOTHERS OF CHILDREN IN PREPRIMARY INSTITUTIONS

Characteristic	No. of Mothers (N = 790)	Distribution
Marital Status		
Single	11	1.4%
Married	691	87.5
Divorced	32	4.1
Separated	26	3.3
Widowed	30	3.8
Educational Status		
Less than 6 yr schooling	137	17.3%
6 yr schooling	273	34.6
12 yr schooling	208	26.3
14 yr or more schooling	168	21.3
No response	4	0.5
Employment Status		
In civil service (including statutory corporations)	259	32.8%
In educational institution	135	17.1
In private industry	73	9.2
In self-employment	315	39.9
No response	8	1.0

Note: Data are from T. O. Fadayomi et al., *The Role of Working Mothers in Early Childhood Education: A Nigerian Case Study* (Ibadan: Institute for Social and Economic Research, 1977).

teacher qualifications, and teacher-pupil ratios is guarded. This information had not been kept by the supervising ministries visited during the author's 1987–88 survey. Table 4 summarizes the information gathered in this survey regarding the situation in seven states. The table gives some idea of the scarcity of preprimary programs vis-à-vis the population of children entering primary school. The ratios for the state capital regions are somewhat better than the ratios statewide, which suggests a preponderance of preprimary institutions in urban areas.

Administration

While the Ministry of Health is in control of the day care centers, the Ministry of Education is in charge of the nursery and kindergarten schools. However, as mentioned earlier, day care, nursery, and kindergarten are often provided under one roof. Proprietors are expected to secure their accreditation from the relevant ministry. (Proprietors in some states complained that their centers were denied registration either because they [the proprietors] were not indigenous to that state or because there was religious bias.) An institution is usually organized according to the philosophy and training of the headmistress/master or proprietor.

Within a given institution, children are grouped according to age. Program names are age-specific rather than function-specific. For example, what is known as a day care center in one place may be called a playgroup or kindergarten in another; so early childhood education

Table 4

NUMBER OF PREPRIMARY INSTITUTIONS COMPARED WITH NUMBER OF PRIMARY SCHOOLS, IN SEVEN STATES

	Number of Schools			
State (year)	Preprimary (Approved)	Primary	Statewide Ratio, Preprimary: Primary	State Capital's Ratio, Preprimary: Primary
Ogun (1987)	11	1,282	1:117	1:37
Oyo (1987)	131	2,519	1:19	1:3
Rivers (1988)	128	1,087	1:8	1:13
Kano (1988)	100	3,119	1:31	1:4
Plateau (1988)	123	1,276	1:10	1:1.4
Bauchi (1988)	16	1,432	1:90	1:11
Borno (1988)	67	1,105	1:16	4:3

Note: Statistics are from O. M. Onibokun, *1987–88 Survey of Preprimary Institutions in Nigeria*, unpublished report, Institute of Education, University of Ibadan.

terms in Nigeria do not have universal application. Admission to an institution is based on availability of space and parents' ability to pay fees, rather than on a child's needs.

The calendar for a preprimary institution usually follows that of the public school system, with quarterly holiday periods. Some of the schools provide boarding facilities. There are no special programs for mildly retarded children; they are educated along with normal children. Seriously disabled children have to wait until age 6, when they attend special primary schools. There also are no preprimary schools running special programs for economically or linguistically disadvantaged children or for gifted children.

Financing

Private preprimary schools receive no form of financial support from the government. No subsidies whatsoever are received from public authorities or from outside philanthropic organizations. The schools are supported by proprietors' capital and by fees collected from parents. No institutions in Nigeria provide free child care, and no law limits the fees that may be charged by the institutions.

Good child care institutions are very costly, and their fees, which are not uniform, range from 40 naira per month in day care centers to over 100 naira per month in nursery and kindergarten schools. Of course, costs of preprimary institutions vary with the quality of child care provided and with the location of the institution (whether in a state capital, in an administrative center, or in a commercial city). In some elitist schools in the capital city of Lagos, for example, the fee is about 400 naira per term (133 naira per month). This is very high when compared with the Nigerian salary structure. The highest-paid civil servant earns about 1,200 naira net per month. The minimum salary is 120 naira per month.

Since there are no free preprimary schools, not every Nigerian child between the ages of 3 and 6 is able to receive the benefits of preprimary education. Also, since the government does not award scholarships for this level of education, it is clear that only children whose parents can pay the fees receive preschool education. Most Nigerian families do not earn the income to support their children in preprimary institutions. In fact, most Nigerian families find it difficult to send their children to any school that charges fees (whether secondary, technical, or commercial).

An analysis of the parental background of children in six preprimary schools in Nigeria shows 86 percent of the children having parents who are professionals (economic elites), such as lawyers, bankers, university teachers, administrators, engineers, architects, and 14 percent having parents who are business executives, entrepreneurs, and highly skilled workers.[17] Children of low-income families are not represented in the "good" institutions because they are too expensive.

Supervision and control

Since 1977 the state government has been charged with the control and supervision of preprimary institutions. Proprietors of day care centers are expected to get approval from the State Ministry of Health; those running nurseries, kindergartens, and primary institutions are approved by the State Ministry of Education. In the author's survey in Oyo State, fewer than 10 percent of the day care institutions were thus approved.[18]

Institutions owned by religious bodies (for example, by Roman Catholic universities) or by government parastatals (that is, by secular universities or teacher-training colleges) are controlled and supervised by a governing board (with government approval). The board is selected from the community. In the case of an institution run by a religious university, the governing board is usually composed of bishops, professors, parents, and the headmistress/master of the preprimary institution, and this board is responsible to the bishop or the council of the university. Staff employment, curriculum matters, finance, admission policy, teacher promotion, and supervision come under the administration of this board. Only daily routines are set by the headmistress/master. Preprimary institutions owned by private individuals (which, in our survey in seven states, was 95 percent of such institutions[19]) may or may not have boards. In most cases, the owner of the school (proprietor) also performs the functions of the administrative head (headmistress/master). This person, with the assistance of some of the teachers, controls and supervises the financial and administrative activities of the institution.

The absence of an efficient central supervisory body results in lack of coordination of the activities of the various preprimary institutions. There are no uniform standards, especially in matters of curriculum, fees, and enrollment policy. Inspectors from each State Ministry of Health and State Ministry of Education are expected to go around ensuring that standards are maintained, but there are usually only one or two such inspectors per ministry. It is very difficult for two experts to supervise more than 200 schools (as is the case in a state like Lagos). Institutions in rural areas are often more neglected than those in urban centers are.

Educational activities and methods

For children under age 6, although there are guidelines, there are no official regulations concerning educational activities. Once a child is 6 years old, he is enrolled in primary one. All primary schools use the government syllabus with some or no modification, since at the end of primary education (at age 12), all children must take a primary-school-leaving certificate examination. (The curriculum is modified, for example, for physically or mentally disadvantaged children who attend special institutions.) At the preprimary institutions, however, each proprietor or headmistress/master formulates policy, objectives, and programs. Among existing institutions, the distinct similarity in their activities is that they are all content-oriented, involving rigorous scholastic education. Reading, writing, and arithmetic are emphasized, especially in the nursery and kindergarten classes. In some schools, children are given summative tests, and parents receive regular progress reports. Many schools stress habit formation, music, physical training (gymnastics, swimming). Free-play activities both indoors and outdoors are also encouraged. English is usually the medium of instruction, and it is also taught as a subject.

Daily schedule

The daily program of the preprimary schools starts between 7:30 a.m. (when public servants start work) and 8:30 a.m., when children settle down to the day's schedule. Parents are free to drop off their children at any time at the day care center, nursery school, or kindergarten. Children's daily activities, which are on a flexible schedule, include singing, drawing, painting, health talk, storytelling, news, numbers, and language activities. Children are encouraged to take part in activities; they are allowed to take their "work" home. Parents collect their children when it is convenient, between 1 p.m. and 3:30 p.m.—the official work-closing time for public servants. Table 5 shows a typical daily schedule for a nursery school.

Teaching methods

Nursery and kindergarten teachers employ no unique methods in teaching. There are no schools using a special curriculum, such as the High/Scope Preschool Curriculum. Even in those institutions where the proprietors claim to have learned Froebelian or Montessori methods, the lecture method is employed. Children's activities are teacher-directed. In the centers visited by the author, many of the teachers did not know their children (perhaps because of frequent teacher-turnover), and there

Table 5

NURSERY SCHOOL DAILY SCHEDULE

Time	Activities
a.m.	
7:30–8:00	Children arrive, free play, outdoor play
8:00–8:15	Tidying up the classroom, morning assembly
8:15–9:15	Mathematics: Developing the basic sense, weighing, counting, seriation, sorting, grouping
9:15–10:00	Teaching sounds, alphabet, letter identification
10:15–11:00	Tea time, washing hands
11:00–12:00	Tracing, art work
p.m.	
12:00–12:15	Cleaning up, tidying up the classroom
12:15–1:00	News: practicing communication skills, speaking, listening
1:00–2:00	Singing, tidying up, departure

was little evidence that programs were planned with the children in mind. There was a conspicuous lack of use of teaching/learning resources. Outdoor play equipment was usually provided, however.

Social aspects

The primary function of early childhood institutions is providing social and educational services in looking after children of working mothers. Thus preprimary institutions tend to be located in towns where the rate of female employment is very high, but nursery school and day care centers are not sited according to children's special social needs. For example, they are not necessarily located in places where the living and working habits of the population deprive children of stimuli for optimum physical, social, and intellectual development. Also, many factories and industrial concerns fail to provide much-needed child care facilities for their workers' children.

Because parents have to pay exorbitant fees for preprimary care and education, they tend to take an active interest in parent-teacher meetings. Most institutions hold such meetings once every 3 or 4 months (once each term), for the discussion of children's problems, progress, and so on.

Health, nutrition, and transportation

Nigerian preprimary institutions aim at making the child's health stronger, yet none of the available institutions provide medical or dental care. Costs incurred if a child is taken to a hospital from school are paid by the parents.

A few schools provide a midday meal, while others expect children to bring their meals from home. Before 1984 some institutions provided midday milk, but this was discontinued when the price of milk became too high.

Usually parents are expected to bring their children to school and to collect them after school. Some schools provide school busses to pick up children.

Buildings and equipment

There are no enforced regulations concerning the premises used for preprimary education in Nigeria. Babyminders use their own homes, which means that private houses (flats, bungalows, storey buildings) are used as schools. In centers, because enrollment is not strictly controlled and there is no regulation of teacher-pupil ratio, it is a common sight to see an overcrowded classroom with 50 children and inadequate facilities, with perhaps 3 children assigned to one seat. The government recommends a teacher-pupil ratio of 1 to 25.

Staffing

Nigeria has had no stipulated requirements for teaching in preprimary institutions. Supposedly, the certification for primary school teachers is also expected of preschool teachers. In fact, the general opinion is that the preprimary level is the area where the least-qualified teachers should work.

A 1988 survey[20] conducted by this author in Ibadan (the capital of Oyo) reveals that a potpourri of adult caretakers operate preprimary institutions. From the 97 schools visited, it was found that nurses, secretaries, social workers, unqualified teachers, administrators, and traders participate in operating preprimary child care and education services. As mentioned earlier, oftentimes those persons running day care centers are nurses—persons trained to look after the health of their wards but not trained to provide appropriate cognitive and emotional stimulation. (More than the initial 3-year nurse's training should be required for nurses who wish to run day care centers.) Nursery schools and kindergartens are usually set up by teachers or nurses.

Available categories of teachers in Nigeria are given in Table 6. Any of these categories of teachers may be found in preprimary programs, either teaching children or acting as proprietors, but only a handful of these teachers have had thorough training in early childhood education. In the 1988 survey in Ibadan, four proprietors claimed to have Froebelian training, while three claimed to have attended a Montessori training institute.

Table 6

CATEGORIES OF TEACHING CREDENTIALS IN NIGERIA

Credential	Type of Training	Years of Postsecondary Education
Grade-III Teacher	Geared towards primary school teaching	2
Grade-II Teacher	Geared towards primary school teaching	4
Grade-I Teacher	Geared towards primary school headship	5
National Certificate of Education (N.C.E.)	Geared either towards secondary and higher-institution teaching or towards primary teaching	3–4
Graduate	B.A., B.S., B.Ed.	4
Higher education	M.Ed.	7

The curriculum of the teacher-training colleges is geared towards primary, secondary, and higher-institution teaching. In these institutions, insufficient attention is paid to training for the teaching of young children. There is urgent need for teacher-training institutions to start intensive courses leading to diplomas and degrees in preprimary education. Recently, the Institute of Education, University of Ibadan, has been organizing summer vacation courses for teachers in preprimary and primary institutions. These courses contain heavy doses of child growth, psychology, and methods of child study; content from elementary science, social studies, language, health, and hygiene is also included. Because of Nigeria's scarcity of teaching aids and toys, artists and technologists are brought in to train the participants in how to improvise and make simple equipment.

In 1987 the federal government issued the following guidelines[21] concerning preprimary school teaching qualifications:

■ ***Head-teacher's qualifications***

It is desirable that the head-teacher receive specialized training in preprimary education. The head-teacher must be one of the following:

1. A Grade-I teacher with at least 5 years experience in lower primary classes or with a Montessori Diploma Certificate or with a diploma of any university or college of education

2. A Grade-II teacher with an Associateship Certificate in Education with specialization in preprimary education

3. A Grade-II teacher with a Montessori Diploma

4. A Grade-II teacher with a diploma in the Froebel Foundation Course

5. A holder of a National Certificate of Education geared towards preprimary/primary education

6. A person with a B.Ed. or a B.A. in education with specialization in preprimary education

7. A person with other qualification in early childhood education approved by the Federal Ministry of Education

- ***Teacher's qualifications*** (one of the following)

1. Grade-III Teacher's Certificate
2. Grade-II Teacher's Certificate
3. Any qualification listed under head-teacher requirements

- ***Helper's qualifications*** (one of the following)

1. Modern III (certificate of 3 years postprimary training)
2. Pre-1976 Standard VI, or Primary IV certificate (both certificates of completion of primary schooling)
3. S.75 (certificate obtained after 4 years of secondary education)

Depending on location, one nurse per school should be provided, and a medical doctor or nursing sister should be on call. The more cosmopolitan the area, the higher the quality of staff found in the schools. In some institutions in Lagos there are staff with master's degrees and Ph.D.'s. In rural areas the quality of staff is poorer.

Research programs

As far back as the *Second National Development Plan* period (1970–74), it was declared that "measures will be taken to encourage and support research programs designed not only to provide solutions to current problems in the field of education but also to make the educational system continuously responsive to the changing needs of the nation."[22] In pursuance of this declaration, the Nigerian Educational Research Council was set up in 1972, but its involvement with preprimary education to date has been minimal. Although individual researchers have studied various aspects of child growth and learning readiness (the universities abound with research reports on children's developmental status, intelligence, social-emotional growth, and achievement), there are no study groups or research centers dealing with the problems of preprimary education. Government support for research concerning this level of education is rare.

SUMMARY

Early childhood care and education today is largely a family responsibility in Nigeria. Completely free health and education facilities are not available at any level. The existing child care arrangements appear elitist, because they are available only to those who can pay for them. Unless the government provides some facilities for economically disadvantaged children, they will continue to be left out of enjoying the benefits of early childhood care and education.

The government has been made aware of the fact that cognitive deficit is cumulative and that it can have roots in early childhood. The least that government could do to participate actively in preprimary care and education would be to set up special centers for underprivileged children, while those who could afford to would continue to finance the care of their own children. The government could reduce its cost of participation by adding preprimary facilities to already-existing public primary schools. These facilities could house 3-, 4-, and 5-year-old children. Middle-class and poor parents could be charged a token fee. This minimal effort would be preferable to the government's current policy of "no direct involvement." (The Kenyan example of preprimary schools attached to primary schools is noteworthy.)

The Federal Military Government, as one of the transition programs to civil rule, recently (1987) launched the Mass Mobilization Program for Social and Economic Recovery (MAMSER). The objective of this program embraces "social justice, economic recovery, and self-reliance"—for all the various groups that make up the Nigerian society, including women, youths, leaders, and workers.[23] Since this program is directed at improving the conditions in rural areas and elevating the status of women, expansion of preprimary care and education facilities should be one of the objectives of MAMSER. If adequate and relatively cheap care and education facilities are available, more women will be helped to combine their mothering and wage-earning roles. Also, more low-income children will be able to participate in preschool education, thus reducing the gap in primary one between them and the rest of the school population. Under MAMSER, it is feasible for the government to give material and financial assistance to preprimary institutions in the rural areas. The fact that MAMSER deals with the society at the grassroots level puts its directorate at an advantage for participating in preschool care and education.

Each state government needs to lay down and enforce regulations regarding preschool location, architectural design, teacher qualifications, teacher/pupil ratio, and safety rules for facilities. This will ensure that children are no longer housed in garages and driveways.

The universities need more funds for research and teacher-training purposes. One of the drawbacks to planning in Nigeria is the lack of data. There is an urgent need for comprehensive data on prechool-aged children; we need to know the total number per age group, the total number per state, and the total number at each socioeconomic level. We also need to know the number of children born per day in the country and the number of various types of child care arrangements now available. Until efforts to collect such data are made at the federal level, Nigeria will be without a basis for planning.

ENDNOTES

[1]Statistics are from *The Nigeria Yearbook, 1986*, a *Daily Times* publication (Lagos: Times Press Ltd.).

[2]Ibid.

[3]From S. Ogunlade and C. Mezue, *Infant and Child Mortality in Nigeria*, paper for Seminar on the Analysis of Infant and Child Mortality in Africa in Cotonou, Benin, November 18, 1985.

[4]National Population Bureau, *Nigeria Fertility Survey 81/82*, principal report.

[5]Statistic is from O. M. Onibokun, "Female Labor Participation in Nigeria" in *EducAfrica* (Dakar: UNESCO, 1984).

[6]At the time of writing, 12 naira is the equivalent of $1 U.S.

[7]A. Bamisaiye and M. Oyediran, *Female Labor Force Participation and the Care of Preschool Children*, paper presented at the National Workshop on Working Mothers and Early Childhood Education in Nigeria, September 13, 1981.

[8]O. M. Onibokun, *1988 Survey of Preprimary Institutions in Oyo State*, unpublished report, Institute of Education, University of Ibadan.

[9]These were the earliest programs that introduced free education at any level in Nigeria. In northern Nigeria, no such program was available. See Ministry of Education, *Free Primary Education*, Ibadan, Western State, 1955 and *Universal Primary Education Scheme*, Enugu, Eastern Region, 1957.

[10]C. Burns (1960) as quoted in E. Maduewesi, *The Development of Early Childhood Education in Eastern Nigeria*, paper presented at Conference on Women and Education in Nigeria, University of Ibadan, 1982.

[11]*Report of the National Curriculum Conference*, Lagos, 1969.

[12]Federal Republic of Nigeria, *New National Policy on Education* (Lagos: Federal Ministry of Information, Printing Division, 1981).

[13]Anambra State Ministry of Education, *Nursery School Regulations*, Enugu, 1977.

[14]Federal Ministry of Education, *Guidelines on Preprimary Education* (Lagos: Author, 1987).

[15]O. M. Onibokun, *1987–88 Survey of Preprimary Institutions in Nigeria*, unpublished report, Institute of Education, University of Ibadan.

[16]T. O. Fadayomi et al., *The Role of Working Mothers in Early Childhood Education: A Nigerian Case Study* (Ibadan: Institute for Social and Economic Research, 1977).

[17]O. M. Onibokun, *1988 Survey of Preprimary Institutions in Oyo State*, unpublished report, Institute of Education, University of Ibadan.

[18]Ibid.

[19]O. M. Onibokun, *1987–88 Survey of Preprimary Institutions in Nigeria*, unpublished report, Institute of Education, University of Ibadan.

[20]O. M. Onibokun, *1988 Survey of Preprimary Institutions in Oyo State*, unpublished report, Institute of Education, University of Ibadan.

[21]Federal Ministry of Education, *Guidelines on Preprimary Education* (Lagos: Author, 1987).

[22]Federal Republic of Nigeria, *Second National Development Plan 1970–74* (Lagos: Federal Ministry of Economic Planning).

[23]J. Gana, "Rigging Is the Bane of Politics," public lecture reported in *Sunday Tribune*, January 22, 1988.

X

Young Children's Care and Education in the People's Republic of China

Shi Hui Zhong, *Professor*
Central Institute of Educational Research
Beijing

Historical Review

How has early childhood education been viewed in China, which has a history of 5000 years' civilization? The following is a brief review.

Early Childhood Education in Ancient China

Recorded history reveals that early childhood education began to receive widespread attention in the 11th century B.C. in the Chinese West Zhou Dynasty. A curriculum for young children called Six Arts Education[1] appeared at that time. According to this curriculum, young children were taught to use their right hands as soon as they were able to serve themselves at table; they were taught to recognize spatial orientations and to read at age 6 and taught courtesy at age 7.

In the 7th century B.C., there appeared a saying that warned the public to pay attention to the proper philosophical orientation in early childhood education. It is said in *Zuo Zhuan*[2] that young children should be taught to know justice instead of material benefits. In the 2nd century B.C. West Han Dynasty, sayings like this one appeared in the ancient book on education *Da Dai Li Ji. Bao Fu:* "To teach a child while he has no question to ask will make him easier to be trained"—evidence that people at that time realized the necessity of early childhood education.[3] Also in the West Han Dynasty, theories of early childhood education began to take shape. Environment and education were thought to have influence in shaping and altering children's knowledge, abilities, and moral character. Therefore a good early childhood education was emphasized. At the same time, reading primers intended for young children were compiled. Later in the 2nd century, the theory developed further. For example, *Yan's Family Instructions*[4] indicates clearly that young children cannot be loved without education; otherwise, when the child is grown, the parents will have no prestige even if they punish the child severely; their anger at his misbehavior can only arouse his resentment and ultimately he will be punished for violating the law. It is also mentioned in *Instructions* that early childhood is a period well suited to various kinds of learning (for example, language learning). From that time on, *Thousand Words*, a reading primer published in the 2nd century B.C., was used in the Tang, Song, Yuan, Ming, and Qing Dynasties.

The foregoing examples indicate that while the ancient Chinese began to pay attention to early childhood education, it consisted mainly of education within the family.

Appearance of Young Children's Educational Institutions

In the 20th century, in the Qing Dynasty, there appeared a number of young children's educational institutions in China, including the Child Care and Enlightenment Institution of Wuchang Mofan Primary School established in 1903, the Nursery School of Shanghai Wuben Women's Private School, the No. 1 Care and Enlightenment Institution of Beijing Normal School created in 1904, and the Foundling Hospital under Jiangsu Education Division. A major impetus for the creation of these institutions was the Qing Government's issuance of the *Zouding School Constitution*, which established a school system prototype to be implemented in 1903. The *Constitution* defined the position, aims, contents, and methods, as well as the age for admission to early childhood education. It stipulated that early childhood education should become a part of the new school system, thus marking the beginning of organized early childhood education in China.

Thereafter, the first half of the 20th century saw a gradual development of early childhood education in China. This development was due in large part to the contributions made by Tao Xingzhi and Chen Heqin, two Chinese modern educators who had a great influence on both the theory and the practice of early childhood education in China.

Tao Xingzhi (1891–1946) regarded early childhood education as the foundation of life. He held that all the important things for a person's life, such as habit, inclination, and attitude, were mostly determined before 6 years of age. Since he believed that primary education was the basis of the country and that early childhood education was the foundation for primary education, he proposed a popularization of early childhood education—the creation of **kindergartens** that did not cost much, served the common people, and fit the country's actual situation. Accordingly, in November of 1927 he set up Nanjing Yanziji Kindergarten, the first rural kindergarten in China, which was followed by the establishment of a number of kindergartens of this kind, including Xiaozhuang Kindergarten, Hepingmen Kindergarten, and Maiaoqiao Kindergarten. In 1934, Mr. Tao created a workers' kindergarten intended for children of women workers in Shanghai. In keeping with his belief—"It is for workers and peasants that we create kindergartens"—all the kindergartens he helped to set up served workers and peasants.

Chen Heqin received his master's degree in education from New York's Columbia University. After he came back home in 1919, besides giving support to Mr. Tao to create Xiaozhuang Normal School, he also began to do research on child development. He conducted a long-term observation of his own child, beginning in 1920, and subsequently published his two books, *Study on Child Psychology*[5] and *Familial Education.*[6] In 1923 Mr. Chen established Gulou Kindergarten in Nanjing, the first experimental center for early childhood education. He conducted a series of experiments on aspects of curriculum and equipment and, as a result, put forward a 15-point proposal for running a kindergarten. Among the 15 points were these:

- The kindergarten must fit the actual situation of China.
- Both kindergarten and family should take responsibility for the child's education.
- The curriculum of a kindergarten should be centered on helping children understand the environment and society.
- The first thing that kindergartens should pay attention to is the children's health.
- Kindergartens should be a place for developing children's good habits.
- Play and games are the major approach for teaching children in kindergartens.
- Teachers should be friends with children.
- Teaching should be in small groups, in most cases.

The results of Gulou Kindergarten's experiments gave Chinese early childhood education some guidance, and the kindergarten has served to this day as a model experimental kindergarten.

Another aspect of the 20th-century development of early childhood education was the appearance of a new kind of kindergarten during the anti-Japanese War. The war gave rise to new kindergartens, aimed at serving common people, in the base areas supporting Chinese militia. In these kindergartens, all the costs for the care and education of those children whose parents fought or worked for the war were paid by the government. Between 1937 and 1949, there were about 90 kindergartens of this type in Shan-Gan-Ning base areas.

The creation of kindergartens by patriotic overseas Chinese was also part of China's early childhood education development in this century. Along the coastline of China there were some kindergartens that were established with the generous help of overseas Chinese. Fujian Province provides one example. Early in 1919, Mr. Chen Jiageng, a leader of patriotic overseas Chinese, helped to set up a kindergarten called Jimei Kindergarten. In kindergartens of this kind, Froebel's and Montessori's theories were usually followed, and American or European curricula and methods of instruction were widely used.

In addition to the three kinds of kindergartens just mentioned, there were other kindergartens run by foreign missionaries, and in some provinces, there were other kinds of privately run kindergartens.

BRIEF INTRODUCTION TO EARLY CHILDHOOD EDUCATION SINCE 1949

The new era of early childhood education began with the founding of the People's Republic of China. Since then, early childhood education has been developing rapidly.

GOVERNMENT ATTENTION TO EARLY CHILDHOOD EDUCATION

After the founding of the Republic, a Division of Early Childhood Education was set up in the Ministry of Education. The government also issued a series of documents that gave direction to the development of early childhood education.

In 1949 *The Guiding Principle of Chinese People's Political Consultative Conference* pointed out that "health of mothers and children should be protected." In *Decisions on School System Reform*, issued by the Government Administration Council in August 1951, the current school system of China was defined. The first item of this document states, "The organization for implementation of early childhood education is kindergarten, which enrolls children from age 3 to age 7." In March 1953 the Ministry of Education issued *Temporary Regulations for Kindergartens (Draft)*, which clearly defined the task of kindergartens as the care and education of young children under the education principle of New Democracy. The purpose of kindergarten was to foster healthy development in children before primary school as well as to lighten mothers' child care burdens so that they could take part in political, productive, cultural, and educational activities. In May 1952 the Ministry of Education published *Contemporary Teaching Outlines for Kindergartens*, which puts forth the content and requirements for kindergarten teaching activities. Later, in January and June of 1955 respectively, the State Council and the Ministry of Education delivered documents calling for factories, the army, and governmental and academic institutions to run their own kindergartens according to their needs and resources and asking the local Boards of Education to help in providing the teachers.[7]

More recently, in November 1979, the Ministry of Education published *Regulations for Kindergartens in Urban Areas*, which deals with such topics as health protection, play and games, activity periods, moral education, and teacher qualifications. In September 1983 the Ministry of Education issued *Points on the Development of Early Childhood Education in Rural Areas*, calling for creating conditions for the development of early childhood education in rural areas, for improving the quality of child care and education, and for training of qualified kindergarten teachers.

In general, all the government documents we have mentioned convey the following ideas: (1) that education for 3- to 6-year-olds is the first stage of national education; (2) that different resources and organizations should be mobilized to develop early childhood education, both in urban and in rural areas; (3) that there should be clear requirements concerning the educational aims, daily routine, and curriculum appropriate for children; and (4) that efforts must be made to train kindergarten teachers.

GREAT DEVELOPMENT OF EARLY CHILDHOOD EDUCATION

Table 1 shows the great development of early childhood education since the 1949 founding of the People's Republic of China. The table indicates that (1) there has been a continuing and remarkable increase in the number of kindergartens since 1949, the number of kindergartens in 1985 being 132.4 times as many as the highest number before 1949; (2) since 1952 there have appeared a great many kindergartens run by factories, by the army, and by various other institutions, and they have been developing rapidly (in 1985 the number of these kinds of kindergartens

Table 1

NUMBER OF KINDERGARTENS IN CHINA FOR SELECTED YEARS, 1949–85

Year	Number of Kindergartens Run by Board of Education	Number of Kindergartens Run by Other Institutions[a]	Number of Kindergartens Run by Local People[b]	Total
Before 1949 (highest number)	824	—	477	1,301
1951	3,238	—	1,595	4,833
1952	4,540	315	1,676	6,531
1957	4,367	3,433	8,620	16,420
1958	4,459	4,833	686,005	695,297
1961	7,555	19,247	33,505	60,307
1962	4,386	4,810	8,368	17,564
1965	4,404	6,260	8,562	19,226
1973	4,812	40,716[c]		45,528
1979	5,041	19,807	140,781	165,629
1984	10,003	30,486	126,037	166,526
1985	11,196	29,794	131,273	172,263

Note. Data are from the *Statistical Yearbook on Education* (1985) published by the Ministry of Education of the People's Republic of China, Beijing.

[a]"Kindergartens run by other institutions" refers to those run by factories, the army, and governmental and academic institutions.

[b]"Kindergartens run by local people" refers to those run by local people in neighborhoods, townships, or villages.

[c]This figure is the combined number of kindergartens run by local people and other institutions.

was 2.7 times the number run by the Board of Education); (3) though the number of kindergartens run by the Board of Education has been increasing steadily, not till the 1980s was there a rapid increase in this kind of kindergarten; (4) for kindergartens run by local people, rapid development has occurred since 1979 (in 1985, their number is almost 12 times the number of kindergartens run by the Board of Education and more than 4 times the number run by other institutions).

Among all the 172,263 kindergartens, there are 26,330 kindergartens in cities, 23,989 in county towns, and 121,944 in rural areas. Rural kindergartens make up 70.7 percent of the total, while city kindergartens make up 15.2 percent, and county town kindergartens, 13.9 percent. This reflects not only the agricultural nature of the country but also the increasing attention paid to the collective care and education of young children in rural areas.

According to 1985 statistics, among 486,999 classes in 172,263 kindergartens, 196,616 (or 40.3 percent) are **preschool classes.**[8] These are a special type of early childhood educational institution, and their numbers have been increasing rapidly in recent years. Different from independent kindergartens, preschool classes are attached to primary school and enroll only 5- to 6-year-olds. Their aim is to provide some education for those children who have not received any collective care and education before entering primary school, so as to facilitate primary education.

Though we can see a continuing increase in the number of kindergartens, the number of early childhood education programs is still far from satisfying public demands. In 1985, there were only 14,796,900 children from age 3 to age 6 in kindergarten, accounting for 19.7 percent of the total of 75,000,000 children in this age-range.

Description of Kindergarten Staff

Table 2 details the staffing numbers in Chinese kindergartens since 1949. A comparison of Tables 1 and 2 indicates that the total number of staff members has been rising with the increase in kindergartens. There were more than 8 times as many kindergarten staff members in 1962 as there were in 1952 and almost 5 times as many in 1985 as there were in 1962. The percentage comparing teachers to total staff fell considerably in 1957 but has been rising again somewhat steadily, so that by 1985 the number of teachers accounted for 68.9 percent of the total staff members. Table 3 shows that the teacher/child ratio has remained fairly stable since 1980.

Overall, the statistics in Tables 1–3 reflect the ever-increasing attention that is being given to the education and care of young children.

Table 2

NUMBER OF KINDERGARTEN STAFF IN CHINA FOR SELECTED YEARS, 1949–85

Year	Total Number of Staff[a]	Teachers[b]	
		Number	Percent of Total Staff
Before 1949 (highest number)	2,500	2,100	84
1951	5,500	4,400	80
1952	19,100	13,600	71.2
1957	101,400	49,800	49.1
1958	1,553,000	1,339,600	86.3
1961	294,800	116,400	39.5
1962	161,400	70,100	43.4
1965	161,700	61,800	38.2
1973	170,200	85,500	50.2
1976	762,600	514,300	67.4
1979	532,700	294,000	55.2
1984	736,700	491,100	66.7
1985	798,000	549,900	68.9

Note. Data are from the *Statistical Yearbook on Education* (1985) published by the Ministry of Education of the People's Republic of China, Beijing.

[a]"Total number of staff" includes administrators, teachers, workers, and other staff members.

[b]"Teachers" refers to those who are directly engaged in teaching children.

TEACHER TRAINING

In China, training of kindergarten teachers is the responsibility of the Department of High Normal Education and the Department of Middle Normal Education, both under the Ministry of Education. Each of these departments provides two kinds of training: preservice training and in-service training. Figure 1, which outlines the training that is provided, indicates that there are four possible levels of formal training that a teacher may have: junior middle, senior middle, college or university (B.A.), and postgraduate (M.A.).[9]

According to the Ministry of Education's *Statistical Yearbook on*

Table 3

ADULT-CHILD RATIO IN KINDERGARTENS IN CHINA, 1980–85

	Teacher-Child Ratio			Staff-Child Ratio		
Year	No. of Teachers	No. of Children	Ratio	No. of Staff	No. of Children	Ratio
1980	410,700	11,507,700	1:28.0	609,700	11,507,700	1:18.9
1981	401,100	10,562,200	1:26.3	598,900	10,562,200	1:17.6
1982	415,200	11,130,900	1:26.8	637,200	11,130,900	1:17.5
1983	433,000	11,402,500	1:26.3	673,500	11,402,500	1:16.9
1984	491,100	12,947,400	1:26.4	736,700	12,947,400	1:17.6
1985	549,869	14,796,900	1:26.9	798,000	14,796,900	1:18.5

Note. Data are from the *Statistical Yearbook on Education* (1985) published by the Ministry of Education of the People's Republic of China, Beijing.

Figure 1

TRAINING OF KINDERGARTEN TEACHERS IN CHINA

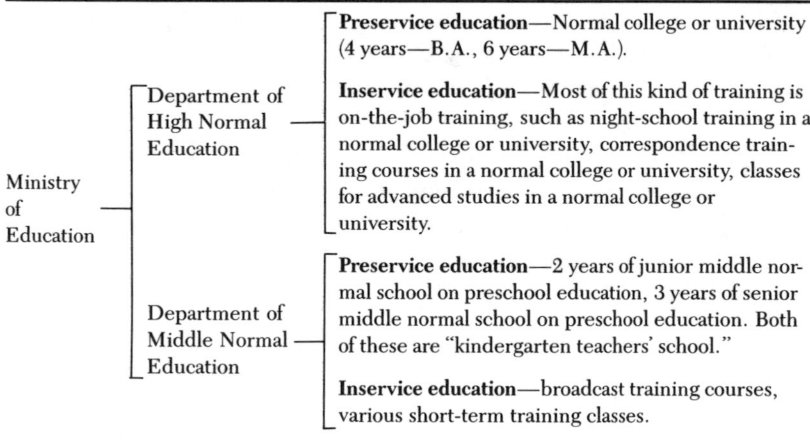

Education (1985), since 1949 the number of kindergarten teachers' schools and the number of normal colleges or universities with specialties in early childhood education have both been growing rapidly. In 1950 there was only one kindergarten teachers' school in the country, while in 1985 there were 57 kindergarten teachers' schools in 24 provinces all over the country. The number of students enrolled at teachers' training schools, which was only 809 in 1950, reached 24,352 in 1985.

Besides this, at that time there were 102,394 students in the kindergarten teachers' classes and vocational kindergarten training classes attached to middle normal schools. All these students are able to serve as kindergarten teachers after graduation.

On the college or university level, to date, 17 departments have established specialties in early childhood education, and these specialties have 5,294 enrolled students who can work after graduation as instructors at kindergarten teachers' schools. Some might choose instead to engage in management or scientific research in early childhood education.

Table 4 shows that among the country's 589,426 kindergarten administrators and teachers, 257,747 (43.7 percent) have at least graduated from senior middle school; 255,418 (43.3 percent) studied for some period in senior middle school or at least graduated from junior middle school. Those 76,261 with an educational level below this make up 12.9 percent of the total. Among the nation's 39,557 kindergarten administrators, those with the above-mentioned educational levels are respectively 48.6 percent, 35.1 percent, and 16.3 percent of the total. Among the 549,869 teachers, the corresponding percentages are respectively 43.7 percent, 43.3 percent, and 12.9 percent.

We can see from Table 5 that there are relatively few kindergarten administrators and teachers with university, college, or normal school training. In particular, only 16.5 percent of teachers have such formal training for their vocation. Consequently, there is urgent need to explore different ways of training kindergarten teachers if early childhood education in China is to improve.

TYPES OF PROGRAMS

With the growing need for greater national productivity, China's system of **kindergartens** for 3- to 6-year-olds has come to include the following types (classified according to sponsors): kindergartens sponsored by the Board of Education; by factories; by the army; by governmental or academic institutions; by neighborhoods in urban areas or by villages in rural areas; and by individuals.

There are four types of kindergarten service offered: **daytime service** (usually from 7 a.m. to 6 p.m.); **boarding service** (except for Sunday, children spend the whole week, day and night, at kindergarten); **half-day service**; and **temporary service** (for example, covering just the busi-

Table 4

Educational Level of Kindergarten Administrators and Teachers, 1985

Position	Total Number	Senior Middle Training or Above	Junior Middle Training	Less Than Junior Middle Training
Administrators	39,557	19,223	13,883	6,451
Teachers	549,869	238,524	241,535	69,810
Total	589,426	257,747	255,418	76,261

Note. Data are from the *Statistical Yearbook on Education* (1985) published by the Ministry of Education of the People's Republic of China, Beijing.

Table 5

Professional Training of Kindergarten Administrators and Teachers, 1985

Position	Total Number	No. of Trained Staff	% of Total Number
Administrators	39,557	9,942	25.1
Teachers	549,869	90,600	16.5
Total	589,426	100,542	17.1

Note. Data are from the *Statistical Yearbook on Education* (1985) published by the Ministry of Education of the People's Republic of China, Beijing.

est seasons, for workers in rural areas, or covering just several hours, according to the needs of various kinds of workers).

A kindergarten may be a single preschool class that is attached to a primary school and usually has only 5- and 6-year-olds, or it may be an independent kindergarten made up of children of several different ages. Some independent kindergartens are rather large, with about 20 classes; some are small, with no more than 3 classes. Generally, the children in an independent kindergarten are grouped into classes according to age: A young children's class is made up of 3- to 4-year-olds; a junior class, of 4- to 5-year-olds; and a senior class, of 5- to 6-year-olds. There are also some classes composed of children of different ages. Such blended classes are more common in rural areas.

Staffing and Curriculum

In *Regulations for Kindergartens* (March 18, 1952) and *Outlines for Kindergarten Education*, (May 24, 1952) the Ministry of Education sets forth requirements regarding kindergarten equipment, materials, organization, staff size, and activities. For example, the number of children for a class of 3- to 4-year-olds is limited to 20–25; for a class of 4- to 5-year-olds, the limit is 25–30 children; and for a class of 5- to 6-year-olds, the limit is 30–35 children. For daytime service kindergartens, each class is staffed with three adults (two teachers and one child care worker); for boarding kindergartens, there are four adults in each class (two teachers and two child care workers). The *Regulations* also sets the number of administrative and support staff members. A kindergarten with at least three classes is staffed with a director; a kindergarten with more than six classes is staffed with a director and a vice-director. For a boarding kindergarten, there are child care workers on night shift, workers for washing clothes, and medical workers who take care of sick children in separate rooms. A boarding kindergarten with more than 100 children is staffed with a doctor and nurse, and a daytime kindergarten with more than 100 children has a nurse and a medical worker.

In the *Regulations*, the following daily routine for daytime kindergartens is outlined: opening at 7:00 a.m.; breakfast at 8:00 a.m.; activity periods at 9:00–10:00 a.m. (one period for 3- to 4-year-olds, two periods for 4-year-olds and above); play at 10:10 a.m.; lunch at 11:30 a.m.; nap from 12 noon–2:00 p.m.; snack at 3:00 p.m.; play at 3:30 p.m.; dinner at 6:00 p.m.; dismissal at 6:30 p.m.

The *Outlines* emphasizes teaching children according to the characteristics of their age, pointing out that play and games are not only the major activities of children but also important means of teaching. It defines, as the major content of teaching, training in daily living and hygienic habits, in physical exercise, in moral character, in language, in general knowledge, in calculation, and in music and art. Regarding the number of activity periods for each week, the *Outlines* sets different limits for different ages: 3- to 4-year-olds have 6–8 periods each week (1 for physical exercise, 1 for language, 1 for general knowledge, 1 for calculation, 2 for music, and 2 for art); 4- to 5-year-olds have 10–11 periods each week (2 for language, 2 for general knowledge, and 2 for calculation, with the rest being the same as those for 3- to 4-year-olds); 5- to 6-year-olds have 12–14 periods each week (3 for language and 3 for art, with the rest being the same as those for 4- to 5-year-olds).

In-Progress Research Work on Early Childhood Education

In the field of early childhood education, the policy followed is one of combining formal research work, done by professional researchers, with more informal research. At the national level, the Research Division of Early Childhood Education has been set up in the Central Institute of Educational Research. At the local level, research on early childhood education has been carried out in the corresponding institutes. So far, 17 provincial institutes of educational research have been staffed with researchers in early childhood education. In addition to this, the National Academy of Early Childhood Education (under the National Academy of Education) and its 27 provincial academies, which have been gradually created, have pushed the research work forward. Other research centers that of their nature are concerned with early childhood are the normal colleges and universities and the Institute of Psychology under the Academy of Science of China.

Practical values play an important role in all Chinese research in early childhood education. The following have been some popular research subjects in recent years: only-child education; moral education; physical culture education; language education; divergent thinking; the concept of number; play and toys; science education; and early childhood education in rural areas.

Current Issues

Although early childhood education has been developing rapidly in China both in quality and quantity, a large number of problems remain to be solved. The most important are the following:

1. Scientific research lags behind educational practice and thus cannot play an important role in policymaking.

2. The quality of teachers, administrators, and researchers of early childhood education at all levels urgently needs improvement.

3. Establishing an early childhood educational system with Chinese

characteristics remains a problematic task, both in theory and in practice.

As a result, we look forward to the IEA Preprimary Project. We hope to make good use of the study to acquire a clear knowledge of young children's care and education in our country. By better understanding the quality of this care and education and its relationship to economic, geographic, and cultural factors, we can establish a scientific foundation for policymaking in early childhood education.

ENDNOTES

[1]Six Arts Education was a curricular program in the slave society of China. It included six kinds of educational content, including morals, courtesy, military training, writing, and mathematics.

[2]These are classical works of the Confucianists in the Spring and Autumn and Warring States periods, 770–221 B.C. "Zuo" is the surname of the editor, Zuo Qiu Min, and "Zhuan" means the style of writing is biography.

[3]This is a book written by Dai De in the West Han Dynasty. It contains 85 chapters, one of which is "Bao Fu"—"Nursing and Teaching."

[4]*Yan's Family Instructions* is a monograph on family education written by Yan Zhi Tui, who was a famous educational theorist. Yan Zhi Tui believed in teaching children as early as possible, even in the prenatal period.

[5]Published in 1925 by Shangwu Press, Shanghai, China.

[6]Published in 1925 by Shangwu Press, Shanghai, China, and in 1983 by Educational Science Press, Beijing, People's Republic of China.

[7]For more information, see *Stipulations Concerning Preschool and Kindergarten Set Up by Factories and Businesses* issued by the State Council, January, 1955.

[8]From the *Statistical Yearbook on Education* (1985) published by the Ministry of Education of the People's Republic of China, Beijing.

[9]Information on teacher training may be found in *Regulations on Normal College and University* and *Regulations on Normal School* published by the Ministry of Education, July 16, 1952.

XI
Philippine Care and Education for Children Aged 3 to 6

Luz G. Palattao-Corpus, *Director*
Child and Youth Research Center
Ministry of Education, Culture, and Sports
Quezon City

This report assembles information from Philippine research, documents, and scientific papers and reports on preschool children. Despite some limitations, the available data approximates the national profile of child care for 3- to 6-year-olds in the Philippines. For a more comprehensive view, however, there is a need for more macrolevel and microlevel early childhood research.

After explaining the historical and philosophical perspective of Philippine early childhood services, our report describes present-day child care options—both school programs and day care programs. We conclude with an overview of child development research and a discussion of future issues affecting young children.

Historical and Philosophical Perspective

Historical Background

Formal early childhood development programs in the Philippines started in 1924 at Harris Memorial School, Manila, under the directorship of Miss Mary A. Evans.[1] After that, interest in the kindergarten movement was picked up by the private schools, with a resultant extensive growth of kindergartens in the religious schools, both Roman Catholic and Protestant. At the same time, civic groups, such as the National

Federation of Women's Clubs, were motivated to set up "playrooms," which became the forerunners of nursery schools in the Philippines.

PHILOSOPHICAL/LEGAL BASES

Recognizing the importance of early childhood development, the Philippine government has not only promulgated laws showing concern for the education and care of young children but has also drawn up subsequent policies to facilitate early childhood development. The following are the legal bases for the development of early childhood services in the Philippines.

The Philippine Constitution

Article II, Section 4, of the Constitution provides that the "state shall strengthen the family as a basic social institution. The natural right and duty of parents in the rearing of youth for civic efficiency and the development of moral character shall receive the aid and support of the government." Section 5 of the same article declares that "the state recognizes the vital role of the youth in nation building and shall promote their physical, intellectual, and social well-being."

Presidential Decree No. 603

More popularly known as the Child and Youth Welfare Code of 1975, Presidential Decree No. 603 echoes a similar concern for the education of children. Article 3 of this decree states, "Every child has the right to an education commensurate to his abilities and to the development of his skills for the improvement of his capacity for service to himself and his fellow man." The more precise articulation of the code for a child's learning is seen in Article 12, which stipulates that "school and other entities engaged in nonformal education shall assist the parent in providing the best education for the child." Article 69 of the same decree mandates that "day care service and other substitute forms of parental arrangements shall be provided a child, where parents and relatives are not able to care for him during the day. Such arrangement shall be the subject of accreditation and licensing by the Ministry of Social Services and Development."

Presidential Decree No. 1567

Known as the Barangay Day Care Law of 1978, Presidential Decree No. 1567 provides for the establishment of a day care center in every *barangay*[2] or for every 100 families with preschool-aged children.

Republic Act No. 232

Otherwise known as the Education Act of 1983, Republic Act No. 232 defines the three levels of formal education, the first level being elementary education. Elementary education traditionally provides basic education for children 7 to 12 years old, with an adjunct that is called preschool education, for children 3 to 6 years old. Preschool education normally consists of both nursery and kindergarten schooling.

PRESENT STATUS: SPONSORSHIP AND COVERAGE OF EARLY CHILDHOOD PROGRAMS

Present-day early childhood programs in the Philippines have a multiplicity of sponsors and provide coverage for about one fifth of the country's preschool-aged population. Based on the 1980 population census and a 2.70 percent annual growth rate, the 1985 projected population of preschool-aged children (3 to 6 years) was 6.3 million, or about 11.5 percent of the total Philippine population (Table 1); roughly two thirds of these children live in the rural areas.[3]

Base-line data on special groups of children obtained from the Min-

Table 1

NUMBER OF PHILIPPINE CHILDREN AGED 3 TO 6 YEARS AND PERCENT OF POPULATION THEY REPRESENTED, 1985

	Preschool Population			Percent of Total Population (All Ages)		
Age (in yr)	Both Sexes	Male	Female	Both Sexes	Male	Female
3	1,650,367	849,183	801,184	3.00	3.08	2.93
4	1,617,353	829,057	788,296	2.94	3.01	2.88
5	1,554,832	800,343	754,489	2.83	2.90	2.75
6	1,506,778	773,326	733,452	2.74	2.80	2.68
Total (3–6)	6,329,330	3,251,909	3,077,421	11.52	11.80	11.24
Total population (all ages)	54,951,985	27,566,849	27,385,136			

Note. These are projected population figures based on a 2.70 percent growth rate and the *1980 Census of Population of the Philippines* from the National Economic and Development Authority, National Census and Statistics Office, Manila.

istry of Education, Culture, and Sports (MECS) reveal that a sizable percentage of the preschool population (aged 3 to 6 years) receive formal educational programs in **non-MECS-registered preschools**—ones sponsored by such service-oriented institutions as the Ministry of Social Service and Development (MSSD); the Ministry of Agriculture, the Bureau of Agricultural Extension (MA-BAEx); the National Federation of Women's Clubs; and other religious and civic organizations. Table 2 shows the enrollment in leading non-MECS-registered public and private schools for the school year 1983–84. The total enrollment of almost 1.2 million represents about 18 percent of Philippine 3- to 6-year-olds. The largest proportion of these 1.2 million children, 50 percent of the total, are serviced by church-related agencies, which demonstrates a present-day preference for this type of preschool setting. This is no doubt due to the strong early beginnings of church-related kindergartens in the Philippines. The Ministry of Social Services and Development services 39 percent of the preschoolers who are in non-MECS-registered preschools, indicating the popularity of MSSD center-based day care centers. This is to be expected, because their setup is the most favorable to the low-income families. Meanwhile, the MA-BAEx serves another 10 percent, and the remaining 1 percent is served by other governmental and private welfare agencies.

The present status of early childhood programs can also be gauged in part by the number of **MECS-registered preschools**—both public and

Table 2

Preschool Children (Aged 3 to 6) Served by Agencies Other Than MECS-Registered Schools, 1983–84

Agency	Enrollment	Percent of Total Enrollment
MSSD, Bureau of Family Life and Child Welfare	464,828	39.64
MSSD, SEA Kalusugan	1,260	0.11
MA, Bureau of Agricultural Extension	115,418	9.84
National Federation of Women's Clubs	4,668	0.40
Church-related centers	586,463	50.00
Private welfare agencies	89	0.01
Total	1,172,726	100.00

Note. Statistics are from the Ministry of Education, Culture, and Sports—Council for the Welfare of Children, *Report on the Situation of Children: Education Sector* (Manila, 1985).

private—that are being established in the country; the total number is estimated to be growing at an average rate of 2 percent annually. Table 3, which gives the 1983–84 distribution of these MECS-registered preschools by region, shows a wide margin between the numbers of public and private preschools. In the National Capital Region, Region IV, Region VII, and Region XI, private preschools predominate; public preschools demonstrate a big margin over the private ones in Regions I, II, VI, VIII and XII. In comparing the total numbers of public and private MECS-registered preschools in Table 3, one sees that overall there are more public than private preschools. However, Table 3 figures may conceal the real situation, since there are many private kindergarten schools not registered with the MECS.

There are no available statistics regarding enrollment in MECS-registered preschools for the school year 1983–1984. While some of these preschools have several sections of 20 to 30 pupils per class, there are also some preschools with only one class of fewer than 20 pupils. As a very rough estimate of the enrollment in MECS-registered preschools, the number of such schools (2,345 from Table 3) can be multiplied by 50,

Table 3

DISTRIBUTION OF MECS-REGISTERED PRESCHOOLS BY REGION, 1983–84

Region		Type of School		
		Public	Private	Total
National Capital Region		191	413	604
I	Ilocos Region	271	43	314
II	Cagayan Valley	103	14	117
III	Central Luzon	72	68	140
IV	Southern Tagalog	66	90	156
V	Bicol Region	53	33	86
VI	Western Region	423	58	481
VII	Central Visayas	23	41	64
VIII	Eastern Visayas	50	8	58
IX	Western Mindanao	22	17	39
X	Northern Mindanao	35	31	66
XI	Southern Mindanao	21	32	53
XII	Central Mindanao	162	5	167
Total		1,492	853	2,345

Note. Statistics are from the Ministry of Education, Culture, and Sports—Council for the Welfare of Children, *Report on the Situation of Children: Education Sector* (Manila, 1985).

which is the estimated enrollment of one morning and one afternoon class of 25 pupils each. This gives a total of 117,250 children enrolled in MECS-registered preschools. With this figure and the total enrollment figure from Table 2, the number of preschool-aged Philippine children receiving some form of structured early childhood education comes to 1,289,976, which is 20.38 percent of the 3- to 6-year-old population.

DESCRIPTION OF CHILD CARE OPTIONS

In this section, we describe the child care options provided by the public and private schools under the Ministry of Education, Culture, and Sports (in other words, the "school programs" for 3- to 6-year-olds). We also describe the home/family-based and center-based day care services provided by the Ministry of Agriculture and the Ministry of Social Services and Development, respectively.[4]

THE SCHOOL PROGRAMS

A school program is the usual form of delivering preschool education to children aged 3 to 6, and it may be within either the public or private sector. The public-sector school program is a preschool class attached to the regular public school and normally held on public school grounds. The private-sector school program can be any one of a number of MECS-registered preschools run by private individuals, institutions, church organizations, or corporations.

Public preschools depend mostly on the financial support of the local government through school board assistance; they also depend on support by parents and by social or civic organizations, such as the Rotary, Lions, and Kiwanis Clubs. Most private preschools depend on parents' support; others depend on sponsorship by religious organizations, social or civic groups, and charitable foundations. A few private preschools are fortunate enough to have private benefactors, either local or foreign.

A major problem for preschools in the private sector is being able to satisfy the regulations or licensing requirements as provided for in the *Manual of Regulations for Private Schools* (7th edition), the Department of Education and Culture Order No. 60 (1975), and the Ministry of Education and Culture Order No. 24 (1978). The public preschools more easily satisfy licensing requirements, since they are adjuncts of regular public elementary schools. Hence there are no problems with compliance regarding size of classrooms, adequate playground areas, equipment, and other school facilities. Likewise, the public preschools have no compliance problem regarding the professional background of teachers, since the preschool teachers are also elementary school teachers, hence professionally trained.

The teaching staff in the preschools have in general (in 93 percent of the cases) completed formal training as teachers; they may have a bachelor of science degree in elementary education, or a bachelor of science degree in kindergarten education, or the equivalent. Salaries of teachers vary according to the type of school a teacher is employed in. In the case of a private school, salaries depend on the location and sponsorship or ownership of the school (whether the school is owned by private individuals or affiliated with an institution), whereas in the public schools, salaries are regulated according to government standards.

Classes in preschools are held from 2 to 3 hours per session, for 5 days a week, allowing for Christmas and summer breaks. Some preschools have double (morning and afternoon) sessions. Ninety percent of the preschool classes are held in regular classrooms, with an outdoor play area, and with the basic equipment and materials. (The amount of equipment and materials varies widely from school to school, with private schools being the best supplied.) About 60 percent of preschool classes have 25 or fewer children per class, suggesting a condition comfortable enough for young children to learn. About 45 percent of the preschool classes maintain a child-adult ratio of 20 to 1. The rest have more than 20 children per teacher. (In a number of cases, the 20 to 1 ratio is misleading, since it may mean that one teacher holds two sessions a day.) There is no apparent attempt to enroll equal numbers of boys and girls per class. Owing to the unequal distribution of children admitted by age level, many classes have vertical enrollment (multi-age classes of 3- to 6-year-olds).

The preschool programs are anchored on the philosophy that every child is a valuable commodity and therefore must be given opportunities to develop his competencies and potential early in life. As such, programs essentially aim at preparing 3- to 6-year-olds for school. This goal is translated into the following program components: teaching preacademic skills (reported in 70 percent of programs); teaching daily living skills (in 98 percent of programs); and providing arts, dance, music, snacks, and rest (in 100 percent of programs). Where schools adopt specific teaching methods like those of Montessori or Piaget, extensive sensory and motor experience is provided, and teachers facilitate children's independent work. In a few of the private settings, medical services add sophistication to the whole program.

Parents' main involvement in their children's preschool education consists of financial support. This is especially true of those parents who send their children to private schools. Although the public schools offer free preschool education, parents are still burdened with financial donations, and about 65 percent of public school parents also render physical assistance to the school, sometimes as occasional volunteers.

THE DAY CARE SERVICES

The day care services in the Philippines are a total departure from the traditional concept of day care centers that serve children 6 years old and below for the whole day while their mothers are at work. More often than not, day care services (which are essentially government-initiated but not necessarily government-funded) are delivered in much the same way as the public and private preschool programs.

Representing the government in helping families facilitate early childhood development are the Ministry of Social Services and Development (MSSD) and the Bureau of Agriculture Extension (BAEx)—Home Economics Division, of the Ministry of Agriculture. The MSSD (then the Social Welfare Administration) first developed a day care service in 1964 under the Philippine Urban Community Welfare Program: This service formed part of the UNICEF-Assisted Social Service Project focusing on the social development of preschool children in communities receiving welfare programs. The program was later, in 1972, strengthened by supplemental feeding, particularly for the malnourished preschoolers in 671 day care centers. The services (mostly center-based) gained support from local governments, voluntary organizations, and parent groups, so that by 1975, more local governments assumed the sponsorship of the centers. With the passing of the Child and Youth Welfare Code (Presidential Decree No. 603, 1975) and the 1978 Barangay Day Care Center Law (Presidential Decree No. 1567, 1978), the program was brought to more and more communities. MSSD statistics for 1985 report serving 13,771 out of 41,114 barangays throughout the country.[5]

With the program getting another boost from additional UNICEF assistance from 1983 to 1987, day care service was expanded to include the training of more child care workers and the training of mothers in families to enable them to develop appropriate teaching and learning devices and play materials. A new concept was introduced—the delivery of day care services to mothers in their homes to enhance the development of the preschoolers who for one reason or another were unable to be in the centers. It entailed introducing into the home materials and devices like those available in the day care centers. Thus, the MSSD day care services took on, in part, a home-based nature.

While the MSSD day care services in centers were gaining strength, growing equally as fast were the Rural Improvement Club (RIC) children's centers, spearheaded by the BAEx. The RIC centers are participated in by mothers in rural communities who are trained by the BAEx home management technicians in homemaking and parenting skills. Along with the emerging home-based MSSD day care services, the RIC centers have been able to serve as another potent venue for reaching out to more mothers/leaders to enrich their knowledge of child growth and development; to train them in the use of stimulating activities and materials—poems, songs, games, stories, and toys; to develop their skills on how to prevent, detect, and intervene in simple childhood problems; and to help them apply these competencies in handling their preschool-aged children right in their own homes. As of 1985, the BAEx reported that some 6,006 mothers/leaders were already trained.[6]

Based on the reports in a survey of 103 child care workers[7] in selected communities, the philosophy behind operation of the center-based and home-based day care services is found to be generally the same as that behind the school programs for children aged 3 to 6. This common philosophy recognizes the importance of the child as a person and therefore provides him the opportunities to fully develop his physical, intellectual, and psychosocial potentials. As strategies for promoting early childhood development, center-based and home-based day care services differ mainly in how structured they are. Whereas home-based day care services are carried out in a very informal manner, center-based day care services are more formal. Sessions in center-based day care programs operate like those in the school system, with children reporting for class for about 2 to 3 hours a day on a 5-day-a-week basis and with program vacations following the school calendar.

Day care services are delivered to children up to 6 years of age principally for psychosocial purposes. About two thirds of day care service activities are geared as well towards children's school preparedness. To carry out the goals of the programs, daily classroom activities include experience in art, dance, and music, (reported in 100 percent of the programs); snacks and rest times (also in 100 percent of programs);

daily living skills (in 85 percent of programs); experiences in pre-academic skills (in 45 percent of programs).

The children served in day care programs range from infancy to 6 years of age, with the youngest (under 3 years old) remaining in their homes to be taught by their mothers (a home-based setting). In other instances, even children older than age 3 are kept from going to the centers, when their mothers do not work outside the home. For such children, it is assumed mothers (who are trained in related programs, such as Neighborhood Parent Education Assistance[8]) will find time to teach their children the basic skills necessary for growth and development.

The physical facilities available for children in center-based programs are reported to be limited. Only about 40 percent of the centers surveyed report having the necessary classroom facilities, outdoor play area, and equipment. Despite the ideal of having a small number of children (25 or below) served in the centers, some 85 percent of the respondents reported that they have more than the ideal number in their classes. Problems with over-enrollment are further reflected in the widespread failure of centers to meet the adult-child ratio of 1 to 20 (only 23 percent of the centers reported meeting this requirement). On the average, there is only one salaried adult staff member per class (the child care worker), with 82 percent of these workers having no formal educational training. Additional services are provided from time to time by parent-volunteers (reported by 98 percent of the respondents), but volunteer services consist mainly in preparing and serving snacks for the children.

National government subsidy for early childhood programs is scarce. Local governments are able to contribute about 65 percent of funding for day care services, while 35 percent comes from individual or institutional donations. Despite the disadvantaged conditions of the families of children served by the day care programs, about 26 percent of the respondents report they are able to generate some funds from the parents.

RESEARCH

The growing interest of researchers in the study of the preschool-aged population, specifically of the population 3 to 6 years of age, indicates a very favorable and active climate regarding early childhood development. Ventura's[9] review of Philippine research on child psychology between 1966 and 1980 reveals that of the 144 studies reviewed, the second most frequently studied group (the subject of 31.25 percent of the studies) was the 3- to 6-year-old population.

OVERVIEW OF RESEARCH

Perhaps the most notable research undertaken thus far in the area of early childhood development is the Impact Evaluation of the Early Childhood Enrichment Program (ECEP), UNICEF-Assisted Project (1983–1987), conducted nationwide by the Child and Youth Research Center, a research agency under the MECS.[10] Using a quasi-experimental design with horizontal approach (1983–1987), the study aims to measure the short-term and long-term impact of ECEP exposure on the learning abilities, value formation, socialization, and school preparedness of children aged 0 to 6 years.

The base-line survey data reveal that the performance of the ECEP and non-ECEP children in four areas (motor, cognitive-adaptive, personal-social, language) falls into three levels: delayed, average, and advanced. On the whole, a majority of the subjects from both the ECEP and the non-ECEP groups are average in each of the developmental areas, with a few isolated subjects with either delayed or advanced performance. In most comparisons, the mean ages at which the developmental tasks are achieved are higher for the non-ECEP children than for the ECEP children. However, none of the differences are significant.[11]

Part of the above-mentioned project was a follow-up evaluation of the academic performance and patterns of social maturity of grade-one children with and without ECEP. Results regarding the academic performance of subjects, indexed by their mean grade in the various subject areas (English, Pilipino, mathematics, and civics and culture) are favorable to the children who had ECEP training. No significant difference between ECEP and non-ECEP subjects is noted in Pilipino or in any of the 10 traits rated in "character-building activities." Furthermore, results regarding patterns of social adjustment—in self-help (dressing), communication, self-help (direction), socialization, locomotion, and occupation (with competence)— also favor the ECEP group. On the other aspects of social adjustment, the ECEP group manifested a significantly favorable performance only regarding "ascendant behavior" (social aggressiveness). No significant differences between the ECEP and non-ECEP groups are evidenced in the other aspects.[12]

A very recent study made by the Child and Youth Research Center (1986), also part of the UNICEF-Assisted Project, is the survey of the early childhood development of 0- to 6-year-olds in 20 disadvantaged and cultural minority communities.[13] The disadvantaged communities include the urban-rural poor in the resettlement areas, farming communities, fishing communities, and so on, while the cultural minorities include the Agtas, Gaddangs, Kalingas, Igorot, Mangyans, and Badjaos. Results disclose that of the total number of children up to 6 years of age, only 24 percent had exposure to some form of formal early childhood training, and of this 24 percent, about 1 in 6 children had ECEP exposure. The general patterns of performance levels of children in the various aspects of development (cognitive-adaptive, language, personal-social, and motor) reveal that a majority fall within the normal range. It appears that the largest percentages of advanced-level performance are found in the personal-social and motor areas, which suggests the potential of the home and community environment for facilitating growth in these areas. The highest percentages of developmental delays, however, are seen in the areas of language and cognitive-adaptive skills.

Research Questions Currently Needing to Be Addressed

The Child and Youth Research Center, on the bases of its research findings and of other related literature on child care, has identified eight research areas that may be considered in future research:

1. Alternative nonformal delivery systems for early childhood services
2. Variances in developmental patterns
3. Parents' perceptions of early childhood development programs
4. Qualities of an effective child care worker
5. Self-reliance models
6. Parent participation in home-based day care
7. The changing family system
8. Social mobility of young children

The MECS has also identified the following directions for future research in conjunction with the planning and evaluation of programs for preschool-aged children:

1. Looking into the existing mechanism for gathering information about, for monitoring the needs of, and for monitoring the services for

children up to age 6, including information on the effects of poverty on children

2. Looking into the possibility of putting all educational services for under-6-year-olds under MECS

3. Looking into the school preparedness of children who have and do not have preschool training

4. Assessing the competencies of teachers in preschool and day care centers

5. Reviewing the effect of small-sized (10–15 children) and large-sized (having more than 20 children) classes on the performance of children

6. Reviewing and producing appropriate and adequate teaching-learning materials for preschool children

7. Reviewing and producing suitable curriculum, books, and similar materials for preschool children

8. Reviewing and translating books and other teaching-learning materials into the vernacular

9. Surveying the numbers of children from cultural minority communities and from disadvantaged families who are served by the preschool programs

10. Conducting evaluations of preschool programs, curriculum, instruction, facilities, resources, and output

11. Conducting continuing parent-education programs to further acquaint parents with their responsibilities to growing children[14]

Child Care Issues of the Next Decade

The *Situation Analysis on Early Childhood Development* (in Endnote 4) describes the present status of early childhood development in disadvantaged and cultural minority communities. Among the policy issues identified in relation to the situation analysis, the following are considered of high priority:

Allocation of Resources

At the highest level of government, the overriding issue is setting priorities for the allocation of resources. The problem concerning provision of early childhood services, be it through preschool or day care programs, is not one of insufficient government awareness. Rather, it is one of competing demands for government resources. The government has enacted a number of legal provisions manifesting its responsibility to provide young children with opportunities to develop their potential. However, the strength of government commitment is not evident in its allocation of resources.

The day care services as presently delivered to 0- to 6-year-olds are principally under the auspices of the MSSD and the MA-BAEx, either in centers or in homes. The lack of national funds to adequately pay child care workers not only prevents the programs from hiring new, qualified day care workers but also makes it difficult to sustain or maintain those workers they have already hired. This situation of inadequate pay for workers results in expensive endless training of personnel, because of the fast worker-turnover, and deprives children of an early childhood program where workers are genuinely committed. This of course does not discount the fact that even among the nonqualified day care workers, there are some who are able to be very effective.

Adequate government funding is also necessary for the purchase or the production of teaching-learning materials and for better classroom facilities to implement programs. At the national level, more aggressive and sensitive policies are needed, including definition of a curriculum for preschool, definition of preschool and day care admission requirements, and standardization of fees.

DOWNWARD EXTENSION OF THE FORMAL EDUCATIONAL SYSTEM

Other than the favorable social adjustment of children who have had preschool education, their favorable school preparedness at age 6, and their subsequent favorable school performance—all of which are reported in a number of local investigations—the advantages of early schooling (that is, exposure to some form of early childhood enrichment program) include reduced dropout rate at the elementary level and an increased literacy rate.[15]

The present practice of pegging the school admission age at 7 years has been prostituted by many administrators who admit children at age 6. Owing to the scanty resources, this illegitimate entry of the 6-year-old to grade one squeezes out many 7-years-olds who deserve priority. Legitimizing admission of 6-year-olds to grade one could further the thrust towards equity and efficiency in the democratization of educational opportunities. The legitimization would likewise make way for the entry of children who have stayed too long (2 or 3 years) in preschool or day care. This new arrangement might eliminate the need for creating a bureau of preelementary education, as proposed by some. The present educational setup (the age-7 admission standard) will still warrant the licensing of preschools registered with the MECS and the accreditation and licensing of day care centers by the MSSD.

CREATION OF PARENT AWARENESS

Anticipating that not all children 0 to 6 years of age can be accommodated in some form of structured early childhood program, we must give serious attention to the need for educating parents about the importance of early childhood development. It is clear that mothers in disadvantaged families especially need assistance in learning how to care for their children beyond just providing for the children's physical needs and safety. (In many disadvantaged homes, even children's physical needs and safety are not assured.)

From another point of view, greater parent awareness might make some parents more willing to share the costs of educating their preschool-aged children, so the burden would not fall so heavily on the government, which operates on very limited resources. A comprehensive parent education program might also help create a greater demand for early childhood education programs. Strengthening existing networks of parent groups, such as the volunteer network in Rural Improvement Clubs, or the Neighborhood Parent Education Assistance network, would be a significant step towards increasing parent awareness.

PRAGMATIC PROGRAM DISPERSAL

Partly because of the limited resources of the national government, it has not gone very far in reaching out to 0- to 6-year-old children in tribal communities. Among the Mangyans of Mindoro and the Agtas of Cagayan, for example, early childhood programs and basic education are pioneered mostly by the religious groups. Most likely this is also the situation in other tribal communities. If parent awareness of early childhood needs can be increased, community resources could be pooled to allow for the operation of more and more preschool/day care services. Perhaps the government can provide some incentives, such as tax exemption, for individuals and groups who are willing to bring similar programs to the far-flung minorities, thereby generating more active collaboration between the government and the people and instilling confidence that people and institutions can be depended on.

CONCLUSION

The need for early childhood development programs exists. Only an estimated 20 percent of the children aged 3 to 6 are benefiting from some form of structured, educational child care.

The strengths of the present status of child care in the country include the following:

1. Sufficient legal bases are provided by the government in support of early childhood programs.

2. Both the public and private sectors show concern for the welfare of preschool-aged children.

3. A number of government agencies with a national network implement the program.

4. Early childhood interventions are aimed mainly at preparing children for formal schooling. This is true for both school and day care programs.

5. The increase in the amount of research undertaken in the area of early childhood is especially noteworthy. Along this line, the UNICEF assistance is definitely commendable.

In examining the foregoing data on early childhood programs, however, we note the following weaknesses:

1. Owing to budgetary constraints, full implementation of legal provisions pertaining to early childhood intervention has not been possible.

2. The confusion over which government agency should rightfully deliver early childhood services has resulted in a conflict between the Ministry of Education, Culture, and Sports and the Ministry of Social Services and Development.

3. Physical facilities needed for center-based early child care are limited.

4. Child care workers in day care centers who do not have proper educational training might be harming rather than helping children.

5. The adult-child ratio in most day care centers does not meet the 1-to-20 requirement.

6. Results of research on early childhood seldom make their way to the policymakers and program planners.

By and large, the nation's present efforts towards early childhood care and education recognize the incalculable value to the Philippines of securing the maximum development of our young children.

ENDNOTES

[1]J. V. Estolas and D. B. Nuñez, *Preschool Education in the Philippines* (Manila: National Bookstore & Publishers, 1974).

[2]A *barangay* is the smallest political unit in the Philippines—similar to a village.

[3]Ministry of Education, Culture, and Sports—Council for the Welfare of Children, *Report on the Situation of Children: Education Sector* (Manila, 1985).

[4]In this section, statistics with no other source cited are from a survey by the Child and Youth Research Center, *Situation Analysis on Early Childhood Development* (UNICEF-Assisted Project, Quezon City, June 1986).

[5]Statistics are from the *Ministry of Social Services and Development Annual Report* (Quezon City, 1985).

[6]*Bureau of Agricultural Extension Annual Report* (Quezon City, 1985).

[7]This paragraph and the following paragraphs in this section refer again to the Child and Youth Research Center's *Situation Analysis* of June 1986.

[8]A program of the Bureau of Child and Family Development, MSSD.

[9]E. R. Ventura, *Child Psychology Research in the Philippines: A Review* (Quezon City: University of the Philippines at Diliman, December 1982).

[10]The Early Childhood Enrichment Program is a national program being implemented by the MSSD and BAEx wherein day care workers and home management technicians who handle preschool-aged children in MSSD day care centers and BAEx Rural Improvement Club centers, and also parents, are given intensive training in early childhood education. They are provided with materials; "how to" manuals; books on caring for children; and children's books, games, toys, and stories. They are also supervised closely by social workers, in the case of MSSD, and by the home economics supervisors, in the case of BAEx. The program's services, materials, facilities, child activities, and teacher competencies are closely monitored by an interagency committee. A child with "ECEP exposure" is a participant in a day care center or Rural Improvement Club center or in a home-based program where the caretaker is ECEP-trained and the ECEP materials are made available to the caretaker. ECEP exposure may be for 1 or more years, depending on the child's age of entrance to the program.

[11]Child and Youth Research Center, *Impact Evaluation of Early Childhood Enrichment Program on the Performance of Children 0 to 6 Years: Initial Report* (Quezon City, 1984).

[12]Child and Youth Research Center, *Impact Evaluation of Early Childhood Enrichment Program on the Performance of Children 0 to 6 Years: Second Partial Report* (Quezon City, 1985).

[13]*Situation Analysis on Early Childhood Development* (UNICEF-Assisted Project, Quezon City, June 1986).

[14]Ministry of Education, Culture, and Sports—Council for the Welfare of Children, op. cit.

[15]See J. C. Sevilla, *Research on the Filipino Family: Review and Prospects* (Pasig, Metro Manila: Development Academy of the Philippines, 1982).

XII

Care and Education for Children Under Age 6 in Portugal

Joaquim Bairrão
Maria Barbosa
Isolina Borges
Orlanda Cruz
Isabel Macedo-Pinto
Faculty of Psychology and Education
Porto University

Introduction

The main purpose of this document is to give a description of early childhood education and care in Portugal.[1] There are important policy choices to be made, and there is no descriptive work of early education that may be used as a frame of reference. Having reviewed the existing documents—legislation, statistical data, theoretical and field works—we will attempt to present issues that are relevant to the decision-making process both at the educational and at the political level. At the same time, by surveying current trends in legislation and in statistical and organizational data, we hope to provide an orientation for early childhood researchers.

It should be understood at the outset that there are two government ministries that share the responsibility of early childhood education and care in Portugal—the Ministry of Work and Social Security (MWSS) (through the Central Bureau of Social Security since 1976) and the Ministry of Education (ME). They function according to different philosophies, with the ME operating in a centralized fashion out of Lisbon and the MWSS operating through fairly autonomous district structures called Regional Centers of Social Security (which is a rare exception in the highly centralized Portuguese administrative system).

Although our initial intention was to survey the most relevant statistical information and legislative developments of the last two decades, for two practical reasons, this turned into a difficult task. First of all, the public kindergartens maintained by the ME were started only very recently (in the 1978–79 academic year), and second, the MWSS has in the last two decades undergone structural modifications. These factors obviously complicated the process of gathering the scarce information that exists.

We begin our description by looking at the history of child care, at relevant demographics, and at national child care policy. Following this, we describe the current child care options and preschool curricula. A concluding section highlights present-day research and future issues.

HISTORICAL AND PHILOSOPHICAL PERSPECTIVE

Early childhood services have undergone the same stages in Portugal as they have in other European countries, although with a significant delay regarding the beginnings and the growth of the kindergarten system. This evolution of children's services has naturally encompassed the sequence of political and economic events that have characterized Portuguese history since the late 19th century, when the first kindergartens were created (Gomes, 1986).

The first institutions specifically designed for children under age 6 date back to 1834, during monarchial rule. Developed under private initiative and for social reasons, they were asylums for the education and protection of impoverished children. These institutions, which are still operative, have in many cases retained their original nature until recent times.

In 1882 the first official kindergarten opened in Lisbon, in commemoration of the centennial of Froebel's birth. The ideas and principles of Froebel, together with those of João de Deus,[2] had been known to those concerned with education for some years. The name of Froebel was even invoked before Parliament by a deputy from Porto, Rodrigues de Freitas, who in 1879 advocated preschool education. By calling the government's attention to the subject, he was able to secure a special budget enabling the local authorities to implement kindergartens. Another Froebelian kindergarten was slated to open in Porto in 1880, although it is difficult to determine whether it actually began operation. Nevertheless, due to the increased interest in preschool education, some primary teachers from Porto were sent to Switzerland to study early childhood education (at this time, the only teacher-training schools operating in Portugal were ones preparing teachers for primary schools).

Although only one (perhaps two) kindergartens had been founded, there was already a large group of intellectuals who were aware of the importance of preschool education and who developed a significant movement in behalf of young children. The name of José Augusto Coelho deserves special mention in connection with this movement. Known as one of Portugal's first modern educators, he is the author of an extensive bibliography on teaching and education. In one of his writings (Coelho, 1893), he analyzes some of the main dimensions of the evolution of the individual and describes a curriculum for "children's school"—for children from 3 to 8 years of age—as well as the main principles on which such a curriculum should be based. He covers all the areas of development: psychomotor, emotional, social, aesthetic, and intellectual. According to him, early education must not only be a pleasant experience for children, providing comfort and security, but must also develop children socially, preparing them for the tasks of the primary school.

Apart from spawning this interesting idea of a "children's school," the growing movement in behalf of young children also gave rise to some legislation concerning preschool education (*Diário do Governo*, No. 141, June 27, 1896). In this legislation, the objectives of preschool education as well as a general program and specifications for teacher training were laid out. The history of preschool education is marked by yet another important event that occurred while the country was still under monarchial rule: the creation of two João de Deus preschools.[3]

On October 5, 1910, when the republican system was proclaimed in Portugal, about 75 percent of the population were illiterate. The republicans were idealistic men, and among their main concerns were the high rate of illiteracy and the lack of primary schools throughout the country, so it is not surprising that the implementation of kindergartens was a part of the *Republican Party Program* (*Boletim do Partido Republicano Portugues*, 1915). Two laws, in 1911, integrate the essentials of the First Republic's ideas on preschool education, establishing the fundamentals of what it should be with regard to objectives, program, teacher qualifications, and so on. The laws also state that other young children's institutions, mainly the asylum-type run by central or local authority, should be transformed into kindergartens. Yet, in spite of the republican concern for legislation, very little was done, mainly because of the country's chaotic economic situation, high percentage of illiteracy, and political instability (46 different cabinets in 16 years). From 1910 to 1926, only 12 new kindergartens were created: 7 public kindergartens in Porto, 4 private kindergartens of the João de Deus type (in the cities of Coimbra, Figueira da Foz, Alcobaça and Lisbon), and the Israelite School.

During the first years of the Second Republic (1926–1937), no further significant changes occurred, with the percentage of preschool-aged children receiving education remaining below 1 percent. By this time, public kindergartens were eliminated (*Diário da República*, No. 28081/1937); the government realized that the existing kindergarten system served only a tiny percentage of children and that the public treasury could not bear extension of that system to the whole population. Consequently, political measures turned to the stimulation of the educational function of the family and to the support of the private institutions, with the João de Deus kindergartens being highly approved by the government. The Ministry of Education thus ceased to be in charge of early childhood education, and other ministries, such as the Ministry of the Interior, the Ministry of Corporations and Social Welfare, and more recently the Ministry of Health and Assistance (created in 1958), progressively developed services for children before their entry into compulsory education. The main purpose of these services was to decrease child mortality by promoting improved hygiene and nutrition. Since these ministries had no staff specialized in early childhood education, the public health nurse had the primary role in providing the services to young children.

In the mid-1950s the Ministry of Education was mainly concerned with the problems of elementary education and was still not directly involved with early childhood education. It nevertheless continued to encourage private initiative. There were by this time several public institutions dependent on the Ministry of the Interior (through the Department of Social Welfare) that assured assistance to children and less-fortunate families. Until 1966, the majority of the existing centers for children under 6 years of age had no educational purposes and were mainly concerned with the care and basic needs of children. The staff had no specific qualifications.

It was not until 1971, with Veiga Simão heading the Ministry of Education, that preprimary education was reinstated as part of the public educational system. This measure was part of a larger plan for reform of the entire Portuguese educational system, which became known as the Veiga Simão Reform.[4] It included plans for the creation of training schools for preschool teachers. In July 1973, preschool education was finally recognized as a constituent part of the public educational system. That same year, the first two public schools for training preschool teachers started to operate in Coimbra and Viana do Castelo. This measure was the result of the government's acknowledgment that most of the existing public services failed to address children's educational needs mainly because staff did not have any professional training.

We should also mention the teacher-training opportunities in existence prior to the founding of the public training schools in 1973. The first two private training schools for preschool teachers, under the initiative of people connected with Roman Catholic movements, appeared as early as 1954 in Lisbon. They were the Child Education Institute (which closed in 1975–1976) and the School of Preschool Teachers (which still operates). In addition, there was a specialized course for "child care nurses," which began in 1939 and which might be considered the forerunner of the training schools for preschool teachers; its original purpose was the training of social workers with a specific vocation in mother-child assistance. Also, in 1958 the School João de Deus was authorized to give professional training to preschool teachers. In the 1960s several private institutions for professional training of preschool teachers were founded throughout the whole country, and most of them were affiliated with religious institutions. Considering its own incapacity for assuming the task, the government highly approved of these private schools. In 1965, because of the number of people working in preschool settings without any kind of professional training, intensive inservice training courses were created for the preparation of preschool assistants and auxiliary staff. Most of the training institutions of the 1960s, however, closed in the wake of political changes after the April 25 Revolution (in 1974).

The April 25 Revolution interrupted the implementation of the Veiga Simão Reform. However, it did succeed in bringing to the fore Portuguese social problems in general, which became the main concern of political measures. Since then, there have been significant increases in the numbers of kindergartens and nurseries as well as training schools for preschool teachers and centers for special education. In many cases, local communities have organized themselves and used local resources for the establishment of new early childhood centers.

After 1974, due to the dispersion of early childhood services among several ministries, coordination of efforts to help young children became an important issue. These services became dependent on two ministries—the Ministry of Education (ME) and the Ministry of Work and Social Security (MWSS). In accordance with the philosophy of the new system that followed the revolution, extending preschool education to the entire population became an important goal, since the philosophy's aims were to reduce, as soon as possible, socioeconomic and cultural differences, to promote social well-being, and to develop the potentialities of the young (*Diário da República*, No. 542/1979).

All these changes in the area of early childhood education, mainly the creation of new kindergartens and nurseries and the reinstatement of preschool education as part of the public system, had an impact on teacher training. Not only was there a recognized need for more teachers, but there was also a general concern about the professional training of all those working with children.

Table 1 shows the increases in the number of trained preschool teachers during this period. It is easily noticeable that from 1981 onwards, the public schools began to show an increasing concern for having professionally trained preschool teachers. In 1977–78, for example, there were only 8 operational training schools, of which 4 were public. In 1984–85 the total number increased to 27, of which 19 were public. Furthermore, in 1977 the Higher Schools of Education were created, designed to graduate teachers for children 3 to 12 years of age.[5] These schools will in the near future replace all existing preprimary and primary training schools, public or private, and will also provide training for special education teachers.[6] In keeping with this general aim, several

Table 1

Number of Licensed Preschool Teachers Graduated From Portugal's Teacher-Training Schools per Year, 1981–86

System	Until 1981	81–82	82–83	83–84	84–85	85–86	86–87	Total
Private training schools	3,874	339	356	439	490	533	551	6,582
Public training schools	806	382	518	490	558	618	612	3,984
Total	4,680	721	874	929	1,048	1,151	1,163	

Note. Statistics obtained from the General Office of Basic and Secondary Education (ME), 1988.

courses for inservice training have been promoted, for auxiliary staff and assistants, throughout the whole country (cf. Gabinete de Estudos e Planeamento, 1986).

DEMOGRAPHIC DATA

As we have mentioned earlier, the national statistics regarding early childhood services are scarce. For the population under age 6, we have only been able to determine the distribution of two age groups: children from birth to age 2, and children from age 3 to age 5. Table 2 shows the distribution of the under-6 population, together with the distribution of the total population. From the table, we can see that although the districts of Lisbon and Porto have the highest percentages of Portugal's under-6 population (23 percent and 18.8 percent, respectively), it is the district of Braga that has the highest percentage of under-6-year-old children in relation to its total district population (12.1 percent). It is also interesting to note the uneven distribution of Portugal's under-6-year-olds among the 18 districts—with 23 percent in Lisbon and 1.2 percent in Portalegre being the two extremes. This unevenness somewhat reflects the distribution of the general Portuguese population, which is more concentrated near the cities that are the most important industrial and trade centers (Lisbon, Braga, and Porto, for example). There is less variation (or unevenness) in the percentages that compare district under-6-year-olds with district residents; these range from 12.1 percent in Braga to 6.2 percent in Setúbal.

Some of the 18 districts are chiefly rural: Bragança, Vila Real, Viseu, Portalegre, Évora, Beja, Castelo Branco, and Guarda; others are chiefly industrialized: Lisbon, Porto, and Setúbal. In this group, but industrialized to a lesser degree, we can also include Braga and Aveiro. The remaining districts would be described as having a moderate level of industrialization.

Table 3 indicates the extent of mothers' employment in Portugal as of the 1981 general census. It shows that the five most industrialized districts, as one would expect, have high percentages of employed mothers under 39 years old—and this potentially includes mothers of preschool-aged youngsters. These percentages range from 26.4 percent to 63.5 percent. The highest percentages are 63.1 percent in Lisbon and 63.5 percent in Setúbal.

Table 4 shows the percentages of Portuguese children up to 6 years

Table 2

PER-DISTRICT RESIDENT, AGE 0–2, AND AGE 3–5 POPULATIONS, 1981

District	Resident Population	Age 0–2 Population	Age 3–5 Population	Age 0–5 Population	District Age 0–5 Population: As % of All-District 0–5 Population	District Age 0–5 Population: As % of District Resident Population
Aveiro	622,988	29,203	31,491	60,694	6.9	9.7
Beja	188,420	7,149	8,072	15,221	1.7	8.1
Braga	708,924	41,817	44,260	86,077	9.7	12.1
Bragança	184,252	8,030	8,416	16,176	1.8	8.8
Castelo Branco	234,230	8,361	9,065	17,426	2.0	7.4
Coimbra	436,324	22,198	22,535	44,733	5.1	10.3
Évora	180,277	7,476	8,507	15,983	1.8	8.9
Faro	323,534	12,023	13,286	25,309	2.9	7.8
Guarda	205,631	7,622	8,078	15,700	1.8	7.6
Leiria	420,229	18,204	18,375	36,579	4.1	8.7
Lisbon	2,069,467	95,718	107,316	203,034	23.0	9.8
Portalegre	142,905	5,019	5,681	10,700	1.2	7.5
Porto	1,562,287	79,853	85,952	165,805	18.8	10.6
Santarém	454,123	17,283	18,711	35,994	4.1	7.9
Setúbal	658,326	17,959	22,698	40,657	4.6	6.2
Viana do Castelo	256,814	11,637	12,338	23,975	2.7	9.3
Vila Real	264,381	12,728	13,734	26,462	3.0	10.0
Viseu	423,648	20,796	22,306	43,102	4.9	10.2
All districts	9,336,760	423,076	460,821	883,627	100.0	9.4

Note. Statistics obtained from the National Institute of Statistics, *XIIth General Census of the Population*, 1984, p. 199.

of age who are served by ME and MWSS early childhood programs. An analysis of this data from 1984 shows that

1. Portugal is far from having total preschool-service coverage of children from birth to age 6. The highest coverage rates for under-3-year-olds are in Setúbal (10.3 percent) and Castelo Branco (10.2 percent), and the highest coverage rate for 3- to 6-year-olds is in Guarda (56.2 percent).

2. The overall percentage of children under age 3 served is considerably less than the overall percentage of 3- to 6-year-olds served—5.8 percent compared with about 32.1 percent.

3. There is a certain inconsistency between some of the districts' preschool-service coverage rates and what we know about parental needs

Table 3

PER-DISTRICT RESIDENT FEMALE POPULATION (AGED 15–39) AND EMPLOYED MOTHERS (AGED 15–39), 1981

District	No. of Resident Females	No. of Employed Mothers	Employed Mothers as % of Resident Females
Aveiro	111,739	33,582	30.0
Beja	54,524	5,422	9.9
Braga	147,917	39,107	26.4
Bragança	40,287	3,910	9.7
Castelo Branco	56,666	7,891	13.9
Coimbra	81,401	20,326	25.0
Évora	41,807	8,053	19.3
Faro	51,559	13,619	26.4
Guarda	47,219	6,026	12.8
Leiria	74,481	17,171	23.1
Lisbon	213,251	134,483	63.1
Portalegre	35,681	4,543	12.7
Porto	276,077	87,331	31.6
Santarém	85,592	17,699	20.7
Setúbal	61,731	39,216	63.5
Viana do Castelo	51,062	9,817	19.2
Vila Real	63,784	5,821	9.1
Viseu	101,896	14,005	13.7
All districts	1,596,674	468,022	29.3

Note. Statistics obtained from the National Institute of Statistics, *XIIth General Census of the Population*, 1984, pp. 199, 397.

for child care (that is, about the districts' industrialization/urbanization and female employment rates, as shown in Table 3). For example, the four districts with the highest ME preschool-service coverage are the *rural districts* Guarda, Bragança, Beja, and Viseu (with 38.6 percent, 26.4 percent, 26.4 percent, and 21.3 percent, respectively). The top three overall coverage rates for 3- to 6-year-olds (56.2 percent for Guarda, 42.3 percent for Castelo Branco, and 41 percent for Beja) also are in *rural districts*. However, this inconsistency is only apparent, as these are inner districts faced with problems such as the geographical isolation of the sparse population groups, which explains the central government's concern with founding new kindergartens to balance the cultural deprivation caused by such isolation. Moreover, in these rural areas children must often be left alone for most of the day while their mothers are working on farms or in other nonprofessional employment.

One might conclude from this that preschool programs are targeted primarily to meet children's educational needs (for cultural experiences and preparation for school) but also to meet the needs of the parents.

4. In 12 of the 18 districts, for 3- to 6-year-olds, the preschool-service coverage rate due to MWSS programs is higher than that due to ME programs.

In comparing the number of Portuguese early childhood institutions dependent on the ME with the number dependent on the MWSS for 1986–87, we find that the number of ME kindergartens (public and private) is substantially higher than the number of MWSS kindergartens—3,302 ME-sponsored institutions versus 1,070 MWSS-sponsored ones.[7] It should also be noted that some of the MWSS institutions in-

Table 4

1984 Per-District Coverage of Children Aged 0–6 by Preschool Services of the ME and the MWSS

	Percent Covered			
	Ages 0–2	Ages 3–6		
District	MWSS Services	MWSS Services	ME Services	Combined Services
Aveiro	8.7	17.3	18.4	35.7
Beja	5.8	14.5	26.4	41.0
Braga	4.0	12.2	7.8	20.0
Bragança	1.6	11.5	26.4	38.0
Castelo Branco	10.2	24.6	17.7	42.3
Coimbra	5.9	19.3	13.2	32.5
Évora	7.1	17.9	12.0	29.9
Faro	4.9	13.1	9.9	23.0
Guarda	9.1	17.6	38.6	56.2
Leiria	6.7	20.4	10.0	30.4
Lisbon	5.5	18.7	11.7	30.4
Portalegre	8.5	17.8	14.8	32.6
Porto	4.4	17.8	10.4	28.2
Santarém	5.8	13.4	19.7	33.1
Setúbal	10.3	24.7	9.4	34.1
Viana do Castelo	2.4	12.8	8.7	21.5
Vila Real	1.3	10.1	9.3	19.4
Viseu	2.2	7.5	21.3	28.8
All districts	5.8	16.17	15.87	32.06

Note. Statistics obtained from the General Office of Basic and Secondary Education (ME), the General Office of Private and Cooperative Education (ME), and the General Office of Social Security (MWSS).

clude nursery schools *and* kindergartens (serving children from age 3 months to age of school entry), while the ME institutions consist of kindergarten programs only (serving children aged 3 to 6 years). Again it must be added that the creation of kindergartens within the public system of the Ministry of Education is recent (1978–79) and that there has been a concerted effort to locate these kindergartens in areas having few preschool facilities.

NATIONAL CHILD CARE POLICY

OVERVIEW: PRENATAL TO AGE OF MAJORITY

The pregnant woman's right to medical assistance is provided by law (*Diário da República*, No. 4/1984): She has the right to free medical assistance and all necessary clinical exams, both during pregnancy and for a period of 60 days after childbirth. However, a significant number of Portuguese women, mainly in rural areas, do not seek any kind of medical assistance during their pregnancy and childbirth. The law (*Diário da República*, No. 81/1984) also gives a pregnant woman work leave for prenatal consultations whenever necessary, and an employed woman is allowed a maternity leave of 90 days. Only rarely is the father allowed to have a paternity leave.

Through Social Security, the government gives families a birth grant for each child (13,350 escudos), a nursing grant (2,450 escudos per month for 10 months after childbirth), and a family grant (1,250 escudos per child per month). ($1 U.S. is approximately 150 escudos.) As a standard of comparison, it should be noted that the minimum national wage is 27,200 escudos per month. The following grants could also be awarded: an orphanage pension (for orphans until the age of majority) and an assistance grant for sick minor children (for a maximum of 30 days per year, totaling no more than the worker's illness compensation.)[8] Beyond this financial support, the law also provides medical assistance and vaccinations to children, as well as twice-a-day work leave (totaling no more than an hour) for nursing mothers throughout the duration of nursing or till the child reaches age 1 (*Diário da República*, No. 81/1984).

Up to age 3 months, a child's main caretaker is considered to be the mother, and only after this age may the child enter into institutional care. For the child 3 months to 3 years of age, the following care options are also possible:

- The child can stay with a paid home day care mother who has no license or specific training in child care.
- The child can stay with a home day care mother who is licensed by the Regional Centers of Social Security.
- The child can attend a nursery.

For children 3 years and above, the informal care options are the same, but the usual formal care option is some kind of kindergarten.

A child may enter Portugal's 4-year primary school at age 6, provided that the 6th birthday is reached by December of the year of school entry. In some cases, primary school entry may be delayed if parents can produce a psychologist's certification that their child has some mental handicap preventing attendance at regular primary school.

Compulsory education normally consists of 9 years of "basic school," although a child can leave the first stage of basic school, primary school, at age 14 regardless of whether this stage has been successfully completed. Children are supposed to have the same teacher throughout the 4 years of primary school, but in the following years of schooling they have as many teachers as academic subjects. In practice, however, children may have two or even more teachers during primary school. This is mainly due to the system of teacher allocation, which is presently under revision by the central government authority because of the problem it causes, namely, instability in primary teachers' careers.

CHILD CARE OPTIONS

In analyzing the child care options, since these options fall under the sponsorship of two different ministries, the Ministry of Education and the Ministry of Work and Social Security, we will introduce the ME and the MWSS options separately and consider both the public and the private parts of the system under each ministry.[9]

Ministry of Education

Table 5 shows the number of both public and private kindergartens for three selected years out of the last decade in all Portuguese districts. Lisbon, unlike all other districts, has fewer public than private ME-sponsored centers—in 1986–87, only 137 public kindergartens compared with 249 private ones (out of a total of 453 private ones for the whole country). Also Table 5 shows a distribution of the ME-sponsored institutions that supports the earlier observation about ME services—that their development follows a compensatory strategy—with the public institutions being located mostly in rural areas, where due to economic difficulties, the private system has little foothold. This is not to say that the private programs that exist in urban areas are able to meet all the urban area's needs, however.

In the year following 1978–79, there was a 186 percent increase in public kindergartens, bringing the total to 406. This was the largest percentage increase for the decade. Private programs however have not developed at the same pace, and their major increase was one of 20.2 percent, in the year following 1983–84, when the total jumped from 483 to 581. During this year, the public system remained unchanged, as can be seen in Figure 1. It is obvious that the increase in ME kindergartens

Table 5

PER-DISTRICT DISTRIBUTION OF PUBLIC AND PRIVATE ME KINDERGARTENS FOR SELECTED YEARS DURING THE LAST DECADE

	No. of Public School Kindergartens			No. of Private School Kindergartens		
District	1978–79[a]	1981–82	1986–87	1976–77	1981–82	1986–87
Aveiro	18	223	354	11	17	16
Beja	4	97	112	2	5	4
Braga	14	100	271	9	9	14
Bragança	3	86	144	—	1	2
Castelo Branco	5	52	84	5	3	2
Coimbra	9	66	136	11	19	18
Évora	4	38	69	2	3	3
Faro	2	24	64	8	14	13
Guarda	12	149	210	—	—	—
Leiria	1	50	135	7	10	8
Lisbon	3	59	137	215	247	249
Portalegre	7	34	67	1	1	1
Porto	4	126	224	65	64	69
Santarém	13	137	264	11	9	8
Setúbal	6	30	61	16	27	33
Viana do Castelo	12	42	60	2	4	3
Vila Real	6	47	103	4	5	5
Viseu	19	188	355	6	6	5
All districts	142	1,548	2,850	375	444	453

Note. Statistics obtained from the General Office of Basic and Secondary Education (ME) and the General Office of Cooperative and Private Education (ME).

[a]There are no data for 1976–77, as the public system was not created until 1977.

has been mainly in public programs, with the private system remaining stable until 1983–84 and then decreasing after 1984–85.

Usually the child-teacher ratio is different for the two kinds of kindergartens. While in public ones the law stipulates a maximum of 25 children per teacher, private kindergartens have less favorable ratios that sometimes reach more than 50 children per teacher. In 1980–81, there was a private-kindergarten average of 30 or more children per teacher in 10 of the 18 districts. However, in 1984–85 the ratios improved throughout the country, with only two districts (Bragança and Viana do Castelo) having more than 30 children per teacher.

Table 6 has important information regarding kindergarten enrollment. As can be seen, a large percentage of public ME kindergartens operate with a small number of children. Those having fewer than 10 children are mainly located in rural districts (Viseu has 132 kindergartens, out of a total of 361 kindergartens, operating with less than 10 children). This fact points out the need for adapting child care options to the characteristics and desires of the local populations, in order to optimize the investments in preschool education. Unfortunately, only 60 percent of Portugal's available kindergarten places are actually occupied

Figure 1

PUBLIC AND PRIVATE KINDERGARTENS OF THE ME FROM 1978 TO 1986

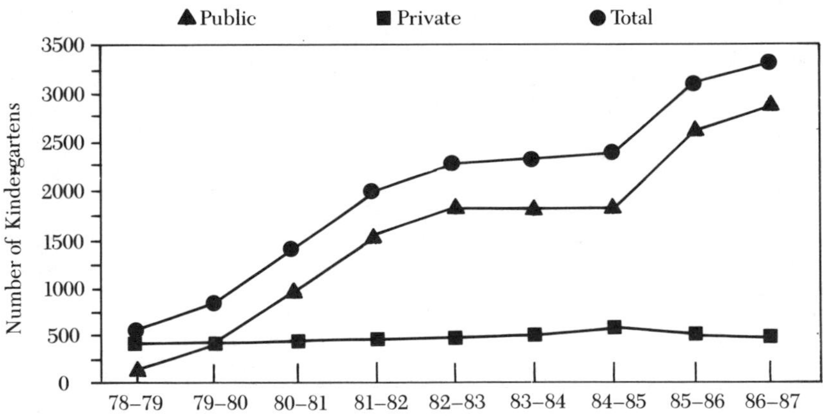

Note. Statistics obtained from the General Office of Basic and Secondary Education (ME) and the General Office of Private and Cooperative Education (ME).

Table 6

PUBLIC SYSTEM (ME)—NUMBER OF OPERATIVE KINDERGARTENS AND PERCENTAGE DISTRIBUTION ACCORDING TO ENROLLMENT, 1987–88

No. of Children per Kindergarten	No. of Operating Kindergartens	Percent of Operating Kindergartens
25	509	17.8
20–24	712	25.0
15–19	884	31.0
10–14	548	19.2
5–9	182	6.4
0–4	17	.6
Total	2,852[a]	100

Note. Statistics obtained from the General Office of Basic and Secondary Education (ME).

[a]Though there are 3,151 kindergartens created by the government, 2,852 is the number actually operating.

by children: There are children where there are no kindergartens, and there are kindergartens where there are not enough children.

Ministry of Work and Social Security

From the MWSS, due to the structural modification that we mentioned earlier, we were able to obtain data concerning only three years—1982, 1984, and 1986. The MWSS sponsors many institutions, all connected with child care and education, which may be categorized as follows:

1. Private institutions of Social Solidarity (IPSS)[10]
2. Public institutions affiliated with the Regional Center of Social Security of each district
3. Institutions of Social Activity, affiliated with the autarchy[11]
4. Cooperatives
5. Private, profit-making institutions
6. Factory-sponsored institutions
7. Casas do Povo (People Houses)[12]
8. Other institutions

The main differences among these categories are administrative and not functional. Kindergartens and nurseries are found in every category, either operating in the same building or separately. Special education centers are included in categories 1, 2, 4, and 5.

Table 7 shows the number of nurseries, kindergartens, and joint nursery/kindergartens under MWSS sponsorship, for the years 1984 (in parentheses) and 1986. There are some obvious conclusions:

■ There is a substantial reduction in all MWSS-sponsored child care options from 1984 to 1986, the main reason being the change in sponsorship (from the MWSS to the ME). This explains the opposite trend—the increase—in ME-sponsored child care options that was observed earlier (Figure 1).

■ The IPSS are by far the most important category for nurseries, kindergartens, and joint nursery/kindergartens.

There is still another MWSS-sponsored child care modality for children up to age 3 that, due to its specific characteristics, is not referred to in Table 7, and that is home day care mothers. For the moment their number, as well as the number served by them, is limited. In 1986 there

Table 7

INSTITUTIONS UNDER THE MWSS, 1986 (1984)

Type of Child Care Institution	No. of Children Served in Nurseries	No. of Children Served in Kindergartens	No. of Children Served in Joint Nursery/ Kindergartens	Total
IPSS	37 (168)	324 (531)	445 (248)	806 (947)
Public institutions	12 (55)	33 (87)	50 (24)	95 (166)
Autarchy-sponsored institutions	6 (20)	32 (58)	21 (19)	59 (97)
Cooperatives	— (5)	1 (13)	2 (—)	3 (18)
Private, profit-making institutions	22 (111)	59 (262)	63 (4)	144 (377)
Factory-sponsored institutions	— (78)	6 (73)	13 (6)	19 (157)
Casas do Povos	1 (3)	8 (17)	11 (5)	20 (25)
Others	— (4)	2 (14)	— (5)	2 (23)
Total	78 (444)	465 (1,055)	605 (311)	1,148 (1,810)

Note. Statistics obtained from the General Office of Social Security, *Social Security Statistics* (Lisbon: Author, 1986), pp. 31–99.

were 158 home day care mothers in the whole country, who served 535 children. Because the demand for child care outstrips the number of available programs, there is an increase in "underground" (unlicensed) home caregivers. These are difficult to survey, because they try to remain unidentified, so that they do not need to be licensed, which entails paying taxes and being regulated. The selection, training, and supervision of licensed home day care mothers, as well as the provision of their equipment, is the responsibility of the Regional Centers of Social Security.

Description of Child Care Options

Child Care From 3 Months to 3 Years of Age

For families with children under 3 years of age, it is the Ministry of Work and Social Security that provides formal options for child care. The following public programs are offered:

- Nurseries (crèches)
- Mini-nurseries (mini-crèches)
- Home day care mothers (licensed)
- Home day care mother groups

The private sector offers only nurseries, which are also under the jurisdiction of the MWSS.

These programs are not enough to meet existing needs, although in recent years there has been a steady increase in the number of available openings for children (about 1,890 per year). The main criterion for eligibility is the family's inability to care for the child.

The **nursery** is a center whose purpose is to care for children from 3 months to 3 years old while parents are working or unable to care for their child for some other reason. It can operate up to 11 hours per day. The nursery staff consists of a director, a nurse, preschool teachers (whose number depends on the number of children), and kitchen and cleaning staff. The children are grouped according to age: babies (3 to 12 months old), a middle group (12 to 24 months old), and an oldest group (24 to 36 months old). A child's age, although officially the main reason for group placement, can be put aside in favor of psychomotor, emotional, cognitive, or social development needs. For the nurseries in the IPSS group, the MWSS provides around 8,000 escudos per child, with small variations depending on a family's resources and the conditions under which the nursery operates.

The **mini-nursery** is a smaller institution—caring for only 12 to 15 children—that more closely resembles the child's family environment. It costs less to operate because it generally shares the services and equipment of a nearby larger nursery. The staff consists of a preschool teacher, two technical assistants, and cleaning staff. The mini-nursery is a new child care option in which the MWSS is very involved, although only four were operative in 1986.

Programs utilizing **home day care mothers** are normally implemented in deprived areas, where presumably the population is less open to traditional out-of-home care. Home day care mothers are self-employed and receive a salary from the MWSS (which amounts to 28,000 escudos for the care of four children, and an extra food subsidy of 760 escudos per child per month). They care for up to four children aged 3 months to 3 years (their own children, if in this age group, may be included, but without subsidy). Their activity is licensed and regulated by the Regional Centers of Social Security, which also provide them with technical and financial support. They operate 5 days a week, between 4 and 12 hours a day. The MWSS also provides the home day care mothers' training, which consists of a course followed by practical experience and for which the mothers are paid half of the wage for caring for one child. The MWSS provides mothers with equipment and, in the case of low-income mothers, with food. Occasional visits by a public health nurse, preschool teacher, social worker, or psychologist provide the mother with ongoing supervision and support.

Another form of care is the **home day care mother group**—a group of 12–20 mothers who are technically and financially supported by a center-based institution, either private or public, although they operate in autonomous buildings. Rules of operation are the same as those for the individual day care mothers. Like the mini-nursery and licensed home day care mother, it is a new care option presently under development, and there are only 10 for the whole country, serving around 390 children under 6 years of age. The legislation concerning home day care appears in *Diário da República*, No. 158/1984.

Child Care From 3 to 6 Years of Age

For children between ages 3 and 6, the main type of care is the kindergarten program. Its objectives and conditions for functioning are stated in *Diário da República*, No. 542/1979 and are mainly these:

■ To provide conditions for social and individual development that are not available at home

■ To collaborate with the family in providing health care and education to children, especially to at-risk and socially deprived children

■ To allow equal opportunities to all children, regardless of family socioeconomic level

■ To compensate for physical, social, or cultural handicaps and diagnose disabilities and deficiencies, mainstreaming the child whenever possible

The two kinds of kindergartens—those under the ME and those under the MWSS—differ in the kind of child care program they offer. The program used by the **kindergartens under the ME** is an "educational model," which implies the following:

■ When the number of applicants is higher than the number of vacancies, the eligibility criterion is the child's age, with priority given to the oldest children.

■ Programs operate 6 hours per day, 30 hours per week; the teachers serve an additional 6 hours per week for meetings, parent conferences, and preparation.

■ Programs close down 45 days for summer holidays and 2 weeks both for Christmas and Easter holidays.

The program used by the **kindergartens under the MWSS** is classified as a "social welfare model," which means that

■ A child's program eligibility depends on the absence or disability of one of the parents, employment of the mother, socioeconomic level of the family, attendance of siblings in kindergarten, and other criteria that may eventually be relevant.

■ Programs operate up to 10 or 12 hours per day, 5 days per week.

■ The kindergartens may function in centers together with nurseries; this is why MWSS kindergartens usually operate in larger buildings with more children and staff (including cook, nurse, and so on), providing meals and other diversified services for the children.

■ Most centers close down for 1 month each year, generally August, for summer holidays.

Since these two official systems of preschool education coexist, the establishment of any new kindergarten requires coordination between them. Whereas the MWSS, in selecting where to establish its kindergartens, takes into account an area's social and cultural deprivation, rate of female employment, and population of 3- to 6-year-olds, the ME considers not only these factors in an area but also the degree of school adaptation or school success in the first level of primary school and the lack of facilities for fulfillment of compulsory education.

Management of public kindergartens (both ME-sponsored and MWSS-sponsored) is handled by

- A director
- The pedagogical body (professional staff)
- The consulting body (board of directors)

In the ME kindergartens, the **director** is a preschool teacher who is elected for this function, while in the MWSS kindergartens, the director is appointed by the directive body of the Regional Center of Social Security. The **pedagogical body** consists of the kindergarten's director and the inservice teachers. The **consulting body**, which is presided over by the director, consists of the preschool teachers, one elected member of the staff assistants, two parent representatives, and one representative of the autarchy. The creation of this body, which occurred at the same time as the definition of these kindergartens, is an innovation that

1. Gives parents the opportunity to defend their own interests and to be involved in the extrafamilial activities of their children.

2. Promotes a closer relationship between the kindergarten and the community through the inclusion of a representative of the autarchy. (It should be noted that only at the preschool education level do we find the inclusion of both parents and autarchy in the school's governing board.)

In the private sector, the management structures of preschool institutions vary, depending on the kind of institution (whether it is a profit-making one, an IPSS one, a factory-sponsored one, and so on).

The kindergarten staff consists of preschool teachers and assistants. The duties of preschool teachers are legislated (*Diário da República*, No. 542/1979). Teachers must have taken an official 3-year course in preschool education, including a year of practical training. This qualification may be fulfilled in a private training school for preschool teachers, as long as it is officially recognized.

Both ministries provide inservice training for preschool teachers, although in different ways. The ME organizes inservice training in several modalities only for the public centers it sponsors, and it provides supervision of the programs. The preschool teachers are the main target of inservice training among all other professionals dependent on the ME. As to the MWSS, it is up to each Regional Center to organize training programs, normally for the staff in the IPSS and the public institutions under IPSS authority.

The salaries of teachers in public ME kindergartens are equal to those of teachers in public MWSS kindergartens, and both are set by the law (*Diário da República*, No. 290/1975). The salaries of teachers in private schools are variable and generally lower. Beyond teachers, other professionals may be temporarily hired by a kindergarten, according to its needs: doctors, nurses, therapists, psychologists, and others. These hiring contracts are not easily drawn up, as they must have the agreement of several state departments. There are no part-time employees in the public kindergartens, although in the MWSS ones, due to the flexibility in hours of operation, auxiliary staff may be hired to work certain shifts during the day. Generally, the only unpaid staff are the parents, and their involvement is minimal, since teachers have a difficult time sharing their educational role in the kindergarten. Whenever a kindergarten functions as a training center for teachers, the trainees (student teachers) might be considered as "unpaid staff."

Provision of kindergarten staff, facilities, equipment, and financing varies as follows, depending on the type of kindergarten:

- **ME-sponsored *public* kindergartens**. The ME allocates preschool teachers and auxiliary staff and provides funding for materials. The autarchies provide the buildings and equipment, and there are no fees for the parents.
- **Both ME- and MWSS-sponsored *private for-profit* kindergartens**. No government subsidy is provided, except in very special circumstances. Families have to pay monthly fees set by the kindergarten, which provides its own staff, facilities, equipment, and materials.
- **MWSS-sponsored *private non-profit* kindergartens**. Usually the institution that runs a kindergarten must provide the facilities, equipment, materials, and staff. Nevertheless the MWSS provides a per-child subsidy that varies according to the socioeconomic status of the family and of the center. Parents are charged fees according to a sliding scale based on income per capita.
- **MWSS-sponsored *public* kindergartens**. Facilities, equipment, and staff salaries are the responsibility of the MWSS. Parents are also assessed fees according to a sliding scale based on income per capita.

As we mentioned earlier, the MWSS kindergartens are usually housed in larger facilities than the ME kindergartens are. The public system however has to fulfill certain requirements concerning the space per child (a minimum of 2 square meters) and the number of children per class and teacher (a maximum of 15 for homogeneous groups of 3-year-olds, and a maximum of 25 for other groups).

PROGRAMS AND CURRICULA

Given the particular features of preschool education in Portugal and the fact that preschool attendance is not compulsory, it is not possible to talk about a single preschool curriculum. Rather, there are several curricula; in each case, the most relevant issues in curriculum implementation are the qualifications, personal characteristics, and years of experience of the teacher.

As a rule, preschool education consists of a set of activities based on general goals and guidelines (with no obligatory character) established by an ME department (General Directory of Basic and Secondary Education). These guidelines describe a program with a strong humanistic trend, valuing activities like art, painting, modeling, storytelling, and role playing (in some rare cases, prereading and prewriting activities may also be implemented). This general program, known as **Project Pedagogy**, is followed in the public ME kindergartens, although public MWSS teachers also commonly base their practice on it. There are, however, some exceptions, like the **João de Deus Schools** and the **Movimento da Escola Moderna** (**Modern School Movement**).

The so-called **Project Pedagogy** consists of a set of activities arising from concrete problems in direct connection with social reality. Children collaborate with the teacher in exploring and dealing with a plan for action that will integrate and give meaning to the children's activities. The teachers act in a semistructured way, coordinating action and giving information. The program is flexible, and the activities are evaluated according to the defined objectives. The main goal is to promote autonomy, creativity, and socialization.

The method of **João de Deus** focuses on the preparation of 4- to 6-year-old children for academic learning. The teacher has a very direct and active role. Children have to fulfill a highly structured plan of activities on a scheduled basis (as in primary school). Activities involving drawing, painting, prereading, and prearithmetic are common.

The kindergarten rooms oriented by the **Modern School Movement** have the appearance of workshops with specific areas for specific activities. These areas, or "corners," like the greeting corner, the press corner, the reading corner, the make-believe corner, contain all the materials needed for the activities. A cooperative organization of the space is adopted, and children go around the areas of interest, working either individually or in groups (small or whole-class). The teacher is the key person, whose main objective is the socialization of the child by promoting free individual expression, participation in the group's life, and a spirit of help and cooperation. The development of logical thinking and an initiation of children to reading and writing through "natural methods" are also goals of the Modern School Movement.

Research

A survey of the research on preschool education in Portugal reveals that there are few relevant studies, a fact that can be attributed to an absence of a tradition of educational research. Two main reasons account for the lack of preschool research:

1. The preschool system is relatively new.
2. Psychology is a relatively new course (created in 1976), and higher-level education courses began only recently. (Although the Higher Schools of Education were created in 1977, they did not start to operate until 1986.)

There are, however, some noteworthy research projects on preschool-aged children. The projects all use an ecological approach and are part of community-aimed programs. They are

- **The Alcácer Project**—a study of child development in a rural environment
- **The Amadora Project**—a study of socioeducational intervention in deprived areas
- **The Águeda Project**—a study of the integration of handicapped children
- **The Paredes de Coura Project**—discovering the child in a rural environment

Begun in October 1981, the 3-year **Alcácer Project**, "Child Development in the Rural Community," was the result of a combined initiative of the Calouste Gulbenkian and the Bernard van Leer Foundations. Implemented in the rural community of Alcácer do Sal (100 km south of Lisbon), the project aimed at the improvement of the educational quality of the preschool centers in the area. These centers started to operate after April 1974, owing among other reasons to the sudden increase in female employment. In the absence of qualified preschool staff, the community hired women whose only training was their experience as mothers. They were the main target of the project.

Since the project's frame of reference was an ecological approach to development, it also focused on other community systems: the directors, the parents, and the remaining staff, apart from the children themselves. Conceptualized as an action-research project, its general goal was "to contribute to the establishment of early education models adapted to the development of children in rural areas" (Campos, 1984).[13]

The **Amadora Project**, "Social and Educational Intervention in Deprived Areas," is a global project in which several resources in the community (such as educational, health, and social welfare agencies) integrate their efforts to

1. Give appropriate answers to the socioeducational needs of at-risk children
2. Promote family and community cooperation in and responsibility for the prevention and remediation of socioeducational problems

The project was undertaken in two of the most deprived areas in the district of Lisbon, districts characterized by slum quarters and government housing. The responsible team belongs to the Regional Center of Social Security of Lisbon, which together with the Bernard van Leer Foundation subsidizes this project. It started in 1985 and will last for 6 years (Centro Regional de Segurança Social, 1986).

The **Águeda Project**, "Community Integrated Education," has as its main goals to commit society to the child's development, to marshal facilities and resources, and to give priority to handicapped children. The project is an intervention one that includes all children who have reached kindergarten age. It started in 1975 as a joint initiative of some local centers (Secretariado Nacional de Reabilitação, 1983).

The **Paredes de Coura Project**, "Discovering the Child in the Rural Environment," is aimed at the reduction of school failure, particularly in the first 2 years of schooling. This community intervention project started in the academic year 1984–85 and is subsidized by UNICEF and the Calouste Gulbenkian Foundation. The project involves collaboration of professionals from several areas—health (public health doctors and nurses), education (preschool teachers), and social welfare (social workers). The main assumption underlying the project is that the quality of the environment for preschool-aged children determines school success and adaptation, particularly for the first years of schooling.

The Financing of Research

There are government and private research financing sources, and in the last category, there are national and international sources. Government financing sources include the following:

■ The National Institute of Scientific and Technological Research—a department of the ME, founded in 1976, that has as its main functions to finance research in higher education, to contribute to the setup of national scientifically based educational policy, and to collaborate in the training of the highly qualified staff necessary for national development

■ The National Junta of Scientific and Technological Research—a department of the Ministry of Planning and Administration of the Territory, founded in 1967, having as its purpose the planning, coordination, and encouragement of scientific and technological research in the national territory

Most of the existing educational research has been financed by private institutions of international scope, such as the Bernard van Leer Foundation, the Aga Khan Foundation, the Rockefeller Foundation, and the Calouste Gulbenkian Foundation. This last one is situated in Lisbon and is the sole financing source of Years 0 to 1 of the IEA Preprimary Project in Portugal.[14] There are other national foundations that finance more regional and limited projects, mostly ones confined to the areas of the country where the foundations are located, for example, Fundação Engenheiro António Almeida, and Fundação Cupertino de Miranda.

Institutions Responsible for Statistical Elaboration

The National Institute of Statistics is responsible for the national system of statistics and belongs to the Ministry of Planning and Administration of the Territory. In addition, there are other organizations responsible for the elaboration of the statistical data related to each ministry, and these should be pointed out because of their relevance to matters concerning the preschool population. They are the Cabinet of Studies and Planning, which is part of the ME; the Institute of Financial Management, which is part of the MWSS; and the Statistical Service of the General Directory of Health, which is part of the Ministry of Health.

Future Needs and Issues

From a survey of the existing literature, and from the opinions gathered through interviews with key people in the area of preschool education, the following may be listed as the main needs of the preschool system in Portugal:

■ Better methods of data collection to obtain more complete statistics

■ Better evaluation of the educational system as a whole and of the preschool system in particular

■ Evaluation/intervention studies of preschool teaching methods, of preschool curriculum, of teacher training, of the new care options now available (home day care mothers and home day care mother groups)

In the near future, the government policy will change to include all existing educational and care options, for all age groups, under the sponsorship of the Ministry of Education. This means that the ME will control the kindergartens presently under the sponsorship of the MWSS, with this control restricted however to the kindergartens' educational program and activities.

Another trend is towards the enhancement of what is considered "preschool education," which refers to the period between birth and age of school entry. For example, already as a start, the continual presence of a "preschool teacher" in each group of children under age 3 is now obligatory. This replaces the traditional "nurse." The phase in which the main concern regarding child care in the first 3 years of life was children's health and nutritional status is gradually being replaced by a new phase that focuses on early development and education. Nevertheless, the prevailing idea is that preschool is not a preparation for school, and consequently its noncompulsory character has been retained in recent legislation.

Finally, the recent government effort through the Ministry of Education to expand the rate of preschool coverage and at the same time to suit the particular characteristics and needs of the specific regions of the country must also be pointed out (Pires, 1987). Among the different programs, "itinerant education" deserves a special reference, although it is still in the experimental stage. It consists of educational intervention programs offered by one preschool teacher who visits several localities in which there are fewer than 10 preschool-aged children. The visiting teacher works with children and their families to foster development and education. This program seems not only well suited to regions with low population density but also quite adaptable to specific regional cultural features, and the outcomes thus far are encouraging.

This diversification in response to the needs of specific geographical groups is one of the factors leading the responsible people in the preschool area to hope for an 80 percent preschool coverage rate by 1991–92. In working towards this ambitious and desirable goal, the country's continued adherence to the European Economic Community certainly plays an important role.

SUMMARY

We have tried to search out what seems to us to be the relevant information concerning preprimary education in Portugal. This information, gathered from various sources, points up first of all the considerable delay that has characterized the evolution of Portuguese preschool education—a delay influenced largely by the political events of our country.

The first impetus for the creation of the current early childhood education system was the Veiga Simão Reform, although most of its plans went awry due to the April 25 Revolution. The Revolution, however, introduced a new dynamic into Portuguese life in general, which ultimately has contributed to the nation's greater interest in sociocultural and educational phenomena, including preschool education. Because of the changes since then, the picture we face today in the field of preschool education is quantitatively and qualitatively different from that of two decades ago, particularly with regard to the following aspects:

■ There is an increase in the number of centers for young children, as well as a greater variety of child care options (for example, the home day care mothers and home day care mother groups). Still, the national coverage of child care needs is less extensive than that of most European countries.

■ There is an increase in the number of training schools for preschool teachers and a greater concern with the development of appropriate preschool curricula.

■ There is a greater sensitivity on the part of policymakers to the educational goals of kindergartens (as is evidenced by the criteria used by the Ministry of Education in the selection of areas for the establishment of new centers).

■ There is a trend towards better coordination of efforts of the Ministry of Education and the Ministry of Work and Social Security, so that all children between ages 3 and 6 might receive appropriate services.

■ There is a growing tendency towards the mainstreaming of handicapped children who are able to benefit from school, although the care of the most profoundly handicapped children continues to depend on the MWSS.

Although Portugal still faces many problems that stem mainly from a lack of economic and material resources, the nation's preprimary education system seems to be undergoing a positive evolutionary process.

AUTHORS' NOTE

This document was produced as a part of the IEA Preprimary Project by the Portuguese National Research Center (NRC), whose directors are Joaquim Bairrão and Maria Isolina Borges. The authors acknowledge the advice of José Garcia de Abreu as well as the contributions of Fernanda Alves Pereira, Antonino do Amaral, Ana Maria Calado, Fernanda Maria Cerquinho, Cristina Figueira, Ana Maria Guardiola, Teresa Leal, Isabel Lopes da Silva, Maria Conceição Moita, Sylviane Neves, Teresa Penha, Maria Armanda Pinto, and Eduarda Ramirez. We also acknowledge the Calouste Gulbenkian Foundation for its financial support and the High/Scope Press editor, Marge Senninger, for her pertinent comments on an earlier draft.

ENDNOTES

[1]This report refers only to Continental Portugal, meaning that no data were collected for the islands of Madeira and Açôres, which are autonomous regions.

[2]João de Deus was a poet and an educator whose writings describing a new method for teaching children to read were published in 1876. Surrounded by a large controversy, criticized by some and praised by others, his nontraditional method was nevertheless quite successful.

[3]The first two kindergartens using the João de Deus method started to operate in 1911, the first year of republican government. The movement towards its foundation was nevertheless initiated under the monarchial government.

[4]Veiga Simão was education minister from 1970, while Marcelo Caetano was prime minister, and remained until the end of the Second Republic in 1974. His reform is described in the "Projecto do Sistema Educativo" [Educational System Project] and in "Linhas Gerais da Reforma do Ensino Superior" [General Guidelines for Higher Education Reform]. Both documents, which include plans for reforming the entire educational system, are published in *Ministério da Educação* (1973)—*A Reforma do Sistema Educativo* [Educational System Reform], Lisboa: Ministério da Educaçáo Nacional. Simão's reform was at the time (and under the political situation) considered very innovative and has been difficult to implement.

[5]At the present time there are 14 Schools of Higher Education in the whole country and plans for others to be created.

[6]Since 1975–76, training schools for preschool teachers have admitted male students. Today there are a few male students training to be teachers and a few male preschool teachers.

[7]These are official statistics from two government agencies: the General Office of Basic and Secondary Education (ME) and the General Office of Social Security (MWSS).

[8]From *Schemes of Pecuniary Lendings of Social Security*, authored and published by the Documentation and Information Center of Social Security, Lisbon, 1986.

[9]In Portugal, *public* agencies or institutions are government controlled and directed; *private* agencies or institutions are nongovernment ones that may nevertheless be regulated and supported by the government to some extent.

[10]The IPSS are a group of private, nonprofit, publicly cosponsored institutions (such as associations of residents, parish centers) that constitute a counterpart to the Social Security system. The IPSS were licensed in 1979, when defined agreements of cooperation were established between the MWSS and the institutions. The MWSS determines the conditions of existence of IPSS institutions and gives them technical and financial support. It also has the right to verify whether the institutions are obeying the conditions of the agreement.

[11]The autarchy is a local authority, with political and administrative power.

[12]In Portugal's rural areas, Casas do Povo are cultural, social, and recreational activity centers that can also act with social welfare purposes.

[13]Some other references are Projecto Alcácer (1982); Campos (1982); and Almeida, Lemos, & Gonçalves (1982).

[14]Year 2 has been cofinanced by the Calouste Gulbenkian Foundation and the National Junta of Scientific and Technological Research.

REFERENCES

Almeida, L., Lemos, M., & Gonçalves, O. (1982). *Primeiro plano de avaliação global do Projecto—Estudo No. 6* [First plan for global evaluation of the project—Study No. 6]. Lisboa: Serviço de Educação da Fundação Calouste Gulbenkian.

Boletim do Partido Republicano Português [Portuguese Republican party journal]. (1915, No. 2). Porto: Imprensa Moderna.

Campos, B. (1982). *Plano Geral de Intervenção/Investigação—Estudo No. 1* [General plan for intervention/research—Study No. 1]. Lisboa: Serviço de Educação da Fundação Calouste Gulbenkian.

Campos, B. (1984). *A formação participante de não profissionais para a inovação em Educação Infantil* [Participatory training of nonprofessionals for innovation in early education]. Lisboa: Serviço de Educação da Fundação Calouste Gulbenkian.

Centro Regional de Segurança Social. (1986). *Projecto Amadora* [Amadora Project]. Lisboa: Fundação Bernard van Leer, Direcção de Serviços de Orientação e Intervenção Psicológica.

Coelho, J. A. (1893). *Princípios de Pedagogia* [Principles of pedagogy] (Vol. 4). Porto: Teixeira e Irmãos.

Diário do Governo [Government diary]. (No. 141, June 27, 1896). Lisboa: Imprensa Nacional.

Diário da República [Diary of the Republic]. (No. 28081/1937). Lisboa: Imprensa Nacional.

Diário da República [Diary of the Republic]. (No. 290/1975). Lisboa: Imprensa Nacional, Casa da Moeda.

Diário da República [Diary of the Republic]. (No. 542/1979). Lisboa: Imprensa Nacional, Casa da Moeda.

Diário da República [Diary of the Republic]. (No. 4/1984). Lisboa: Imprensa Nacional, Casa da Moeda.

Diário da República [Diary of the Republic]. (No. 81/1984). Lisboa: Imprensa Nacional, Casa da Moeda.

Diário da República [Diary of the Republic]. (No. 158/1984). Lisboa: Imprensa Nacional, Casa da Moeda.

Gabinete de Estudos e Planeamento. (1986). *Sistemas de Formação de Professores. Contributo para a sua análise* [Teacher-training systems. Contributions for analysis]. Lisboa: Author.

Gomes, J. F. (1986). *A Educação Infantil em Portugal* [Early education in Portugal]. (2nd ed.). Lisboa: Instituto Nacional de Investigação Científica.

Pires, E. L. (1987). *Lei de Bases do Sistema Educativo. Apresentação e comentários* [Public laws of the educational system. Presentation and comments]. Porto: Edições Asa.

Projecto Alcácer. (1982). *Apresentação Geral do Projecto Alcácer e programa de acção do primeiro ano* [A general presentation of the Alcácer Project and an action program for the first year]. Lisboa: Fundação Calouste Gulbenkian/Fundação Bernard van Leer.

Secretariado Nacional de Reabilitação. (1983). *Experiências inovadoras no campo da integração. Um projecto de educação-integração na comunidade. A experiência de Águeda* [Innovation in the area of integration. A community education-integration project. The Águeda experiment]. Lisboa: Author.

XIII
Child Care and Early Education in Spain

Jesús Palacios, *Professor*
Department of Developmental Psychology
University of Sevilla

Introduction

This report presents a general overview of the state of care provided for preprimary-aged children in Spain. The report focuses on children between the ages of 3 and 6 years, since this is the group of most interest to us, but frequent reference also is made to the situation of children under 3 years of age. In general, these references allow us to illustrate some of the important aspects of the past, present, and future of the care provided for Spain's preprimary-aged children.

Publications concerning the child care situation in Spain are scarce and often fragmentary. For the most part, they present statistics obtained from the Ministry of Education. Yet such statistics, especially in the case of children under 4 years of age, do not always reflect the reality of the situation; some situations fall outside government control, as will be explained in later sections of this report.

To the extent possible, this report attempts to familiarize the reader with the present Spanish situation—to explain where we have come from, where we are headed, and which elements constitute potential threats in the future. The report is divided into seven sections covering these topics: historical perspective, demographic data, types of care provided, distribution of children by type of care, research trends, future problems, and finally, a brief summary of the general state of care provided for preprimary-aged children.

Historical Perspective

A comprehensive history of preprimary education in Spain has not yet been written. However, the data that have been collected by some researchers (for example, Faubell, 1974) reveal that throughout its development, preprimary education has depended on town hall initiatives, state initiatives, and the initiatives of private individuals or institutions. The roles played by each of these types of initiatives and the extent to which they have been effective depend on the historical moment being considered, the ages of the children in question, and the regions of Spain subjected to analysis.

Available evidence shows that town halls generated the first initiatives; some of the contracts established between town halls and schoolmasters are still in existence. The contracts were formulated so that schoolmasters could teach a certain number of pupils. An example of a town hall contract is the September 1415 agreement between the town hall of Castellón and Schoolmaster Arnau de Peralta. The town halls also formulated similar contracts with religious orders dedicated to teaching, as reflected in an agreement signed in 1677 between the town hall of Barbastro (Huesca) and the Order of the Escolapians, which allowed members of the Escolapian order to offer schooling in the elements of the alphabet, writing, reading, and counting. Although neither of these types of contracts specified the age of the pupils, they outlined activities best suited to young children, which suggests that they were concerned with preprimary education (Faubell, 1974).

Other well-established institutions in the area of Spanish education below primary level were the "friendly women's schools," or *escuelas de amigas* (sometimes called friendlies or *migas*). Although they were found throughout Spain, "friendly women" were mostly associated with southern Spain. The friendlies were women in the villages or towns who looked after children with mothers who worked outside the home or who preferred that their children be tended by another woman, so they could carry out their domestic chores more efficiently. Although, as Faubell (1974) points out, it would not be strange to find that the friendly women originated in the Middle Ages, there is no documentation of this. It can be proved, however, that friendly women existed in the 16th century. For example, the poet Luís de Góngora (born in 1561) begins one of his ballads as follows: "Sister Marica/Tomorrow's a holiday,/You won't go to the friendly woman,/I shan't go to school." Friendly women not only cared for the children but also prayed aloud with them and taught them to read and write. The friendly women worked for a moderate amount of money, usually receiving a coin of little value according to the monetary system of the time. They collected their pay each day as they inspected the children's hands for cleanlinesss upon their arrival.

For centuries, then, the care of Spain's youngest children was the responsibility of three institutions: schoolmasters under contract to town halls, schools run by religious orders, and friendly women's schools. But in the 19th century, the state became involved in the education of very young children in Spain.

The origin of state intervention in the education of preprimary children is directly related to the efforts of Pablo Montesino (1840). He was a reformer who, while exiled in England, became familiar with pedagogical innovations. After that, Montesino inspired Spanish educational politics between 1835 and 1849, and his campaigns for reform resulted in the Royal Ordinance of 1836, which directed the political leaders of each province to set up preprimary schools. In 1857 the so-called Moyano's Law was instituted, the general outline of which would have repercussions in Spain for over a century. This law required the government to set up preprimary schools in population centers with more than 10,000 inhabitants, but the masters who worked in these schools were not required to have any academic credentials (Ministry of Education and Science, 1979). The Law of Primary Education of 1868 established that "there should be preprimary schools in every town where the town hall may have sufficient funds available for this purpose" (Ministry of Education and Science, 1979, Vol. 2, p. 303). By the end of the 1880s, there were 815 preprimary schools in Spain, of which 347 were state-run and 468 were private. Children could be admitted to them at 3 years of age and remain there until the beginning of primary school, at the age of 6. During the last three decades of the 19th century, "kindergartens" began to appear in Spain, and Froebel's methods became popular. The concern with methodology is also evident in the work of Andrés Manjón, priest and defender of popular education who established Ave María Open-Air Schools following the foundation of an earlier friendly women's school in Granada.

The New School (Ecole Nouvelle) movement and its concern with active methods became influential in Spain at the beginning of the 20th century. The new educational methods were introduced in children's programs in Cataluña and Spanish Levant mainly through private initiatives. One of the most influential approaches was that of Maria Montessori, who lived in Barcelona for quite a long period.

The experience of active, experimental preprimary education was suddenly interrupted by the Spanish Civil War (1936–39) and by the victory of those sectors that opposed modernization, progress, and social justice. As happened in other aspects of life, the education of preprimary-aged children suffered; there was a return to traditional methods and content, and the role of prevention and compensation in preprimary education was virtually ignored.

This trend was not reversed until 1945 when the Law of Primary Education established a "period of initiation" for young children during which they would attend maternal schools (up to the age of 4) and infant schools (between the ages of 4 and 6). According to this law, the teachers in both schools were to be female, and their work was to be more concerned with child welfare than with academics and to be based on "the intelligent care and custody of the children under 6 years of age" (Ministry of National Education, 1945, p. 389).

In 1970 a General Law of Education was established, the general outline of which is still applicable. This law required two levels of education below the primary level: nursery school (for children aged 2 to 4) and kindergarten (for children aged 4 and 6). However, as a recent official report of the Center of Educational Research and Documentation (CIDE) recognizes, education below primary level did not constitute a priority within the General Law of Education of 1970 (Rivière et al., 1988). In fact, during the first years of this law's application, not only were no new places created for children under age 6, but the number of existing places decreased. This decrease was due to the high birthrates of the 1960s and early 1970s, which required resources that otherwise might have flowed into preprimary education to be directed towards compulsory programs for children of school age. Since the government was overwhelmed by the increasing demand for primary schools, it was the private preprimary sector that developed most during that period. The development continued, as will be subsequently shown, within a legal framework that was almost nonexistent and that made few demands upon this sector. As a result, the reality that materialized was of little interest in educational terms.

After 1975—at the beginning of the new period of democracy—preprimary education programs in the state-owned sector began to increase, although they remained concentrated in the 4–6 age group. In 1977 a series of social and political agreements (the Moncloa Pacts) were reached by the leaders of Spain's political parties. In the area of educational policy, these agreements set the following goal for preprimary education: a general increase in the number of places, with the aim of eventually providing a place for each child within the age group immediately before that of compulsory school-age (4- and 5-year-olds), together with a certain amount of surplus that allows for a minimum level of schooling within the lower age groups (Presidency of the Government, 1977).

As noted in a recent report published in one of the journals of the Ministry of Education and Science, preprimary education in Spain today may be best described as a "conglomeration of schools over which there is little control" (Report on Preprimary Schools, 1984). The most well-defined group is that of children between the ages of 4 and 6, which is distributed in state-run and private schools according to the statistics offered in this discussion. The level of preprimary school attendance within this age group is very high as a result of a number of interrelated factors: (1) the existence of a large number of preprimary school places in the state sector, (2) a growing awareness of the preparatory role of preprimary education with regard to later schooling, and (3) the increasing recognition that a child's preprimary school placement is important in guaranteeing access to primary school. (This last factor pertains especially to the situation in cities and the industrial belts that surround them, where there has been a shortage of primary school places and where having a place in the preprimary level can guarantee a child's acceptance into the primary school program in the same school.)

At this point it is worth analyzing some of the data provided by a study carried out by the Center for Sociological Research (CIS) in 1983. Project Staff interviewed 1,573 Spanish mothers between the ages of 20 and 40 with children under 6 years old. The women lived in cities with populations of 30,000 or more.

As Table 1 shows, the social and academic learning children acquire through preschool education were the reasons most often given by mothers when asked why they sent their children to a preprimary school. It is interesting to note that mothers with the lowest level of educational attainment were most often the ones who emphasized the importance of preprimary academic learning as preparation for later schooling (see Table 2).

In all state-affiliated schools (public schools that are either state-owned or state-supported), teachers of children between the ages of 4 and 6 frequently have official qualifications in the preprimary educational field. Schools belonging to the Ministry of Education and Science are free, while schools linked to other ministries (as in the case of some day care centers) either are free or have a system of fees based on parental income. Private schools (those dependent on the Roman Catho-

Table 1

Reasons Mothers Give for Sending Their Children to a Preprimary Center

Primary Reason	Percent of Mothers Giving Reason
So that they can learn to live alongside other children	33
So that they can acquire learning skills	37
Convenience	12
So that they are occupied	3
Because of the mother's employment	3
Because the mother is not able to pay the necessary attention to the child at home	3
Other types of reply	1
No reply	8
Total	100

Note. From Center for Sociological Research (1983, p. 93).

Table 2

Percentage of Women Interviewed, in Relation to Their Level of Educational Attainment, Who Place Emphasis on Academic Learning During the Preprimary Years as Preparation for the School Years

Level of Educational Attainment	Percent
Below primary school	45
Primary school	39
Secondary school	33
University diploma (3 yr)	25
University honor degree (5 yr)	32

Note. From Center for Sociological Research (1983, p. 94).

lic church or on some other kind of entity or individual) charge fees that are directly related to the school's prestige or to the type of facilities provided.

In the case of the under-4 age group, the heterogeneous nature of the system (which often becomes chaotic) is its most significant feature.

The most common type of center is the **day care center**, which exists in a variety of forms, and few such centers are provided by the Ministry of Education and Science. Other ministries (such as the Ministry of Employment) provide day care centers that can be used by employed mothers, but here again, such centers are scarce and the staff are usually qualified more in the area of welfare than in education. Something similar may be said about **care centers at places of work**, which are set up by business with state assistance. They too are scarce, and focus more on custodial care than on education of children. It should be pointed out, however, that many of these centers seem to be changing their custodial-care approach to one that is more educational in nature.

If there is little state provision for the care of children under the age of 4, the same may be said of town hall provision. During the past decades, town halls have exerted less and less influence in the area of preprimary education. It is only recently that some of them have again begun to develop activities in this area. The municipal trustee boards already in existence in some towns have initiated and supported preprimary educational programs that, although small in number, offer parents an appealing method of child care and provide interesting educational experiences for the children.

The friendly women's schools, which have continued to exist over the centuries, have begun to disappear little by little during recent decades. Nowadays, most of the centers in Spain concerned with the education of children under age 4 are the privately owned day care centers (also called kindergartens, nurseries, or preprimary schools), and their setup varies from those concerned with custodial care of children to those clearly educational in nature. They have grown in number as a result of the increasing demand and because of the complete lack of regulations concerning their operations.

Setting up a day care center in Spain is easier than setting up a butcher shop or a bar, in terms of satisfying licensing and regulation requirements. A day care center operation must obtain a ground license from the town hall, and when meals are to be provided in the center, a permit from the Industry Ministry that guarantees the premises are sufficient for this purpose. Once these requisites have been satisfied, the owner of the center can do exactly as he or she wishes with regard to the qualifications of center staff, the kind of program offered, the number of children per class, and so on. This situation has resulted in worthwhile programs as well as programs that are deplorable. These centers have diverse owners (religious institutions, private individuals) and a variety of fees. In the best of situations (although this is not the most common case), teachers or nursery school specialists (a specialty within the vocational track of Spain's educational system) are in charge of children in these institutions. Quite often however, the people employed in the centers have no official qualifications other than work experience.

To form a preliminary idea about the extrafamilial child care options Spanish parents use, we refer again to the CIS study data (Center for Sociological Research, 1983). Out of the 1,573 women who participated in the study, 54 percent sent their children (under age 6) to some type of day care center or preprimary school; in the case of employed mothers, close to 75 percent chose such child care options. In general, the higher the mother's educational attainment and the higher the parental income, the greater the possibility that a child would be attending an educational center outside the family circle.

To bring this historical review to a close, we should point out that in 1987, the Ministry of Education and Science opened a public debate on the education system in Spain (Ministry of Education and Science, 1987b), which has not been modified since 1970. The ministry's proposal suggests a major change in attitudes towards preprimary education. Preprimary school, which stretches from birth up to 6 years of age, is now to be viewed as the first link in the educational chain; it is not a compulsory stage, but the ministry's proposal also emphasizes that preprimary educational centers should not be viewed merely as care centers. Two age groups are contemplated in preprimary education—birth to 3 years, and 3 to 6 years— and the ministry proposes expanding state education for children between ages 3 and 6 until all children are assured places. In connection with the cycle involving children from birth to age 3, the ministry offers support, by means of specific agreements, for the initiatives of nonprofit groups or cooperatives. A maximum number of children per class is suggested (between 8 and 10 children to 1 adult in the case of the younger age-groups, and a maximum of 25 children to 1 adult in the older age-groups). Teachers will be responsible for the education of children between the ages of 3 and 6, while in the case of children between birth and age 3, these teachers may be helped by other child education specialists. The ministry's proposal favors adoption of teaching methods that encourage active learning and parent participation. Finally, an inspection system is proposed for the preprimary education area. The inspectorate will insure that establishments caring for children of preprimary age satisfy certain requirements in relation to building characteristics, hygiene, staff qualifications, and teacher-pupil ratios. At present this proposal is being debated within society and will give rise to a new law that should be promulgated by 1989.

Demography

The most reliable data available in connection with demography come from the *1981 Population Census* (National Institute of Statistics, 1985). The 1981 figures are especially useful because some of the statistics that follow (see Tables 8 and 9, for example) are related to the 1985–86 school year (the year in which the children born in 1981 ended their preprimary cycle). In any case, some of the most interesting figures in this report (such as the number of preprimary children at each age level at the present moment) have been updated with regard to the 1981 census. Before analyzing Spain's demographic situation, however, we will discuss the general characteristics of the country, which in turn may contribute to a better understanding of the data contained in this report.

Situated in southern Europe, having frontiers with both Portugal and France, and separated by only a few kilometers from the African continent, Spain is a country forging a new social, administrative, and political identity. Spain acceded to a new democratic way of life in the middle of the 1970s, after 40 years of dictatorial rule under General Franco. Following decades of isolation, Spain recently has become a member of such international organizations as the European Economic Community. The old centralized state has gradually acquired a structure similar to that of countries organized on a federal basis. At present, Spain is made up of 17 autonomous communities, some of which occupy a large geographical area (for example, Andalucía takes up one quarter of the country), while others occupy smaller areas (for example, La Rioja's geographical area is less than the size of any of the eight provinces that make up Andalucía). In addition, two cities situated on the African continent belong to Spain (Ceuta and Melilla).

Each autonomous community has its own parliament and its own government. The communities differ mainly in the level of administrative and political responsibility delegated to each of them by the central state government. Some of these communities already have responsibilities in areas formerly reserved for the central government, while others have fewer responsibilities and therefore less autonomy. It must be kept in mind that Spain, having emerged from decades of rule by a centralized government, is a new state that is gradually acquiring its identity. It is therefore understandable that among the autonomous communities, there might be different degrees of autonomy and different rhythms of evolution as a result of the politics of the past and the present.

According to the census figures of 1981 (National Institute of Statistics, 1985), the population of Spain is 37,746,260, and the number of women (19,216,496) is greater than that of men (18,529,764). The population is spread among the 50 Spanish provinces that are grouped within the 17 autonomous communities and in the 2 African cities that are part of Spain. Some autonomous communities have large populations (Andalucía, for example, has 6,440,985 inhabitants), while other communities have much smaller populations (La Rioja, for example, has 245,349 inhabitants). The large populations centered in and around the two major Spanish cities (Madrid and Barcelona) cause the autonomous community of Madrid to have 4,686,895 inhabitants and the autonomous community of Cataluña, with Barcelona as its capital, to have 5,956,414 inhabitants. (This is close to the total for Andalucía, despite the fact that Cataluña occupies an area less than half the size of Andalucía.) A little over half of the residents of Spain (51.3 percent) live in townships of more than 50,000 inhabitants, and approximately one quarter (26.8 percent) live in population centers with fewer than 5,000 inhabitants.

The number of preprimary children living in Spain is shown in Table 3, and the national totals are indicated for each age through age 5. Table 4 presents Spain's numbers of preprimary children for two different years, showing the significant drop in the birthrate in Spain between 1981 and 1986. In fact, in 1981 Spain's birthrate dropped below that needed for generation replacement (a birthrate of 2.1 children per woman)—a phenomenon that had already occurred in the mid-to-late 1970s in Spain's neighboring countries.

Nevertheless, Spanish children under age 6 make up almost 3.2 million of Spain's population, and they live primarily in the provincial capitals. Their families are among the thousands who in recent decades have steadily migrated into the cities from rural areas. In the case of the country's two largest cities (Madrid and Barcelona), many of those who emigrated from rural zones settled in nearby villages rather than in the urban centers themselves. As a consequence, these villages have grown to such an extent that they are now recognized as part of the greater metropolitan areas. They are "dormitory" towns; the resident families earn their living by working in the big cities. Dormitory towns are also

Table 3

SPAIN'S PREPRIMARY POPULATION BY AGE, ACCORDING TO 1981 POPULATION CENSUS

Age (in yr)	Both sexes	Boys	Girls
0	587,020	302,092	284,928
1	586,962	301,673	285,289
2	615,316	317,775	297,541
3	632,432	325,364	307,068
4	653,623	337,006	316,617
5	663,827	341,312	322,515

Note. From Ministry of Education and Science (1987a, p. 20).

Table 4

NUMBER OF PREPRIMARY CHILDREN IN SPAIN IN 1981 AND IN 1986

Age (in yr)	1981	1986
0	587,020	480,941
1	586,962	505,372
2	615,316	528,264
3	632,432	549,582
4	653,623	569,284
5	663,827	588,457

Note. Data obtained from the General Board of Planning and Investment, Ministry of Education and Science.

evident around other large cities, such as Valencia, Sevilla, Zaragoza, and Bilbao.

Unfortunately, the greatest expansion of these cities took place in the 1960s—a time when the ambition of speculators was not regulated by adequate urban and social policies. As a result, the areas surrounding Spain's largest cities often have unsatisfactory living conditions. It is possible to find housing that consists of multistoried buildings built side-by-side with very little recreational or green space between them. This type of housing also has very few social amenities. As a result of the arrival of democracy in Spain, institutions such as the town halls are trying as much as possible to alleviate some of the negative aspects of the situation they have inherited.

Parallel with this state of things in the great cities, we find rural centers of population that have long suffered because of the little attention paid to them. The unattractive living conditions in rural communities have contributed greatly to the migration of Spain's rural population to the cities. For decades, one of the distinctive features of rural centers in Spain has been the significant lack of social services (for example, health, educational, cultural facilities). As in the case of cities, many smaller towns are changing gradually for the better because of political and social changes that have occurred in recent years.

Another demographic fact of special significance in understanding young Spanish children's social milieu concerns family structure. According to the figures available from different sources (Del Campo, 1982, p. 73; Institute of Women, 1986, p. 86), over 90 percent of Spanish families have two parents living together in the home. Spanish families are very stable. Of the few one-parent families, 82 percent are headed by women. Divorce became legal in Spain in 1981, but the percentage of divorced or separated couples remains low.

In a typical family, it is the husband who seeks outside employment, while the wife is in charge of the home. This pattern is especially true in the case of parents in the period following the birth of their first child and in the case of older and less-educated parents. According to the figures provided by Del Campo (1982, p. 140), only an average of 18 percent of married women are employed outside the home. Whether a mother works outside the home or not depends not only on her status regarding children but also on the mother's age, since, as Del Campo (1982, p. 140) shows, childless married women with less than 6 years of marriage work in 54 percent of cases; married women with a child younger than 6 work in 24 percent of cases; women with the oldest offspring between 13 and 20 years of age work in 15 percent of cases (a percentage that decreases to 12 percent for mothers with at least one offspring living outside the home); and women with all offspring already living outside the home work in 10 percent of cases. However, as the report of the Institute of Women reveals (1986, p. 381), this employment pattern could very well change in the future for various reasons; among these, the most notable is the fact that giving up paid work for several years lessens a woman's chances of reentering the work force at the same level, which is one of the consequences of the high level of unemployment in Spain (presently about 20 percent of Spain's working population is unemployed). The report of the Institute of Women (1986, p. 454) also shows the existence of a strong positive relation between a woman's level of educational attainment and level of employment.

As a general rule, the typical Spanish family's lifestyle provides a favorable context for the upbringing of small children. This pattern is most frequently broken in large cities and, in such cases, in families with better-educated parents. It is difficult to pinpoint exactly why Spain's families have a lifestyle so conducive to the upbringing of small children without the need for additional resources outside the family circle. We cannot say whether this situation is a consequence of the population's high regard for family values and recognition of the importance of child-rearing, whether it results from the scarcity of favorable alternatives, or whether it is a result of both factors.

A clear example of how the organization of the Spanish family is geared towards the care of its youngest members is found in the information presented in Table 5, which is taken from the CIS study (Center for Sociological Research, 1983). One of the questions put to the mothers who were interviewed concerned the number of hours each day they and their husbands played with their children. As shown in Table 5, the percentage of mothers who spend 2 hours or more is very high (78 percent). Equally high is the percentage of fathers who spend 1 hour or less (46 percent), which also illustrates the marked difference that exists between mothers and fathers with regard to tasks involved in the care and education of young Spanish children.

Table 5

TIME PARENTS PLAY WITH THEIR CHILDREN

Hours per Day	Percent of Mothers	Percent of Fathers
1 or less	18	46
Between 2 and 3	36	29
More than 3	42	18
No time spent	3	6
No reply	1	1
Total	100	100

Note. From Center for Sociological Research (1983, p. 91).

The Care of Young Children in Spain

As indicated later in this report, the types of child care in Spain fall within a small range. There are two major forms of care: Children either remain at home or receive some kind of child care or education outside the home. Most children who are cared for at home are in their mother's care; some are cared for by other family members; and some are supervised by a paid caregiver, a situation that occurs primarily in cities and in upper-middle-class and very wealthy families. In discussing Spain's child care policies, we must consider Spain's policies in support of families with young children as well as the types and characteristics of the centers that care for or provide education facilities for preprimary children.

Spain's Policies in Support of Families

Government policies in support of the family date from relatively recent times (the Workers' Statute, which contains most of these policies, was approved in 1980), and some of them will be modified soon in accordance with a bill that is being considered in Parliament. The synthesis that follows takes advantage of the updated information collected by the Spanish commission acting within the Commission of the European Communities, which studies the kinds of child care that exist throughout Europe (Durán, 1987).

Maternity leave
New mothers are allowed up to 14 weeks leave without losing their employment. This leave can be taken according to the mother's needs. (The bill being considered in Parliament would allow for an extension of this period to 16 weeks.) This leave is considered to be the same as temporary disability leave and cannot be denied the mother.

Long-term maternity leave
Fathers as well as mothers may take advantage of this kind of leave. This long-term leave may last up to 3 years and may be extended if there are additional births. Such periods begin at the moment of the birth, and the birth of each successive child gives one the right to an entirely new period of long-term leave. In the case of long-term leave, however, the right of accumulated years of service is forfeited, as is the right to accede to the same post. However, if a vacancy occurs in the same or in a similar post, employment preference is given to the employee returning from long-term leave. (The bill being considered in Parliament allows for the

possibility of extended leave for a period of 1 year, without the risk of job loss and without the loss of accumulated years of experience in a firm.)

Breast-feeding leave

Mothers have the right to daily leave to breast-feed their babies during the first 9 months following birth. Mothers can be absent from work for 1 hour each day, or for two shorter periods of time. If the mother wishes (this right is exclusively applicable to women), this hour during which she is absent from work may be replaced by a reduction of her working day by 30 minutes, at either the beginning or the end of the workday.

Leave for family reasons

Leave of absence from work is also possible as a result of the illness of one's child. A 2-day leave is allowed in the case of a serious illness and needs to be justified with a doctor's certificate. In a situation in which a child's illness requires leave for more than 2 days, parents must obtain special permission from their employers. Some collective bargaining labor agreements regulate such cases.

Worktime flexibility

The Workers' Statute does not allow for flexible hours to accommodate child care arrangements. Workers can, however, choose their holidays to accommodate their children's school holidays. Also, a shorter workday is possible for those (either male or female) with children under age 6 (or over age 6, if the child is mentally or physically handicapped). However, in these cases, the worker takes a corresponding pay cut, which may be as much as one third to one half of the regular salary.

Financial benefits

Parents who work outside the home have the right to economic help (merely symbolic in character) for each child in their care, but for married couples, only one member can receive such help. Couples with children also enjoy certain tax benefits.

All these means of family support are, in fact, directly related with women's work outside the home. Support that would benefit *all* parents who are bringing up and educating small children (for example, parent education programs) is still scarce in Spain. However, some of the autonomous communities are taking steps to rectify this situation.

Extrafamilial Child Care for Preprimary Children

As indicated earlier, most small children in Spain who are not cared for at home attend some kind of day care or educational center for children under 6 years of age, which is the age of compulsory school attendance. These child care centers exhibit great variation in terms of both quality and service provision, especially those serving children in the under-4 age group. In this latter case, the majority of children go to private centers whose services range from custodial care in questionable conditions to educational programs that are very worthwhile. There are not many worthwhile programs, however, and those that do exist are expensive. Thus, many parents have trouble finding a young children's educational center that really inspires their confidence and that they can afford. It is clear that the state needs to become more involved to improve program quality and availability, especially in programs for children under age 4. As was stated earlier, Spain's Ministry of Education and Science is planning to modify the existing situation by increasing the number of places available in state-run schools for children under the age of 4 and by introducing improvements in the quality of the service being provided (for example, a reduction in the number of pupils per teacher). The introduction of government-sanctioned regulations for all preprimary schools (for example, staff safety measures, health and hygiene norms) is also envisaged.

STATISTICS AND DESCRIPTION OF EXTRAFAMILIAL CHILD CARE PROGRAMS

The education of preprimary children outside the family circle occurs within a narrow range of situations, primarily **day care centers** and **kindergartens**. There may be a few cases of children being cared for in small groups in caregivers' homes (perhaps a continuation of the traditional friendly women's schools, but more probably the result of urban lifestyles). In some areas of Spain where the population is spread out among small rural centers, **traveling preschools** or **home-based preschools** also have developed. For the most part, however, centers and kindergartens provide child care and education programs outside the family unit. Therefore, the statistics for Spain relating to the extrafamilial education and care of preprimary children can be grouped as follows: by children's ages, by whether the center is privately owned or state-owned, and by region.

As has already been indicated, Spain as a democratic country has developed the model of a state that is becoming more and more decentralized and that is divided into 17 autonomous communities, together with 2 Spanish cities on the African continent. In the field of education, some decision making is centralized (for example, the design of the overall structure of the educational system), while some responsibilities have been transferred to the autonomous communities (for example, policy regarding the setting up of schools). A similar situation exists in the case of social services. It has already been pointed out that the communities have been taking on their autonomous character at differing rates, so that at present some have already acquired all the decision-making capacity that the Constitution and the laws of the country allow, while others still depend on the Ministry of Education and Science to varying degrees. These varying situations, and the reality of decentralizaton itself, make it difficult to present statistical data that refer to the country as a whole. The Center of Educational Research and Documentation (CIDE), which is a division of the Ministry of Education and Science, was established to ease this difficulty. In fact, the majority of the statistics presented in this section have been taken from a report prepared by CIDE (Rivière et al., 1988). Decentralization is not the only difficulty encountered when attempting to formulate accurate statistics. Illegally established centers do not appear in the official statistics. Nevertheless, the figures presented in this section are useful, since they give a reasonably accurate picture of preprimary education in Spain.

The terms "preprimary education" and "preschool education" are used interchangeably to refer to either of the two kinds of programs initiated since the General Law of Education was passed in 1970: the nursery schools for ages 2 to 4 and the kindergartens for ages 4 to 6. The figures take us up to the 1985–86 academic year, the most recent one for which detailed figures are available. The general trends have not changed in the years following 1985–86.

Developments During the Last 15 Years

As shown in Table 6, preschool education has grown rapidly in Spain over the past 15 years. Enrollment grew from only 819,914 in 1970–71 to a record level of 1,197,897 pupils in 1981–82, which was the largest number of preschool pupils ever registered in Spain. A subsequent drop in the birthrate has caused preschool enrollments to fall since then, however.

As may be observed in Table 6 and Figure 1, the evolution of the state-owned sector differs considerably from that of the private sector. In the years immediately following the passage of the General Law of Edu-

Table 6

SPAIN'S 1970–86 PREPRIMARY SCHOOL ENROLLMENTS

Academic Year	Total Enrollment	Enrollment, State-Run Schools	Enrollment, Private Schools
1970–71	819,914	362,940	456,974
1971–72	760,277	365,253	395,024
1972–73	801,119	343,258	457,861
1973–74	829,155	322,697	506,458
1974–75	853,322	322,685	530,637
1975–76	920,336	347,026	573,310
1976–77	956,184	389,026	567,158
1977–78	1,008,796	455,594	553,202
1978–79	1,077,652	521,928	555,724
1979–80	1,159,854	611,496	548,358
1980–81	1,152,425	651,338	531,087
1981–82	1,197,897	670,950	526,947
1982–83	1,187,617	683,220	504,397
1983–84	1,171,062	699,943	471,119
1984–85	1,115,968	669,170	446,798
1985–86	1,127,348	702,057	425,291

Note. From Rivière et al. (1988, p. 68).

cation (1970), the number of places for preprimary-aged children in the state system dropped because service provision was concentrated on those children of compulsory school-age (6 years and up). In the middle of the decade, there was a sharp rise in enrollments in state-run centers. This increase continued through the 1985–86 academic year, culminating in an enrollment (702,057) nearly double that of 1970–71 (362,940). The evolution of private centers has been the exact opposite of that of state-run programs: a growing provision up to 1975–76 and then zero-growth and a subsequent decrease to the point at which the provision made in 1985–86 is somewhat less than that offered in 1970–71.

FIGURES FOR THE 1985–86 SCHOOL YEAR

The distribution of education programs for preprimary children between state-owned and private centers is seen more clearly in Figure 2, which

Figure 1

NUMBER OF PREPRIMARY PUPILS BETWEEN 1970 AND 1985 IN STATE-RUN AND PRIVATE SCHOOLS

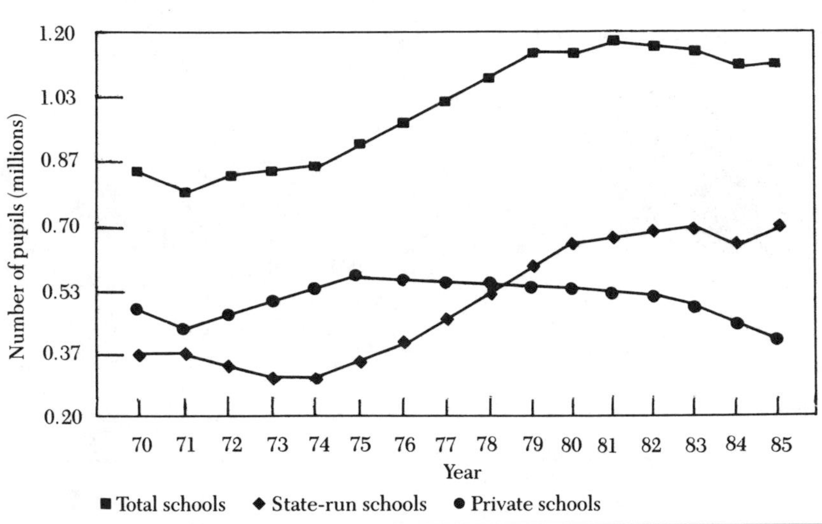

Note. From Rivière et al. (1988, p. 67).

shows the percentages of classrooms for preprimary children according to whether they are linked to the state or to the private system. As illustrated, of the 39,668 classes that existed in the school year 1985–86, the state sector provided almost twice as many (64.6 percent) as did the private sector.

Figure 3 shows the types of organizations that both the state-owned and privately owned units (classes) depend on. As may be seen, almost all units for preprimary children in the state-run sector belong to the Ministry of Education and Science or to the autonomous communities with decision-making capacity in this area. In the private sector, the majority of the units are the result of the initiatives of private individuals or organizations, with the Roman Catholic church accounting for a large number of units.

The distribution of these units for preprimary children according to the autonomous communities in which they appear reveals clear differences between the state and the private sectors (Table 7). In some autonomous communities the private sector is more predominant than the state sector (Baleares, Madrid); in others the state and private sec-

Figure 2

NUMBER OF CLASSES IN PREPRIMARY SCHOOLS, BOTH STATE-RUN AND PRIVATE, 1985–86

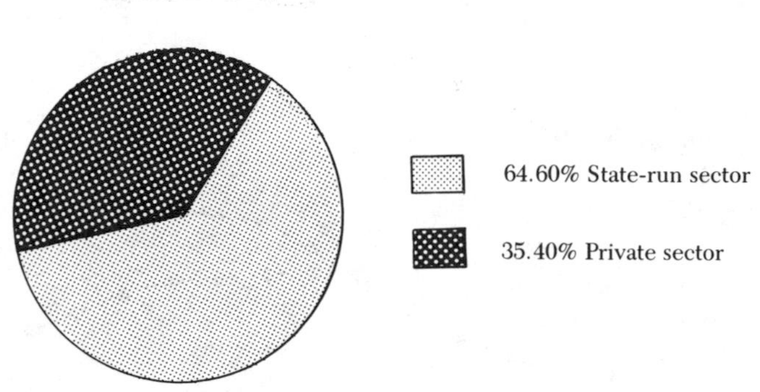

Note. From Rivière et al. (1988, p. 68).

tors are more or less equal (Cataluña, País Vasco, Navarra); and in still others the state sector clearly predominates (for example, Andalucía, Castilla-La Mancha, Extremadura, Comunidad Valenciana).

Also, the autonomous communities have variable teacher-pupil ratios, as shown in Table 8. Table 8 also shows that there are more pupils per teacher in the private sector than in the state sector.

In another respect, differences can also be found among autonomous communities concerning how well they are meeting the demand for services for preprimary-aged children. According to the Center of Educational Research and Documentation report (Rivière et al., 1988, p. 73), in the country as a whole, 17 percent of places in preprimary classes are vacant; in some communities, the vacancy rate reaches 30 percent (Navarra), while in others the rate is only 5 percent (Andalucía).

Table 9 contains information concerning the number of preprimary children enrolled in school during 1985–86 academic year. The growth of the number of places provided in the state sector, together with the drop in the birthrate in recent years, has meant that the level of schooling has been high, especially for 5- to 6-year-olds, for whom the level is almost 100 percent. For the reasons already mentioned, the figures in Table 9 are more reliable for older children than for younger children.

Figure 3

STATE-RUN AND PRIVATE SECTOR ENTITIES THAT PREPRIMARY SCHOOL CLASSES ARE LINKED WITH, 1985–86

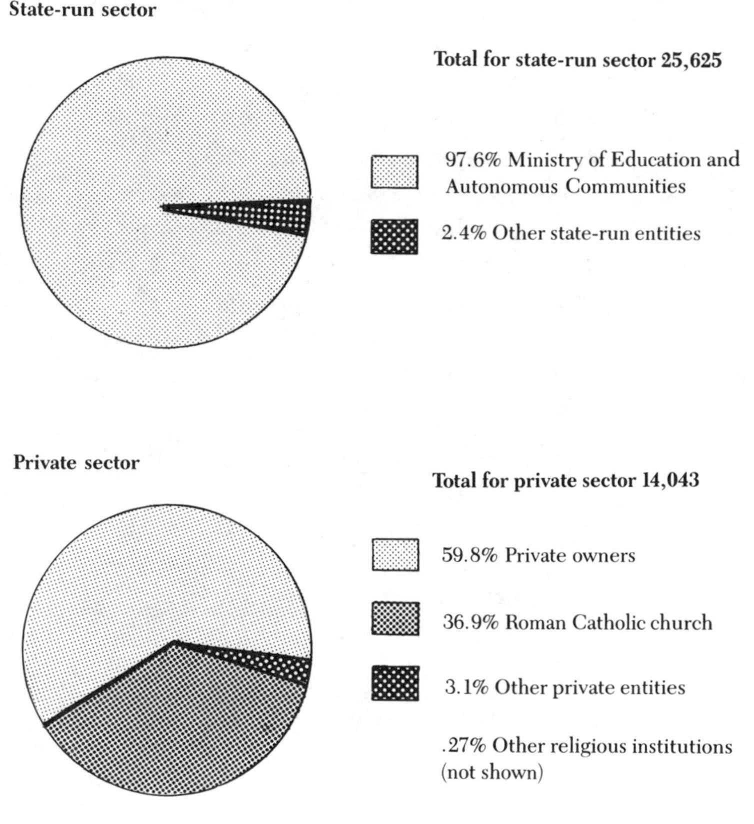

Note. From Rivière et al. (1988, p. 69).

As Figure 4 shows, the majority of children in nursery schools attend schools that are run by the Roman Catholic church or otherwise privately owned. During the 1985–86 school year almost 17 percent of the children attended state-run nursery schools. In fact, state-sector provision for this age group is very limited; very few state schools admit children between the ages of 2 and 4. When they do so, it is either by

Table 7

DISTRIBUTION OF PREPRIMARY PUPILS BY AUTONOMOUS COMMUNITY FOR BOTH STATE AND PRIVATE SCHOOLS, 1985–86

Autonomous Community	Total		State-Run		Private	
	Pupils	Teachers	Pupils	Teachers	Pupils	Teachers
Andalucía	193,577	6,269	146,896	4,893	46,681	1,376
Aragón	31,901	1,136	18,332	715	13,569	421
Asturias	24,962	877	16,856	627	8,106	250
Baleares	20,909	700	7,761	303	13,148	397
Canarias	43,097	1,481	34,213	1,215	8,884	266
Cantabria	13,877	475	7,986	289	5,891	186
Castilla-Mancha	50,107	1,648	38,146	1,305	11,961	343
Castilla-León	67,940	2,447	46,917	1,813	21,023	634
Cataluña	181,924	8,805	94,162	3,622	87,762	3,183
Ceuta-Melilla	4,102	122	2,842	93	1,260	29
Extremadura	31,544	1,066	25,196	893	6,348	173
Galicia	71,210	2,695	50,518	2,038	20,692	657
La Rioja	7,335	256	4,575	171	2,788	85
Madrid	140,283	4,902	60,638	2,153	79,645	2,749
Murcia	36,871	1,162	27,052	882	9,819	280
Navarra	15,819	625	7,378	333	8,441	292
C. Valenciana	118,049	3,852	76,683	2,655	41,366	1,197
País Vasco	73,841	3,055	35,934	1,648	37,907	1,407
Total	1,127,348	41,573	702,085	25,648	425,291	13,925

Note. From Rivière et al. (1988, p.72).

way of an experiment or because the demand for compulsory schooling has been met and there are still classrooms and teachers available. The opposite is seen to happen in the case of kindergartens, since almost 67 percent of the children between the ages of 4 and 6 attend state-run kindergartens.

The final set of figures gleaned from the 1988 Center of Educational Research and Documentation report (Rivière et al., 1988) on the education of preprimary children in Spain concerns teachers. Noteworthy in this respect is that 93 percent of teachers who work at this level (39,573 in the 1985–86 school year) are women. The distribution of teachers by

Table 8

TEACHER-PUPIL RATIOS IN STATE AND PRIVATE SCHOOLS BY AUTONOMOUS COMMUNITY, 1985–86

	Number of Pupils per Teacher		
Autonomous Community	Schools Overall	State-Run Schools	Private Schools
Andalucía	31.09	29.94	35.31
Aragón	27.64	25.53	31.12
Asturias	28.72	27.06	32.95
Baleares	30.00	25.53	33.46
Canarias	27.77	28.00	26.92
Cantabria	29.03	27.73	31.01
Cataluña	26.68	26.00	27.35
Castilla-Mancha	30.33	29.30	34.17
Castilla-León	28.13	26.39	33.00
Ceuta-Melilla	34.18	30.89	45.00
Extremadura	29.76	28.34	37.11
Galicia	26.39	25.00	30.56
La Rioja	28.76	26.75	32.80
Madrid	28.50	27.92	28.96
Murcia	31.76	30.67	35.19
Navarra	25.55	22.22	29.11
C. Valenciana	30.15	28.87	32.86
País Vasco	24.49	21.82	27.02
Overall ratio	28.42	27.40	30.28

Note. From Rivière et al. (1988, p. 70).

type of school is presented in Figure 5. As the figure illustrates, 64.8 percent of teachers work in state-owned centers.

In relation to teacher specialization, as Rivière et al. (1988, p. 74) point out, the different professional qualifications of those who teach cannot be precisely defined, given the heterogeneous character of the situations that exist. As illustrated in Figure 6, in state-run centers most teachers are specialists in the area of preprimary education ("specialist" is used here in a very loose sense). The situation in private schools is also reflected in Figure 6: Out of all the qualified teachers who work in

Table 9

PERCENTAGE OF SCHOOL ENROLLMENT AMONG THE PREPRIMARY POPULATION, 1985–86

Age (in yr)	Population	Number in School	Percent in School
2	477,291	22,657	4.75
3	511,511	83,559	16.34
4	534,314	452,016	84.60
5	587,020	569,116	96.95

Note. From Rivière et al. (1988, p. 71).

private schools, approximately half are specialized in the area of preprimary education. What Figure 6 does not show, however, is the situation that exists in many unregistered or unofficial private centers, where children are not even looked after by *qualified teachers*, let alone by specialists in preprimary education. It is precisely for this reason that many of these establishments are not officially recognized by the Ministry of Education and Science and therefore not included in official statistics. If they do appear in the statistics, it is on an irregular basis.

The data presented thus far in this section allow us to obtain an idea of the different situations of care and education of young children in Spain. Some additional comments about the characteristics of the different kinds of young children's centers may be of interest.

The easiest situation to describe is, once again, the one for children aged 4 to 6. The most typical provision for 4- to 6-year-olds is found in the state sector, in the primary schools attended by children between the ages of 6 and 14 (the present age-limits of compulsory education). These primary schools also provide some classes for children below school age, usually for those between ages 4 and 6, and these classes usually follow the normal school timetable in Spain (9 a.m. to 5 p.m.). In some primary schools (still few in number, but on the increase) that already have been affected by Spain's decreasing birthrate, children between the ages of 3 and 4 are filling places that otherwise would have been filled by older children.

Spain has no official curriculum for children below school age, although the Ministry of Education and Science and also some autonomous communities have established "preschool experimental plans." The state's latest official guidelines date from 1981 and establish six major

Figure 4

PERCENTAGE OF PREPRIMARY PUPILS ENROLLED IN NURSERY SCHOOLS AND KINDERGARTENS, STATE-RUN AND PRIVATE, 1985–86

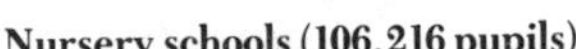
Nursery schools (106,216 pupils)

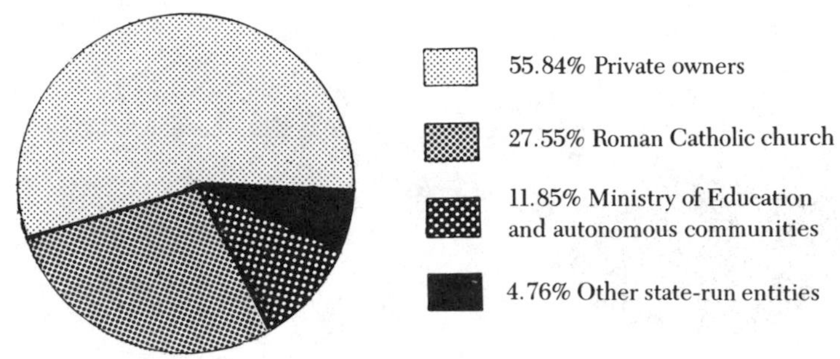

Kindergartens (1,021,132 pupils)

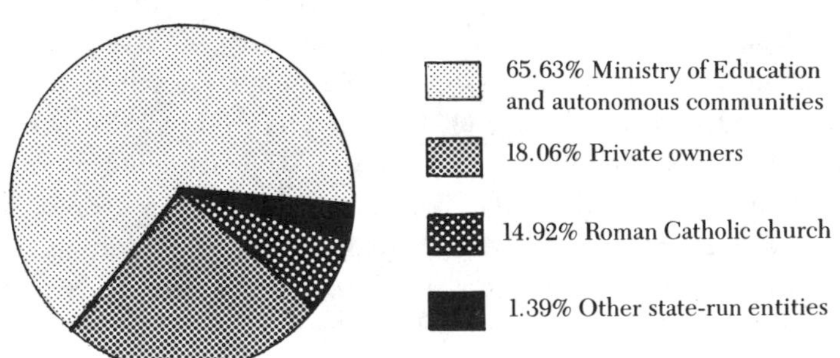

Note. From Rivière et al. (1988, p. 71).

educational areas (Spanish language, mathematics, social and natural experiences, artistic education, physical education, affective and social behavior) to which the autonomous communities that have their own language have added the corresponding content. Pupils in Spain may or may not receive religious education, depending on the wishes of their

Figure 5

PERCENTAGE OF PREPRIMARY TEACHERS IN STATE-RUN AND PRIVATE SCHOOLS

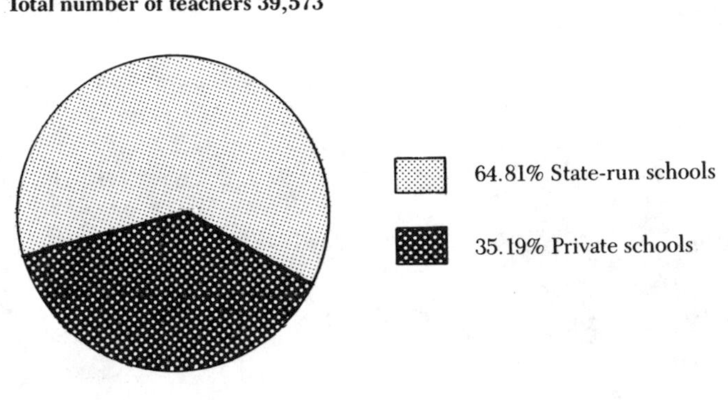

Note. From Rivière et al. (1988, p. 73).

parents. Besides those developed by the Ministry of Education and Science, some autonomous communities (for example, Cataluña and Galicia) have developed specific preschool curricula. All in all, Spain's official guidelines are not highly prescriptive, and what actually happens in classrooms reflects great diversity. Teachers with a certain level of specialization who are interested in pedagogic techniques are more likely to experiment with and develop innovative programs for preprimary children; usually these curricula focus on the developmental levels of children and emphasize activities and experimentation. In contrast, teachers with little or no training depend more on textbooks designed for preprimary children. Frequently the content of these books is academic and encourages passive learning, with excessive emphasis being placed on pupils working on their own with paper and pencil. In classrooms staffed by trained preprimary teachers, activities directed towards the acquisition of reading and writing skills are usually of preparatory nature, while in the case of untrained preprimary teachers, classroom activities are focused on acquiring skills that are more appropriate for older children.

As a result of a 1985 decision of staff in the Ministry of Education and

Figure 6

Number of Preprimary Teachers by Degree of Specialization in Both the State-Run and Private Sectors

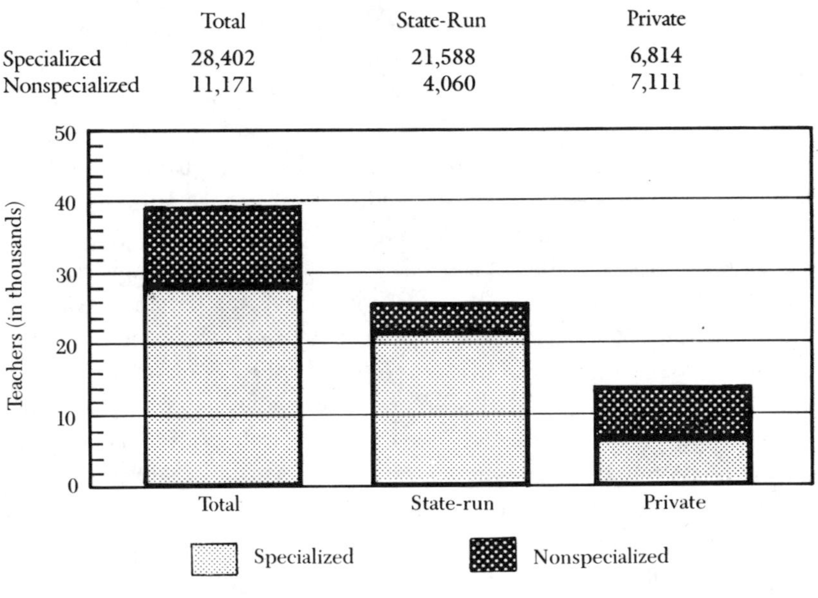

	Total	State-Run	Private
Specialized	28,402	21,588	6,814
Nonspecialized	11,171	4,060	7,111

Note. From Rivière et al. (1988, p. 74).

Science, Spain practices the mainstreaming of handicapped children in the normal school-system. Before 1985 the majority of handicapped children had been attending schools set up for special education. The participation of a particular school in the integration project is voluntary and is based on the approval of a majority of parents and teachers. There are supposed to be no more than two handicapped children per class, and participating schools receive additional support from the ministry (for example, a better teacher-pupil ratio, additional teaching materials, and access to specialized personnel). On the whole, the schools participating in the mainstreaming experience are state-run, although there are some in the private sector. The integration program began with preprimary children and has since been extended to include the older age groups within the compulsory educational levels.

Since the beginning of the 1980s, the provision of equipment for the new classes in the state-run preprimary sector has been acceptable, having improved over the years. In fact, equipment is readily available for new classes (although no provision is made for the replacement of used, broken, or lost materials). Equipment sent to preprimary classes supported by the Ministry of Education and Science and also by the autonomous communities includes the following: carpets, mats, building blocks, logic blocks used in acquiring mathematical concepts, toys used in symbolic play and observation, a range of material for language work (books, work cards, flash cards, puppets), painting material, movement and rhythm materials (hoops, skipping ropes, balls, tricycles, skates), and malleable materials to develop manual skills. Also supplied are teacher materials (books, teacher guides) and school equipment (tunnels, water trays, and sand trays), along with playground equipment that can be used by a number of schools (swings, slides, climbing frames).

It is much more difficult to describe the situation that exists in Spain's private schools in all these respects. A large number of them only provide classes for children under age 6; only the larger ones also provide places for children at the different stages within the educational system (preprimary, primary, secondary). Those schools that have a clear educational philosophy and qualified teachers share many of the characteristics already seen in similar cases in the state sector; within them, there is great variety in educational planning as well as in organizational framework. Other schools, in which the caregiving role is seen to be more important than the educational role, usually have teachers who are less qualified and whose educational programs are less defined, if they exist at all. As a general rule in most kinds of school, the younger the children, the greater the flexibility of the school timetable and the less academically oriented the curriculum. Of course, the types of activities, facilities, and materials offered by schools depend primarily on the quality of the individual programs and are closely linked with the amount of fees paid.

With regard to parent participation, in general, there is very little involvement of parents in Spanish schools. In the case of state-run schools, parent participation consists of parent representatives serving on various school governing bodies. With regard to the education of their children, parents usually have only sporadic contact with the teachers, and this may be only when the teachers take the initiative. Much less frequently, parents attend informative parent-teacher meetings. In contrast to the heterogeneous nature of preprimary education in Spain, which we have referred to repeatedly in this report, the homogeneity that characterizes the low level of parent participation both in state-run and private schools is, unfortunately, a reality.

Our observations about preprimary education become more complete if we take into account the additional information taken from the CIS study (Center for Sociological Research, 1983). Although this information is useful, it should be approached with a certain degree of caution for several reasons: (1) It refers to environments that are fundamentally urban or semiurban, (2) it does not distinguish between age levels under 6 years, and (3) it does not take into consideration the type of school involved. Even so, the data help complete the picture we have painted of Spain's preprimary school programs and policies.

As frequently happens in urban environments, many children must be transported to their preprimary centers. Very few of these centers are set up within walking distance of children's homes. Table 10 summarizes different transportation methods used by CIS study mothers in getting their children to preprimary centers.

As shown in Table 11, the schools attended by most children are open during Spain's normal school hours (9 a.m. to 5 p.m.), with short breaks in both morning and afternoon, and with a longer break at lunch time, about 1 p.m. Table 12 shows the amount of time the children usually spend in school per day. The vast majority of these schools (89 percent) are not open on Saturdays, and in 75 percent of the cases, the schools are closed during July and August.

In most cases, the classrooms occupied by the preprimary children are part of a larger complex of school buildings housing primary school classrooms as well (Table 13). Many of these schools have a yard or playground (Table 14) as a basic open space.

The types of services provided in these schools are shown in Table

Table 10

METHODS OF TRANSPORTING CHILDREN TO PREPRIMARY SCHOOLS

Method	Percent Using Method
Public transport (bus)	8
Public transport (subway)	1
Private car	36
School bus	52
Other type	2
No reply	1
Total	100

Note. From Center for Sociological Research (1983, p. 102).

Table 11

DISTRIBUTION OF PREPRIMARY SCHOOLS ACCORDING TO OPERATING HOURS

Hours	Percent of Preprimary Schools
School-day (9 a.m. – 5 p.m.)	89
School-day plus 2 hours before and after (7 a.m.–7 p.m.)	9
Don't know	0
No reply	2
Total	100

Note. From Center for Sociological Research (1983, p. 99).

Table 12

NUMBER OF HOURS CHILDREN SPEND IN PREPRIMARY SCHOOLS

Time Spent (in hr)	Percent of Children
2–3	3
4–5	52
6–7	33
8–10	12
Total	100

Note. From Center for Sociological Research (1983, p. 101).

15. Nevertheless, it should be pointed out that not every child has the same opportunities of access to the services. Tables 16 and 17, for example, show the relation that exists between parent's educational level and family income, respectively, and the existence of psychopedagogic services in the schools attended by these children.

More than half (54 percent) of the 1,573 women interviewed in the CIS project reported here (Center for Sociological Research, 1983) indicated that the school to which they send their children receives a full or partial government grant (in 79 percent of the cases, government aid comes from the central government, the autonomous communities, or the town halls). For about 30 percent of the women interviewed, the

Table 13

PREPRIMARY EDUCATION ACCOMMODATION

Type of Accommodation	Percent of Preprimary Schools
Detached building (bungalow type)	26
Bottom floor of a building	19
Entire floor	8
Large school building	47
Total	100

Note. From Center for Sociological Research (1983, p. 103).

Table 14

OUTDOOR SPACES IN PREPRIMARY SCHOOLS

Play Space	Percent of Preprimary Schools
Having school grounds	26
Having a yard/playground	60
Having a terrace or a roof-top area	3
Having a nearby public park	6
Having no opportunity for outdoor play	4
No reply	1
Total	100

Note. From Center for Sociological Research (1983, p. 104).

education of their children was free or they were asked to pay a token amount. Approximately half of the women interviewed paid an amount that varied between 2,000 and 10,000 pesetas per month (in 1983, the minimum wage in Spain was 1,072 pesetas per day). Of the remaining 20 percent, 15 percent paid between 500 and 2,000 pesetas, and 5 percent paid more than 10,000 pesetas every month (at the moment of writing this profile, $1 U.S. is equivalent to 125 pesetas).

In support of what we have said earlier, the CIS research (Center for Sociological Research, 1983) reveals that parents' relations with the schools are not very strong; although 67 percent of the CIS study mothers stated that they had a certain amount of incidental school contact,

Table 15

SERVICES PROVIDED IN PREPRIMARY SCHOOLS

	Percent of Schools		
Type of Services	Yes	No	No Reply
Educational activities	95	4	1
Dining room	50	48	2
School bus	31	64	5
Medical service	60	33	8
Psychopedagogic services	42	42	16
Extracurricular activities (for example, sports, creative manual skills, ballet)	69	26	5

Note. From Center for Sociological Research (1983, p. 105).

Table 16

PERCENTAGE OF PARENTS, ACCORDING TO PARENT'S EDUCATIONAL ATTAINMENT LEVEL, USING A PREPRIMARY SCHOOL WITH PSYCHOPEDAGOGIC SERVICES

Parent's Educational Attainment Level	Percent Using a Preprimary School With Psych. Services
Less than primary school education	29
Primary school education	39
Secondary school education	46
University Diploma (3 yr)	49
University Honors Degree (5 yr)	60

Note. From Center for Sociological Research (1983, p. 106).

only 57 percent reported that they had received some kind of report about their children's progress. Even so, the most outstanding feature concerning parents' participation is that the women's replies to interview questions do not differ with regard to their level of educational attainment, income, or profession, which indicates that we are dealing with a problem that is widespread among the Spanish. The fault, it seems, lies within the system itself.

Table 17

Percentage of Parents, According to Parent's Income Level, Using a Preprimary School With Psychopedagogic Services

Parent's Income Level (in pesetas[a])	Percent Using a Preprimary School with Psych. Services
Up to 50,000	34
50,001–75,000	38
75,001–100,000	51
100,001–150,000	52
Over 150,000	63

Note. From Center for Sociological Research (1983, p. 106).

[a]One U.S. dollar is equivalent to 125 pesetas at the time of this writing.

Research

Researchers in Spain are showing a growing interest in young children. Such topics as children's language, cognitive, and social development are the foci of many important research projects. Although they receive very little private support, researchers are gradually beginning to receive more funding from the public administration—either from the central government (Ministry of Education and Science, Interministerial Committee for Science and Technology) or from the various autonomous communities. Unfortunately, however, there is more emphasis on studying child development issues than on studying early childhood education issues. In general, it can be affirmed that as a context for development and learning, the family receives much more attention than the school receives at any of its stages, including the preprimary stage. For example, the research that is focused on the process of language acquisition and development, which is abundant in Spain, rarely considers contexts outside the family circle. True, many researchers test and interview children in the schools, but their motive for doing so seems to be to locate a large number of children to study. Quite often they take one child after another into a separate room, where they study each child as they would have been able to do in the home setting or in the laboratory. Thus it may be stated that research on preprimary children is largely carried out by developmental psychologists whose primary interest is not education issues. Of course, there are also educators who publish articles on young children and their educational development. In general, however, the articles describe specific educational innovations and are not "research" in the strictest sense of the word.

There are, naturally, exceptions that disprove the rule. These exceptions are the result of a new kind of sensibility and a new professional outlook: The proliferation of psychopedagogic teams linked with central government or with autonomous or local governments is at times contributing to the unification of the two areas of research that have been seen as separate up to now. Sometimes linked also with university departments, such teams carry out tasks that go beyond mere intervention and reach into areas of basic research.

The fundamental problem is one of lack of research (to say nothing of the need for more accurate statistics). There is need for **more psychopedagogic research** into the processes that develop within schools, the determining and the differentiating factors, the impact of one kind of curriculum or another; **more longitudinal research** is necessary to evaluate the long-term effects of different educational approaches and the differences between children who have experienced only home care and those who have experienced a formal preprimary program.

One example of psychopedagogic research of a longitudinal kind is the evaluation of the process of integrating handicapped children within the normal school, a process set in motion by the Ministry of Education and Science in 1985. Children with different types of handicaps who attend schools in which the mainstreaming process is approached in different ways are the subject of a long-term investigation that also includes nonhandicapped children. The researchers are studying both developmental and educational variables. Their interest is not only in the children but also in their parents, in their teachers, and in the characteristics of their classes and their schools. An initial report concerning the objectives and the context of this research was authored by the Commission for the Evaluation of Mainstreaming (1987) and published in the journal *Revista de Educación.*

The Ministry of Education and Science itself set up an Experimental Program in Preschool Education in 1985, in which about 70 schools began to implement a very open curriculum. As far as we know, no rigorous, systematic longitudinal evaluation has been planned for this program. What this probably means is that at the end of the experimental period, it will be impossible to answer scientifically such basic questions as what the effects of the program have been, what the duration and scope of its effects might be, in what different ways the project has materialized, and what its long- and short-term consequences are. In this case, we find ourselves faced with a situation that should be avoided in the future.

FUTURE PROBLEMS

According to demographic predictions in the near future, the population of preprimary children will not change much; the most significant reductions are expected in children aged 3 to 5. Table 18 illustrates these trends.

In future years there probably will continue to be two types of care situations available for Spain's preprimary children: the family and preprimary schools. Some problems may arise in the future with regard to both situations.

As far as family care situations are concerned, there should be greater involvement of public authorities in providing support for (not substituting for) parents in their childrearing responsibilities. Parent programs and social and welfare aid for families (not just for working mothers) are both scarce and insufficient. Without a doubt, this is an area in which the rhetoric of good intentions always runs the risk of finding itself followed only by the absence of real action.

As for the preprimary school situation, the main challenge of the coming decade involves putting into practice the plan of the Ministry of

Table 18

POPULATION PREDICTIONS FOR PREPRIMARY CHILDREN IN SPAIN

Age (in yr)	1986 Population	Projected 1991 Population	Projected 1996 Population
0	587,020	571,853	575,927
1	586,962	539,572	567,545
2	615,316	517,539	558,672
3	632,432	504,644	549,673
4	653,623	499,795	540,902
5	663,827	480,405	565,913

Note. Data obtained from General Board of Planning and Investment, Ministry of Education and Science.

Education and Science, which is under debate at present. Within a few months' time, the education of preprimary children in Spain will be outlined and regulated by a new law for the educational system. However, real change results not only from the institution of new laws but also from the manner in which they are applied. To satisfy existing needs, this application should take into account the following concerns:

1. Teacher-pupil ratios should be significantly improved, and new places for preprimary children should be created in schools. The danger lies in assigning only residual importance to preprimary education. The same education law that will regulate preprimary education also will extend compulsory education in Spain up to the age of 16 (instead of the present age-14 limit); this extension will call for a rerouting of funds, which could jeopardize other education sectors, such as preprimary education. Putting it simply, it is possible that the declared good intentions of the present ministerial project with regard to preschool education may only be seen in practice in the form of the token schooling of children between the ages of 3 and 4 in the classes at primary schools that have vacancies.

2. Young children should not spend their time at school in work areas and recreational areas designed to be used by older pupils with different needs.

3. There is the risk that the education sector involving children up to the age of 3 may be completely ignored. It seems that the Ministry of Education and Science is not going to make large investments in this area. Since preprimary education will depend on agreements between education authorities and nonprofit institutions, there is a danger that such agreements will become excessively dependent on two factors that are difficult to control: political intention and the availability of economic resources. There needs to be a high degree of conviction (and also a large dose of political courage) for both of these variables to be turned in favor of preprimary education.

4. It remains to be seen what will be done with the hundreds of preprimary centers that are not in good condition because of inadequate space, inadequate educational programs, and inadequate staff training. Some special projects exist that are geared towards training teachers who do not have adequate qualifications but are already working in centers for the care or education of preprimary children. This is a difficult problem to solve, and special attention will have to be paid to it in the coming years.

5. For education of children up to the age of 6, the ministry pro-

poses to put forward curricular areas, general objectives, and methodological guidelines. The extent to which these intentions end up as innovative educational practice will prove whether the new law has been worthwhile or not.

6. In the future, an important increase should be made in the number and the quality of the psychopedagogic teams concerned with preprimary education. At present they exist in very small numbers, and they sometimes only focus on issues related to the mainstreaming of handicapped children. Preprimary education of high quality is costly and demands the collaboration of multidisciplinary teams. Such teams already exist in many places in Spain, but they usually have such a heavy workload that their work is geared towards the most problematical cases.

The way in which these and other tensions can be ironed out may serve to indicate the extent to which the public authorities are convinced that preprimary education is worthwhile and that it, together with other measures, can prevent future problems and inequalities. It will be one of the indices that, as the years go by, may be used to show whether Spain has become a modern society, not only in an administrative and a political sense but also in an educational, social, and cultural sense.

Conclusion

Spanish children up to the age of 6 basically grow up within two contexts: the family and centers dedicated to their care and/or education. In general, Spanish families are organized in such a way as to provide a suitable context for the upbringing and education of children. In the case of employed mothers, there are provisions involving maternity leave, leave of absence from work, and so on. Nevertheless, whether mothers are employed or not, families do not receive enough support in the care and education of young children; almost no social or community resources are available for this type of aid.

Those parents who wish to send a child under 4 years of age to an educational center are practically obliged to make use of a privately owned center, since the provision made in the state-run sector is negligible. For 4- to 6-year-olds, state sector provision is more extensive than that of the private sector and consists of centers belonging to the central government or to the autonomous communities. Be it in one kind of center or in another, about 85 percent of 4-year-olds and 95 percent of 5-

year-olds spend a large portion of their day in a formal educational setting.

While in general the high level of schooling for these older children is a positive development, the lack of attention paid to the needs of younger children, the poor quality of the programs offered, and the slight (or nonexistent) control maintained over centers outside the state sector are clearly negative developments. "Day care centers" are widespread, and although some of these centers offer developmentally appropriate educational experiences, most of them merely provide custodial care. Research studies related to these younger age groups have been more developmental than educational in nature, with little emphasis on the assessment of innovative educational projects.

At present there is a national debate under way concerning the project of the Ministry of Education and Science that, with regard to preprimary children, emphasizes the educational character of the preschool experiences (in contrast with the custodial orientation so widespread nowadays). Among other things, the project is establishing basic requirements concerning teacher qualifications and regulations concerning the conditions that have to be met by centers. While this project may be jeopardized by the way in which it may materialize (one wonders whether more than a token attention will be paid to younger children, whether the project under discussion will be the means by which substantial changes in educational practice may come about . . .), there is no doubt that it will be a major improvement with regard to the previous situation. The political will to make the content of the project feasible, together with its ultimate materialization, will be the means by which an assessment can be undertaken of the extent to which advances have been made in the transformation of a reality, which although it already shows some positive signs, is still susceptible to no end of improvements.

Author's Note

The Spanish research of the Preprimary Project counts on funding from the Interministerial Committee for Science and Technology (CICYT) of the National Agency for Evaluation and Prospective. The study is being carried out by three teams belonging respectively to the Universities of Barcelona, Santiago de Compostela, and Sevilla, with this last university acting as the National Research Center for the Preprimary Project.

This article has been translated into English by Michael Gronow.

REFERENCES*

Center for Sociological Research (CIS). (1983). *Preprimary education: Mothers* (Report 1373) (in Spanish). Madrid: Center for Sociological Research.

Commission for the Evaluation of Mainstreaming. (1987, special issue). Report on the evaluation of mainstreaming: General framework, hypotheses, and phases of the study (in Spanish). *Revista de Educación*, pp. 7–44.

Del Campo. (1982). *Evolution of the Spanish family in the 20th century* (in Spanish). Madrid: Alianza.

Durán, T. (1987). *European network on child care* (in Spanish). Barcelona. Unpublished report.

Faubell, V. (1974, July–September). Historical remarks on preprimary education in Spain (in Spanish). *Revista de Ciencias de la Educación*, pp. 1–30.

Institute of Women. (1986). *Women's social situation in Spain* (in Spanish). Madrid: Ministry of Culture.

Ministry of Education and Science. (1979). *History of education in Spain* (3 vols.) (in Spanish). Madrid: Author.

Ministry of Education and Science. (1987a). *Data and statistics of education in Spain 1984–85* (in Spanish). Madrid: Author.

Ministry of Education and Science. (1987b). *Project for educational reform—Preprimary, primary, secondary, and vocational education. Proposal for a debate.* Madrid: Author.

Ministry of National Education. (1945, July 18). Primary Education Law I (in Spanish). *State Official Gazette, 199*, 385–417.

Montesino, P. (1840). *Nursery school handbook* (in Spanish). Madrid: National Press.

National Institute of Statistics. (1985). *1981 population census (Vol. 1)* (in Spanish). Madrid: National Institute of Statistics.

Presidency of the Government. (1977). *The Moncloa Pacts* (in Spanish). Madrid: Central Service of Publications/Technical General Secretary.

Report on Preprimary Schools. (1984, April 1–15). A conglomeration of schools over which there is little control (in Spanish). *Comunidad Escolar*, pp. 17–23.

Rivière, A., Muñoz-Repiso, M., Gil, G., Ferrándis, A., Lausín, P., López, M., Medrano, G., and Rodríguez, M. (1988). *Spain's educational system* (in Spanish). Madrid: Ministry of Education and Science.

---

*The editors would like to express their appreciation to Jesús Palacios for translating all elements of each entry in the reference list into English.

XIV
Child Care and Early Education in Thailand

Nittaya Passornsiri, *Assistant Professor*
Pusadee Kutintara, *Associate Professor*
Arrome Suwannapal, *Instructor*
School of Educational Studies
Sukhothai Thammathirat Open University
Nonthaburi

Introduction

The purpose of this paper is to describe the national profile of child care and early education in Thailand as background information for the International Association for the Evaluation of Educational Achievement (IEA) preprimary study. Whereas the information included in this profile should be useful to policymakers dealing with care and education for 3- to 6-year-olds, further studies need to be carried out to have a more complete picture regarding the children in this age-range.

This national profile includes the history of preprimary care and education in Thailand, the national policy on child care and early education, and the current organizational structure for the delivery of early childhood services. Preschool curriculum, supervision, personnel training, and financing are discussed. Finally, problems and issues concerning child care and early education in Thailand are presented.

History of Child Care and Early Education

Until the late 19th century, child care in Thailand was mainly the responsibility of parents and relatives. Education for the very young was provided informally; when children were ready to learn, they were taught the three Rs in their own homes or in monasteries. The Western concept of formal schooling was not introduced until the reign of King Chulalongkorn the Great (Rama V), when the first formal school was founded in the Royal Palace in 1871. Later, more schools were opened for the public, and by the end of the reign of this great monarch (1910), a large number of schools had been founded all over the country (Ministry of Education, 1964).

Child care and early education in the institution-based form in Thailand can be traced back to 1890 when Her Royal Highness Princess Sai Savali, a consort of King Chulalongkorn, decided to build Phra Akra Chaya Thoe's Orphanage with her own money. The orphanage was built in memory of the loss of her daughter, who had died in 1889 at the age of 5 years. This first orphanage in Thailand rendered services to children aged 1 month to 10 years. Apart from care services, the children also received training and education to prepare them for future occupations (UNICEF, 1982).

Froebel's and Montessori's concepts of child care were introduced in Thailand at the end of the reign of King Chulalongkorn, as is recorded in a book on child care published in 1910 (Prasert-Aksorn). In 1911, which marked the beginning of the reign of King Rama VI, kindergarten classes were founded at Wattanawittayalai School, a famous private school, through the effort of Miss Edna Sara Cole, an American missionary and the principal of the school. Thereafter, additional private kindergartens were set up, and some government primary schools began to add preprimary classes (Rungsinant, 1981).

In 1938 the Ministry of Education sent two educators to Japan to observe and study early childhood education for 6 months, and in 1939 three more persons were sent to Japan on a similar mission. After that, the Ministry of Education was able to set up a model government kindergarten in Bangkok in 1940; more government kindergartens were subsequently founded in Bangkok and in urban areas in other provinces. Besides these 2-year kindergartens, other forms of child care and early education were gradually established by various government institutions. These forms included 1-year preprimary classes (annexed to primary schools), child development centers, child nutrition centers, and day care centers.

The private sector has also continued to play an important role in Thailand's early education. As of 1985, for example, 1,930 private kindergartens were operating throughout the country. In addition, a large number of private day care centers were operated by individuals, foundations, and various nongovernmental organizations.

To better understand the development of programs for child care and early education in Thailand, the evolution of national policy in this regard should be examined.

NATIONAL POLICY AFFECTING YOUNG CHILDREN

The Thai government has recognized the importance of preprimary care and education since the reign of King Rama V. A history of the Ministry of Education (Ministry of Education, 1964) describes the National Education Program 1898 as requiring that preprimary classes and kindergartens be set up to prepare children for primary education. However, curriculum and instructional methods were not yet well defined. After the change to a constitutional monarchy in 1932, the first constitution (drafted in the same year) called for the establishment of kindergartens to prepare children for formal schooling. It was this that led to the founding of the model government kindergarten in 1940. Although gradual expansion of early education followed, education for the very young was emphasized mainly in the capital city and other urban areas.

From the promulgation of Thailand's first constitution in 1932 to the present, the government's view of early education has changed considerably. The emphasis on formal teaching has gradually been replaced by an emphasis on promoting the child's total development. The most recent government policies and plans regarding early education are outlined as follows:

1. In 1975 a major step in improving the quality of preprimary education and care was the government's acceptance of the principles proposed in the *Report of the Committee for Establishing the Framework for Educational Reform* (Office of the National Education Commission, 1976). The report proposed that the responsible agencies in every locality cooperate in the mobilization of resources to provide children with proper care and training before compulsory education. Taking care of the young child was to be the joint responsibility of the family, the community, and the government. In organizing services, efforts were to be coordinated on all fronts, including health, community development, nutrition, and education (Passornsiri, 1983).

2. The *National Scheme of Education 1977*, initially implemented in 1978, established the groundwork for the government's acceleration and promotion of preprimary education. According to the *Scheme*, the responsibility for implementation was to lie mainly with local districts and

the private sector, on the condition that young children's centers remain under government supervision. At the preprimary level of education, the government was to provide some model kindergartens and do relevant research (Office of the National Education Commission, 1977b; Passornsiri, 1983).

3. The policy stated in the *National Scheme of Education 1977* was expanded and made more operational in the *Fourth National Education Development Plan (1977–1981)*. This plan stated that precompulsory education could be of different types, depending on what was appropriate to local conditions. Preschool models could be arranged as either formal or nonformal education. Preschool might, for example, take the form of a nursery home, a child care center, a class for small children, or a kindergarten. The purpose of preprimary education should be to lay a foundation so that a child might go on to the next stage of his or her education properly prepared (Office of the National Education Commission, 1977a; Passornsiri, 1983).

Educational policy relating to preprimary services also appears in the *Fourth National Economic and Social Development Plan (1977–1981)* under "public health, food, and nutrition policies." In that document, government policy on public health called for "improvements in the health of mothers and their children and in nutrition in general, especially among infants and preprimary children, to ensure that the nutritional content of foods provides the necessities for physical growth" (Office of the National Economic and Social Development Board, 1977). The policy on food and nutrition required that children between 6 months and 2 years of age with nutrition problems receive the necessary food supplements at various service centers maintained by the Ministries of Public Health, of the Interior, and of Education, and by the Bangkok Metropolis; that stations be set up in the villages to distribute such food; and that food be distributed directly to the houses of children with serious problems (Office of the National Economic and Social Development Board, 1977; Passornsiri, 1983).

4. The *Fifth National Economic and Social Development Plan (1982–1986)*, which includes child and youth development, aimed at expanding service centers and reducing the nutritional problems of babies and preprimary children (Office of the National Economic and Social Development Board, 1982). First priority was to be given to the areas of poverty in 37 of Thailand's 73 provinces. Cost-effective 1-year preprimary classes annexed to primary schools were to be set up, with

the goal of having in each district at least one primary school with a preprimary class. With regard to childrearing, mothers were to be trained to have a basic knowledge of baby and child care, including especially knowledge about nutrition and mental development of children through age 14.

5. The *Sixth National Education Development Plan (1987–1991)* states that preprimary education will be expanded to serve at least 37 percent of 3- to 5-year-old children, and disadvantaged children will be given more opportunity to receive readiness training (Office of the National Education Commission, 1986). The quality of preprimary education is emphasized in terms of the development of service models appropriate to local conditions, the improvement of methods of readiness training in accordance with the psychology of child development, the upgrading of health and nutrition standards, and the improvement of supervision and evaluation.

Evidently there has been a lack of cooperation among various agencies responsible for organizing preprimary services. To remedy this problem, the *Sixth Plan* also states clearly that different agencies should coordinate and cooperate so that services can effectively be given to children throughout the country.

6. Since the beginning of the academic year 1986, the government has approved the expansion of preprimary classes annexed to primary schools. The expansion project, called The Rural Kindergarten, can provide preprimary education services for many more children. Therefore, the target set by the *Sixth Plan*—to serve 37 percent of 3- to 5-year-old children—is likely to be met in the very near future.

Current Delivery of Preprimary Education and Care

Organizational Structure

Preprimary services in Thailand are provided by both government and private agencies. The private agencies include, for example, the National Women's Council, the YWCA, S.O.S. (Save Our Soul) Children's Village of Thailand, and Ban Tantawan Foundation for Children. The government agencies include local governments of three different kinds (Bangkok Metropolis, the municipalities, and Pattaya City Province) and various departments of the ministries, as follows:

1. Ministry of Education
   - Department of General Education
   - Department of Religious Affairs
   - Department of Teacher Education
   - Office of the Private Education Commission
   - Office of the National Primary Education Commission
   - Special Education Division
2. Ministry of Interior
   - Department of Community Development
   - Department of Public Welfare
   - Royal Thai Police Department
3. Ministry of Public Health
   - Department of Health
4. Ministry of University Affairs

The numbers and types of preprimary centers and the related operating departments are shown in Table 1. As indicated in the table, there are three major types of preprimary programs:

1. Two-year formal education in kindergarten for children aged 4 to 6. Some private kindergartens provide a 3-year program.

2. One-year preprimary classes annexed to primary schools for children aged 5 to 6.

3. Nonformal education in centers of various types, such as child development centers, child nutrition centers, day care centers, and child care centers. In these centers, the children's ages can range anywhere from birth to 7 years.

The kindergartens and preprimary classes aim at preparing children for primary education. The various kinds of centers aim at providing child care services for employed mothers; also, some center programs aim at improving children's health and nutrition.

CURRICULA

As stated in the curricula, preprimary education in Thailand has changed from a traditional perspective of teaching the three Rs to a readiness-oriented perspective in which the objectives are to develop children in four ways: physically, emotionally, socially, and intellectually. The principles of today's preprimary education are to instill morale and morals in children; to encourage them to learn how to think, to act, and to solve their problems; and to prepare them to be ready for elementary education.

Table 1

PREPRIMARY EDUCATION AND CARE IN THAILAND, 1985

Type	Ministry/Dept. Responsible	No. of Preschool Institutions (No. of children)		Aims and Programs	Age Group (yr)	Catchment Area	Staffing
		Bangkok	Other Provinces				
Government-operated kindergartens (since 1940)	Ministry of Ed. (MOE), Office of the National Primary Education Commission (ONPEC)	4 (2,264)	73 (33,283)	Demonstration programs to encourage the expansion of other kindergartens in the provinces.	4–6	Urban	Trained kindergarten teachers.
	Ministry of University Affairs, universities	3 (293)	1 (115)	Programs to train teachers and conduct research.	4–6	Urban	Trained kindergarten teachers.
	MOE, teacher-training colleges	2 (496)	9 (383)	Same as above.	4–6	Urban	Same as above.
	MOE, Special Education Division	5 (391)	5 (180)	Special education programs for preschoolers.	4–6	Urban	Trained teachers for special education.
Private kindergartens	MOE, (ONPEC)	711 (86,273)	1,219 (186,826)	2- to 3-year programs, preparation for formal school.	3–6	Urban and a few rural	Variety: trained and untrained teachers.
Preprimary classes in primary schools	Bangkok Metropolis	155 (3,875)	—	One-year preprimary classes, preparation for primary.	5–6	Bangkok	Trained primary teachers.
	Municipalities	—	361 (21,988)			Urban	

Table 1—Cont.

Preprimary Education and Care in Thailand, 1985

Type	Ministry/Dept. Responsible	No. of Preschool Institutions (No. of children)		Aims and Programs	Age Group (yr)	Catchment Area	Staffing
		Bangkok	Other Provinces				
	ONPEC	7 (360)	10,368 (338,698)			Rural	
	Ministry of Interior (MOI), Royal Thai Police Dept., Border Patrol Police General Headquarters		50 (1,133)			Rural	
	MOE, Special Education Division	1 (48)	1 (13)			Urban	
Head-Start-type centers (started in 1968)	MOE, Dept. of Teacher Education	1 (24)	11 (613)	Centers operated in conjunction with rural schools in selected areas.	4–6 or 5–7	Rural	Village teachers and supervisors from Teacher's College in the area. Staff are given a special course designed for this program by the Department of Teacher Education.

Child development centers (started in 1967)	MOI, Community Development Department	1 (37)	3,255 (121,684)	Community-based preschool centers aimed at child development, early preparation for schooling, and child care for working mothers. Programs provided are not highly structured.	3–6	Rural	Trained child care attendants usually with grade-7 background and a 3-month training in basic knowledge related to child development or early childhood education.
Preschool centers	MOE, Department of Religious Affairs	11 (737)	275 (18,446)	Stated purposes are almost the same as those of child development centers.	3½–6	Urban and rural	Monks and some child care attendants with grade-7 (or less) background. Some attend short-course.
Child nutrition centers (started in 1968)	Ministry of Public Health, Department of Health	—	1,271 (50,840)	Services of comprehensive early childhood type emphasize the improvement of the nutritional condition of rural children, with better health care and day care services similar to other day care centers.	2–5	Rural	Health workers and helpers are native village girls with primary education background and a 2-week training in childrearing techniques and knowledge in nutrition.
Government day care centers	Bangkok Metropolis	32 (1,898)	—	Day care services for working mothers.	3–6	Bangkok	Grade 10 and above, inservice training.
	MOI, Department of Public Welfare	5 (660)	3 (120)		3–6	Bangkok	

Table 1—Cont.

PREPRIMARY EDUCATION AND CARE IN THAILAND, 1985

Type	Ministry/Dept. Responsible	No. of Preschool Institutions (No. of children)		Aims and Programs	Age Group (yr)	Catchment Area	Staffing
		Bangkok	Other Provinces				
Private day care centers (registered at the Dept. of Public Welfare)	MOI, Department of Public Welfare	474 (19,728)	294 (16,123)	Day care centers operated by individuals, groups, foundations, factories, etc.	0–5 (varied)	Bangkok and urban	Variety: trained and untrained child care attendants.
Children's homes	MOI, Department of Public Welfare	4 (1,076)	—	Residential care for needy infants, both boys and girls.	0–7	Bangkok	Social workers, nurses, and child care attendants.
	Private	8 (443)	10 (1,642)	Same as above.	0–7	Bangkok and urban	Same as above.
Nongovernmental organizations	National Women's Council	7 (350)	21 (1,050)	Day care centers for employed mothers.	3–5	Bangkok and rural	Variety: trained and untrained child care attendants.
	YWCA	—	—				
Total		1,431 (118,953)	17,227 (793,137)				

Preprimary programs consist of at least 40 weeks per academic year. In the formal education system, the activities are highly structured. Having children learn through play is the main technique in almost all government kindergartens. In child development centers, child nutrition centers, and other types of child care centers, activities are less structured than in the government kindergartens.

For organizing curriculum activities, government kindergartens have their own guidelines, which were developed in 1979 by a committee under the Ministry of Education (Department of Curriculum and Instruction Development, 1979). These guidelines, which are also used by some private kindergartens and centers, list three "experience groups" that should form the curricular framework: (1) mathematics and Thai language, (2) life experiences, and (3) character development. These experience groups are to be integrated into class activities, which include sharing time; music, movement, and rhythm activities; creative activity and corner play; academic time; storytelling and listening time; manipulation of materials; work time; and playground time.

Although the activity schedules in all centers are quite similar, the teaching methods are not the same. For example, because of pressure from parents, especially from parents living in urban, competitive environments, considerable academic and formal teaching is done in private kindergartens; less emphasis is put on free activities. Children learn reading, writing, arithmetic, the Thai language, and in some instances, also the English language.

The progress of preprimary children is evaluated by observation, interviews, work assessment, and readiness tests. Evaluation occurs during school activities, at the end of each week, and at the end of each school term.

SUPERVISION

Supervision plays an important role in preprimary education, as it does at other educational levels. Centers, preprimary classes, and kindergartens administered by the government agencies are subject to inspection and supervision by their operating departments. Voluntary agencies provide their own supervision and support for centers under their control. For example, kindergartens and preprimary classes under the control of the Office of the National Primary Education Commission (ONPEC) are served by supervisors of ONPEC. ONPEC's supervisors are divided into three levels—national, provincial, and district. Supervisors at the district level are responsible for giving supervision to preprimary classes and kindergartens. Their guidance and monitoring of field staff is inadequate, however, because the authorized supervisors are not well trained in early childhood education. While supervision is a function of district supervisors, inspection is the responsibility of supervisors at the national level.

Private kindergartens in Bangkok are supervised by central officers of the Office of the Private Education Commission, but in the rural areas, the education officers at the provincial and district levels are responsible for this job. None of the mentioned officers are trained for preprimary supervision, but they do have some experience in working with kindergartens.

Child development centers under the Department of Community Development are supervised by community development supervisors, but child development center supervision is not the only job of these supervisors; they are also involved in other work concerning the community. Child nutrition centers are supervised by responsible authorities at all levels, ranging from provincial health officers to obstetricians at health centers. The officers who work closely with the centers are obstetricians and district nurses who have 2-week training in nutrition. Other types of centers generally are subject to supervision by their own department officers. Because these officers are not necessarily specialists in early childhood education, the supervision is not always of the kind needed.

Training of Personnel

The training of personnel in preprimary education is the responsibility of the government. However, some nongovernmental organizations also take part in organizing various inservice training courses.

As regards preservice training, although the 2-year certificate program (a secondary-level program) was discontinued in 1985, there are still 2 teacher-training colleges granting 2-year postsecondary diplomas in preprimary education. There are also 14 teacher-training colleges and 3 universities offering a bachelor's degree in preprimary education. The universities are Chulalongkorn University, Srinakarinwirot University, and Sukhothai Thammathirat Open University. Both Chulalongkorn University and Srinakarinwirot University offer a master's degree in preprimary education as well.

To carry out the most recent government policy concerning expansion and improvement of preprimary education services, trained personnel are urgently needed. Statistics from 1981 show only 56 percent of personnel as having formal teaching qualifications (Office of the National Education Commission, 1985). In general, teachers in government kindergartens have higher qualifications than teachers in private kindergartens have. According to a recent study, 34 percent of preprimary education personnel have never received inservice training (Office of the National Education Commission, 1985). In a 1984 survey of staff in community development centers, child nutrition centers, child care centers in monasteries, and many private child care centers, 38 percent of child care workers reported receiving no inservice training, despite the fact that 63 percent had only a 10th-grade education (Office of the National Education Commission, 1987).

The organizations participating in the inservice training of preprimary education personnel include the following:

- **Office of the National Primary Education Commission**—provides inservice training for teachers in government kindergartens and for teachers of preprimary classes annexed to primary schools
- **Teacher-training colleges**—organize inservice training courses for teachers and child care workers
- **Department of Religious Affairs**—provides training for monks and child care workers in the centers attached to the monasteries
- **Private School Association**—provides inservice training for unqualified kindergarten teachers

In addition to this, training courses for child care workers are conducted by many of the other government organizations responsible for various types of child care centers, such as the Child and Youth Welfare Division, the Department of Public Welfare, and the Department of Community Development (all of which are under the Ministry of Interior); the Department of Health (under the Ministry of Public Health); and the Department of Social Welfare (under the Bangkok Metropolis). Some nongovernmental organizations also provide inservice training for kindergarten teachers, child care workers, and parents. These include the National Women's Council, the YMCA, and the Thai-Israel Friendship Group (a Thai group who studied and trained in Israel).

Since there are a limited number of experts in preprimary education, most agencies render assistance to one another by way of exchanging experts. If Thailand is to reach the goal set in the *Sixth National Education Development Plan (1987–1991)*, it will be necessary for the organizations involved in personnel training to coordinate and cooperate even more than they do at present, to improve the quality of personnel in preprimary education and care.

FINANCING

Since preprimary education is not compulsory, the government allocations for this level of education are far from adequate. In 1984 most of the financial support (71 percent) was provided by the private sector (parents, foundations, and private donations), while the government supplied only 29 percent of the support (Office of the National Education Commission, 1987).

The government support varies with the type of preprimary program. In private kindergartens, parents usually pay all fees and other expenses, although some schools do receive a little government support. In government kindergartens, which are located in the urban areas, buildings, equipment, supplies, and teachers' salaries are all provided by the government. However, the government allocates very little for child development centers in the rural areas; it provides equipment, supplies, and a monthly salary of approximately 400 baht for each child care worker (26 baht is equivalent to $1 U.S. at the time of writing). Therefore, parents have to cover the rest of the cost of the services provided by the centers. In 1984 parents' annual fees for all types of centers ranged from 94 baht to 1,000 baht per child (Office of the National Education Commission, 1987).

DEMOGRAPHICS

Table 2 shows that from 1979 to 1987, Thailand's preschool-aged population (aged 3 to 6) increased from 4,927,960 to 5,099,991, an overall growth of only 3 percent. The number of these children enrolled in preschool grew at a much greater rate during this time. Enrollments in 1979 totaled 405,489, whereas in 1987 they were 1,329,777—more than triple the 1979 figure. As a result, the proportion of preschool-enrolled children, which was 8 percent of 3- to 6-year-olds (or 11 percent of 3- to 5-year-olds) in 1979, reached 26 percent of 3- to 6-year-olds (or 35 percent of 3- to 5-year-olds) in 1987. At this rate, it is expected that the target set for the *Sixth National Education Development Plan* (which is enrollment of 37 percent of 3- to 5-year-olds) will easily be achieved.

The number of preschool institutions has been growing at ever-

Table 2

NUMBERS OF PRESCHOOLERS (AGED 3 TO 6) AND OF PRESCHOOL INSTITUTIONS, 1979–87

Year	Preschool-Aged Population (Aged 3–6)	Enrollment at Preschool institutions: Number	Enrollment at Preschool institutions: % of Population	Number of Preschool Institutions
1979	4,927,960	405,489	8.23	7,338
1980	4,895,966	467,948	9.56	7,972
1981	4,990,224	513,617	10.29	8,435
1982	5,059,596	551,374	10.90	9,286
1983	5,041,042	635,357	12.60	11,427
1984	5,035,335	708,120	14.06	13,132
1985	5,042,342	869,468	17.24	18,658
1986	5,076,177	1,185,841	23.36	27,077
1987	5,099,991	1,329,777	26.07	28,804

Note. Unpublished data from Office of the National Education Commission, Office of the Prime Minister; Office of the National Economic and Social Development Board, Office of the Prime Minister; and Ministry of Education. Also, data from Office of the National Education Commission, *An Evaluation Study of Preschool Services in Thailand* (Bangkok: Srideja Press, 1985), pp. 15–16.

increasing rates. During 1979–80 and 1985–86 the growth rates were 9 percent and 45 percent respectively (Table 2). Enrollments and preprimary institutions grew very rapidly during 1982–86, leveling off somewhat after 1986. It should be noted, however, that beginning in 1986, the Office of the National Primary Education Commission has added 2,000 preprimary classes every year.

Table 3 shows preschool statistics for 1984–85, with some breakdown according to location of preschool facilities and teacher-training facilities. In 1985 there were approximately 18,658 preprimary centers in Thailand, with 8 percent in Bangkok and 92 percent in the 72 other provinces. Of the 18,658 centers, 85 percent are government centers (made up of the 1 percent in Bangkok and the 84 percent in other provinces); 15 percent are nongovernment centers (made up of the 7 percent in Bangkok and the 8 percent in other provinces). Thus, there are more government centers than nongovernment ones in areas other than Bangkok. The situation is just the opposite for Bangkok. With reference again to Table 1, preprimary children in Bangkok are served mainly by private kindergartens and private day care centers, whereas children in other areas are served mainly by child development centers,

Table 3

PRESCHOOL STATISTICS, 1984–85

Area	Number of Preschool-Aged Children (3–6 yr)	Number Attending Preschool Programs	Number of Preschool Institutions						Number of Institutions Training Preschool Personnel		Per-Child Cost for Preschool Education[c] (Baht per Year)	Gross Domestic Product per Capita[d]
			Govt.		Non-govt.[b]		Total					
			No.	%	No.	%	No.	%	Govt.	Non-govt.		
Bangkok	N.A.[a]	N.A.	231	1	1,200	7	1,431	8	4	—	7,823	N.A.
Other provinces	N.A.	N.A.	15,683	84	1,544	8	17,227	92	15	—	4,442	N.A.
Total	5,042,342	869,468	15,914	85	2,744	15	18,658	100	19	—	5,697	19,551

[a]N.A. means data not available.

[b]Private kindergartens under the Ministry of Education, private nurseries under the Ministry of Interior, and preschool centers operated by private agencies and the National Women's Council.

[c]Average cost (recurrent plus capital costs) from a sample survey of preschools, 1985, Office of the National Education Commission, unpublished data. $1 U.S. = 26 baht.

[d]1984 statistic from the Office of the National Economic and Social Development Board, *National Income Statistics of Thailand* (Bangkok: National Accounts Division, 1986).

child nutrition centers, and preprimary classes annexed to primary schools.

It is estimated that demand for preprimary institutions is increasing, as indicated by the following evidence:

1. Female labor force participation rates have increased from 58 percent in 1980 to 63 percent in 1983, and then to 65 percent in 1985 (National Statistical Office, 1983, pp. 113–114; 1984, p. 21; 1986, p. 48).

2. Family structure has changed from the extended to the nuclear family. In the 1970 census, 4.5 percent and 8.0 percent of the total number of households had family sizes of one and two persons respectively. By the time of the 1980 census, 6.7 percent and 15.5 percent of the total number of households had family sizes of one and two persons respectively (National Statistical Office, 1973, p. 5; 1983, p. 183).

Regarding the costs for preprimary education, the figures in Table 3 are for 1984 and are the average recurrent and capital costs based on a sample survey in 1985. The figures show that per-child costs for preprimary education in Bangkok and in other provinces are 7,823 baht and 4,442 baht respectively, which means that the cost of providing preprimary services in Bangkok is almost two times that of other provinces. In comparison with the gross domestic product per capita, the cost of services for children of preprimary age is fairly high, and that may be the reason why such services do not reach the most disadvantaged children in rural areas.

PROBLEMS AND ISSUES CONCERNING CHILD CARE AND EARLY EDUCATION

Even though it is evident that the importance of preprimary education has been realized by all parties concerned, a number of problems still exist. Some of the main problems are these:

1. **Too many different agencies are involved in preprimary education.** At present, preprimary education in Thailand is organized by four ministries, local governments of three different kinds, and various private agencies. Each agency has different objectives in setting up preprimary centers. For example, the Office of the National Primary Education Commission emphasizes a school-readiness program, while the Department of Health, in keeping with its primary task, aims at solving children's health and nutrition problems. Besides the differences in their objectives, the lack of coordination among the many agencies is a major

problem. In some localities, there is a duplication of services because several different departments have set up centers; in other localities, there are no services available for large numbers of poor children who need them (Department of Technical and Economic Cooperation, 1978; Office of the National Education Commission, 1983).

2. **There is wide variation in the quality of services provided by the different types of agencies**. This is partly due to the variations in training of caregivers, in government funding, in equipment, in supplies, and in facilities. It is also due to the fact that each agency has its own policies and objectives and therefore its own guidelines for program implementation. Often a program's weak point is supervision. A number of agencies do not consider the supervision of preprimary centers as their main task, and the supervision that is carried out is not systematic (Office of the National Education Commission, 1983).

3. **The training of personnel in preprimary education needs improvement**. Even though a number of colleges and universities offer preservice training, their training emphasizes theory rather than needed skills and practice. Also, a large number of untrained child care workers in the rural areas have no access to inservice training. Moreover, preprimary education is growing rapidly because of the expansion of preprimary classes in primary schools. Since 1986 the Office of the National Primary Education Commission has added 2,000 preprimary classes every year. Eventually these will become 2-year rural kindergartens, and preprimary education will be treated as a downward extension of primary schooling. However, since most of the primary school teachers lack training in preprimary education, inservice training for those teachers who will be responsible for rural kindergartens is most urgently needed.

4. **Although preprimary curricula emphasize readiness training, in practice the majority of preprimary teachers and caregivers teach the three Rs to preprimary children**. This is due partly to lack of training on the part of teachers: Many caregivers and teachers perceive "learning" and "reading" as synonymous and do not know what activities to organize if they do not teach the three Rs. Parental pressure is another reason for teaching the three Rs: Parents often demand that preschools teach their children to read and write, believing that such early learning leads to success in primary school. Also, parents want children to be prepared for the competitive examinations that are required before entering some better-known primary schools (Office of the National Education Commission, 1979, 1985).

However, some studies have recently been conducted to measure the primary school impact of different kinds of preschool programs. One of the studies compared primary school children who had gone through an overall readiness program with those who had learned the three Rs before entering grade one. The results of the measurement of student achievement were that both groups performed the same, but the overall readiness group achieved higher scores in social development (Thai-Israel Friendship Group, 1980). Another study showed that children who had gone through a readiness program enjoyed learning in the primary school more than did those with early exposure to the three Rs (Thai-Israel Friendship Group, 1980).

5. **The problem of inequality of educational opportunity clearly exists in preprimary education.** The evidence is that (1) in 1987 only 35 percent of the 3- to 5-year-olds (or 26 percent of 3- to 6-year-olds) attended preprimary institutions, (2) there are vast differences in the quality of existing services, and (3) the government has invested more in children with the best opportunities, with the poor having to pay more than the rich because of the differing degrees of government support for various types of preprimary schools and centers (Passornsiri, 1983). Nevertheless, it is hoped that the expansion of rural kindergartens through the efforts of the Office of the National Primary Education Commission will help increase the educational opportunity of children in rural areas.

CONCLUSION

At present, it is generally accepted that the current system of preprimary education in Thailand is meeting the needs of young children and their families, even though this level of education is not compulsory. Evidence of this acceptance can be seen in the increasing numbers of children enrolled in preprimary services (now 35 percent of 3- to 5-year-old children); the target of 37 percent set by the *Sixth National Education Development Plan (1987–1991)* will no doubt be met in 1989.

Nevertheless, besides the need to expand services to children all over the country, there is need for improvement in many other areas. First of all, various government agencies must coordinate their efforts and cooperate so that children's services can be provided most effectively and so that the problem of duplication of services can be solved. With regard to the improvement of quality, appropriate supervision models should be set up to ensure the successful implementation of preprimary education programs.

To improve the training of personnel, the preservice degree programs of colleges and universities should put greater emphasis on practical training. At the same time, various types of resources should be employed for inservice training, so that personnel already engaged in preprimary education can improve their skills. Educational radio and television programs by some universities and government agencies could be useful for training personnel who work in remote areas. Besides the training of preschool personnel, one of the most important factors affecting the quality of Thailand's preprimary education is parents' attitudes. Therefore promotion of parent education should have high priority.

REFERENCES

Department of Curriculum and Instruction Development. (1979). *Guidelines for organizing kindergarten experiences*. Bangkok: Karnsasna Press.

Department of Technical and Economic Cooperation. (1978). *Report on the evaluation of the child nutrition center and child development projects* (Mimeographed report). Bangkok.

Ministry of Education. (1964). *History of the Ministry of Education (1892– 1964)*. Bangkok: Kurusapa Press.

National Statistical Office. (1973). *1970 population and housing census*. Bangkok: Author.

National Statistical Office. (1983). *1980 population and housing census*. Bangkok: Author.

National Statistical Office. (1984). *Yearbook of labor statistics, 1984*. Bangkok: The Daily Trade News Office, Department of Commercial Relations.

National Statistical Office. (1986). *Report of the labor force survey, Whole kingdom (Round 1), February 1985*. Bangkok, Thailand: Romsaikarnpim.

Office of the National Economic and Social Development Board. (1977). *Fourth national economic and social development plan (1977–1981)*. Bangkok: Tawanna Press.

Office of the National Economic and Social Development Board. (1982). *Fifth national economic and social development plan (1982–1986)*. Bangkok: Choomnoom Sahakorn Karnkaset Press.

Office of the National Education Commission. (1976). *Education for life and society: A report of the Committee for Establishing the Framework for Educational Reform*. Bangkok: Choomnoom Sahakorn Karnkaset Press.

Office of the National Education Commission. (1977a). *Fourth national education development plan (1977–1981)*. Bangkok: Author.

Office of the National Education Commission (1977b). *National scheme of education 1977*. Bangkok: Srimuang Press.

Office of the National Education Commission. (1979). *The organization of preprimary centers in Thailand.* Bangkok: Charoenphol Press.

Office of the National Education Commission. (1983). *Perspective policies and planning for the development of children.* Bangkok: United Production.

Office of the National Education Commission. (1985). *An evaluation study of preschool services in Thailand.* Bangkok: Srideja Press.

Office of the National Education Commission. (1986). *Sixth national education development plan (1987–1991).* Bangkok: Roongruengsarnkarnpim.

Office of the National Education Commission. (1987). *Resource allocation for preschool education.* Bangkok: Chuanpim.

Passornsiri, Nittaya. (1983). Preschool services in Thailand. In *Preventing school failure: The relationship between preschool and primary education* (pp. 103–107). Proceedings of a workshop on preschool research held in Bogota, Colombia, May 26–29, 1981. Ottawa: International Development Research Centre.

Prasert-Aksorn. (1910). *Narangkurowat* [Proper behavior for young children]. Bangkok: Supakarn-Chamroon Press.

Rungsinant, A. (1981). Development of early childhood education in Thailand. In *Teaching behavior in early childhood education* (pp. 119–161). Bangkok: Sukhothai Thammathirat Open University Press.

Thai-Israel Friendship Group. (1980). *Understanding preprimary children.* Bangkok: Erawan Press.

UNICEF (United Nations Children's Fund). (1982). *200 years of child care in Thailand,* A UNICEF publication in observance of the Rattanakosin Bicentennial. Bangkok: Author.

XV
Early Childhood Care and Education in the United States

Patricia P. Olmsted
Research Associate
High/Scope Educational Research Foundation
Ypsilanti, Michigan

> *Who can compute the value of the first seven years of life? Who can tell the strength of impressions, made ere the mind is pre-occupied, prejudiced or perverted? Especially, if in its waxen state, it is softened by the breath of a mother, will not the seal which she stamps there, resist the mutations of time, and be read before the Throne of the Judge, when the light of this sun and moon, are quenched and extinct? (Sigourney, 1838, p. 89)*
>
> *The industry displayed in the various trades and occupations, should be a stimulant to the mother, who modifies a material more costly than all others, more liable to destruction by brief neglect. . . . Is the builder of a lofty and magnificent edifice, careless of its foundations, and whether its columns are to rest upon a quicksand, or a quagmire? (Sigourney, 1838, pp. 90–91)*

In 1838 *Letters to Mothers* by Lydia Sigourney was published in the United States. It is a book giving advice to mothers about child care and education—advice that reflects the attitudes of that period in America regarding the critical nature of a child's early years, the important role of religion in childrearing, and the pivotal role of the mother. Around the year of publication of Sigourney's book, out-of-home child care by groups and institutions was just beginning in the U.S. A history of these extra-familial services for children appears in this national profile, along with other general information about early care and education. We begin with a presentation of the demographics of children in the U.S., followed by a brief historical overview and a short discussion of national child care and early education policies. A description of child care arrangements available for 3- to 6-year-olds appears next, followed by a summary of key research studies conducted in the U.S. We conclude with a discussion of the nation's early childhood issues for the coming decade.

THE DEMOGRAPHICS REGARDING CHILDREN

POPULATION TRENDS

Based on the detailed population statistics collected every 10 years in the United States, Table 1 shows the change in the nation's number of 3- to 6-year-old children during the past century. Although there has been a general increase in this age group during the 100-year time period, the size of the group relative to the total population has decreased from 8.2 percent to 4.2 percent. Thus, although over the years the number of preschool-aged children has increased, their rate of increase has been slower than that of the total population. The increasing U.S. life span is clearly one reason for the decreasing percentage of the population represented by these young children.

As indicated in Table 1, the number of 3- to 6-year-old children in the U.S. in 1980 was 9,484,000. When this number is compared with the estimated number for 1987 (10,879,000; U.S. Bureau of the Census, 1988), the increase between 1980 and 1987 is calculated to be about 15

Table 1

NUMBER OF 3- TO 6-YEAR-OLD CHILDREN AND PERCENT OF THE POPULATION THEY REPRESENTED, 1880–1980

Year	Number of Children (Thousands)	Percent of U.S. Population
1880	4,140	8.2
1900	5,464	7.1
1920	7,032	6.6
1940	6,409	4.9
1960	11,938	6.6
1980	9,484	4.2

Note. Statistics are from U.S. Bureau of the Census, *1980 Census of the Population*, Volume 1 (Washington, DC: Government Printing Office, 1983).

percent. However, the percentage of the nation's population represented by this age group has remained essentially constant over this time period—growing only from 4.2 percent in 1980 to 4.5 percent in 1987.

MOTHERS ENTERING THE LABOR FORCE

A major change in the United States during the last 30 years that has important implications for 3- to 6-year-old children is the increasing participation of women in the labor force. Although employed women are not the only ones utilizing child care, they make up the largest proportion of the group. Available national statistics regarding employed mothers do not provide separate figures according to the ages of their young children, only aggregate numbers for women with children "under the age of 6." In 1950, 12 percent of women with children under the age of 6 were employed, while the comparable figure for 1985 is 57 percent (U.S. Department of Labor, 1988). While the employment rate has increased substantially for all women during this period (growing from 34 percent in 1950 to 55 percent in 1985; U.S. Bureau of the Census, 1987), the employment rate increase for mothers of children under the age of 6 has been even greater. These mothers come from both "two-parent" and "single-parent" households. There are 12.8 million employed mothers from two-parent households (having both parents in the work force) with an estimated total of 8.8 million children younger than 6. In addition, there are 3.5 million employed single mothers who have 1.8 million children younger than 6. Of all these mothers of young children, approximately 70 percent are employed full-time (35 or more hours per week) and 30 percent are employed part-time (U.S. Department of Labor, 1988).

CHILDREN LIVING IN POVERTY

The U.S. government has developed a definition of poverty that uses an index based on money income and family size, with the poverty threshold adjusted yearly to reflect changes in the consumer price index. In 1985 the average poverty threshold for a family of four was $10,989 while the threshold for a family of six was $14,696. Using the poverty threshold, we can determine the number of children living in poverty (that is, living in families with incomes below the poverty threshold). For all children combined, the poverty rate in 1985 was 20.1 percent. The poverty rates for children for selected years prior to 1985 were 26.9

percent for 1959, 13.8 percent for 1969, and 16.0 percent for 1979. For this time period, the highest rate occurred in 1959, with a large decrease occurring between 1959 and 1969. From 1969 to 1985, the rate increased but did not reach the 1959 rate (U.S. Bureau of the Census, 1986).

Two major factors are related to the poverty rates for children, their racial group and their family structure. Table 2 presents poverty rates for white, black, and Hispanic children for selected years. Figures are included for all families combined and for the subcategory of female-headed, no-male-present families. For all families combined as well as for female-headed, no-male-present families, the poverty rate is higher in black and Hispanic families than in white families. In addition, in all racial groups, the percentage of children living in poverty is higher for female-headed, no-male-present families than for all families combined. In 1985, the percentage of families that were female-headed, no-male-present families ranged from 13 percent for whites to 42 percent for blacks. The trends in poverty rates across years for racial subgroups are similar and resemble the general trend mentioned earlier. That is, the highest rate occurred in 1959, followed by a large decrease between 1959 and 1969 and generally increasing rates between 1969 and 1985.

Table 2

Percentage of Children (Under 18) in Poverty, by Family Structure and Race, for Selected Years

Type of family	1959 (%)	1969 (%)	1979 (%)	1985 (%)
White families				
All	20.6	9.7	11.4	15.6
Female-headed, no-male-present (13%[a])	64.6	45.2	38.6	45.2
Black families				
All	65.5	39.6	40.8	43.1
Female-headed, no-male-present (42%)	81.6	68.2	63.1	66.9
Hispanic[b] families				
All	n/a	n/a	27.7	39.6
Female-headed, no-male-present (23%)	n/a	n/a	62.2	72.4

Note. Statistics are from U.S. Bureau of the Census, *Current Population Reports*, Series P-60, No. 154 (Washington, DC: U.S. Government Printing Office, 1986).

[a]Percent of female-headed, no-male-present families for 1985.

[b]Hispanic children may be of any race.

In summary, the demographics of children in the U.S. indicate a leveling off in the proportion of the population represented by the 3- to 6-year-old age group, a large increase since 1950 in the percentage of employed mothers with children under the age of 6, and large variations in the percentages of children living in poverty, depending on racial subgroup and family structure.

Historical Background

The history of early childhood care and education in the United States has consisted of two major strands of activity. The first strand, with roots in a social welfare tradition, has been associated with the **provision of care** for young children, particularly for those from poor and troubled families. The second strand, with roots in the German kindergarten movement, has been associated with the **provision of early education**, especially for children from affluent families. After presenting the major events forming these two strands, we will discuss the current state of early childhood care and education in the United States.

The history of the United States has contributed in a unique way to a national set of attitudes towards child care that includes, for example, beliefs about the primacy of the family regarding childrearing and beliefs about the value of personal fulfillment through work. Cochran (1982) discusses the former beliefs by noting that "There is a strong feeling that childrearing is a family affair, to be carried out by the mother, with help from the father, separate from public life. A national commitment to pluralism, stimulated by successive waves of immigration, has carried with it an agreement that different peoples rear their children differently, and reinforced the belief that childrearing practices are the private province of family members" (Draft, pp. 3–4). Regarding beliefs about personal fulfillment through work, Cochran points out that both church and state have promoted the value of work throughout the history of this country. Furthermore, with the industrial revolution, work increasingly implied paid employment away from home. The historical movement of women into the labor force can be related to the combination of the growing mechanization of household tasks, the desire for more consumer goods, and a desire for personal fulfillment through paid employment. Cochran states, "The tension created by combining the belief that childrearing is a private affair, to be carried out primarily by the mother, with a desire to maximize human potential, individual freedom, and socioeconomic participation through work for pay, is being felt both inside the family and at every other level of American society" (pp. 4–5). This tension manifests itself both in the individual arrangements made by families for child care (often informal, family-based arrangements) and in the diverse views found among people in the United States about who (family, community, national government) should be responsible for child care.

The Care Strand

Day nurseries, the original social welfare day care centers, first appeared shortly after the flood of immigration that brought more than 5 million foreign families to the United States between 1815 and 1860 (Clarke-Stewart, 1982; Kahn & Kamerman, 1987). As Kahn and Kamerman state, "The early cases cited by Greenblatt and others involve instances of 'day orphans' who were to be protected while their mothers worked or of charitable groups that were responding to alleged or potential child neglect" (p. 121). During the 1870s and 1880s philanthropic agencies began sponsoring day nurseries, seeing such child care assistance for poor or immigrant mothers as the best way to help preserve the family (Steinfels, 1973).

Based on the French model of the crèche, the main purpose of the day nursery was physical care of the children (feeding, bathing, keeping them safe from the dangers of the street) 6 days a week, 12 hours a day. Day nurseries also generally expressed a strong concern for the moral care and proper upbringing of the children by assisting them in developing habits of cleanliness and order as well as obedience and industry (Steinfels, 1973).

The Education Strand

The beginnings of the second strand, early childhood education, can be traced to the 19th-century development of the kindergarten. "The idea that some form of education outside the home might be appropriate for children before they entered the first grade paved the way for the later development of nursery schools" (Almy, 1982, p. 478). Specific elements of early childhood education in the United States can be traced to earlier programs developed in Europe by Froebel and Montessori (Spodek, 1973). Froebel's ideas that the role of education was to support the child's natural development and that play was an essential part of the educational activity of childhood have been maintained in many U.S. early childhood programs. Similarly, such U.S. program features as prescribed sequences of activities, self-correcting materials, and indirect teaching styles can be traced to the work of Maria Montessori.

During the 1930s middle-class families began to enroll their children in early childhood education programs in large numbers (Clarke-Stewart & Fein, 1983). Most of these early education programs were based on Froebel or Montessori or were derivatives of the nursery school programs developed in England by such educators as Robert Owen and Margaret McMillan.

Combining the Strands

The first large-scale early childhood care *and* education programs occurred in the 1930s, when such programs were authorized under the federally sponsored Work Projects Administration (WPA) to provide jobs for unemployed professionals (Clarke-Stewart, 1982; Scarr & Weinberg, 1986). By 1937, there were 1,900 programs established and approximately 40 thousand children being served. Located mainly in public schools, the year-round, all-day programs were basically viewed as child care, although they clearly had educational components. With the demise of the WPA, most of the programs were phased out because of a lack of funds.

During World War II, early childhood care again attracted public attention as many women went to work in defense-related industries. In 1941 Congress passed the Lanham Act, which provided matching federal funds for states to establish day care centers and nursery schools. In 1945 between 105,000 and 130,000 children were enrolled in Lanham centers (Zigler & Goodman, 1982). Following the end of World War II, the Lanham centers and other wartime child care programs were dismantled everywhere except in California and New York City. As men returned from the battlefield, there was a general assumption that women would return to the home.

The 1960s brought renewed interest in early childhood care and education, with one attendant result being a closer meshing of the two strands, child care and early education programs. As women began participating in the labor force in greater numbers, the need for child care increased—for all families, not just for poor or troubled families, which was the earlier focus of the "social welfare" movement (Kahn & Kamerman, 1987).

There was also an academic "rediscovery" of early childhood education during this time, as evidenced by the increased interest in the work of Jean Piaget, Jerome Bruner, J. McV. Hunt and others (Almy, 1982). More families began to see early educational programs as helpful for their children, as a routine part of children's experience. During the 1960s several studies of the effectiveness of early childhood education, particularly for children in low-income families, were launched. Examples of these studies include David Weikart's Perry Preschool study (Berrueta-Clement, Schweinhart, Barnett, Epstein, & Weikart, 1984), Susan Gray's Early Training study (Gray, Ramsey, & Klaus, 1982), and Phyllis Levenstein's Mother-Child Home program (Levenstein, O'Hara, & Madden, 1983).

In 1964 the Head Start program, which is still the largest national effort in the area of early childhood education, was initiated. One important aspect of the Head Start program is that it is developed on the premise that early education and enrichment are important for all children, not just for children from affluent families such as those served by the early nursery schools. Also, Head Start has a strong educational emphasis and therefore continues the trend (started in the Lanham centers) towards the provision of early education as well as daytime supervision for children from low-income families.

During the 1970s the use of early childhood care and education programs increased as mothers continued to enter the labor force in greater numbers and as more families saw early education programs as beneficial for their children. During this period different models of early childhood education were tested in the national Head Start Planned Variation program, with most of the models developed by child development scholars or early childhood education researchers at universities or research institutions (Miller, 1979). Examples of planned variation models included the Behavior Analysis program (University of Kansas), the Cognitively Oriented Curriculum (High/Scope Educational Research Foundation), and the Bank Street Model (Bank Street College of Education).

In the area of child care during the 1970s, many professionals in the field consider the major event to be President Richard Nixon's veto in 1971 of the Comprehensive Child Development Bill. This bill, sponsored by Senator Walter Mondale and Congressman John Brademus and passed by both houses of Congress, would have established a national child care program for the first time in the United States. In vetoing the bill, President Nixon stated that the legislation "would commit the vast moral authority of the National Government to the side of communal approaches of childrearing over against the family-centered approach" (Nixon, 1971).

The Beginning of Decentralization, Privatization, and Deregulation

According to Kahn and Kamerman (1987), "**Decentralization**, **privatization**, and **deregulation** became the guiding principles in federal child care policy in the 1980s" (p. 3). The **decentralization** has occurred through a combination of federal funding cutbacks and the elimination of matching-fund requirements for states. Federal funds for child care services (Title XX) were converted into Social Services Block Grant funds in 1981 and were passed through to the states. Under this latter funding mechanism, policy and program decisions were made by the individual states. **Privatization** has included open support for a diverse child care market: providing incentives to employers, easing requirements regarding for-profit providers, and giving tax benefits to families. These forms of support have been accompanied by a decrease in federal funding and policymaking.

The major instance of **deregulation** involved the failure to enact the Federal Interagency Day Care Requirements. These regulations, developed by federal agency experts and child development advisers and based on research, would have established minimum standards for child care services, at least for those receiving federal funding, and would have served as general guidelines for all child care services. However, these standards have never been adopted by the Congress, and consequently U.S. child care services are subject only to state standards. These standards vary considerably from state to state, and in some states certain forms of care (for example, family day care homes) are subject to *no* requirements for licensing or registration.

With decentralization, privatization, and deregulation characterizing the federal involvement in child care during the 1980s, the roles of state and local agencies have become increasingly more important. In some states, new child care programs, generally targeted to serve the children of special populations (such as low-income working families, adolescent parents), have been created with state, or combined state and local, funding. States with programs of this nature include Minnesota, Massachusetts, Virginia, and New York. In other states, no additional state or local funds have been allocated for child care, and the federal funds (Title XX through Social Services Block Grants to states) have failed to keep pace with inflation, resulting in the provision of services to fewer children each year. During 1988 twenty-eight states provided some funding for early childhood education programs (Children's Defense Fund, 1988). Some states have made concerted efforts to integrate early childhood education and child care into one system, while others continue to have the two parallel strands. The resulting overall picture of early childhood care and education is one of great variation from state to state.

At present the United States has a highly decentralized system of early childhood care and education services. Some special programs, usually those of compensatory nature for children from low-income families, are funded and organized according to the federal guidelines (Head Start, for example). Other federal financial support for the provision of child care comes in the form of tax credits for families. State governments set general policy, regulations, and licensing standards for services and programs. Individual providers—for-profit as well as non-profit, center-based as well as home-based—organize, administer, and operate their own programs. As a result of this decentralized system, various forms of early childhood care and education exist. We describe these forms more fully in a later section of this profile.

NATIONAL CHILD CARE AND EDUCATION POLICIES

THE EDUCATIONAL SYSTEM

In the U.S., education in general is the responsibility of individual states, and the states share this responsibility with local communities. In each state, there is a system of free public schools covering kindergarten (for 5-year-olds) and 12 additional years. Although there is variation among states, schooling is generally compulsory between the ages of 6 and 16. Following kindergarten, three different patterns of schooling are common: (1) 8 years of elementary school followed by 4 years of high school, (2) 6 years of elementary school followed by 3 years of junior high school and 3 years of senior high school, and (3) 5 years of elementary schooling followed by 3 years of middle school and 4 years of high school. For most students, high school graduation occurs at age 17 or 18. According to Eckstein (1988), about 10 percent of students in the U.S. attend private institutions, the majority of which are religious schools. At present, about 75 percent of an age group complete high school.

Child and Family Policy

U.S. policy regarding families with young children is based on the idea of noninterference in family affairs relating to the care and education of children. Traditionally, there has been a consensus that the family as an institution should remain independent of government unless special circumstances warrant otherwise. Thus, any specific government policies generally target families with special needs or families at risk because of economic or social circumstances.

The policies that do exist at present are intended to promote family choice in the selection of child care and to encourage the development of many forms of child care services. These policies are a combination of social benefits for specific types of families, tax benefits for families paying income taxes, services for specific children, and tax incentives for employers.

Aid to Families with Dependent Children (AFDC) is a social benefit program primarily for low-income mothers with at least one minor-aged child. The program gives money directly to mothers for basic living expenses. In addition, AFDC-eligible families usually qualify for food stamps, Medicaid, and, in some cases, public housing. In some states, AFDC is available only to single-parent families (female-headed, no-male-present). Consequently, in these states two-parent families can have an income far below the poverty level and still not qualify for AFDC, a situation that may encourage family breakups.

The primary child care tax benefit for families is the **Child Care Tax Credit**. This credit is available to two-parent families with children under age 15 in which one or both parents work full-time, to divorced or separated parents with custody of children, and to single parents. Under the system, a family can deduct between 20 and 30 percent of child care expenses from their federal income tax, up to a maximum of $2,400 per year for one child and $4,800 per year for two or more children. However, since there are many low-income families who are not required to pay federal income taxes or who pay such a small amount that they only partially benefit from the tax credit, one can see that the child care tax credit does not benefit all families equally.

At present, the federal government provides direct early childhood care and education services through **Project Head Start**. As indicated in the previous section, this project, started in the 1960s, is designed primarily for children from low-income families. During the 1987–88 school year, Head Start operated approximately 1,200 centers across the U.S. serving approximately 446,500 children between the ages of 3 and 5 (Administration for Children, Youth, and Families, 1988). Head Start is a comprehensive program in that it provides education, health, nutrition, and social services to 3- to 5-year-old children and their families. Heavy emphasis is put on involving parents in various ways: as teachers of their own children, as classroom volunteers, as program decision-makers. Whereas other child care and education programs have experienced funding cuts during the 1980s, Head Start has not; indeed, it has consistently been supported by both major U.S. political parties.

Indirectly, the federal government provides support for child care through **Social Services Block Grants**. These funds, originally distributed directly by the federal government under Title XX, are distributed to states according to their population, so that states can design their own social services allocation programs within broad federal guidelines. States use the funds primarily to purchase low-cost child care and to support training and counseling services for low-income mothers.

The federal government has recently encouraged employer-sponsored child care through the provision of incentives to employers. In 1981, legislation established a tax advantage program for employers, the **Dependent Care Assistance Plan**. This program "permits an exclusion from gross income for the value of employer-provided child-care services." In addition, there is a "depreciation system for employers who improve facilities by creating on-site or nearby child care centers for employees' children" (Kahn & Kamerman, 1987, pp. 195–196). These efforts on the part of the federal government have contributed to the increase, although small, of employer-sponsored child care. Finally, changes in the tax laws now allow employers and employees to develop flexible plans that shift salary monies from direct payment to various benefit plans that can include child care services. These changes allow the employee to select child care as a fringe benefit, an attractive choice when two parents are employed and traditional fringe benefits (for example, health, life insurance) are available through either employer.

Recent Policy Changes

In October 1988 Congress passed the **Family Support Act** (otherwise known as the welfare reform bill). This act includes several provisions that will affect AFDC and, potentially, the regulation of child care services. By October 1, 1990, all states will be required to establish programs for providing education, training, and employment services to AFDC recipients and will have the option of requiring participation by one or both parents of children aged 3 and older. Concurrently, states will have the responsibility to guarantee child care for those families participating in Job Opportunities and Basic Skills Training (JOBS) program activities. The state agency will be required to provide information on accessible child care, provide assistance in selecting appropriate care, and, upon request, assist participants in obtaining child care services. The Family Support Act also requires that participating states endeavor to develop basic health and safety requirements that would apply to "all family day care provided through the JOBS or AFDC programs that is currently exempt from state and local standards" (Children's Defense Fund, 1988, p. 18). The Family Support Act also makes grants available in 1990 and 1991 for states to improve their child care licensing and registration requirements, to monitor child care provided to AFDC children, and to fund demonstration programs aimed at developing innovative programs for AFDC children.

Other early childhood care and education measures currently under consideration at the federal level include (1) increased funding to states for the provision of child care to low- and moderate-income families and for the improvement of quality and availability of all child care services within a state, (2) an increased child care tax credit for families, (3) increased funding for the Head Start program, and (4) increased federal involvement in other early childhood education programs.

The current high level of public and political interest in early childhood care and education issues has resulted in the articulation and proposal of several federal efforts to broaden the availability and improve the quality of programs for young children. In general, however, the individual states would continue to hold most of the responsibility for the actual design and implementation of programs.

Early Childhood Care and Education Arrangements

Child care arrangements for preprimary children aged 3 to 6 vary widely according to parental needs, income level, and education. The arrangements may involve individual care in the child's home or someone else's home; in a family or group child care home; in a part-day public or private educational program; or in a child care center. Families in which all adults are employed often use multiple care arrangements that typically include some combination of a part-day educational program, a family day care home, or care by relatives.

TYPES OF ARRANGEMENTS

Descriptions of the major early childhood care and education arrangements used in the United States are given in this section. The arrangements are as follows:

■ ***Care in own home, by relative or nonrelative.*** In this arrangement, an adult comes into the child's home to provide care and supervision. The in-home sitter is often a relative who may or may not be paid.

■ ***Care in another home by relative.*** A common child care arrangement in the United States is care of a child by a relative in the relative's home. In some cases, these services are provided without cost, while in others, money, goods, or an exchange of services may be involved.

■ ***Family day care home.*** This arrangement involves child care on a regular basis by a nonrelative in a home other than the child's home. Family day care home arrangements can vary from an informal, shared-caregiving agreement between friends to a highly formal network of licensed homes.

■ ***Part-day educational program.*** These programs, which can be under private or public sponsorship, are housed in a variety of settings, such as community centers, public schools, churches, and buildings specifically built for this purpose. Educational programs generally consist of a large group of children with two or more adults and are traditionally concerned with children's growth in several areas (social, cognitive, creative). There are likely to be scheduled activities, clearly defined play areas with associated routines, and a specific curriculum (for example, Montessori, High/Scope). At present, most educational programs for 3- to 5-year-olds are still limited to half-day sessions, usually 3 hours a day for 5 days a week during the school year. However, there are many institutional efforts currently under way to coordinate educational programs with other child care arrangements, to better meet the child care needs of families throughout the entire working day and throughout the entire year.

■ ***Child care center.*** In this arrangement, care is provided by groups or individuals in special facilities devoted to child care. The average number of children served by a center is 50, but the number may range from 15 to 300. In large centers, children are usually divided into groups according to age. There are several types of centers, including: (1) private for-profit; (2) private nonprofit; (3) publicly operated; (4) parent cooperative; and (5) employer-provided.

Private for-profit centers may be either proprietary or commercial. Proprietary centers are usually small, serving approximately 30 children, and are typically family-run. They are often located in converted shops or homes and may accept only children within a specified age-range (for example, 3- to 5-year-olds) whose families can pay the fee. Commercial centers are generally operated as franchises: A specific program is developed and replicated on a large scale, which results in uniform facilities and procedures. Such centers may accommodate as many as 70 to 100 children in groups of approximately 20.

Private nonprofit centers are usually operated by churches or by private community or charitable organizations and are often located in churches, schools, or community halls.

Publicly operated centers serve children from low-income families who receive government subsidies for child care, as well as children whose parents pay for child care. Because they receive public funding, these child care centers must meet required standards that insure adequate physical facilities, equipment, staff, and educational programs. For many centers, adequate parent involvement is another requirement.

Parent cooperative centers are those in which parents play a major role in providing child care, management, and decision making, usually with the guidance of a paid director and teachers. As a result of this in-kind service by parents, fees tend to be lower than those for other types of centers, but cooperative centers tend to attract high-income families because the parents must have the time flexibility to work at the center. Parent cooperative centers typically offer part-day programs for young children.

Employer-provided centers are offered by a small number of corporations, factories, hospitals, universities, and trade unions to provide child care as a fringe benefit for their employees. These centers are typically large (approximately 80 to 100 children, divided into appropriate groups) and are usually located close to the parent's workplace.

Availability and Use of Arrangements

In the United States, 96 percent of 5-year-olds attend public or private kindergarten programs (Center for Education statistics, 1987). Data on child care arrangements for 5-year-olds when they are not attending kindergarten are limited, and thus the remainder of this section will cover only services for children under 5 years of age.

The collection of data regarding availability and use of different child care arrangements in the United States is a piecemeal effort. For example, at the federal level, the U.S. Department of Labor gathers child care information for families with mothers in the labor force (*Child Care: A Workforce Issue*, April 1988), while the National Center for Education Statistics collects data on preschool enrollment (*The Condition of Education*, 1986). Information about state-level efforts in early childhood care and education is collected annually by the Children's Defense Fund (*State Child Care Fact Book*, 1982 through 1988). In addition, information is available from surveys conducted by professional groups, such as the National Association for the Education of Young Children, and from large-scale studies, such as the National Day Care Study. Because these various sets of data have included different types of child care arrangements, have been collected at different times, and have utilized different data collection procedures, it is difficult to combine them to obtain an overall picture of Americans' use of early childhood care and education arrangements.

Recently, however, an attempt was made to develop such an overall picture by using data from different sources; the result is shown in Table 3. Statistics are presented separately for children with mothers in the labor force and for those with mothers not in the labor force. The care arrangement categories given in Table 3 have been constructed from the many diverse categories covered in each of the different sources of statistics.

For children with mothers in the labor force, the most frequently used type of care is different for the two ages of children in the table: Relative or in-home care is most frequently used for ages 0–2, while centers or schools are most frequently used for ages 3–4. For children with mothers not in the labor force, parental care is the most frequently used type of care, regardless of the child's age. The percentages attending centers or schools are nearly equal for 3- and 4-year-olds whose mothers are in the labor force (18 percent) and for 3- and 4-year-olds whose mothers are not in the labor force (16 percent).

When changes in the availability of various types of child care settings are examined over the past 10 to 15 years, a large overall increase is seen, but variations in the size of increase are found among the different settings. This section includes data for two major settings, family day care homes and child care centers.

Table 3

U.S. EARLY CHILDHOOD CARE AND EDUCATION IN 1987

	Group Size in Thousands (% of Age Group)		
Population Category	Aged 0–2	Aged 3–4	Aged 0–4
All Children[a]	**9,629 (100%)**	**6,454 (100%)**	**16,083 (100%)**
With mothers in labor force[a]	**4,921 (51%)**	**3,497 (54%)**	**8,418 (52%)**
In parental care during work[b]	1,226 (13%)	783 (12%)	2,009 (12%)
In relative or in-home care[b]	1,628 (17%)	908 (14%)	2,536 (16%)
In nonrelative care in other homes[b]	1,265 (13%)	621 (10%)	1,886 (12%)
In centers or schools[b]	802 (8%)	1,186 (18%)	1,988 (12%)
With mothers not in labor force[a]	**4,708 (49%)**	**2,957 (46%)**	**7,665 (48%)**
In parental care only	4,708 (49%)	1,940 (30%)	6,648 (41%)
In centers or schools[c]	0 (0%)	1,017 (16%)	1,017 (6%)
In any form of extrafamilial, out-of-home care or education[d]	**2,013 (21%)**	**2,888 (45%)**	**4,901 (30%)**

[a]From U.S. Bureau of Labor Statistics, unpublished data, November 30, 1988.

[b]From U.S. Bureau of the Census, *Who's Minding the Kids? Child Care Arrangements: Winter 1984–85*, Series P-70, No. 9 (Washington, DC: U.S. Government Printing Office, 1987), p. 5. Given figures multiplied by 1.058 for ages 0–2 and .995 for ages 3–4 to match 1987 totals.

[c]From National Center for Education Statistics, *The Condition of Education—1986 Edition* (Washington, DC: U.S. Government Printing Office, 1986), pp. 5, 13. In 1984, 34.4 percent of 3- and 4-year-olds of mothers not working were enrolled in centers or schools.

[d]Percent totals in this row were affected by rounding of component percents.

Family day care homes

In 1978 there were over 100,000 licensed or regulated family day care homes with an estimated total capacity of 400,000 children, using an estimate of 4 children per licensed home (Ruopp, Travers, Glantz, & Coelen, 1979). By 1988 the number of licensed or regulated family day care homes had increased to approximately 170,000 (Children's Defense Fund, 1988) with an estimated total capacity of 680,000 children. Exact figures are not available, but this author estimates that in the United States, only 10 to 40 percent of family day care homes are licensed, which would suggest an actual total number of family day care homes between 425,000 and 1,700,000 with an actual total capacity between 1.7 million and 6.8 million children. This child care setting typically serves both preschool-aged children (full-day or part-day) and school-aged children (before and after school).

Child care centers

In 1978 the number of licensed or regulated child care centers was estimated to be 18,300 with a total capacity of 1.0 million children (Ruopp et al., 1979). By 1988 the number of licensed centers had increased to an estimated 66,400 (Children's Defense Fund, 1988) with a total capacity of 3.7 million children.

The variety of settings available for child care and early education in the United States is a direct reflection of the variety of needs of families. A family's choice of setting is the result of several factors, including family income, family preferences about setting characteristics (such as opportunities for peer-group interaction, availability of health services), and availability of care and education settings within a community.

STATE LICENSING OF ARRANGEMENTS

In the United States, regulation of early childhood care and education is a state rather than a federal responsibility. All states have regulations for child care centers and regulations for preschool educational programs that are part of the public school system. The latter are typically included under licensing and regulation for regular public school programs. For child care centers, a typical licensing procedure consists of an initial inspection visit and additional visits prior to renewal of the license (the license period may be 1, 2, or 3 years).

The states vary widely in their licensing of family day care homes. Eight states do not regulate homes or regulate only for subsidized care; 3 states have voluntary registration; 13 states register but do not license homes; and 26 states license homes. The minimum enrollment requiring a family day care home to be licensed also varies among states, with half the states requiring licensing when one or more children are enrolled and the other half requiring licensing when from three to six children or more are enrolled (Morgan, 1987).

Also, individual states have various categories of "noncovered" settings. For example, 12 states exempt from regulation all church-sponsored day care centers; 21 states exempt from regulation all nursery schools and other part-day or full-day educational programs other than those affiliated with the public schools. Additional examples of settings that one or more states choose not to regulate include programs run by private colleges and universities, programs where the parents are on the premises (parent cooperatives), and programs run by the military (Morgan, 1987).

State Educational Qualifications for Early Childhood Staff

The professional standards and salaries of those who work with young children are issues presently receiving great attention in the United States. Although there are large variations among states, salaries of teachers in public school preschool programs are basically equivalent to those of other teachers in the school system. (For state-funded preprimary programs, the salary range for a beginning teacher is $12,000 to $20,000, and the range for an experienced teacher is $16,000 to $24,000; Mitchell, 1988.) Salaries of teachers in private preschool programs are generally about half of what is earned by public school teachers. Salary levels and certification procedures are related; that is, for public school preschool programs, a college educated, certified teacher is required, whereas for private preschool programs, certification requirements are a program-specific decision (Morgan, 1987; Schweinhart & Mazur, 1987). At present, some states have a separate certification for early childhood education; other states have programs for this specific certification under development (Seefeldt, 1988).

States tend to have two basic types of educational requirements for staff in child care centers: education prior to employment (preservice) and ongoing training (inservice). In addition, many states recognize the Child Development Associate (CDA) credential, which is a national competency-based credential that usually involves a training program and a competency assessment. The duration of CDA training varies between 2 months and 2 years, but is generally 1 year. States differ greatly in the educational qualifications they require for directors, teachers, and assistants in child care centers. For center teachers, 24 states have preservice qualifications, while 26 states do not. Among the states with preservice qualifications, there are 4 different patterns of college course work or previous experience requirements. Among the 26 states with no preservice qualifications, 17 require inservice training, while 9 do not. A few states have entry-level educational requirements for center classroom assistants: some require a high school diploma; others, only basic orientation given by the center (Morgan, 1987).

For family day care providers, 27 states require neither experience nor any form of education; 13 states require at least preservice training; and 8 states (including 4 of the 13 just mentioned) require some inservice training. The remaining states do not regulate family day care homes and thus have no educational qualifications for day care providers (Morgan, 1987).

Considering their minimal educational qualifications, it is not surprising that child care workers in centers and family day care homes receive very low salaries. According to the Bureau of Labor Statistics, two out of every three child care workers earn wages below the poverty threshold, regardless of their education, training, or experience. In 1984, the median annual income of a full-time child care worker was $9,200 (if employed in a center) or $4,400 (if employed in a private household). It is estimated that over 2 million persons, mostly women, are employed as child care workers. Related to low salaries are the high staff turnover rates found in both centers and homes. Turnover in child care centers averages 42 percent per year, while the rate is even higher among family day care providers (Children's Defense Fund, 1987).

STATE LICENSING STANDARDS FOR KEY PROGRAM CHARACTERISTICS

Child-staff ratios and group size

Research conducted in 1977 (the National Day Care Study reported later in this profile) indicated that staff-child ratio and group size were strongly related to program quality. Guidelines for number of staff and group size for children of different ages were developed from the research study. For 4-year-olds, according to the study, group size should not exceed 20 children, and there should be at least 1 staff member for every 10 children. However, 32 states do not regulate group size at all for preschool children, and of the states that do regulate it, only a small number fall within the range recommended by the research study. For 4-year-old children, 1 state sets the child-staff ratio at 7 to 1, or 8 to 1; 16 states set the child-staff ratio at 10 to 1; 10 states set a 12 to 1 ratio; and the remaining states set ratios ranging between 13 to 1 and 20 to 1 (Morgan, 1987).

Space requirements for centers and family day care homes
Most states require centers to have 35 square feet of indoor space and 75 square feet of outdoor space per child. For family day care homes, 21 states have no space requirements. In states with space requirements, the minimums are generally similar to those for centers (Morgan, 1987).

Age-appropriate program content
Nearly every state requires centers to provide a written plan for a developmental program, and 34 states have similar requirements for family day care homes. In addition, 24 states require centers to express their educational philosophy in writing (Morgan, 1987).

Cost of Child Care

The estimated typical cost of full-time child care in the United States is $3,000 a year for one child. In a survey of child care professionals in seven major cities, the yearly cost for a 3- to 5-year-old in a child care center was found to range from $2,600 to $5,200, while the yearly cost for a child in the same age-range in a family day care home was found to range from $2,000 to $6,000. It is reasonable to assume that U.S. child care costs are slightly lower in rural areas than they are in major cities (Children's Defense Fund, 1987).

Summary

In this section of the profile, we have tried to provide a picture of the diversity present in the United States—the diversity in types of settings available for preschool-aged children, in licensing systems used by various states, and in educational qualifications required of adults who work with preschool-aged children.

The complex makeup of the U.S. early childhood care and education system has several ramifications. We will mention only a few here. First, in states with minimal regulation systems, parents have difficulty obtaining information about the availability or quality of specific settings. Second, considering the high staff turnover rates, a parent cannot assume that the staff present in a center is the staff that was present at the time of the latest licensing inspection nor that a given family day care home will still be in operation even 6 months in the future. Finally, with the lack of educational qualifications required of child care staff in both centers and homes, there are few assurances for parents regarding the quality of care in most settings.

RESEARCH ON EARLY CHILDHOOD CARE AND EDUCATION

The earliest American studies of the effects of care and education environments on the intellectual development of young children were those carried out during the 1930s at the Iowa Child Welfare Research Station (for example, Skeels, Updegraf, Wellman, & Williams, 1938, and Wellman, 1932, as cited in Thompson & Grusec, 1970). These studies were part of a large-scale inquiry into the effects of various environments on intellectual development. During the next 25 years, the level of activity in this area of research was relatively low. In the early 1960s, however, there was a resurgence of interest in the field. This was due to a heightened awareness of the importance of the early years in a child's life, as evidenced by the work of Piaget and Hunt, and also to the changing nature of the American family—increasing numbers of children were requiring out-of-family care. Support for research into early childhood care and education in the United States has come primarily from two sources, the federal government and private foundations, with the proportion of research studies funded by each source fluctuating from year to year.

Our discussion of research in early childhood care and education is organized into three major categories: (1) **studies providing national statistics** about a specific form of early childhood care or education; (2) **studies of effects**, both short-term and long-term, of early childhood care and education; and (3) **studies making comparisons** between types of programs or between different program contents.

The number of U.S. research studies in early childhood care and education is so massive that it would be impossible to present even a summary of the findings in this document. Consequently, we mention specifically only two major studies from each of the three categories and attempt to provide a balance between studies that focus on early childhood care and studies that focus on early childhood education.

Category 1: Studies Providing National Statistics

Two significant studies in this category are the **National Day Care Study** funded by the federal government, and the **Public School Early Childhood Study** funded by two private foundations (Carnegie Corporation of New York and the Ford Foundation).

The **National Day Care Study** (NDCS), a study of federally subsidized day care, provides basic information about a small number of regulatable features (ones currently or potentially subject to government regulation) of day care centers and explores the relationships among these features, program quality and costs, and effects on children (Ruopp et al., 1979). The three variables studied were staff-child ratio, group size, and caregiver qualifications. Sixty-four day care centers in Atlanta, Detroit, and Seattle were selected for the study, and the major forms of data collection included observations (of adult and child behaviors) in the settings, assessment of children served by the settings, and interviews with the caregivers to ascertain education/training and experience. The two major phases of the NDCS were (1) a study of naturally occurring characteristics of centers and (2) a systematic alteration of the three center characteristics of primary interest and an associated assessment of the changes this produced in program quality and costs and in children.

A summary statement of the results indicates: "NDCS findings show that certain regulatable center characteristics are consistently associated with measures of day care quality. Composition of the day care classroom—the number of caregivers and the number of children grouped together—is linked to day-to-day behavior of children and caregivers and to children's gains on the Preschool Inventory (PSI) and the revised Peabody Picture Vocabulary Test (PPVT). Smaller groups of children and caregivers and, to a lesser extent, higher staff-child ratios are associated with more desirable classroom behavior; smaller groups are also associated with higher test score gains. Moreover, aspects of caregiver qualifications, especially education/training relevant to young children, are associated with positive classroom dynamics and superior test score gains" (Ruopp et al., p. 77).

The NDCS was a well-executed study from which policy recommendations were developed. It is important, however, to remember that the

NDCS was limited to one type of child care setting (child care centers) and only included those centers receiving federal support; also, it only looked at regulatable characteristics of the centers. These were important points, considering the policy focus of the study, but when considered from the larger perspective of the nation's multiplicity of forms of preschool care and education, the findings must be seen as limited.

The second national study we consider is the **Public School Early Childhood Study** (Mitchell, 1988), which collected descriptive data on public school programs for "prekindergarten" children (aged 0 to 5). The study, which was a collaborative effort of Bank Street College and the Wellesley College Center for Research on Women, had three parts: a telephone and mail survey of all 50 states and the District of Columbia (1986–1987), a mail survey of 1,200 public school districts (1986), and case studies of 13 programs in 12 states (1986–1987). We present only the school-district mail survey results.

Through a variety of data sources, approximately 2,800 districts throughout the United States were identified as having an early childhood supervisor or operating a prekindergarten classroom (including Head Start), and survey questionnaires were mailed to these districts. Only 44 percent of the questionnaires were returned, but when responding and nonresponding districts were compared on a number of characteristics, no differences were found. From the districts returning the survey, program information was obtained for 1,681 prekindergarten programs.

Mitchell (1988) states, "Public schools currently operate a diverse set of programs for children younger than kindergarten entry age. Most are for 4-year-olds. Most operate part day, for the school year only, with state funds as their major source of support. Class sizes and staff-child ratios are within generally accepted limits of appropriate practice." She also writes, "Public schools currently provide a modest portion of early childhood services nationwide. Close to 200,000 children attend those public school programs represented in this survey. In contrast, about one million children under five are enrolled in publicly subsidized child care and Head Start programs nationwide. An indeterminate number of young children, but certainly a few million, attend non-public early childhood programs such as nursery schools and day care centers" (p. 48).

When considering the role of the public schools in the United States in providing early education programs for prekindergarten children, Mitchell notes that these programs are still relatively few in number and operate only part-day, making them, at present, a less-than-viable early childhood education/care option for the millions of families needing child care for the total work day. In closing the report, Mitchell (1988, p. 49) states, "Given superintendents' views and the current operational facts, it seems somewhat unlikely that public schools will rapidly expand services in ways that support families to support themselves, much beyond what is currently offered. The appropriate question now is: What other institutions, along with public schools, can be encouraged to create and expand programs to meet the growing needs of children and families?"

As noted earlier, public schools operated early childhood programs during the 1930s (WPA programs) and again during the 1940s (Lanham Act centers). However, the current major involvement of the public schools in early childhood programs began during the early 1980s, and the Mitchell study is the first attempt to gather detailed information about such programs. The project report contains data about a large number of program characteristics, including program types, class size and staff-child ratio, staff educational requirements and salaries, and parent participation. This information should be helpful to other public school systems as well as to state policymakers as they consider new public school prekindergarten programs.

CATEGORY 2: STUDIES OF EFFECTS

Studies in this category generally compare two groups of children, one group that participated in a program and one group that did not participate. Both short-term and long-term effects of programs have been examined in these studies, using a variety of child-outcome measures. We present the Perry Preschool Project and the work of the Consortium for Longitudinal Studies as major representatives of this category.

The Perry Preschool Project (Berrueta-Clement et al., 1984; Schweinhart & Weikart, 1980), funded by various foundations and government agencies, is a landmark study of the effects of early childhood education. This study has had a major impact on policy and funding for early childhood programs at federal and state levels.

Children from low-income, black families in Ypsilanti, Michigan, who were at risk of failing in school were selected for the Perry Preschool study. At ages 3 and 4, the 123 children were randomly divided into an experimental group that received a high-quality preschool program, and a control group that received no program. Assessment of these children on a variety of measures has continued through age 19, with data available for 98 percent of the original sample. At age 19, the preschool group, compared with the no-preschool group, were significantly more likely to have graduated from high school, to be enrolled in postsecondary education, and to find themselves employed. Also, compared to the no-preschool group, the preschool group was significantly less likely to have been assigned to special education classes, to have committed crimes, to have borne children during their teen-age years, or to be receiving welfare assistance. A benefit-cost analysis of the Perry Preschool program based on 15 years of follow-up data indicated a benefit-cost ratio of 6 to 1 for a 1-year program and 3 to 1 for a 2-year program (Berrueta-Clement et al., 1984).

A key strength of the Perry Preschool Project was the inclusion of assessment measures for the young adults in the areas of early socioeconomic success and social responsibility as well as in the area of academic success. With these multiple outcome measures, it was possible to examine the relationship between preschool participation and adult behaviors beyond school success. A second strength of the project was the benefit-cost analysis, which allowed policymakers to consider a preschool program from an economic point of view.

During the late 1970s the 12-member Consortium for Longitudinal Studies operated under the direction of Irving Lazar of Cornell University (Consortium for Longitudinal Studies, 1983). Members of the consortium included Martin Deutsch, Susan Gray, Phyllis Levenstein, Francis Palmer, and David Weikart. Each member of the consortium, while conducting a longitudinal study of an early childhood program, elected to collaborate in a study of long-term effectiveness of the various programs. Consortium members agreed to collect data in common and to make these data available for both individual and pooled analyses. As a group, the collection of 12 experimentally designed and well-implemented early childhood programs provided a wealth of data that allowed for the study of program impact on such variables as achievement, attitudes, school competence, and occupational outcomes.

In summarizing the findings of the pooled analyses of data across the various projects (including the Perry Preschool Project), Royce, Darlington, and Murray (1983) state, "When evaluated over a 15-year period, early education had significant effects in five areas: developed abilities in early to middle childhood, school competence in middle childhood and adolescence, attitudes toward achievement in adolescence, educational attainment in late adolescence, and occupational attitudes in early adulthood. For the sixth outcome area, occupational attainment in early adulthood, indirect preschool effects were found" (p. 450).

The consortium findings are particularly important because of the variety of types of early childhood programs represented in the group of studies—home-based, center-based, and combination programs. In addition, the programs varied on length of intervention, age of the child when the intervention began, staff training, and intensity of program. Lazar (1983) notes, "We can conclude that any well-designed, professionally supervised program to stimulate and socialize infants and young children from poor minority families will be efficacious. It is certainly possible that finer-grained outcome measures might reveal differential effectiveness of the programs, settings, durations, and intensities" (p. 462). The differential effectiveness of programs is the subject of Category 3 research studies.

Category 3: Program-Comparison Studies

The effects of early childhood care and education programs are assessed in both Category 2 and Category 3 studies. However, whereas "program vs. no-program" was the focus of Category 2 studies, different types of programs are compared in Category 3 studies. Two major representatives of Category 3 studies are the High/Scope Preschool Curriculum Comparison study and Alison Clarke-Stewart's study of child care in Chicago.

In the High/Scope Preschool Curriculum Comparison study, sixty-eight 3- and 4-year-old children from low-income families were randomly assigned to one of three well-implemented preschool curriculum models—a direct-instruction program, a High/Scope program, and a child-centered nursery school program (Schweinhart, Weikart, & Larner, 1986). When school achievement was assessed through age 10, the three groups of participants generally showed similar patterns of scores over time. At age 15, 79 percent of the participants were interviewed regarding various aspects of social behavior, including school activities, family relations, juvenile delinquency, and mental health.

The authors state, "In this study, the group that received a preschool program using the teacher-directed Distar model, when compared to groups receiving preschool programs that encouraged children to initiate their own activities in a specially prepared environment, evidenced substantially higher rates of self-reported juvenile delinquency and associated problems" (p. 41). Later in the same article, the authors say, "The

Curriculum study's most recent data suggest that there are important social consequences to preschool curriculum choices. . . . The other two preschool curriculum approaches in this study [High/Scope and nursery school] did have social-behavior goals and did appear to produce favorable long-term social effects indicated by lower rates of juvenile delinquency and other social-behavior problems, as well as equivalent academic outcomes" (pp. 41–42).

Whereas different preschool curricula were compared in High/Scope's study, different forms of child care were compared in Clarke-Stewart's Chicago Study. First, four different child care forms were identified: (1) care in child's own home, (2) family day care home, (3) full-time child care center, and (4) part-time nursery school program. Then, 2- and 3-year-old children who were cared for in these different types of settings were identified. For all children in the study, this was the first child care setting, and families were intact and self-supporting (Clarke-Stewart, 1987). Data were collected through observation, interviews, and assessment of child competencies.

Clarke-Stewart (1987) writes, "Thus we see that the four forms of child care were associated with predictable patterns of competence in the children attending them. The educational orientation of the nursery school was reflected in advanced cognition and adult-oriented competence. The lengthier separation of mothers and children using full-time child care centers was reflected in the child's greater physical independence from mother coupled with more involved social interactions with her. Children from family day care homes, who had less familiarity than center children with an institutional setting, stayed closer to their mothers in our university setting, but, consistent with their opportunity for intimate social interaction with peers, played more comfortably, cooperatively, and actively with an unfamiliar child than children with in-home caregivers. Children with untrained caregivers in their own home, with one other (usually younger) child at most, and with no educational program did not excel in any domain of competence" (pp. 32–33).

The two studies included here are representative of the finer-grained approach to program evaluation mentioned earlier by Lazar. Each study examined the effects of several programs (or settings) by using the same set of multiple outcome measures, and then reported the differential patterns of results for each type of program (or setting). Such information regarding the differential effects of various types of settings can be helpful to parents as they make decisions about the care of their young children.

FURTHER INFORMATION ON U.S. RESEARCH STUDIES

The six studies that have been described here are major research efforts, either because they were large-scale or long-term studies or because they have had a significant impact on practice or policy in early childhood care and education. In the U.S., research in early childhood is also conducted using small controlled studies, each of which makes only a minor contribution to the overall research knowledge-base, but combined with other studies, assists in identifying trends and patterns. Thus the field advances as patterns of results are discerned across many studies that are similar in some respects while different in others.

The following resources are recommended for additional information on research studies in early childhood care and education in the United States: (1) *Handbook of Research in Early Childhood Education*, edited by Spodek, 1982; (2) *Early Childhood Programs*, Clarke-Stewart and Fein, 1983; (3) *Quality in Child Care: What Does Research Tell Us?* edited by Phillips, 1987; and (4) *Keeping Current in Child Care Research: An Annotated Bibliography*, Howes, 1988.

ISSUES OF THE NEXT DECADE

Early childhood care and education issues are presently capturing public attention in the United States. Education and child care were issues during the 1988 presidential campaign, and there were over 100 child care and education bills considered during the last session of Congress (1987–88). As noted earlier in this profile, this high level of interest is fueled primarily by increased maternal employment and by the recent research results concerning the effects of early childhood education.

The issues for the next decade in early childhood care and education are defined by projecting trends and examining the implications of these trends and of the information presented earlier in this profile. For example, although a stable birthrate is predicted for the United States during the near future, the number of 3- to 6-year-old children who will need extrafamilial care will continue to increase owing to the anticipated increase in the number of mothers of young children entering the labor force. If recent trends continue, by 1995 the proportion of children under age 6 with mothers in the labor force will reach an estimated 66 percent (Hofferth & Phillips, 1986).

This increasing demand for early childhood services, the complex nature of the present system of services, and the historical roles of federal and state governments in early childhood care and education together point to several issues needing to be addressed in the next decade.

Staffing Concerns

Considering past national policies, we can assume it is unlikely that the federal government will provide substantial support for early childhood services for the majority of families in the United States. When this assumption is combined with the increasing need for child care, the following questions must be asked: Who will pay for these services (that is, for the salaries of providers, since staff salaries is the largest category of a services budget)? What caregiver (or teacher) training will be required? How can parents be assured of qualified staff in a high-quality early childhood setting?

Earlier in this profile, we noted the very low salaries for most categories of early childhood staff and the accompanying high turnover rate among these workers. Higher salaries might decrease the turnover rate, justify the individual worker's investment in preservice education, and allow states to increase staff educational requirements without creating staff shortages. However, with only limited federal government support likely for the near future, the families using the services must bear most of the financial burdens related to those services. When one considers that many families in need of services are those in which all adults are working to maintain a desired standard of living, and that the salary levels of parents when they have young children are often lower than later in their employment careers, it becomes clear that families will not be able to significantly increase their payments for services to allow for increased salaries for early childhood staff. This issue of salaries for providers of early childhood services is a critical one for the United States and one with no easy solution.

Related to salaries is the issue of educational qualifications for providers of early childhood services. With the currently low salaries, what types of training or experience can one reasonably expect a service provider to have? Earlier we presented information about the minimal level of educational qualifications required by most states for early childhood care and education staff. This information, though understandable in light of the low salaries, is surprising considering that the National Day Care Study found staff qualifications, "especially education/training relevant to young children," to be positively related to both classroom interactions and increases on children's test scores (Ruopp et al., 1979). Also, it is important to remember that even in states with staff requirements, the requirements apply to only licensed settings. It was noted earlier that estimates of the proportion of family day care homes that are licensed range between 10 and 40 percent. Thus, even in states requiring staff qualifications, the requirements apply to only a subgroup of providers. Finally, from a national perspective, the differing requirements among states pose problems for service providers moving from one state to another as well as for families moving between states. The issue of qualifications for early childhood staff in the United States is closely linked with the issue of salaries, and it is unlikely that the two issues will have separate resolutions.

Quality of Services

The quality of early childhood services is clearly related to the staffing issues (salaries, qualifications) just discussed. However, there are additional issues related to quality that need to be addressed during the next decade. Research on "quality" services and the specification of dimensions of quality for different types of settings and different groups of children needs to continue. In addition, we need to determine the best public policies and systems for developing and maintaining high-quality early childhood services. Are the present state systems of regulating early childhood services adequate? Would a set of national guidelines that states would be required to follow ensure a higher level of quality? In the United States, could a set of national guidelines apply to all early childhood settings—or only to those settings receiving public funding (for example, Head Start or Social Services Block Grant monies)?

The current licensing system used by states serves primarily to set minimum standards (staff qualifications, adult-child ratios). However, in many cases these minimum standards are lower than the levels found to be related to positive child outcomes in research studies. In addition, many states do not regulate certain types of settings or do not regulate specific characteristics within settings (for example, 32 states do not regulate group size for 4-year-old children in centers). Even if regulation systems only establish minimum standards, increasing the levels to ones recommended by research studies, increasing the number of setting characteristics included in the system, and including all major types of early childhood settings in the system would be steps towards improving the development of high-quality early childhood programs.

During the past several years, the National Association for the Education of Young Children (NAEYC; 1984) has been working through its National Academy of Early Childhood Programs to improve the quality of early childhood services by the development of accreditation criteria and procedures. The NAEYC accreditation system covers several program components, including curriculum, physical environment, and staff qualifications and development, and specific criteria are established for each component. Presently, only a very small portion of the total number of early childhood care and education settings in the U.S. have participated in the NAEYC accreditation procedures. It is a good beginning, but much more needs to be done to improve the quality of early childhood services during the next decade.

Parent Information

As we observed earlier, it is unlikely that the federal government will provide substantial support for early childhood services in the near future. Consequently, parents will continue to assume the major responsibility for supporting, locating, and evaluating early childhood services. Parental support of services was discussed earlier, and thus only the locating and evaluating of services will be discussed here. A major issue for the next decade will be the development and dissemination of information to parents to allow them to become better, more informed consumers of early childhood services.

In some communities in the U.S., parents have few early childhood service alternatives from which to choose, and therefore the locating of services is not a complex process. However, in other communities (such as large cities) a variety of types of settings may be in operation (for example, family day care homes, public school preschool programs, child care centers, church-sponsored programs). The parents' task then consists of deciding which type of care or education service is most appropriate for the child and family, obtaining information about settings in the local area that provide the service they want, determining which of these settings have openings (available spaces), and making a final selection by evaluating the settings with openings. In communities with a great variety of services, many parents spend vast amounts of time searching out information about settings and possible openings in settings.

The process is further complicated by the high turnover rate of providers. Parents often ask experienced neighbors or friends for advice about early childhood services and then find that this advice (which perhaps recommends a specific caregiver at a center or a specific family day care home) may no longer be relevant when the parents are searching for services several months later. Also, parents frequently find that satisfactory services, once located, eventually cease operations, and then parents must begin the search process anew.

During the past 15 years "resource and referral" agencies have been increasing in number throughout the U.S. These agencies, funded by various sources (state, local community, employers), provide information to parents, employers, and others about early childhood services within their communities. Some resource and referral agencies prepare a listing of community early childhood services, which they provide upon request. Others prepare information about the characteristics of various types of care and about making a care choice; they are often willing to discuss individual care situations with parents and to assist them in their search process. During the 1980s resource and referral agencies have been operating in at least some areas of nearly every state.

The resource and referral agencies are providing an important service for everyone involved with early childhood services, but the funding of these agencies is a continual struggle, and many communities still do not have such an agency. Also, since some agencies provide only a basic listing of services, there is a need for preparation and dissemination of other information to help parents better select and utilize existing early childhood services. For example, some parents may need information about different types of settings and how to make decisions about the "best" setting for their child and family. Other parents may need information about how to identify a "quality" setting, that is, about questions to ask and things to look for when visiting a potential setting. Some parents may need information about what to expect from a provider (the procedure followed by the provider if a child becomes ill, for example), what their own responsibilities are (whether parents must pay for days when their child is unable to attend, for example), and how to clarify these matters when initially making arrangements with the provider. Those resource and referral agencies that have had sufficient funding have been instrumental in assisting parents and others. However obtaining additional funding to allow for an increase in the number of agencies as well as an increase in the types of assistance provided by agencies is a major issue to be dealt with during the next decade.

CONCLUSION

The U.S. has experienced great changes in the area of early childhood care and education since the time of Lydia Sigourney's book *Letters to Mothers*, but especially during the last 20 years. In recent years vast numbers of various types of settings have come into operation to meet the large increase in the need for early childhood services. However, the early childhood service system has remained a decentralized one, and to a large degree, each family is responsible for locating and supporting the services for their own children.

Now is the time to step back to assess the current system of early childhood care and education services in the United States. We must assess it in terms of its ability to meet the needs of young children and their families, in terms of its viability as an employment system for adults, and in terms of its relationships with other societal systems, such as employment and education. Most important, we need to assess the impact of the system on the children it is serving, to insure that we have developed a system that will help children develop and grow into productive adult members of the American society.

AUTHOR'S NOTE

I thank Jennifer Smith and Elizabeth Mazur, both of whom worked on an earlier draft of this profile. In addition, I thank Helen Barnes, Jenni Klein, Mary Larner, and Karen Pinner for their assistance.

REFERENCES

Administration for Children, Youth, and Families. (1988). *Project Head Start statistical fact sheet*. Washington, DC: Department of Health and Human Services.

Almy, M. (1982). Day care and early childhood education. In E. F. Zigler & E. W. Gordon (Eds.), *Day care: Scientific and social policy* (pp. 476–496). Boston: Auburn House.

Berrueta-Clement, J. R., Schweinhart, L. J., Barnett, W. S., Epstein, A. S., & Weikart, D. P. (1984). *Changed lives: The effects of the Perry Preschool program on youths through age 19* (Monographs of the High/Scope Educational Research Foundation, 8). Ypsilanti, MI: High/Scope Press.

Center for Education Statistics. (1987). *The condition of education—1987 edition*. Washington, DC: U.S. Government Printing Office.

Children's Defense Fund. (1982–87). *State child care fact book*. Washington, DC: Author.

Children's Defense Fund. (1987). *Child care: The time is now*. Washington, DC: Author.

Children's Defense Fund. (1988). *State child care fact book.* Washington, DC: Author.

Clarke-Stewart, K. A. (1982). *Daycare.* Cambridge, MA: Harvard University Press.

Clarke-Stewart, K. A. (1987). Predicting child development from child care forms and features: The Chicago Study. In D. A. Phillips (Ed.), *Quality in child care: What does research tell us?* (pp. 21–43). Washington, DC: National Association for the Education of Young Children.

Clarke-Stewart, K. A., & Fein, G. G. (1983). Early childhood programs. In P. H. Mussen (Ed.), *Handbook of child psychology* (4th ed., Vol. 2, pp. 917–1000). New York: Wiley.

Cochran, M. (1982). Profits and policy: Child care in America. In R. Rist (Ed.), *Policy studies annals* (Vol. 6, draft version of article).

Consortium for Longitudinal Studies. (1983). *As the twig is bent . . . Lasting effects of preschool programs.* Hillsdale, NJ: Lawrence Erlbaum.

Eckstein, M. A. (1988). United States. In T. N. Postlethwaite (Ed.), *The encyclopedia of comparative education and national systems of education* (pp. 698–707). Oxford: Pergamon Press.

Gray, S. W., Ramsey, B. K., & Klaus, R. A. (1982). *From 3 to 20: The Early Training Project.* Baltimore: University Park Press.

Hofferth, S. L., & Phillips, D. A. (1987). Child care in the United States, 1970 to 1995. *Journal of Marriage and the Family, 49,* 559–571.

Howes, C. (1988). *Keeping current in child care research: An annotated bibliography.* Washington, DC: National Association for the Education of Young Children.

Kahn, A. J., & Kamerman, S. B. (1987). *Child care: Facing the hard choices.* Dover, MA: Auburn House.

Lazar, I. (1983). Discussion and implications of the findings. In Consortium of Longitudinal Studies, *As the twig is bent . . . Lasting effects of preschool programs* (pp. 461–467). Hillsdale, NJ: Lawrence Erlbaum.

Levenstein, P., O'Hara, J., & Madden, J. (1983). The Mother-Child Home Program of the Verbal Interaction Project. In Consortium of Longitudinal Studies, *As the twig is bent . . . Lasting effects of preschool programs* (pp. 237–265). Hillsdale, NJ: Lawrence Erlbaum.

Miller, L. B. (1979). Development of curriculum models in Head Start. In E. Zigler & J. Valentine (Eds.), *Project Head Start: A Legacy of the war on poverty* (pp. 195–221). New York: Free Press.

Mitchell, A. (1988). *The public school early childhood study: The district survey.* New York: Bank Street College of Education.

Morgan, G. (1987). *The national state of child care regulation, 1986.* Watertown, MA: Work/Family Directions, Inc.

National Association for the Education of Young Children. (1984). *Accreditation criteria and procedures of the National Academy of Early Childhood Programs.* Washington, DC: Author.

National Center for Education Statistics. (1986). *The condition of education—1986 edition.* Washington, DC: U.S. Government Printing Office.

Nixon, R. M. (1971). *Veto message—Economic Opportunity Amendments of 1971.* (S. 2007), 92nd Cong., 1st sess., Senate Doc. 92–48.

Phillips, D. A. (Ed.). (1987). *Quality in child care: What does research tell us?* Washington, DC: National Association for the Education of Young Children.

Royce, J. M., Darlington, R. B., & Murray, H. W. (1983). Pooled analyses: Findings across studies. In Consortium for Longitudinal Studies, *As the twig is bent . . . Lasting effects of preschool programs* (pp. 411–461). Hillsdale, NJ: Lawrence Erlbaum.

Ruopp, R., Travers, J., Glantz, F., & Coelen, C. (1979). *Children at the center: Summary findings and their implications* (Final report of the National Day Care Study, Vol. 1). Cambridge, MA: Abt Associates.

Scarr, S., & Weinberg, R. A. (1986). The early childhood enterprise: Care and education of the young. *American Psychologist, 41*, 1140–1146.

Schweinhart, L. J., & Mazur, E. (1987). *Prekindergarten programs in urban schools* (High/Scope Early Childhood Policy Paper No. 6). Ypsilanti, MI: High/Scope Press.

Schweinhart, L. J., & Weikart, D. P. (1980). *Young children grow up: The effects of the Perry Preschool program on youths through age 15* (Monographs of the High/Scope Educational Research Foundation, 7). Ypsilanti, MI: High/Scope Press.

Schweinhart, L. J., Weikart, D. P., & Larner, M. B. (1986). Consequences of three preschool curriculum models through age 15. *Early Childhood Research Quarterly, 1*, 15–45.

Seefeldt, C. (1988). Teacher certification and program accreditation in early childhood education. *The Elementary School Journal, 89*, 241–252.

Sigourney, L. H. (1838). *Letters to mothers*. Hartford, CT: Hudson & Skinner.

Spodek, B. (1973). *Early childhood education*. Englewood Cliffs, NJ: Prentice-Hall.

Spodek, B. (Ed.). (1982). *Handbook of research in early childhood education*. New York: Free Press.

Steinfels, M. O. (1973). *Who's minding the children?* New York: Simon & Schuster.

Thompson, W. R., & Grusec, J. (1970). Studies of early experience. In P. H. Mussen (Ed.), *Manual of child psychology* (3rd ed., Vol. 1, pp. 565–657). New York: Wiley.

U.S. Bureau of the Census. (1986). *Money income and poverty status of families and persons in the United States: 1985* (Current Population Reports, Series P-60, No. 154). Washington, DC: U.S. Government Printing Office.

U.S. Bureau of the Census. (1987). *Statistical abstract of the United States: 1987* (107th ed.). Washington, DC: U.S. Government Printing Office.

U.S. Bureau of the Census. (1988). *United States population estimates, by age, sex, and race: 1980 to 1987* (Current Population Reports, Series P- 25, No. 1022). Washington, DC: U.S. Government Printing Office.

U.S. Department of Labor. (1988). *Child care: A workforce issue, Report of the Secretary's Task Force*. Washington, DC: Author.

Zigler, E. F., & Goodman, J. (1982). The battle for day care in America: A view from the trenches. In E. F. Zigler & E. W. Gordon (Eds.), *Day care: Scientific and social policy* (pp. 338–351). Boston: Auburn House.

Afterword: Young Children in Cross-National Perspective

Lilian G. Katz
Professor of Early Childhood Education
Director of ERIC Clearinghouse on Elementary and Early Childhood Education
University of Illinois
Urbana

Introduction

The national profiles in this book document how the worldwide interest in preprimary care and education has mushroomed during the past 20 years. Some profiles note that this interest is due primarily to the increasing number of parents who are employed in environments in which the presence of their young children is neither desirable nor practical. Other profiles attribute the interest to a slow but steady improvement in child health: Once basic survival risks have been addressed within a society, issues concerning children's quality of life in general, and their care and education in particular, begin to command attention.

Converging with these trends is the growing conviction among specialists in education as well as among the wider community that experience during the early years may have significant, if not irreversible, effects on children's subsequent development, including effects on their responsiveness to schooling. Paradoxically, there seems to be more agreement about the lasting damage from early negative experiences than about the lasting benefits from early positive experiences. Nonetheless, whether they are viewed as a means of minimizing early negative experiences or of maximizing early positive experiences, expanded or improved preprimary services seem to be on many a national agenda.

International Themes in Preprimary Education and Care

The descriptions of current preprimary education and care in the IEA Preprimary Project countries present a surprisingly consistent picture.

Each country suggests that much remains to be done to fully meet the needs of its young children. Deficits in service availability, in agency coordination, and in personnel quality seem to be recurring themes.

The Availability of Preprimary Services

The discrepancies between children's needs and the resources available to meet those needs—which all countries experience—seem to have different causes from one country to another. In some countries, the needs/resources gap stems primarily from a low level of economic development, a severe competition for scarce resources, and intense demographic pressures. In many countries—even those where the economic level, the competition for resources, and the demographic pressures are not critical issues—the increasing participation of mothers in the work force has exhausted the supply of out-of-home settings for their children's care. Although at one time, adult extended family members or older siblings might have cared for the very young, the former are now frequently themselves employed, and the latter are unavailable because they are staying in school longer. Thus, traditional ways of caring for the young have broken down, but alternative care arrangements have not yet been fully developed. In some countries, the discrepancy between what services are needed and what services are available is primarily the result of national policies concerning the role of government versus the role of the family.

The Multiplicity of Agencies

The national profiles also highlight the fact that preprimary provisions in many countries fall under the purview of a wide variety of agencies—health, public welfare, social service, public assistance, religious, or charitable agencies. This sometimes results in interagency rivalries and disputes concerning which agency has the most appropriate knowledge and expertise or which has the best interests of children and families at heart. Also, in many of the participating countries, the quality of preprimary services varies with the income of the families being served. One gets an overall impression that the fact that a country has great wealth does not necessarily preclude the existence of discrepancies in the quality of services for children of different socioeconomic levels.

THE QUALITY OF PREPRIMARY PERSONNEL

Another theme threaded through the descriptions of preprimary education in the various nations is the relatively low status of teachers, even though there is general agreement among specialists in the field that the competence of the teacher is a central determinant of the quality and effectiveness of a program. As Crahay (1988) points out, one of the most reliable generalizations about education around the world is that the younger the pupils being taught, the less adequate the training, the lower the status, and the smaller the salaries of their teachers. It is probably true that in most countries, the public believes that the care or education of young children requires little, if any, special preparation on the part of the caregiver or teacher. It is anticipated that the cross-national findings of the IEA Preprimary Project will illuminate the outcomes for children that result from such a generalization.

CROSS-NATIONAL VARIATIONS AS A NATURAL LABORATORY

Cross-national studies can be illuminating in some ways that within-nation studies cannot. For example, a cross-national study is particularly suited to studying the *processes of development*. In principle, the younger the child being studied, the more that the processes of *development* rather than those of *learning* are taken into account. While theories of learning address the processes by which behaviors and knowledge are acquired or changed within a relatively short time, theories of development address the sequences, transformations, and stages apparent in the individual's capacities as observed over a relatively long period of time. As Rogoff and Morelli point out, cross-national studies allow researchers to use cultural and national variation in experiences and environments as a "natural laboratory" (1989, p.343) for the study of development, helping them to disentangle the variables impinging on children's development in a way that research within a single culture cannot.

On the basis of extensive cross-cultural research on children's development, it has been shown that there are both "impressive regularities across cultures in developmental phenomena" as well as "consistent findings that behavior and development vary according to cultural context" (Rogoff & Morelli, 1989, p. 343). Applying such generalizations to the study of educational and child care settings reminds us to look for both regularities and variations in the ways children and their families respond to the developmental and environmental exigencies confronting them.

Contexts and Meanings of Behavior

As many of the profiles have stated, the research on preprimary education initiated by IEA has the potential to provide information and knowledge useful to countries in addressing issues of policy with respect to the education and care of young children. The study will provide cross-national data on many aspects, including the long-term effects, of the preprimary experiences of children and their parents. However, interpretation of the findings of such a study is no simple matter. Experience from cross-cultural and anthropological research indicates that such studies present a number of ecological and methodological problems that introduce important risks in interpretation of findings (LeVine, 1989).

By way of example, LeVine points out that parents' use of praise in guiding behavior is not universal. In some parts of Africa, "children grow up without experiencing praise from their parents or others for behaving in a socially approved way or for learning a socially desirable skill" (LeVine, 1989, p. 63). Yet for most American families, and even child psychologists, such an approach to childrearing is likely to be incomprehensible! At issue for a cross-national study, however, is how variations in the frequency of teachers' or parents' praise might be interpreted. If it is found that such cross-national variations in adult-child relationships are not associated with differences in children's current or later competence, early childhood professionals as well as parents in many countries may choose to reexamine their assumptions and practices.

LeVine (1989) further points out that children experience their environments not directly but through the mediation of local cultural beliefs, concepts, norms, and so forth. For example, examination of the quality and variety of equipment available to young children in their preprimary settings cannot consist of simple quantification. The stimulus potential of a given preprimary environment is very likely a function of the stimulus level of the environment children experience outside that setting. When a child's home contains very few play materials, little play space, and no television, a small supply of over-used toys in the preprimary setting may have considerable stimulus value—sufficient to attract the child's attention. However, if the home environment is full of distractions, activity/play materials, open space, and varied television fare, a relatively meager supply of equipment in the child care center may have a depressing effect on the child. The IEA Project's cross-national analyses of the material provisions in preprimary settings will help us to understand more about the larger context in which the material provision occurs and about ways that both context and materials determine the quality of children's experiences.

Another issue under examination by early childhood specialists is the development of young children's attachments to adults (see, for example, Belsky, 1988). Much of the concern over this issue, in the U.S. at least, is related to the fact that many preprimary settings are characterized by very high staff turnover. This constant changing of staff means that children are faced with frequent breaking of relationships at the very time in their development when secure attachments to caregivers are assumed to increase the chances of developing successful attachments later in life. LeVine (1989) points out, however, that assumptions about the importance of "secure" attachments between children and their caretakers suffer from an American bias. Evidence gathered outside the U.S. shows that "secure" attachment reactions are not always the mode. Furthermore, societies in which "insecure" and "avoidant" attachments are more typical than "secure" attachments are not marked by greater incidence of psychopathology than countries where "secure" attachments are typical (LeVine, 1989, p. 61).

Early childhood specialists are also interested in adult-child ratio and how it impinges on children's development. It has often been noted that in many settings where the number of adults is low compared with the number of children (for example, 1 adult for 40 or more children), children appear very respectful and compliant. Conversely, preschool children in relatively small classes with high numbers of adults (for example, 2 adults for 15 children) seem to exhibit less impulse control and to provoke more limit setting and rule enforcing on the part of adults than children in very large groups do. Logically, one would expect that the smaller the number of adults for a given group of children, the greater the likelihood that the children would push or at least challenge the boundaries of adult authority. It may be, however, that the central variable accounting for these differences in children's responses is the extent to which they experience *choice making*. For children who have frequent opportunities to choose between alternatives (whether to have orange or apple juice, whether to cook or to paint, for instance), perceiving and acting on options in the environment would seem appropriate, if not natural. However, in a context in which there are few, if any, choices—for whatever reason—the consideration of alternatives would be dysfunctional, and compliance would very likely be easily obtained. Observations taken in the international array of various preprimary settings included in this project should shed new light on this and similar issues confronting early childhood educators.

CONCLUSION

As the countries participating in this important project gather and report their findings, and as cross-national analysis and comparisons become possible, the field of preprimary education is bound to gain knowledge and insights not obtainable solely from experience within each country's borders. The fruits of IEA labors are anticipated with eagerness and appreciation for the large-scale effort they require.

REFERENCES

Belsky, J. (1988). The "effects" of infant day care reconsidered. *Early Childhood Research Quarterly*, *3*(3), 235–272.

Crahay, M. (1988, November). *Discussant's remarks*. Paper presented at the Annual Conference of the National Association for the Education of Young Children, Anaheim, CA.

LeVine, R. A. (1989). Cultural environments in child development. In W. Damon (Ed.), *Child development today and tomorrow* (pp. 52–68). San Francisco: Jossey-Bass.

Rogoff, B., & Morelli, G. (1989). Perspective on children's development from cultural psychology. *American Psychologist*, *44*(2), 343–348.

Appendix

IEA Preprimary Project Phase 1 National Research Centers

Belgium

Laboratoire de Pédagogie Expérimentale B32
Université de Liège au Sart Tilman
par 4000 Liège 1

Director: Arlette Delhaxhe

Federal Republic of Germany

Universität Münster
FB Erziehungswissenschaft Institute III
GeorgsKommende 33
4400 Münster

Director: Hans-Günther Rossbach

Finland

Early Childhood Education Department
University of Joensuu
P.O. Box 111
80101 Joensuu

Director: Mikko Ojala

Hong Kong

Department of Education
University of Hong Kong
Pokfulam Road

Directors: Alan Brimer (1986–1987)
Sylvia Opper (1987–)

Hungary

National Institute of Research for Education
Gorkij fasor 17–21
1071 Budapest

Director: Zsuzsa Kereszty

ITALY

Centro Europeo dell'Educazione
Villa Falconieri
00044 Frascati
Rome

Directors: Filomena Pistillo (1985–1986)
Lucio Pusci (1986–)

KENYA

Bureau of Educational Research
Kenyatta University
P.O. Box 43844
Nairobi

Director: George S. Eshiwani

NIGERIA

Institute of Education
University of Ibadan
Ibadan

Director: Olayemi M. Onibokun

PEOPLE'S REPUBLIC OF CHINA

Central Institute of Educational Research
Beisanhuan zhong lu 46
100088 Beijing

Director: Shi Hui Zhong

PHILIPPINES

Department of Education, Culture, and Sports
National Educational Testing and Research Center
Meralco Avenue, Pasig
Metro Manila

Director: Luz G. Palattao-Corpus

PORTUGAL

Faculdade de Psicológia e de Ciências de Educaçáo
Universidade do Porto
Rua das Taipas, 76
4000 Porto

Director: Joaquim Bairrão

SPAIN

Departamento Psicologia Evolutiva
Universidad de Sevilla
Apartado 3128
41071 Sevilla

Director: Jesús Palacios

THAILAND

School of Educational Studies
Sukhothai Thammathirat Open University
Pakkred
Nonthaburi 11120

Director: Nittaya Passornsiri

UNITED STATES

High/Scope Educational Research Foundation
600 North River Street
Ypsilanti, Michigan 48198-2898

Director: Helena Hoas

INTERNATIONAL COORDINATING CENTER

High/Scope Educational Research Foundation
600 North River Street
Ypsilanti, Michigan 48198-2898

International Coordinator: David P. Weikart
Deputy International Coordinator: Patricia P. Olmsted